OSWALD, MEXICO, AND DEEP POLITICS

OSWALD, MEXICO, AND DEEP POLITICS

Revelations from CIA Records on the Assassination of JFK

Peter Dale Scott

Skyhorse Publishing

Skyhorse Publishing books may be purchased in bulk at special discounts for sales promotion, corporate gifts, fund-raising, or educational purposes. Special editions can also be created to specifications. For details, contact the Special Sales Department, Skyhorse Publishing, 307 West 36th Street, 11th Floor, New York, NY 10018 or info@skyhorsepublishing.com.

Skyhorse® and Skyhorse Publishing® are registered trademarks of Skyhorse Publishing, Inc.®, a Delaware corporation.

Visit our website at www.skyhorsepublishing.com.

10 9 8 7 6 5 4 3 2 1

Library of Congress Cataloging-in-Publication Data is available on file.
ISBN: 978-1-62636-009-9

Printed in the United States of America

ACKNOWLEDGMENTS

Help and inspiration for the writing of this book have come from two kinds of sources. First, those who proved to me that the careful scrutiny of documents is both rewarding and hopefully useful towards a less oppressive world. I should mention first the late I.F. Stone, even if when we finally came to know each other our talk was only of Socrates and Catullus. Sylvia Meagher's book was and remains my bible on the Kennedy assassination. In the collective enterprise I think especially of Bernard Fensterwald, Mary Ferrell, Larry Haapanen, Edwin Lopez, Richard Popkin, Anthony Summers, Dick Russell, David Scheim, Josiah Thompson, William Turner, and Harold Weisberg. In the Vietnam era I learned from many: among them Franz Schurmann, Daniel Ellsberg, and (despite our differences) Noam Chomsky.

In the last year, I have once again been indebted to the sharp eye and pencil of Paul Hoch. To colleagues in the Coalition on Political Assassinations, especially Jim Lesar, John Newman , John Judge and Dan Alcorn, who helped me dip into the river of new documents. To Bill Adams, Mary LaFontaine. Gary Aguilar and others with whom I have had stimulating discussions. To Patrick Fourmy, who published one of these chapters. I owe a special debt to Alan Rogers for his previous research and publications, as well as assembling, indexing, and publishing the present work. Thanks also to innumerable other colleagues with whom I have exchanged telephone conversations and email. I apologize to those who, under the pressure of a deadline, have forgotten to mention.

Once again, and in ways that defy counting, my greatest debt is to that most reluctant conspiratorialist, my wonderful wife.

OSWALD, MEXICO, AND DEEP POLITICS

Revelations from CIA Records on the Assassination of JFK

I. INTRODUCTION

August 1995

This is an unusual interim publication, responding to an unusual time in the protracted history of the John F. Kennedy assassination. Until October 1996 we have a window of opportunity to press for the release of withheld documents, by bringing them to the attention of the newly-created Assassination Records Review Board. All Americans have a great stake in the fruitfulness of the procedures established by the JFK Records Act, not just to learn more about the government's secretiveness with respect to this one assassination, but also to create a precedent for ending the rule of secrecy that has so vitiated democracy in this country since World War II.

In response to this opportunity, and in response also to the flood of new documents we have been given since 1993, I have been writing a series of essays on the general theme of Oswald, Mexico, and Cuba. Until now they have mostly circulated among a few other researchers and/or members of the Review Board staff. But cumulatively these essays make a case for the review and release of specific records still withheld; and so far many of these records have not yet been released.

I have therefore decided to arrange for limited publication of these essays, more or less as originally written, to a larger select audience. I am not altogether happy about this. The first essay, on the Lopez Report, needs revision in the light of of the flood of documents to which I gained access later. What needs to be changed are not the specific details, which have borne up well, but the whole perspective of the essay. I suspect that while new researchers may prefer to start at the beginning of the book, experts may prefer to begin with the latest essays.

When I began these researches, I like most people focused on events portrayed in government documents, trying to resolve such familiar questions as: who was the person who identified himself as Lee Oswald to someone in the Mexico City Soviet Embassy, and just when did he visit the Cuban and Soviet Consulates? By the end of these essays, the events on which I focus have become the documents themselves. More clearly than at the beginning, I postulate that the Oswald documents, far more than a person or persons calling themselves Lee Oswald, are the key to a sophisticated CIA operation: an operation which became entangled in, even if it did not directly engender, the Kennedy assassination.

More specifically, three different deceptive stratagems need to be distinguished: a sophisticated intelligence operation (or complex of operations), the conspiracy to kill the president, and the ensuing cover-up. All three are intertwined, and each can tell us something about the others. We should expect that government records will tell us more about the first and third than about the second, but I have been saying for thirty years that this oblique path to the truth about the murder is the best hope which the documents give us.

Even on the limited topic of Oswald, Mexico, and Cuba, there is far more to be written than I have been able to achieve in these limited essays. Two areas in particular are under-represented here: disagreements between Kennedy and the CIA over specific strategies and Cuban personnel to displace Fidel Castro, and Oswald's intriguing relations with the Cuban exile groups such as the DRE (discussed to some extent in my book *Deep Politics and the Death of JFK*). In both of these areas I am still awaiting publication of work by other researchers.

In any case, readers should not expect these essays to lead us to a full understanding of the Kennedy case. Rather they lead towards key anomalies of resistance, suppression, and above all falsification of major documents. Just as the mapping of geophysical anomalies can aid in the search for petroleum, so the mapping of these documentary anomalies can aid us, and hopefully the Review Board, in isolating the key factors which led to the governmental cover-up of America's most important political assassination in this century.

Only special readers will have the patience to pursue this difficult route. I invite them, which is to say you, to join in the task of facilitating the Review Board's work. There are two ways to do this. The first is to join in the search for further anomalies: there remain thousands of documents in the Archives which have not yet been seen by anyone outside government. And second, as this golden year of opportunity draws to a close, to join in the outcry for those key documents which have not yet been released.

We know already one area where the FBI has so far refused to comply with the Review Board's unanimous recommendations: this is with respect to FBI documents pertaining to their informants. Behind this robust resistance, one suspects, may be documents still surviving which would indicate the use of Oswald as an agent or informant. I myself have waited now for a year with respect to action on one possible relevant file, the FBI's Mexico City file 105-2137, with subject "Harvey Lee Oswald."

There is another key area where the Board has hitherto failed to show results. This is with respect to military intelligence, and in articular the Army Intelligence Agent, Edward Coyle, and the unidentified OSI agent, whose entanglement in the events of Dealey Plaza has not yet been satisfactorily explained (see Chapter VII).

In these provisional essays, I have by no means presented the full case for demanding the review of documents such as those on these military intelligence personnel (and others in military intelligence reserve). But time is running out, and it takes time to build momentum for the kind of informed citizen pressure that will encourage the release of the truth.

It is towards this end that I offer, to a special readership, these provisional essays on the theme of Oswald, Mexico, and Cuba.

II. A DIFFERENT OSWALD IN MEXICO?

THE LOPEZ REPORT AND THE CIA'S OSWALD COUNTERINTELLIGENCE SECRETS

January 1994

Much of the government's failure to investigate thoroughly and honestly the murder of President Kennedy can be traced. it appears, to highly embarrassing secrets buried in the CIA's files. Indeed a central part of the cover-up can be attributed to one such secret alone. This secret, found in pre-assassination CIA cables, is that Oswald had been falsely linked to a senior Soviet KGB agent in Mexico, Valeriy Kostikov, in such a way as to create a misleading impression of a sinister KGB assassination plot.

As we shall see, the evidence is far from clear that the CIA itself was responsible for this false incrimination of Oswald. On the contrary, it is at least possible that the false impression was planted on the CIA by someone else impersonating Oswald, whose allegiance and purposes remain unknown. Another possibility is that the deception was created and fostered for unrelated intelligence purposes; and that other conspirators, not necessarily inside the CIA, took advantage of this embarrassing secret to blackmail the government into covering up.

What is clear that the CIA records on Oswald, from when a file was opened on him in 1960, had been loaded with false information, even to such elementary matters as his name (misrecorded as "Lee Henry Oswald") and physical description (see Chapter III). CIA officers continued after the assassination to transmit false information to their superiors, and later to Congress, about the Oswald records and these officers' true relationship to them, especially to the Oswald-Kostikov story.

This fact, long known, is further confirmed by new evidence recently declassified by the CIA and released through the National Archives. Many of the new revelations come in the so-called "Lopez Report," an anonymous staff study (entitled "Lee Harvey Oswald, the CIA and Mexico City") prepared in 1978 for the House Select Committee on Assassinations by two junior members of the Committee's staff, Edwin Lopez and Dan Hardway. The declassification and release of this Report were not authorized by the CIA until August 1993. Even today, parts of the sections dealing with Oswald and Kostikov remain heavily censored, and one short key section is deleted entirely.

The new evidence does not clear up the mystery; indeed it deepens our sense of what we do not know. But we can see more clearly the areas in which the CIA has been covering up: alleged links (which were probably false) between Oswald, on the one hand, and Soviet and/or Cuban intelligence on the other. And we can trace how the disclosed secret, of the falsified Oswald-Kostikov link in CIA cables, leads back to larger secrets in CIA files which are still undisclosed, and still actively protected by the CIA.

In the recent 1993 CIA releases, which I have so far barely skimmed, it is clear from the large numbers of redactions and withheld documents that extensive secrets are still being hidden in CIA files. That the secrets are there, however, does not necessarily mean that they originated with the CIA. On the contrary, one is reinforced in the impression that the files of other government agencies are involved: of Army, Navy, and Marine Intelligence, and the FBI.[1]

The Alleged Oswald-Kostikov Conversation

At the heart of this mystery was an alleged intercept by CIA electronic surveillance of a phone call on October 1, 1963, from someone who identified himself as "Lee Oswald." This was a local call to the Soviet Embassy in Mexico City, in which the alleged "Oswald" talked of his contact with a KGB Agent called Valeriy Kostikov. We shall see that there are reasons to suspect that the man who

---

[1] Cf. Peter Dale Scott. *Deep Politics and the Death of JFK* (Berkeley and Los Angeles: University of California Press, 1993), 257-60, etc.

represented himself as Oswald in this call was in fact someone else impersonating him.

The truth about this phone call has remained obscure ever since its interception, partly because the CIA reaction to it has been so consistently mysterious, and misleading. On October 8, 1963, the CIA station in Mexico City, in their report on the phone call, supplied a physical description (and later six photographs) of someone who was in fact not Lee Harvey Oswald but someone else.[2] This so-called "mystery man" (as he has been known since photographs of him reached the public) was described as "approximately 35 years old," with a receding hairline.[3]

This confusion, or falsification, was compounded by CIA officials at Headquarters two days later. They responded with two messages, both misnaming Oswald as Lee Henry Oswald. One of these messages transmitted back to Mexico City the quite different description of the 24-year-old Lee Harvey Oswald in their files.[4] The other forwarded to the FBI and other agencies the description, as if it was Oswald's, of the mystery man, "approximately 35 years old."[5]

We now know that the same people drafted both messages at the same time, and that the first, drafted by at least three people, was signed off by a high-level officer, the Assistant Deputy Director for Plans.[6] The misinformation in the cables is unlikely to have been accidental, from inattention, as CIA officers have since claimed. The Mexico City cable "caused a lot of excitement" at Headquarters, because it appeared that a former defector had made contact with a KGB agent.[7]

We shall consider later the hypothesis that these three Oswald cables were deliberately falsified, as part of what the CIA itself calls a "deception program." What emerges immediately is that Oswald, supposedly an insignificant loner, had been the subject of high-level CIA cable traffic shortly before the assassination. It will not be easy to determine why in this traffic numerous key details about Oswald had been systematically falsified. (Even his name, as in earlier CIA documents going back to 1960, was misrendered as "Lee Henry Oswald.")[8] What is clear is that this false information about Oswald came chiefly from one particularly secret section of the Agency, that concerned with Counterintelligence.

There is nothing in this new evidence, still partly censored, to implicate these CIA elements in the Kennedy assassination. What is indicated rather is some embarrassing secret or series of secrets about Oswald or his CIA file, which would appear to have originated some three years earlier in a possibly unrelated operation.

This secret evidence, which implicated Oswald falsely with an alleged KGB assassin, may however have been exploited by the Presidents' murderers: to ensure that the U.S. Government, to protect world peace and also its operations from disclosure, went along with the hypothesis that Lee Harvey Oswald acted alone. The "lone assassin" hypothesis about Oswald, even if as implausible as the "KGB assassin" hypothesis, had the advantage of not threatening nuclear war.

One can speculate further that if the truth about the CIA's Oswald secret had been disclosed to a court of law, the FBI's legal case against Oswald as a deranged lone assassin might well have collapsed. In this case, the CIA, by suppressing and lying about its internal secrets about Oswald, would have allowed Oswald to be framed.

---

[2] Lopez Report, 137-38. According to an uncorroborated source cited by the Lopez Report, this man may have been "Yuriy Ivanovich Moskalev, a Soviet KGB officer" (Lopez Report, 179).

[3] Lopez Report, 138.

[4] CIA outgoing cable DIR 74830 Oct 10, 4 AH 216; Lopez Report, 144. By falsification I mean, not complete fabrication, but contamination of true information with details that are clearly false (chiefly, but by no means uniquely, the false name "Lee Henry Oswald" that the CIA originated back in 1960).

[5] CIA outgoing cable DIR 74673 Oct 10; 4 AH 219; Lopez Report, 146.

[6] Lopez Report, 144.

[7] Lopez Report, 143.

[8] Lopez Report, 144-47 Cf. discussion of Oswald in FBI, Secret Service, and Dallas Police files as "Harvey Lee Oswald," in Scott, Deep Politics, 277, 374-75.

CIA Counterintelligence and the Oswald-Kostikov Story

Although this CIA secret remains hidden, recent declassifications make it clear who was lying about Oswald, and when. False information, often the daily business of CIA officers, appears to have been generated about Oswald from two sources. One was a very small but very powerful unit, the CI/SIG (Counterintelligence Special Investigation Group), within the CIA's Counterintelligence (CI) staff. The other source was a group of officers within the CIA's station in Mexico City, at least one of whom was allegedly a Counterintelligence officer.[9]

From these two sources we can guess that the CIA Oswald secret had to do with a sensitive CIA counterintelligence operation. We know that CI/SIG's primary mission, since it had been set up by CI Chief James Angleton in 1954, was in effect to spy on the rest of the CIA. As Angleton himself told the House Select Committee on Assassinations in 1978, he set up the CI/SIG in 1954 to investigate the allegations (promoted at the time by FBI chief J. Edgar Hoover) that the CIA itself might have been penetrated by the KGB.[10]

Partly to ensure that the CI/SIG would not be too sympathetic to the rest of the CIA, Angleton entrusted it to an ex-FBI agent, Birch D. O'Neal.[11] O'Neal had been part of a wartime FBI overseas operation (the SIS) that had been bitterly competitive with the CIA's predecessor agency, the OSS. It has been suggested that Hoover so mistrusted the CIA that he arranged for some of his FBI/SIS veterans to resign from the FBI and join the CIA as penetration agents. FBI veterans in the Agency (many of them close to Angleton) included O'Neal, William Harvey (Angleton's predecessor as Counterintelligence Chief), Mexico City Station Chief Win Scott, and at least one other relevant officer (George Munroe) of the Mexico City CIA station.[12] According to Dick Russell, Munroe was "the CIA's leading surveillance man in Mexico City, responsible for the electronic bugging of the Soviet and Cuban embassies."[13]

The falsified "Lee Henry Oswald" cables of October 1963, which became part of a CI/SIG file on "Lee Henry Oswald" going back to 1960, were supervised by officers of this small Angleton-FBI veterans clique in CI. One can imagine that this clique had used their falsified file on "Lee Henry Oswald" as part of the CI/SIG's search for a KGB penetration agent, or "mole," within the CIA's ranks. This search became particularly active in 1963, the year of falsified cable traffic about Oswald.[14]

It is certain however that the effect of the falsified Oswald documentation, consciously or accidentally, was to incriminate him falsely as an apparent KGB assassin. One day after the assassination, the CIA Counterintelligence staff speculated on the sinister implications of Oswald's alleged contact with Kostikov; and it continued to do so for years after.[15] For Kostikov was not just a known KGB agent; he was suspected by Counterintelligence officials in the FBI and CIA of working for the KGB's Department Thirteen, which according to a contemporary CIA memo was "responsible for sabotage and assassination."[16] This falsified picture of Oswald as a potential KGB assassin, though never used by the Warren Commission against him, almost certainly contributed to the Warren Commission's determination to close the case as the work of a lone assassin.[17] The alleged Oswald-

[9] Lopez Report, 101; interview with Edwin Lopez, 10/9/93.

[10] HSCA, Deposition of James Angleton, 145-47, as summarized in Tom Mangold, *Cold Warrior* (New York: Simon and Schuster/Touchstone, 1991), 57.

[11] David Wise, *Molehunt* (New York: Random House, 1992), 158, 160.

[12] Curt Gentry, *J. Edgar Hoover* (New York: Norton, 1991), 392.

[13] Dick Russell, *The Man Who Knew Too Much* (New York: Carroll and Graf, 1992), 239.

[14] Mangold, 108; Edward Jay Epstein, *Deception* (New York: Simon and Schuster, 1989), 75-77.

[15] CIA Doc. # 34-538, Memo of 23 Nov 1963 from Tennant ("Pete") Bagley, Chief, SR/CI; Schweiker-Hart Report, 25; Peter Dale Scott, *Deep Politics*, 54.

[16] Bagley memo of 23 Nov 1963; Schweiker-Hart Report, 92; Scott, *Deep Politics*, 39; Edward Jay Epstein, *Legend* (New York: Reader's Digest Press/ McGraw-Hill, 1978), 16, 237; U.S. Cong., Senate, Committee on the Judiciary, *Murder International Incorporated, Hearing*, 89th Cong., 1st Sess. (Washington: G.P.O., 1965).

[17] Scott, *Deep Politics*, 113; William Manchester, *Death of a President* (New York: Harper and Row, 1967), 730; see also below.

Kostikov-Department Thirteen connection must have seemed particularly ominous after the Commission was informed by Richard Helms that

> The Thirteenth Department headquarters, according to very reliable information, conducts interviews or, as appropriate, file reviews on every foreign military defector to the USSR to study and to determine the possibility of utilizing the defector in his country of origin.[18]

CIA and FBI officials have since said that their respective agencies made mistakes in their handling of the Oswald case prior to Kennedy's murder. Yet the Counterintelligence staffs of CIA and FBI, who were responsible for the alleged mistakes, were also given the responsibility for investigating the Kennedy assassination afterwards. The CI/SIG in particular, which had misrepresented Oswald within the CIA, was given responsibility for liaison on the assassination with the CI staff in the FBI, who were given secret FBI reprimands for having failed to put Oswald on the FBI's Security Index.[19]

FBI and CIA officials, especially those in CI, continued to conceal and misrepresent the facts, first to the Warren Commission, and later to the House Committee.[20] A typical example was a CIA Counterintelligence memo recommending that Helms "wait out the Commission" in its request for CIA documents, which justified the withholding of information about the "mystery man" problem in Mexico City, because the "items refer to aborted leads."[21] The least damning excuse for CI personnel having been put by their superiors in a position to do this is that Oswald (or at a minimum the erroneous Oswald record, salted with errors) was indeed part of some covert intelligence operation.

Possibility of an Oswald Impostor in Mexico City

Thanks to the Lopez Report, we now know how shaky, if not implausible, were the foundations of the original CIA claim in 1963 that Oswald had met with Kostikov.[22] On October 1, 1963, two months before the assassination of President Kennedy, CIA surveillance at the Soviet Embassy in Mexico City overheard a man, who apparently spoke in broken Russian, identify himself as Lee Oswald, and talk of his contact with Kostikov, an Embassy Consular official.[23]

The newly released evidence in the Lopez Report makes it likely that this man, who identified himself as Oswald, was in fact an impostor. It is almost certain, moreover, that a Mexico City CIA official misrepresented the conversation in order to prevent this likelihood from being disclosed.[24]

From the time of the Warren Report to the present, key facts about this alleged Oswald-Kostikov contact have continued to be suppressed. Despite these gaps in the public record, there is

---

[18] Memo of 1/31/64 from Helms to Warren Commission Counsel J. Lee Rankin, "Information Developed by CIA on the Activity of Lee Harvey Oswald in Mexico City, 28 September - 3 October 1963," CIA Document 509-803.

[19] 11 AH 476, 485; Scott, *Deep Politics*, 61-67.

[20] Schweiker-Hart Report, 54; 3 AH 535; Scott, *Deep Politics*, 63 (FBI CI); Lopez Report, 141, 148-50, 183-84, etc.

[21] 11 AH 63, 491; CIA internal memo of 3/5/63 from Ray Rocca of CI, reporting the recommendations of CI Chief James Angleton.

[22] This section was written before the publication by Oleg Nechiporenko of a book corroborating the meeting from sources who would normally appear to be definitive: Kostikov himself, supported by two of his colleagues in the Soviet Embassy, Pavel Yatzkov and Nechipenko. At this point in my text, I originally expressed skepticism about the book, on the basis of the advance report of it in Posner (p. 183). Having since both read the book and spent hours with Nechiporenko himself, I am now convinced that both the man and the book have to be taken seriously (see below). For reasons I shall explain later, however, I still believe that the Lopez Report hypothesis of a possible Oswald impostor in Mexico remains a viable one, neither proven nor disproven.

[23] Lopez Report, 78-79. The transcript is in English, which is said to indicate "either English or Russian." But the translator of an earlier conversation on September 28, which was in broken Russian, later identified the two speakers as being the same, while his wife identified the October 1 conversation from the transcript as being in Russian (Lopez Report, 83).

[24] Lopez Report, 171; cf. discussion below.

new evidence for four propositions indicating a conspiracy in Mexico City to incriminate Oswald.

--- The first is that Oswald was impersonated at the Cuban Consulate in Mexico by someone else, a man over thirty, about five foot six, thin, with blonde hair. (The Oswald arrested in Dallas was aged twenty-four, five foot nine, and had brown hair.)

--- The second is that someone who phoned the Soviet Embassy in Mexico City, identified himself as Lee Oswald, and referred to his meeting with Kostikov, was in fact not Oswald at all, but someone whose Russian (unlike Oswald's) was extremely poor.

--- The third is that a tape of this phone conversation, which could have proven conclusively whether Oswald was or was not being impersonated, was preserved by the CIA for some time longer than was originally claimed; almost certainly (despite misleading denials) it survived the assassination.

--- The fourth is that CIA officials in Mexico City helped to conceal the truth about these matters, by lying to their own superiors in Washington, and later to the House Select Committee on Assassinations. In particular these officials, along with members of the CI/SIG staff in Washington and others, complicated the matter still further, by circulating a false description of the alleged impostor, one that in fact fitted neither him nor the man he impersonated.

It is important to repeat that these CIA lies do not prove the involvement of CIA officials in the conspiracy to kill the President. As we shall see, however, CIA behavior appears to have augmented the fear at that time of unnecessary war, which is said in turn to have motivated Chief Justice Earl Warren's pursuit of Oswald as a lone assassin.

The Short Blonde Older Oswald Impostor

In 1978 the House Select Committee heard testimony from two former Cuban Consulate officials, Consul Eusebio Azcue and Silvia Duran. Each testified separately that the "Oswald" whom they dealt with was short, blonde, and over 30.[25] The corroboration was the more significant in that Azcue was first deposed by the Committee in Cuba, and Duran, a Mexican national, in Mexico City. The two witnesses said they had not been in touch with each other for some years.

Nevertheless critics were reluctant to make too much of this discordant testimony. One reason is that Duran (3 AH 118). unlike Azcue (3 AH 139), thought that the visitor to the Consulate was the same as the man killed by Jack Ruby in Dallas. Another reason was because the Warren Report contained an alleged summary of a Duran interview in 1963, containing nothing which would distinguish the man she interviewed from the assassin in Dallas. This summary is cited by Gerald Posner, in his recent book *Case Closed*. to support his statement that Silvia Duran "positively identified the visitor as Oswald," and to suggest, wrongly, that Azcue is alone in describing the visitor as a short older blonde.[26]

One new revelation is that Duran's interview summary from 1963, as published in the Warren Report, was rewritten and censored. For the first time we learn that the original report of Duran's interview by the Mexican Security Police (DFS), seen in November 1963 by the Mexico CIA station but never by the Warren Commission, was significantly different. More specifically she described him as an "individual who was blonde, short, dressed unelegantly and whose face turned red when angry."[27]

---

[25] 3 AH 69-70 (Duran); 3 AH 136, cf. 152 (Azcue). For what it is worth, Duran described Oswald as as blond and balding (poco pelo. 3 AH 104). This description recalls the description of Oswald, or "Oswald," by Alfred Osborne alias John Bowen, the mysterious Englishman who sat next to him in the bus that brought him to Mexico City. Osborne/Bowen also described "Oswald"'s hair as "blond and thin" (25 WH 37; 25 WH 573).

[26] Posner. *Case Closed*. 188-89.

[27] Lopez Report, 186.

This description actually reached the staff of the Warren Commission from the CIA.[28] But some months later these words were removed from a rewritten summary of Duran's testimony, and only the rewritten, censored summary was published by the Warren Commission.[29] According to the Lopez Report, it was the CIA who "deleted Duran's description of Oswald as blonde and short."[30] The public record indicates that the rewritten summary came from the Mexican Security Police or DFS (Dirección Federal de Seguridad) in their Ministry of Government.[31] But as the House Committee recognized, these Mexican authorities collaborated very closely with the CIA. (The Minister was said to be "in Scott's pocket" and may have been on the CIA payroll.)[32]

One can see why it would have been embarrassing to the Warren Commission's lone assassin hypothesis to have published Silvia Duran's description of him as blonde, short, and "dressed unelegantly." The visa application submitted by Oswald to Duran showed a photograph, said by Posner to have been taken the same day "at a nearby shop recommended by Duran."[33] As in no other photo or description of Oswald, the "Oswald" in this unique photograph is dressed like a Harvard student, with a dress shirt, necktie, and pullover sweater. As we shall see, former KGB officer Oleg Nechiporenko, describing his encounters with "Oswald" in the Soviet Embassy, denies that the visitor wore such attire, and agrees with Duran that he was dressed inelegantly. Thus Nechiporenko, used by Posner and others to rebut the "impostor" hypothesis, can also be cited on the other side, to support the discordant testimony of Duran and Azcue.

Further evidence that the Oswald in the Cuban Consulate was an impostor has just been made public in a new book by former House Committee investigator Gaeton Fonzi. According to Fonzi, the CIA actually had two "assets," or double agents, working inside the Cuban Consulate at the time of the "Oswald" visit. These two assets were located and interviewed in 1978 by Ed Lopez, without the Agency's permission. The assets told Lopez

> that the consensus among employees within the Cuban Consulate after the Kennedy assassination was that it wasn't Oswald who had been there. The assets said that they reported that to the Agency but there were no documents in the CIA file noting that fact.[34]

In any case, anti-conspiratorial books like *Case Closed* will no longer be able to claim that Azcue was unsupported in his allegations of a short blonde impostor. Azcue's claim is further supported by the fact, long rumored but never before officially corroborated, that the CIA, with thorough photographic surveillance of both the Cuban and Soviet Embassies, had at least ten opportunities to photograph Oswald, yet CIA records at the time of the assassination allegedly did not contain a single photograph matching the man arrested in Dallas.[35]

---

[28] WCD 347 (CIA Document # 509-803); CIA memorandum of 31 January 1964. Also WCD 426; memo of 14 February 1964 from Richard Helms to Commission Counsel J. Lee Rankin.

[29] 24 WH 565.

[30] Lopez Report, 190.

[31] WCE 2123; 24 WH 680, 682. Cf. Scott, *Deep Politics*, 105.

[32] Scott, *Deep Politics*, 123, 336; Philip Agee, *CIA Diary* (Harmondsworth, Middlesex: Penguin, 1975), 275-76, 524-26, 553.

[33] Posner, *Case Closed*, 182. The FBI could never locate the shop; thus the Warren Report concluded that Oswald brought with him "passport photographs which he may have obtained in the United States" (WR 734; cf. 25 WH 589).

[34] Fonzi, *The Last Investigation*, 293-94. The presence of HUMINT or human intelligence assets inside the Cuban Consulate appears to explain some of the extensive redactions in the released Lopez Report. It may also help explain the astonishing footnote 319 to the Report, on page A-23. This refers to a call between "a woman named Silvia" and a Consulate employee named Guillermo Ruiz (the cousin of Alpha 66 leader Antonio Veciana, another CIA asset). Silvia asks Ruiz for the Consul's telephone number, and "Ruiz says that the number is 11-28-47." This number, which critics had hitherto assumed to be the publicly available one, is the number for the Cuban Consulate entered with Duran's name in Oswald's address book (16 WH 54). If it was publicly available, it is hard to understand why Silvia Duran would have had to telephone Ruiz to obtain it.

[35] CIA Doc. # 59-23, MEXI (Mexico City CIA cable) 7035 of 23 Nov 1963.

We now learn from the Lopez Report that CIA experts told the Committee it was unlikely that the surveillance could have failed to photograph Oswald. Some of them, furthermore, reported that photos of Oswald were taken and delivered to CIA headquarters near Washington. Winston Scott, then Chief of the Mexico City CIA station, later wrote in an unpublished memoir that "persons watching these embassies photographed Oswald as he entered and left each one, and clocked the time he spent on each visit."[36] After Scott died, this memoir was retrieved and sequestered by CIA Counterintelligence Chief James Angleton. Allegedly Angleton also made off with a profile photo of Oswald entering the Soviet Embassy.[37]

It remains to be learned whether a search of the photographic surveillance product would show photos of a man who was short, blonde, and over thirty. The CIA did release some photographs to the Committee, and Silvia Duran, when shown these, failed to identify any of them as her visitor. But the CIA never released the photos from the special "pulse camera" which they had just installed to watch the Cuban Consulate, shortly before Oswald's visit. Worse, when the Committee asked for the "pulse camera" photos, the CIA replied, falsely, that this camera had not been in operation until three months later.[38]

Did an Oswald Impostor Phone the Soviet Embassy?

The possibility of an impostor at the Cuban Consulate raises the question of why, on October 8, 1963, the CIA Station reported that one week earlier someone had telephoned the Soviet Embassy in Mexico City, identified himself as Lee Oswald, and referred to a previous meeting with the Soviet Consul.[39] According to the cable of October 8, 1963 sent from the Mexican City CIA Station to Headquarters, this individual said he "spoke with Consul whom he believed to be Valeriy Vladimirovich Kostikov" (4 AH 212). In contrast, according to the summary of the transcript quoted in the Lopez Report, "Oswald...said that he did not remember the name of the Consul with whom he had spoken. Obyedkov [the guard with whom "Oswald" was currently speaking] asked if it had been Kostikov....The man outside replied affirmatively and repeated that his name was Oswald."[40]

The difference could be immensely important. If the cable is accurate, "Oswald" (whether the real Oswald or an impostor) is responsible for initiating the impression of a sinister KGB connection. If the transcript is correct, and the name of Kostikov did not come from the lips of the alleged "Oswald," that impression was created by a misleading CIA cable. In the first case, a conspiratorial deception could have been foisted on the CIA by someone else. In the second case, the deception arose within the CIA itself.[41]

Whatever the facts, the report of this conversation cast a lengthy shadow over the investigation of the President's murder. After the assassination, it led senior CIA officials to talk of an Oswald-Kostikov meeting, which they took as possible evidence of a high-level Oswald-KGB plot. (These

---

[36] Lopez Report, 23.

[37] Lopez Report, 87-88, 88-89; Posner, 187; Fonzi, 295. On November 16, 1993 a PBS Frontline television report on Oswald referred to Win Scott's claim that "persons watching these embassies photographed Oswald as he entered and left each one." PBS also elicited from Richard Helms the response, "He [Scott] couldn't produce the photograph."

[38] Lopez Report, 13-30; footnote 363 on p. A-25.

[39] Lopez Report, 78-79, 136.

[40] Lopez Report, 79.

[41] A third account of this conversation, transmitted by House Committee investigator Gaeton Fonzi, would, if accurate, be even more conspiratorial. According to Fonzi, the CIA told the Warren Commission it had "tape recordings of Oswald telephoning the Soviets and asking for a 'Comrade Kostin.' (That, the Agency said, was a code name for Valery Kostikov, a Russian officer in charge of the KGB's Department Thirteenth [sic], which was responsible for assassinations and sabotage.)" (Fonzi, 283). This version raises the question of how "Oswald" could have known a KGB code name, "Kostin," which the real Lee Harvey Oswald allegedly used afterwards in a letter of November 9, 1963, to the Soviet Embassy in Washington (WR 309-11; Scott, *Deep Politics*, 39-40). So far I have found no documentary evidence for Fonzi's claim.

senior officials included Win Scott, the head of the Mexico City CIA station, James Angleton, the chief of CIA Counterintelligence, Angleton's deputy Ray Rocca, and Angleton loyalist Tennant Bagley at CIA Headquarters.)[42]

For some time it has been suspected that the caller was not Oswald. The newly declassified Lopez Report and CIA cables reveal that CIA translators who listened to the tape identified the caller as someone who had phoned the Embassy three days earlier and spoken "broken," indeed "terrible, hardly recognizable Russian."[43] This could hardly be Lee Harvey Oswald, who reportedly spoke Russian reasonably well even before his three years in the Soviet Union. (Oswald had spoken Russian for two hours in California with a friend's aunt, Rosaleen Quinn, who had been studying Russian for over a year with a Berlitz tutor in preparation for the the State Department's foreign language examination. Ms. Quinn reported to author Edward Jay Epstein that Oswald "had a far more confident command of the language than she did.")[44] Marina Oswald, when she met Oswald in 1961, "found his Russian so fluent that she simply believed he was from a different Russian-speaking region."[45]

Furthermore the misleading incrimination of Oswald, by linking him to the alleged KGB assassinations expert Kostikov, was reinforced by members of the Mexico City CIA Station. A memo was prepared (by an unidentified Ms. X) stating that it had been "determined" (as opposed to "claimed") that Oswald "had been at the Soviet Embassy on 28 September 1963 and had talked with" Kostikov. Though the discussion concerned a visa, which would make the Kostikov contact seem more innocent, the memo did not show this. Instead it claimed, in language which the Lopez Report found "misleading," that "we have no clarifying information with regard to this request."[46] Almost certainly these allegations were "determined" by comparing the intercepts and transcripts of September 28 and October 1, which a) were indeed determined to have been made by the same caller, b) contained no further evidence of an actual Oswald-Kostikov meeting, and c) were known to be part of a sequence of intercepts which clearly had as their subject Oswald's request for a Soviet visa.[47]

CIA Headquarters, which was concerned about the Kostikov contact and had asked to be informed, did not learn about the visa request until after the assassination. According to the Lopez Report, witnesses suggested that information not directly transmitted to CIA Headquarters may have been provided to them indirectly through the FBI.[48] It is clear that some information not in the CIA cables (such as alleged Oswald visits to the Embassies on September 27) did reach CIA Headquarters. It is possible that this information was communicated through a CIA Counterintelligence back channel, since CI maintained its own communication network and cipher that was independent of the regular CIA cable traffic.

Was the Tape of This Conversation Destroyed?

[42] CIA Document # 34-538, Memo of 23 November 1963 from Bagley to ADDP Karamessines.

[43] Lopez Report, 77; MEXI (Mexico City CIA cable) 7023 of November 23, 1963; DIR (CIA HQ cable) 84915 of November 23, 1963.

[44] Epstein, *Legend*, 87; Summers, *Conspiracy*, 154; WR 685; 24 WH 130.

[45] Hurt, *Reasonable Doubt*, 211; WR 703; WCE 1401, p. 261; WCE 994, p. 5. Posner recognizes that the caller's broken Russian on September 28 is a problem. His response is to distinguish between the two callers on September 28 and October 1: "the tape referred to," Posner writes, "may not even have been a recording of Oswald" (Posner, 187). This solution does not deal with the fact that the CIA translators and officers identified the speaker of broken Russian on September 28 with the caller on October 1 who introduced himself as 'Lee Oswald.' Someone, not Oswald, who introduced himself as Oswald, could only be an impostor.

[46] CIA Document # 9-5, Memo of 16 October 1963 to the Ambassador from [deleted]; Lopez Report, 170-72; Scott, *Deep Politics*, 41. In *Deep Politics* I wrongly suggested that the author might have been David Phillips; we now learn that the author was a woman with "very much the Counter-Intelligence mentality" (Lopez Report, 171, 101).

[47] Lopez Report, 73-79, 162, 170-72. The House Committee determined that by October 16, the date of Ms. X's memo, all four intercepts "had been linked to Oswald" (Lopez Report, 170). A post-assassination cable confirmed that "no other info available" (Lopez Report, 183).

[48] Lopez Report, 181.

The evidence is extremely confused as to how long the CIA preserved its tape of the October 1 phone conversation, which could have proven conclusively that Oswald was being impersonated. Having studied the CIA files and listened to many witnesses, the authors of the Lopez Report concluded that tapes of the two conversations, on September 28 and October 1, were preserved at least until mid-October, by which time Langley had expressed interest in the Oswald-Kostikov contact. A key piece of evidence was a note placed in the files by Annie Goodpasture, an officer in the Mexico City station. She wrote "The caller from the Cuban Embassy [on September 28] was unidentified until HQ [Langley] sent traces on Oswald and voices [on the two tapes] compared by [deleted: (the translators)]."[49] All of a brief section of the Lopez Report, entitled "Voice Comparisons," is deleted.

Yet the same officer sent a cable on November 23 saying, in part, "Station unable compare voice as first tape [of September 28] erased prior receipt of second call [of October 1]." The Lopez Report twice called this statement "highly unlikely," as inconsistent with sworn testimony, other CIA cables, and what was known of CIA procedures. Once we question this account of the destruction of the tapes, all CIA accounts of when they were destroyed become more suspect.

In both FBI and CIA records, there are indications that the tapes, which could have proven a conspiracy to incriminate Oswald, survived the assassination, yet were withheld from authorities after Oswald had been arrested for the murder of President Kennedy. This would of course appear to be a serious, possibly criminal, interference with a criminal investigation, one denying both justice to Oswald and the truth to law enforcement and the American people. It is likely moreover that numerous attestations by officials to the tapes' erasure are either false or deliberately misleading.

According to an FBI message to the Secret Service on November 23, that was not released to the public until 1975, a CIA source

> had reported that an individual identified himself as Lee Oswald, who contacted the Soviet Embassy in Mexico City inquiring as to any messages. Special Agents of this Bureau, who have conversed with Oswald in Dallas, Tex., have observed photographs of the individual referred to above and have listened to a recording of his voice. These Special Agents are of the opinion that the above-referred-to individual was not Lee Harvey Oswald."[50]

We learn now for the first time that this memo was based on a telephone conversation between J. Edgar Hoover's subordinate Alan Belmont, and Gordon Shanklin, head of the Dallas FBI. This phone call took place just before noon on November 23. At 7:30 PM, CST, Shanklin cabled Hoover and said, "It should be noted that the actual tape [of the October 1 call] has been erased." On the same day the Mexico City CIA Station informed its Headquarters "Regret complete recheck shows tapes for this period already erased."[51]

Because these two cables do not say when the tapes were erased, they do not refute Hoover's statement that FBI agents in Dallas had listened to them. The House Committee, in its published report, cited yet another FBI report that "no tapes were taken [from Mexico City] to Dallas." But this does not refute Hoover's statement either, since the FBI agents could, and indeed very probably would, have listened to the recordings in a long-distance telephone call. The Committee's Report concluded that the FBI and CIA in the U.S. never received "a recording of Oswald's voice."[52] But this language, repeated three times, does not address the real issue: did they receive a recording of the voice of someone else, not Oswald, who identified himself as Oswald?

The inconsistencies in the CIA's accounts of the tapes, as revealed by the 1978 Lopez Report, suggest that officers in the Mexico City Station acted, as early as one day after the assassination, as if they had something to hide from their own Headquarters. It seems likely, moreover, that they were prevaricating when they said that the tapes had been erased.

---

[49] Lopez Report, 162.

[50] AR 249-50; Scott, *Deep Politics*, 41-43.

[51] Lopez Report, Addendum, 1-3.

[52] AR 250. I am reliably informed that the Report used this evasive and misleading phrase after careful deliberation and consultation.

Warren Commission Counsel David Slawson has since confirmed to investigators, including myself, that he listened to an Oswald tape inside the Mexico City CIA station in the spring of 1964.[53] His memory on this crucial point has been corroborated by two other Warren Commission counsels, William Coleman and David Belin. Members of the Win Scott family recall that a vinyl recording, which Scott had identified to his wife as being of Oswald, was retrieved by Angleton after Scott's death and taken to CIA headquarters.

Key redactions in the Lopez Report, as censored by the CIA before release in 1993, still prevent the American people from knowing what the Mexico City CIA station was up to in 1963. On the basis of what has been released, however, one can tentatively conclude that Oswald was indeed impersonated in Mexico, that a false trail was laid which linked him to an alleged KGB assassin agent, and that some individual officers in the Mexico City Station acted conspiratorially: first to strengthen this false trail, and later to cover it up.

Oleg Nechiporenko and the Oswald Impostor Hypothesis

Informed readers are no doubt asking themselves why I have spent so much time discussing the possibility of an Oswald impostor in Mexico City, without mentioning the rebuttal testimony that might seem to be definitive, from three former KGB officers in the Soviet Embassy, including Kostikov himself. All three have said that the Oswald of Dallas did visit the Soviet Embassy on September 28, and that he brandished a revolver much like that which is said to have been used by Oswald on November 22 to murder Officer Tippit.

The answer is that I first drafted a version of this essay before Col. Nechiporenko's book had appeared. I have since had occasion, not only to read and re-read his book, but to spend several hours with the Colonel himself, an intelligent and engaging person. Indeed I had the post-Cold War and post-structuralist historical experience of standing with the Colonel and many others on the grassy knoll in Dealey Plaza, each of us holding a candle in a commemoration of the 30th anniversary of President Kennedy's murder.

And yet prolonged reflection on this topic has persuaded me, not only that the hypothesis of a possible Oswald impostor remains a viable one, but that portions of what the Colonel has to tell us can be used in support of it.

It is important first of all to distinguish between what we learn from the Colonel himself, and what we learn from his book, which is less reliable. I learned this when I asked the Colonel at breakfast about his relations with the DFS and their senior official Miguel Nazar Haro, who as we shall see I consider important, perhaps crucial, in this case. On hearing the name of Nazar Haro, he laughed and said first, "I knew him well;" and then "He's in my book!" I then gave him my copy; his brow furrowed as he searched but failed to find what he was looking for. He finally fixed on page 83, and said, "This is the place, but they must have taken him out." On the page there were references to an "FDS-a" -- clearly the DFS (Federal Directorate of Security), but the "-a" made no sense to me. He looked at the page again, and said: "That's a mistake; I don't know where that came from."[54]

It is relevant here that the DFS in general, and Nazar Haro in particular, were both important assets of the CIA Mexico Station in 1963, and also significant sources of disinformation about Oswald as part of an international Communist conspiracy. I assume that the "they" who deleted Nazar Haro from the book may well be from the same part of CIA that is said to have edited Khrushchev's memoirs before their publication, and possibly the memoirs of Stalin's daughter Svetlana Allelueva.

---

[53] Fonzi, *The Last Investigation*, 286-87n. Slawson explained to me that he was concerned only to establish the accuracy of the transcripts, not the identity of the speaker

[54] Cf. Oleg M. Nechiporenko, translated by Todd P Bludeau, *Passport to Assassination* (New York: Birch Lane/Carol, 1993), 83.

I was already suspicious of the book because it seemed to fit so well into the "Posnermania" of late 1993. On the one hand it validated the Warren Report precisely where it was weakest, in its otherwise unsubstantiated portrait of Oswald as a deranged gunman. (Before these three KGB agents came forward, the only credible sighting of Oswald with a gun had been made by Marina Oswald; others had claimed to have seen him shoot, in concatenated and possibly conspiratorial testimony, but the Warren Commission had systematically refuted them.)[55]

On the other hand, Nechiporenko's book rebutted the newly-declassified Lopez Report precisely where it was most indicative of a conspiracy. It first reassured us that the Oswald in contact with the Soviet Embassy in Mexico City was indeed no impostor. The book seems virtually to have in mind the alleged impostor who was short, blonde, and over thirty, when it writes that the Oswald visitor to the Consulate was "apparently twenty-five to twenty-seven... of medium height...and...a brunet."[56]

Additionally, and perhaps even more importantly, it appeared to determine that Lee Harvey Oswald had indeed met with Valeriy Kostikov on September 28, 1963, just as Ms. X had "determined" in her memo of October 16.[57] The CIA station, in other words, was validated in what threatened to become the most controversial features of their pre-assassination handling of the Lee Harvey Oswald matter.

I was admittedly prejudiced against the forthcoming Nechiporenko book by other favors which in recent months KGB files and veterans had performed for post-Cold War propaganda campaigns in this country. I thought particularly of the alleged KGB report of an 1970s interview with a senior North Vietnamese official, allegedly confirming that the Vietnamese had indeed used significant numbers of American MIA's (Missing in Action) as slave labor in that period. Thanks to anachronisms in this alleged KGB document, it had been easily exposed as a forgery; and eventually it was debunked by the CIA and other U.S. intelligence agencies.[58]

Another reason to doubt the Nechiporenko story of the September 28 visit is that it has been told again, differently, by another ex-KGB officer, Gen. Nikolai Leonov. Though the substance of the story remains the same (Oswald appearing at the Embassy, and brandishing a revolver), the date of the alleged visit is one day later, on Sunday, September 29, and Leonov recalls that, other than the guard at the front gate, he was the only person to receive Oswald.[59] The near duplication of the story, far from increasing its credibility, makes us realize how easy it would be, in the year of Posnermania, for penurious KGB officers to pick up a little hard currency by joining the Warren Commission chorus.

Both Leonov and Nechiporenko claim that they reported Oswald's flamboyant visits to KGB Headquarters.[60] Nechiporenko adds that when Anastas Mikoyan came to President Kennedy's funeral in November 1963, he brought with him the KGB "materials" on Oswald in the Soviet Union, "to give to the Americans."[61]

This draws our attention to what is, with or without the Oswald-revolver story, one of the more intriguing "black holes" in the documentation of the case. The CIA and FBI both drew heavily on the Oswald correspondence supplied at the time by the Soviet Embassy in Washington, which corroborated the fact that both Oswalds had been in correspondence with the Embassy about returning to the Soviet Union. Soviet (presumably KGB) documentation on Oswald was also used to corroborate the details of his supposed defection (WR 692, WCE 985). But there is no use by the Warren Commission of Soviet documentation to corroborate or refute the questionable stories about Oswald's visits to the Soviet Embassy in Mexico. Other Soviet-supplied materials on Oswald were used to

---

[55] Scott, *Deep Politics*, 284, 291.

[56] Nechiporenko, 68.

[57] Nechiporenko, 75-81. This is the meeting at which Oswald allegedly brandished a revolver.

[58] *San Francisco Chronicle*, January 25, 1994, A10.

[59] *National Enquirer*, November 22, 1993.

[60] Ibid.; Nechiporenko, 81.

[61] Nechiporenko, 110.

bolster the Warren Report, but no effort was apparently ever made to obtain their Mexico Oswald documents, on a matter which in November 1963 was considered crucial to the proof or disproof of an international conspiracy.

It is striking that Nechiporenko's book, which quotes liberally from KGB documents on Oswald in the Soviet Union, has no citations from the documents which he and Kostikov allegedly filed from Mexico. A search should be made in Moscow to find the alleged reports of the Oswald-revolver story from Nechiporenko and Leonov. One should also, apparently for the first time, request the Mexican Government to supply its files on Oswald's Mexico visit. (Nechiporenko claims that the Oswald-revolver story was "forwarded to Mexican authorities through their foreign affairs ministry.")[62]

We have just seen that, whatever one makes of the Oswald-revolver story, there are useful facts in Nechiporenko's book. Though he often draws on some of the West's more unreliable sources (Priscilla McMillan, Eddowes, Hugh MacDonald, even David Phillips), at other times the book is startlingly accurate. For example, Nechiporenko excerpts from the Schweiker-Hart Report the important information that FBI information on Oswald was directed in mid-November to the counterintelligence branch of the Special Affairs Staff in charge of Cuban operations (SAS/CI), and thereafter, on November 22, to counterintelligence (specifically CI/SIG).[63]

In my present state of imperfect understanding, Nechiporenko is a mystery, not unrelated to the mystery of Nosenko, that other volunteer of KGB information about Oswald. Readers of this essay will recall that the core of Nosenko's story, in 1964 and again to the House Committee in 1978, was that Oswald was of "no interest" to the KGB (2 AH 464). The same message is the core of Nechiporenko's book as well, which repeats the same words, "no interest," at least six times.[64]

How Nechiporenko Raises New Questions About the Oswald-Kostikov Story

Whatever the full background, neither Nechiporenko nor his book can be simply dismissed. His account is detailed, plausible, corroborated by two other intelligent plausible eyewitnesses: Pavel Yatzkov and Valeriy Kostikov himself. I am now satisfied that some form of Oswald (or "Oswald") - Kostikov meeting may well have occurred. At the same time, one cannot use Nechiporenko to "close" the case, as Posner tried to do without having seen his published book.[65] On the contrary, Nechiporenko introduces a number of new pieces of evidence which complicate the already murky story of Oswald in Mexico still further.

I have already mentioned that Nechiporenko corroborates Silvia Duran's description of Oswald as "dressed unelegantly," and definitely not in the shirt, tie, and sweater of his visa photograph allegedly taken the same day.[66] Much more important, in my view, is his emphatic denial that there could have been any telephone calls to the Soviet Embassy on September 28, a Saturday on which, he insists, the Embassy was closed down, and the only personnel present were those who had gathered for a volleyball game.[67] In other words, if Nechiporenko is right, we have to question what has

---

[62] Nechiporenko, 179.

[63] Nechiporenko, 171-72; Schweiker-Hart Report, 24; cover-sheets to DBA 55777 (FBI de Brueys Report of 25 Oct 1963) and DBA 55715 (FBI Kaack Report of 31 Oct 1963). David Phillips, detached temporarily from Mexico City to Washington, appears to have been the recipient of the documents in SAS/CI.

[64] Nechiporenko, 94, 96, 109, 111, 221, 231. The words allegedly occur in the November 1963 report of KGB Chairman Semichastny to the Soviet Party Central Committee (p. 111). Nechiporenko's book is sympathetic neither to Nosenko, who is accused of "moral bankruptcy" (p. 228), nor to the view of his CIA tormentors, Angleton and Bagley, that Nosenko was a KGB plant" (p. 245).

[65] Posner, *Case Closed*, 183, etc. Nechiporenko's book is by no means a simple defense of the Warren Report, against whose narrative he raises a number of subtle and cogent points (e.g. p. 209).

[66] Nechiporenko interview, November 20, 1993, Dallas.

[67] Ibid. As for the October 1 phone call, he reports that Obyedkov does not remember it. The Nechiporenko story of Embassy volleyball games on Saturdays is corroborated by declassified CIA Cable MEXI 7060 of 26 November.

hitherto been considered the hardest evidence of all: the record of electronic surveillance transcripts, which show a Duran-Oswald-Soviet Consulate telephone conversation on September 28.

Here too Nechiporenko corroborates Silvia Duran on a point where, given the transcript record, no one (except possibly the authors of the Lopez Report) has hitherto believed her. She has maintained that the Cuban Consulate was closed on Saturday, September 28, and that on that day she neither met with Oswald nor telephoned the Soviet Embassy about him.[68] This is flatly at odds with the transcript record, hitherto deemed unimpeachable, which says that "at 11:51 a.m. [September 28] Silvia Duran called the Soviet Consulate [and] said there was an American citizen at the Cuban Consulate."[69]

Having contemplated this conundrum at some length, I am now inclined to question the transcript record, which at a minimum can be shown to have been altered (or censored). This alteration may have been either accidental, or deliberate, perhaps in order to reinforce the October 16 memo, which "determined that Oswald had been at the Soviet Embassy on 28 September 1963 and had talked with...Kostikov." A fuller, and presumably more accurate account of the transcript, in Mexico City Station cable 7023 of 23 November, separates the visit to the Consul from the visit of the same day. 28 September:

MEXI 7023 of 23 Nov 63:	TRANSCRIPT of 28 Sept intercept (Lopez Report, 76-77):
On 28 Sep 63 Silvia Duran Cuban Emb called Sov Consul saying Northamerican there who had been Sov Emb and wish speak with Consul.	At 11:51 a.m. Silvia Duran called the Soviet Consulate. She said that there was an American citizen at the Cuban Consulate who had previously visited the Soviet Consulate. The Soviet asked Silvia to wait a minute. Upon his return to the telephone, Silvia put the American on the line....
Uniden Northamerican told Sov Consul quote "I was *in your Emb and spoke to your Consul. I was just now at your Emb and they took my address.*"	Russian: What else do you want?
Sov Consul says "I know that".	American: *I was just now at your Embassy and they took my address.*
	Russian: I know that.

---

[68] Lopez Report, 246; 3 AH 49. Duran testified that she made only one telephone call to the Soviet Embassy, on Friday September 27 (3 AH 51); and that on Saturdays the Cuban Consulate doorman never let people in (3 AH 50). Since as early as CIA Cable MEXI 7023 of 23 November 1963, the CIA has maintained that its transcript record shows a second, independent call by Duran, with Oswald present, on Saturday, September 28 (Lopez Report, 76-77). Consul Azcue, who also spoke to Oswald, recalled three visits, and deduced that the third was probably on September 28 (3 AH 132-33; Lopez Report, 204). But he confirmed that on Saturdays the Consulate was not open to the public (3 AH 133). So did Consul Alfredo Mirabal Diaz, a witness who did not speak to Oswald, and who only recalled two visits (3 AH 173-74; Lopez Report, 205-06).

[69] Lopez Report, 77. Nechiporenko's book (110-11) reminds us that the initial post-assassination KGB report on Oswald "states that Oswald visited the Soviet Embassy in October 1963 and requested political asylum in the USSR." The report cited a KGB "special report from Mexico no. 550 dated 3 October 1963." Nechiporenko and his book are insistent that the only Oswald visits were on September 27 and 28. The allegation of an additional October visit should be set against what the Lopez Report has to say about a possible missing intercept transcript in which Oswald asked for assistance from the Soviet Consulate (Lopez Report, 83-88).

Note that the Cable provides no evidence of an Oswald-Kostikov meeting at the Soviet Embassy on September 28. as had been "determined" in the October 16 memo of Ms. X.[70] (The meeting could just as easily have been on September 27, a date corroborated by Duran, Kostikov and the September 27 transcripts).[71]

However the two visits had been collapsed into one when CIA Headquarters transmitted the contents of cable MEXI 7023 to the FBI (who already possessed the October 16 memo):

DIR (CIA HQ cable) 84915 of 23 Nov 63 to FBI:

On 28 September 1963 Silvia Duran of the Cuban Embassy in Mexico City telephoned the Soviet Embassy and said there was a "North American" with her who wanted to speak with the Soviet Consul. The "North American" came on the line and said that he had *just* been to the Soviet Embassy *and had spoken to their Consul* adding that the Soviets had "taken his address." The Soviet Consul acknowledged he knew this was true.

With the cables declassified, we can now see that this corroboration of the September 28 Oswald-Kostikov meeting (and thus of the October 16 memo) had no foundation in the cable from Mexico City it purported to transmit. This corroboration surely added to the swirl of foreign involvement stories that led to the creation of the Warren Commission. It was however an artefact which emanated from an office in CIA Headquarters.

Believers that the case is closed will say that these minute falsifications in the post-assassination cable traffic are of no significance, now that Nechiporenko and Kostikov have corroborated that the September 28 meeting did take place. Their critics may in rebuttal raise questions about the timing of the new Nechiporenko revelations, precisely when the shaky basis for the October 16 allegations has first been exposed.

For the present I must remain in the middle. The conflicting data we now have on Oswald's (or "Oswald"'s) visits in Mexico City demand a resolution we cannot currently provide. No source is above suspicion; and Nechiporenko's insistence that there could not have been a telephone call on September 28 should probably persuade us to look more critically at the transcript record than anyone has done in the past.

Thus my conclusion is much like that of the Lopez Report itself, whose authors concluded that "Oswald himself probably visited the Cuban Consulate at least once," probably on September 27, but that the individual involved in subsequent visits and telephone contacts "may not have been Oswald."[72] If the man who identified himself as Oswald was not, then the case against Oswald as a likely assassin was grounded, at least in part, on a pre-assassination deception.

For the time being I shall continue to take seriously the hypothesis, as yet neither proven or disproven, that a false trail was laid in Mexico City, linking Lee Harvey Oswald to the KGB's assassination capabilities.[73]

---

[70] By the rules of palaeography one is accustomed to prefer the more difficult or complex variant (the *difficilior lectio*) -- in this case, MEXI 7023. At the same time, one of the commonest errors of transcription comes from *homoioteleuton* or common endings: the eye of the naturally lazy transcriber skips from the first instance of a repeated passage (in this case "your Emb and") to the second instance, and thus accidentally deletes what falls between ("spoke to your Consul. I was just now at"). By this accident of *homoioteleuton* the impression of a Saturday September 28 meeting at the Soviet Consulate may have been falsely, but innocently, created, perhaps even before the October 16 memo. The re-creation of this impression in the DIR 84915 cable of 23 November (see below) has no such excuse, only that of the bureaucratic tendency to preserve allegations already in the file.

[71] There is additional testimony that the transcript record was edited to omit one additional intercept, in which Oswald asked for financial assistance (Lopez Report, 83-88, mentioned above at footnote 58).

[72] Lopez Report, 242, 245.

[73] According to Nechiporenko in interview, Department Thirteen of the KGB dealt not with assassinations but with the development of assets and contingency plans for future war situations. The two accounts are not necessarily incompatible. Others have suggested that Department Thirteen, concerned with war plans in response to a sneak nuclear attack, did in fact plan for teams with a future sabotage and assassination capability.

The Oswald Cables: An Unrelated Deception Operation?

One can only speculate as to the reasons why this false trail was laid. It seems unlikely however that those responsible acted without some kind of authorization, and even more unlikely that this authorization would have overtly contemplated the murder of the president. It is far more likely that these cables were sent as part of a CIA deception operation, and that this deception operation went back at least three years, to the time of Oswald's alleged defection to the Soviet Union.

As I write in November 1993, it is premature to speculate with too great precision what that deception operation (or operations) might have entailed. In the course of writing this essay I have received some three thousand items from the CI/SIG's 201 file on Oswald. The cover sheets on the pre-assassination reports on Oswald (from State, FBI and the Navy) show these reports being circulated to ten or more sections of the CIA's Clandestine Staff, not only in CI but in the SR or Soviet Russia Division, including SR's Counterespionage (later renamed Counterintelligence) Branch. This was headed by Tennant "Pete" Bagley, one of Angleton's "closest allies and strongest supporters in the Soviet division."[74] And Counterespionage, as defined by Angleton, involved not just understanding of but hostile operations against an enemy.[75]

Oswald may have been part of these hostile operations; alternatively he (or someone using his name) may have been a target. In June of 1960 an FBI memo to the State Department, signed by J. Edgar Hoover (and later added to Oswald's 201 file), raised the possibility that the person using Oswald's passport and other credentials in the Soviet Union was in fact an impostor.[76] Oswald was subsequently watched within the State Department by Otto Otepka and other members of its Office of Security, who collaborated with the FBI's Counterespionage Division and the CIA's Counterintelligence Staff in the search for Soviet penetration agents.[77]

Otepka's frustrations in pursuing the Oswald matter, which he shared with me fifteen years ago, are instructive. As a right-winger who shared Angleton's profound mistrust of the Soviet Union, he feared that Oswald's defection had something to do with the KGB. He found it anomalous that Oswald received a visa to enter the Soviet Union from Finland in only two days (rather than the one-to-two weeks it normally took); and also that the USSR granted Oswald an exit visa a month and a half early.[78] Above all, as a security officer who had spent a lifetime studying State Department procedures, he claimed to know for a certainty that Oswald in 1963 had been granted a passport when he should not have. His efforts to learn why were resisted by his own superiors at State, which compounded his suspicions of a subversive conspiracy.[79] Otepka was not alone in his suspicions.

Six months after the Hoover memo, in December 1960, Ann Egerter of the CI/SIG staff opened a 201 file on Lee Harvey Oswald, but gave it the falsified name of "Lee Henry Oswald." The same Ann Egerter was one of the CIA officials who in 1963 drafted the falsified cables about "Lee Henry Oswald" in Mexico City.[80]

The CI/SIG, which opened the 201 file on Oswald, also had a file on him through their mail-opening or HT/LINGUAL program, operated jointly with the FBI and the CIA's Office of Security.[81]

---

[74] Wise, *Molehunt*, 234. Cf. Mangold, *Cold Warrior*, 249.

[75] Mangold, *Cold Warrior*, 61.

[76] 11 AH 432; *New York Times*, February 23, 1975, 32.

[77] 26 WH 45; cf. 22 WH 21.

[78] William J. Gill, *The Ordeal of Otto Otepka* (New Rochelle, NY: Arlington House, 1969), 324-26. The one-to-two-week figure is confirmed by the Warren Report (WR 258).

[79] Interview with Otto Otepka, September 1978.

[80] AR 201 at footnote 40; Lopez Report, 143-46. Though Ms. Egerter is not specifically named in the Assassination Report as "the individual who was directly responsible for opening the 201 file," the document number of her classified interview on 5/17/78, 014731, is identified as Ann Egerter's in the Lopez Report on page 143 at footnote 570.

[81] CI/SIG's responsibility for HT/LINGUAL can be deduced by comparing AR 205 at footnote 74, with the footnote to 11 AH 476. Both make reference to the testimony of an ex-FBI agent heading CI/SIG (i.e. Birch D. O'Neal, 11 AH 476) who "had jurisdiction over the HT-Lingual project files" (AR 205). This HT/LINGUAL project may well explain why a CI card was opened on Oswald in 1959 with the notation "CI/Project/RE" (AR 206). The

And the letter "D" on the cover-sheet of Oswald's 201 file suggests yet another super-secret Counter-intelligence operation. The CIA's STAFF D was a SIGINT or signals intelligence operation, run in conjunction with the National Security Agency, or NSA.[82] Because of the ultra-secrecy involving NSA and SIGINT, Staff D became the hiding place for other CIA ultra-secrets as well. In 1961, when William Harvey headed Staff D, he was assigned the task of developing the CIA's assassination project, ZR/RIFLE, because "D was the perfect cranny in which to tuck a particularly nasty piece of business."[83]

The false name of Lee Henry Oswald may have been used by the CI/SIG to deceive investigators into the death of President Kennedy. The FBI reported that Birch D. O'Neal, the Chief of the CI/SIG, told them that the CIA had no CIA-generated material "in CIA file regarding Oswald," perhaps since all of the CIA cables in the CI/SIG file had been about a slightly different name.[84]

But it is hardly likely that the CI/SIG 201 file on Lee Henry Oswald, opened in 1960, was opened for this purpose. It is more likely that Angleton's spies in the CI/SIG, mistrustful not only of the KGB but also the rest of the CIA, set up the 201 file with the same motive as Otepka's researches in State, to learn more about suspicious operations in their own agency.

The false "Lee Henry Oswald" cables of 1963, for example, have the features of what Angleton himself called a "marked card" operation. This is a special form of deception operation, in which falsified information, "like a bent card, is passed through an intelligence channel to see where it ends up."[85]

In other words if Angleton (like Hoover and Otepka) mistrusted what "Lee Harvey Oswald" was up to, it made sense to put "marked cards," or falsified cables, in his CI/SIG 201 file on "Lee Henry Oswald." By this means he could learn who wanted to gain access to this false information, and also who they shared it with. With its special taint, "Lee Henry Oswald" information, if it turned up in the KGB, could have come from no other source. The "mole" (if one existed) could thus have been found.

Such a hypothesis may sound more like the fiction of LeCarré than the dreary realities of Washington bureaucracy. But by all accounts the mentality of LeCarré characters was the mentality of those in CI/SIG. Angleton allegedly believed, and the CI/SIG files contained, charges that Kennedy's roving ambassador Averell Harriman was a KGB agent; just as ten years later CI/SIG files would contain similar charges about Henry Kissinger.[86]

The issuance of a passport to Oswald in June 1963, which according to Otepka he should have been denied, would certainly have aroused the suspicions of those who could imagine that Harriman was a KGB agent. Nor should we trivialize the Oswald matter by comparing Lee Harvey Oswald, or even Lee Henry Oswald, to the paranoid Harriman allegations.

Quite the contrary. On the basis of what we know about the story of Lee Harvey Oswald as a lone defector to the Soviet Union, it is indeed possible, if not likely, that Angleton, Hoover, and Otepka, were all quite justified in mistrusting it.

Did the Oswald Cables Become Part of the Assassination Plot?

Even if the "Lee Henry Oswald" deception began as an unrelated matter, however, there are reasons to suspect that at least some of the falsified Oswald cable traffic of October 1963 was

"Projects Branch" within CI processed the information from HT/LINGUAL, and indexed the names (David C. Martin, *Wilderness of Mirrors* [New York: Harper and Row, 1980], 70).

[82] 4 AH 206 (cover-sheet); Peter Wright, *Spycatcher*, 145; Martin, 127; (STAFF D).

[83] Martin, 121. The ZR cryptonyms (e.g. ZR/KNICK, ZR/BEACH) were normally assigned to CIA radio monitoring projects collecting data for the NSA (Agee, 348, 351, etc.).

[84] WCD 49.22; Peter Dale Scott, *Crime and Cover-Up* (Santa Barbara: Open Archive Press, 1993), 12.

[85] Epstein, *Deception*, 77.

[86] Mangold, 330.

instigated (whether inside or outside the CIA) as part of a plot to assassinate President Kennedy.

As I have argued in my book *Deep Politics* and elsewhere, the key to this successful conspiracy appears to have been the false incrimination of Oswald in two successive phases of what I have called a dialectical cover-up. In the first phase, false but credible evidence was planted in government files to suggest that Oswald was part of a Soviet or Cuban conspiracy. The resulting threat of a devastating and unnecessary nuclear war was then used to persuade men of high status to accept a "phase two" fiction, equally false but much less disastrous in its consequence, that Oswald was not a "KGB assassin," but a "lone assassin."

This two-phase account of how the "lone assassin" theory came to be promoted is quite consistent with Earl Warren's narrative of how he reluctantly accepted the chairmanship, which he initially declined, of the Warren Commission. Warren said that President Johnson

> then told me of the rumors floating around the world. The gravity of the situation was such that it might lead us into war, he said, and, if so, it might be a nuclear war. He went on to tell me that he had just talked to Defense Secretary Robert McNamara, who had advised him that the first nuclear strike against us might cause the loss of 40 million people. I then said, "Mr. President, if the situation is that serious, my personal views do not count. I will do it."[87]

Why was the situation that serious? Rumors by themselves, "floating around the world," have virtually never caused a major accidental war. The Oswald-Kostikov rumors, however, unlike virtually all other "phase one" stories of Oswald as a KGB assassin, were floating around at the very top of the Counterintelligence staff of the CIA, as well as elsewhere in the government. It remains to be proven whether the falsified cables contributed to the decision at this time to place the nuclear forces of the U.S. on an alert, mobilized for possible retaliation against either Cuba or the Soviet Union.[88]

James Angleton and Ray Rocca, the head of the CIA CI staff and his aide, continued for some time thereafter to promote the importance of the Oswald-Kostikov meeting, and the resulting "phase one" case that Oswald was a KGB assassin. In this they were not alone, but were joined by others, notably Mexico City CIA Station Chief Win Scott.[89]

But their advocacy, while influential, was countered by the "phase-two" lone-assassin advocacy of others in government who were even more powerful, above all FBI Chief J. Edgar Hoover and Chief Justice Earl Warren. This could have been an honest disagreement among colleagues, in their assessment of the degree of Soviet (or Cuban) involvement.

Another, more conspiratorial possibility is that, from the outset, some of the "phase one" ("KGB-assassin") and "phase two" ("lone-assassin") advocates had colluded, in order to activate the dialectical cover-up. One is particularly struck by the on-going, and ultimately unauthorized intimacy between CI Chief James Angleton, perhaps the leading "phase one" advocate in the CIA, and FBI Counterintelligence (or Counterespionage) Chief William Sullivan, perhaps the chief architect of the ultimate "phase two" story that Oswald acted alone.

Investigation of the Kennedy murder led to a great institutional rift between two longtime collaborators: CI in the CIA and Counterespionage in the FBI. In January 1964 an alleged KGB defector, Yuri Nosenko, arrived in Washington with important but controversial backing for the "phase two" story. He claimed that he himself "had had an opportunity to see the KGB file" on Oswald, and thus "was able to state categorically that Oswald was not a Soviet agent and that no officer of the KGB had ever interviewed or debriefed him."[90]

This convenient but suspicious assurance found almost immediate backing from a power not usually friendly to KGB gifts: J. Edgar Hoover. In the CIA however, Nosenko was handled by CI

---

[87] Earl Warren, *Memoirs* (Garden City, NY: Doubleday, 1977), 357-58; reprinted in 11 AH 7.

[88] Michael R. Beschloss, *The Crisis Years: Kennedy and Khrushchev 1960-1963* (New York: Edward Burlingame/HarperCollins, 1991), 675.

[89] Lopez Report, 23-24.

[90] AR 101.

officials who treated him from the outset as a false defector with a false story.[91] This disagreement soon led to a permanent estrangement between Hoover and Angleton, and an order from Hoover that FBI agents should henceforth have no further dealings with the CIA.[92]

What is most striking in this split between the two agencies is that the friendship between Angleton, the Nosenko-attacking "phase one" advocate in the CIA, and Sullivan, the Nosenko-supporting "phase two" advocate in the FBI, continued unabated. "Contrary to Hoover's instructions," Curt Gentry has written, William Sullivan continued to meet with Angleton, "although both were careful to keep such meetings discreet."[93] Ultimately Sullivan's closeness to the CIA was one of the factors leading Hoover to force his resignation.

Angleton and Sullivan are said to have expressed opposing views about the credibility of Nosenko, and indeed about the whole issue of whether Oswald was a "KGB" or a "lone" assassin. These were among the most divisive issues separating the two agencies, so it is hard to imagine that two men who disagreed ideologically on them could have remained such close friends.

An alternative possibility is that the "phase one" and "phase two" views expressed by these two friends did not express their innermost convictions. One can speculate that perhaps, despite their promotion of opposing views, the two men were actually in agreement for some other agenda, whether dealing with the assassination or an unrelated counterintelligence matter. In this case Angleton and William Sullivan may well have been the key to an integrated, dialectical cover-up.

It is of course not conceivable that Angleton and Sullivan could by themselves have pulled off the cover-up. But what heightens the possibility of the two men's collusion in cover-up is precisely the special treatment given them at this time by their superiors. Angleton's CI/SIG was clearly responsible for the falsified "Lee Henry Oswald" cables that constituted the CIA's most recent embarrassing Oswald secret: yet Richard Helms, Angleton's superior as CIA Deputy Director of Plans, arranged for Angleton to co-ordinate the CIA's investigation of Kennedy's murder. He further directed that CI/SIG itself be responsible for liaison with the FBI on this matter, and for Angleton's deputy Ray Rocca to handle liaison with the Warren Commission.[94]

The situation within the FBI was even more paradoxical. Hoover was so angry at Sullivan's pre-assassination oversight of the Oswald matter that he approved a secret reprimand of Sullivan and other members of his counterintelligence staff. Yet Sullivan, and some of his reprimanded subordinates, were given tight control of the Oswald investigation (in liaison with CI/SIG) after Kennedy's murder.[95]

The least conspiratorial explanation for this collusive cover-up is that the Oswald secret overlapped with some on-going project concerning both the CIA and FBI. Yet it is hard to believe that this on-going project had nothing whatever to do with the assassination. One is particularly struck by the apparent coincidence (already noted) that William Sullivan, during World War Two, had been the head of the FBI's Special Intelligence Service (SIS) in Latin America. As such he had been the superior of Mexico City Station Chief Win Scott, as well of CI/SIG Chief Birch D. O'Neal, and of others who have figured prominently in the Kennedy assassination story. One of these was Dallas District Attorney Henry Wade, who on November 22 allegedly planned to indict Oswald for murder "in furtherance of an international Communist conspiracy."[96] (Among the others are also William Harvey and Robert Maheu, who oversaw the CIA-mob assassination plots against Fidel Castro, and William Gaudet, whose Mexican travel permit immediately proceeded Oswald's).[97]

It appears there may have been a clique within the government who cooperated with outside elements to kill the President, and that this clique included elements in Counterintelligence. For as

[91] Mangold, 173-91; Wise, *Molehunt*, 134, 139, 143, etc.

[92] Gentry, 418, 645-46.

[93] Gentry, 646; cf. 418, 734.

[94] 11 AH 57, 476.

[95] Scott, *Deep Politics*, 63-67; AR 243.

[96] PBS, Frontline show on Lee Harvey Oswald, November 16, 1993. Cf. Posner, 348n.

[97] Scott, *Deep Politics*, 96-97, 107, 112.

we have been showing they would have had the power to manipulate the "Lee Henry Oswald" deception operation, in such a way as to activate a "phase-one/phase two" dialectical cover-up.

Collusion to Promote a War?

As early as one day after the assassination, CIA Headquarters acted, correctly, as if they feared that independent actions, by the CIA station in Mexico City and its Mexican assets, might embroil the CIA in a war against Cuba. On November 23, after the Mexico City Station had requested the Gobernación Ministry of Mexico to arrest Silvia Duran, Headquarters reacted urgently, both by telephone and by Flash Cable. Langley rightly feared that the arrest "could prejudice U.S. freedom of action on the whole question of Cuban responsibility."[98] Indeed the interrogation of Duran was conducted in just this way by the Mexican Security Police (DFS), controlled by the Gobernación, so as to pressure her, vainly, to admit she was the "link for the International Communists" in a conspiracy to kill Kennedy.[99]

Such a confession, if it had been obtained, could indeed easily have led to war. At the time, the U.S. nuclear forces were on an alert; and senior U.S. officials, notably U.S. Ambassador to Mexico Thomas Mann, were arguing that Cuba was indeed involved in the assassination.[100] Transcripts of President Johnson's telephone calls in this period, newly released fom the National Archives, confirm that he talked repeatedly of the threat of nuclear war.[101]

Citing an internal FBI source, retired FBI agent James Hosty, who was disciplined (some say scapegoated) for his preassassination handling of the Oswald file in Dallas, has alleged that

> President Johnson and Robert F. Kennedy ordered intelligence agents in Mexico to stop pursuing a possible Cuban or Soviet connection. His informants tell him CIA agents in Mexico City were [in] "near mutiny" at this order....Mr. Hosty's theory has drawn support from...Thomas Mann, who has said he received "peremptory instructions to stop" investigating those issues.[102]

At least one of the declassified cables, signed by Richard Helms, confirms the concern in the CIA, FBI, and State, that Ambassador Mann was "pushing this case too hard."[103]

A first perusal of the newly declassified CIA documents indicates that proponents of the KGB or Cuban hypothesis were to be found inside Langley as well as the Mexico City Station. There were apparently also forces inside the Defense Department poised to use Oswald's record as a pretext to strike against Cuba.[104]

Could those pressuring to retaliate against Cuba have included in their numbers those who plotted to kill the President? One clue is the involvement of the DFS, the Mexican police who attempted to extract an inflammatory confession from Silvia Duran, with international drug trafficking, and hence with American organized crime. In *Deep Politics* I focused on the double role of DFS Chief Miguel Nazar Haro as both a major CIA asset (close to Win Scott) and also as a major figure in organized smuggling, both of drugs and of stolen cars, between the U.S. and Mexico.[105] I related this to pre-assassination reports in FBI files that Jack Ruby, as well as the Chicago mob in general, had

---

[98] CIA FLASH cable 84916 of 23 Nov 1963 (CIA Doc. 37-529). Lopez Report, 185; Schweiker-Hart Report, 25.

[99] 3 AH 91, cf. 86, 102; Scott, *Deep Politics*, 123.

[100] John Davis, *The Kennedys* (New York: McGraw-Hill, 1985), 549-52. Cf. Mann's cables MEXI 7072 of 26 Nov 1963 and MEXI 7104 of 27 Nov 1963.

[101] *Wall Street Journal*, October 18, 1993, A16.

[102] *Wall Street Journal*, October 18, 1993, A16. Cf. Schweiker-Hart Report, 41; 3 AH 568-69.

[103] DIR 85469 of 27 Nov 63 to Mexico City (CIA Doc # 178-620).

[104] Scott, *Deep Politics*, 275.

[105] Scott, *Deep Politics*, 104-05, 336. See also Peter Dale Scott and Jonathan Marshall, *Cocaine Politics: Drugs, Armies, and the CIA in Central America* (Berkeley and Los Angeles: University of California Press, 1991), 34-36.

also been important in Mexican-U.S. drug trafficking.[106]

Only with the release of the Lopez Report do we learn that in 1978, Nazar Haro, then still only the assistant chief of the DFS, was the senior DFS official coordinating with the visit of Edwin Lopez and other HSCA staffers to Mexico City.[107] This is indeed relevant to the assassination story, because the DFS in 1978 appears to have been less than fully cooperative with the House Committee investigators. In particular they failed to make available one of their members, Manuel Calvillo, who was apparently also a Mexico City CIA asset with a "pen name."[108] Juan Manuel Calvillo Alonso was involved in, and an apparent CIA source for, an inflammatory story (from the Mexican writer Elena Garro de Paz) linking both Oswald and Silvia Duran to an international Communist plot.[109]

How eloquent then is the implication of the Lopez Report, that with respect to Calvillo, the Mexican government was possibly lying.[110] And that, even more importantly,

The Committee believes that there is a possibility that a U.S. Government agency requested the Mexican government [i.e. the DFS] to refrain from aiding the Committee with this aspect of its work.[111]

There is no pretext in this area of "sensitive" sources or "on-going operations." The appearance of this particular cover-up is one of a lying co-conspirator being protected by his employers in two government agencies. It is the recurrence in the record of this kind of cover-up that suggests that the CIA's hidden Oswald secrets involve not just unknown intelligence operations, which might hypothetically be defensible, but also collusion by some individuals that is on the surface indicative of guilt.

[106] Scott, *Deep Politics*, 131-33, etc. I wish now that I had written more about the Mexican crime connections of Sam Giancana and Richard Cain (both allegedly involved in the CIA-mafia plots against Castro). Cain is additionally reported to have assisted the DFS, possibly in bugging operations against the Cuban and Soviet Embassies.

[107] Lopez Report, 270.

[108] Lopez Report, 209, 231-32, 279-80, 286, A-58.

[109] Lopez Report, 209; 3 AH 304; Scott, *Deep Politics*, 123.

[110] Lopez Report, 232.

[111] Lopez Report, 232.

III. CIA FILES AND THE PRE-ASSASSINATION FRAMING OF LEE HARVEY OSWALD

March 1994

Were CIA Files Manipulated to Prepare the Way for the Warren Commission?

The U.S. media responded to the 30th anniversary of the John F. Kennedy assassination by reviving the Warren Commission picture of Lee Harvey Oswald as a neurotic frustrated by neglect, and "angered" (in the words of Gerald Posner) "that others failed to recognize the stature he thought he deserved."[1] The newly released government files, we were assured, would add nothing to this picture.

In fact the recently released documents tell us a great deal that is new, and important, not so much about Lee Oswald the man, who remains mysterious, but about "Lee Oswald" the file subject. The man may or may not have been neglected, but the file subject was the focus of sustained governmental interest. This lasted from the time of his alleged defection in 1959, and was particularly active in the crucial eight weeks preceding the President's murder.

The clearest new picture of this sustained interest comes from the files of the CIA, the fullest new release that we have to date. Although the CIA had professedly no intelligence interest in Oswald the man, incoming FBI documents on "Lee Oswald" the file subject were always distributed to widely scattered sections of the CIA's Counterintelligence Staff, from a minimum of four persons in different sections, to as many as eleven. At least two FBI documents on "Lee Harvey Oswald" were reviewed by SAS/CI/Control, in the Counterintelligence section of the CIA's anti-Castro Special Affairs Staff, on November 21, 1963, the day before the assassination.

These details by themselves prove nothing. More serious is the evidence that the CIA files were being fed false information from without, while in the same period CIA officers were further distorting and falsifying the Oswald file with additional false information from inside, both prior to the assassination and subsequent to it.[2] The cover-up in this area can presumably be taken as an indication of some important issue at stake.

With the new releases, the number of unanswered questions about "Lee Oswald" the file subject is now greater, not less, than before. However one hypothesis at the center seems more and more reasonable. This is that the CIA's files were being both fed and doctored in late 1963 to present a continuous flow of apparent evidence, always plausible but never conclusive, and above all never true, that Oswald was a possible agent of Soviet or Cuban intelligence.

This alleged evidence was never at any time strong enough to justify an armed response against either the Soviet Union or Cuba. On the other hand it was cumulatively enough for Lyndon Johnson, by November 29, 1963, to persuade Chief Justice Warren and other recalcitrant leaders of the need for a Warren Commission. According to Warren, Johnson spoke of the "rumors floating around the world" that "might lead us into war," and possibly "a nuclear war."[3]

"Rumors floating around the world" were of course far less likely to lead to war than apparent evidence in government files of Oswald's involvement in KGB or Cuban assassination plots. I have called such claims "phase one" stories, because their real purpose may have been no more than to produce the desired "phase two" hypothesis (no more true, but much less dangerous) that Oswald was a lone assassin. Two of these "phase one" stories particularly concern us because in each case the claim, inherently flimsy, was actively promoted by individuals inside the U.S. government.

---

[1] Gerald Posner, *Case Closed* (New York: Random House, 1993), 220.

[2] By falsification I mean, not complete fabrication, but contamination of true information with details that are clearly false (such as replacing the name "Lee Harvey Oswald" in files with the false name "Lee Henry Oswald" that the CIA originated back in 1960).

[3] Earl Warren, *Memoirs* (Garden City, NY: Doubleday, 1977), 357-58; quoted at 11 AH 7. Cf. Peter Dale Scott, *Deep Politics and the Death of JFK* (Berkeley and Los Angeles: University of California Press), 113.

The first, which we shall look at more closely, was that Oswald had met in Mexico City with a Soviet KGB assassination operative, Valeriy Vladimirovich Kostikov. As we shall see, this allegation had been essentially stripped of its ominousness by November 27, 1963, when one of its original proponents had acknowledged there was no strong evidence of Kostikov's role as an assassin.

A Digression: The Timing and Consequences of the Alvarado "Phase One" Story

By this time, however, a second "phase one" story had surfaced. On November 25, 1963, a Nicaraguan double agent, Gilberto Alvarado, told a Mexico City CIA officer that he had seen Oswald recruited to kill Kennedy inside the Cuban Consulate in Mexico City. The second story had three points in common with the first one.

1. It had enthusiastic proponents within the government (in this case U.S. Ambassador Thomas Mann and CIA officer David Phillips in Mexico City).

2. It received apparent corroboration from other sources.

3. Nevertheless the story was inherently so flawed it was destined to be discredited.

The fatal weakness of the Alvarado story was his claim to have seen Oswald in the Cuban Consulate on September 18, 1963, at a time when Oswald had not yet left New Orleans. Faced with this problem, Alvarado retracted his story on November 30. We do not yet know if CIA Director McCone told President Johnson this when he discussed Alvarado with him on November 30 and December 1.[4] No matter: by November 29 Lyndon Johnson had announced the formation of the Warren Commission. (It would appear that the Alvarado story delayed the FBI's official report on the assassination, originally scheduled for November 29, until December 5.)[5]

Lyndon Johnson's conversation with Congressman Charles Halleck the same day gives the clearest picture of the role played by false "phase one" allegations: "This thing is getting pretty serious and our folks are worried about it...it has some foreign implications...CIA and other things...and I'm going to try to get the Chief Justice on it." Johnson added that "we can't have Congress, FBI and others saying that Khrushchev or Castro ordered the assassination:" "This thing is so touchy from an international standpoint....This is a question that could involve our losing 39 million people."[6]

Johnson drew particular attention to the plans which Senator Eastland had revealed to him the previous day, of holding hearings before his Senate Internal Security Subcommittee. Speaking to House Speaker John McCormack, Johnson explained that he had to announce the Warren Commission quickly: "I better get him [Senator Eastland] to call off his investigation." He added that some Dallas official would testify that Khrushchev planned the assassination.[7] This last detail is supported by the recurring reports that Dallas District Attorney Henry Wade, and his Assistant, William Alexander, had been preparing to charge Oswald with murdering the President as part of an international Communist conspiracy.[8]

But the Eastland Committee may have got wind of the still secret Alvarado allegation as well. Their staff person Al Tarabochia, a Cuban exile, claimed to "know someone who has access to confidential information about the Cuban Embassy in Mexico City."[9] Although Committee Counsel

---

[4] Schweiker-Hart Report, 103. An LBJ-McCone telephone transcript at 3:14 PM November 30 is withheld on grounds of national security.

[5] AR 244; Scott, *Deep Politics*, 38.

[6] LBJ telephonic transcripts: conversation at 18:30 11/29/63.

[7] LBJ telephonic transcripts: conversation at 16:55 11/29/63.

[8] Scott, *Deep Politics*, 270.

[9] Warren Commission staff memorandum of March 27, 1964 from W. David Slawson to J. Lee Rankin, reproduced at 11 AH 176; cf. 11 AH 65, 175, WCD 351. Warren Commission Document 351, which discussed this matter, also revealed that the Staff of the Senate Internal Security Subcommittee had been in touch with Ed Butler, whose right-wing propaganda organization INCA managed the Oswald radio debate in New Orleans. Cf. Peter Dale Scott, *Crime and Cover-Up* (Santa Barbara: Prevailing Winds Research, 1993), 53.

Julien Sourwine refused to reveal the identity of this informant, the thrust of the Eastland inquiry would seem to suggest that he was someone conversant with the Alvarado allegations.[10]

As far as we know, support within the CIA for the Alvarado "phase one" story was confined to the Mexico City Station. The Kostikov story, although short-lived, was potentially more serious. Not only did it have high-level proponents at Headquarters, it would appear that the Oswald-Kostikov contact had been reported by CIA officers in such a way as to ensure that its potential significance would not be realized at the time.

In short the key to the Kostikov story, as to the Alvarado story, would appear to have been its timing. Just as the Alvarado story contained a fatal flaw that led to its timely disposal, so the key · explosive element in the Kostikov story (his KGB status and alleged assassination activity) would appear to have been suppressed, with the result that no alarms went off until after the assassination.

The Kostikov Story and Falsifications in the CIA Documentary Record for October 1963

In October 1963, the month before the President's murder, the CIA produced five documents on Oswald: three cables, a teletype, and a memo. In late November the cumulative effect of these was to give investigators the impression, superficially provocative but in fact misleading, that Lee Harvey Oswald, the leading suspect in the assassination, had met in Mexico City with KGB agent Valeriy Kostikov, a suspected Soviet assassinations operative.[11]

1. The Mexico City Station Cable of October 8, 1963

Of these five documents, at least three show signs of CIA doctoring; and the first, which does not, was nevertheless so misleading as to be possibly dishonest. This was a cable to CIA Headquarters from the Mexico City Station on October 8, 1963, reporting that on October 1, an individual, who "identified himself as Lee Oswald," had been overheard telling the Soviet Embassy that three days earlier, on September 28, he had been at the Soviet Embassy when he "spoke with Consul whom he believed to be Valeriy Vladimirovich Kostikov."[12]

This cable has been the subject of much speculation since the belated release in 1975 of an FBI memorandum, saying that FBI agents in Dallas who had spoken to Oswald had "listened to a recording" of the voice of this individual, and were of the opinion that he "was not Lee Harvey Oswald."[13] The House Committee's devious treatment of this memo in their Report reflects their suspicion that the individual was in fact not Oswald but an impostor.[14]

This impression of an impostor was further complicated by the second paragraph of the cable:

Have photos male appears be American entering SovEmb 1216 hours, leaving 1222 on 1 Oct. Apparent age 35, athletic build, circa 6 feet, receding hairline, balding top. Wore khakis and sport shirt.

This 35-year old visitor to the Soviet Embassy was not the 24-year old Oswald. But neither (we now suspect) was he the individual who identified himself as Lee Oswald.

---

[10] Julien Sourwine was involved in other CIA-supported covert operations that may have had a bearing on the Kennedy assassination and cover-up. See Scott, *Deep Politics*, 116; cf. 215-16, 260, 262, 264-66.

[11] Peter Dale Scott, *Deep Politics*, 39-44.

[12] MEXI 6453 of 8 October 1963; Incoming 36017 of 9 October, CIA Document #5-1A; text in Lopez Report, 136-37.

[13] FBI Letterhead Memorandum of February 23, 1963, reprinted in AR 249-50; Scott, *Deep Politics*, 41-42.

[14] AR 250. The Report says that the CIA Headquarters, "never received a recording of Oswald's voice," leaving room for the possibility that they received a recording of someone else impersonating Oswald. This evasive language ("recording of Oswald's voice") is used three times: see Peter Dale Scott, "The Lopez Report and the CIA's Oswald Counterintelligence Secrets, in *Oswald in Mexico: A Research Document Compendium*, Book Three: The Lopez Report (Evanston, IL: Rogra Research, 1994), 11-14.

It is hard to justify the mention of this so-called "mystery man" in the cable. The intercepted telephone conversation had taken place at 10:45 A.M. that day; in it the man identifying himself as Oswald had spoken of a visit on September 28 only. There was nothing to suggest that he intended to visit the Embassy on October 1.[15]

The author of the cable's second paragraph, Ann Goodpasture, was an assistant to Station Chief Winston Scott, who supervised the work of three photo bases operating against the Soviet Embassy.[16] Her explanation to the House Select Committee (supported in part by other Station officers) was that, out of the four or five day period of Oswald's visit, this "was the only non-Latin appearing person's photograph that we found that we could not identify as somebody else."[17]

For various reasons Edwin Lopez and Dan Hardway, the authors of the House Committee's staff report on "Lee Harvey Oswald, the CIA, and Mexico City," found this explanation "implausible." One of these reasons was that the photo, allegedly taken on October 1, was in fact taken one day later. They also found it suspect that this alleged mistake was not discovered until 1976, even though CIA Headquarters, the day after the assassination, had told MEXI (the Mexico City station) that the "mystery man" was not Oswald, and added, "Presume MEXI has double-checked dates of these photos."[18]

If Ms. Goodpasture's testimony was accurate, then the photo surveillance of the Soviet Embassy failed to turn up any photos of the Lee Harvey Oswald arrested in Dallas. The House Committee was however unable to confirm this; the CIA declined to make the photo take from the Soviet Embassy available for review.[19]

2. The Headquarters Cable and Teletype of October 10 about Lee Henry Oswald

However suspicious we find the first cable's description of an irrelevant "mystery man," the Mexico City CIA Station's role in transmitting this information seems relatively innocuous, compared to the devious Headquarters response to it. Two messages were sent out within two hours of each other on October 10, a cable to Mexico City and a disseminating teletype to the FBI, Navy, and State Department. Although (according to one of the authors) "the cable and the teletype had been prepared simultaneously by three knowledgable people,"[20] the two messages contained falsified information and were mutually incompatible. While the teletype transmitted the misleading description of the 35-year-old mystery man, the cable informed Mexico City of the age and height of the 24-year-old former Marine Lee Harvey Oswald. Not by this name however: both outgoing messages misidentified the "Lee Oswald" in Mexico City with a "Lee Henry Oswald" who had since 1960 existed in CIA files and documents and nowhere else.[21]

CIA counterintelligence officer Ann Egerter, one of these "three knowledgable people," had invented the name "Lee Henry Oswald" back in November 1960, when information about Lee Harvey Oswald was collected in response to a request from the State Department's Director of Intelligence and Research. In December 1960 Ms. Egerter then opened a 201 file on "Lee Henry Oswald," which then became the repository for information on Lee Harvey Oswald, plus her lone misleading report on Lee Henry Oswald.[22]

[15] Lopez Report, 78-79.

[16] Lopez Report, 47-48, 136-37.

[17] Ann Goodpasture Testimony to House Select Committee on Assassinations, 4/13/78; reproduced in Lopez Report, 138.

[18] DIR 84888 of 23 Nov 1963; Lopez Report, 139-41.

[19] Lopez Report, 139; telephone interview with Edwin Lopez, 10/4/93.

[20] Lopez Report, 149.

[21] CIA teletype 74673 of 10 Oct 1963; CIA cable 74830 of 10 Oct 1963; both reproduced in Lopez Report, 144-46.

[22] File Request for "Lee Henry Oswald" reproduced at 4 AH 206. Without being directly named, Ann Egerter is identified by a reference in the House Committee Assassination Report (AR 201) to the individual who "responded to the [State Department] inquiry and then opened a 201 file on each defector [including 'Lee Henry Oswald'] involved." The footnote cites an interview of May 17, 1978 (JFK Classified Document 014731) which is identified in

This falsification in 1960 appears to have been deliberate. In her report for the State Department, Ms. Egerter also altered an FBI account from Oswald's mother of Oswald's coming "to *Fort Worth* for a visit of about three days" into a visit to "his mother in *Waco*, Texas for about three days."[23] The effect of the two alterations was to make "Lee Henry Oswald" much harder to trace.[24]

I will show in a moment that the falsification and distortion in the two messages of October 10, 1963, was in fact far worse than the supplying of two incompatible physical descriptions for a man with an invented name; and that it was possibly concerted (I suspect) so as to create an impression of KGB intrigue that would only surface after the assassination. But let us first dispense with the standard CIA explanation that the confusions in the cables are attributable to Murphy's Law, and the inattention of those drafting the cables. Ann Egerter told the House Committee that Oswald's "contact with Kostikov" "caused a lot of excitement" at Langley; and that Oswald "had to be up to something bad." Another of the officers drafting the messages (whom we shall call Ms. A) thought it possible that Oswald "really was working for the Soviets." The key to this excitement was the "contact with Kostikov;" yet Kostikov's KGB identity and allegedly sinister reputation were, inexplicably, not mentioned in either cable.[25]

These two employees should have to explain why, if the Kostikov contact excited them so much, they chose not to mention it to the FBI. It can safely be said that, if they had, the reaction of the FBI to their teletype would have been very different; and with it American history. The FBI already had a file on Kostikov, and knew him to be at the least a KGB agent. Thus Oswald would very likely have been interviewed, and possibly put under surveillance. If he had, he would probably not have been in a position to be, or be fingered as, the assassin.

What was left out of the two messages in fact created a far greater distortion than the misinformation included. What most strikes us about the two messages is not the falsification of Oswald's name (as Henry rather than Harvey) and of his wife's (as Pusakova rather than Prusakova); it is the staggeringly false claim in the cable that the "latest headquarters info" was a State Department report "dated May 1962:"

> Latest HDQS info was [State] report dated May 1962 saying [State] had determined Oswald is still US citizen and both he and his Soviet wife have exit permits and Dept State had given approval for their travel with their infant child to USA.[26]

---

the Lopez Report (142-43, footnote 570 at A-39) as that of Ann Egerter. This identification has been confirmed to me.

[23] CIA Document # 596-252F (copy of #1371-447); Attachment to letter of 21 Nov 1960 to Hugh S. Cumming, Jr., Director of Intelligence and Research, State Department, from Richard M. Bissell, Jr., CIA Deputy Director (Plans); submitted for signature by S.H. Horton, Acting Chief, Counter Intelligence Staff; CIA Document # 596-252F. Cf. FBI Interview of Marguerite Oswald, 4/23/60; in Fain Report of 5/12/60, "Funds Transmitted to Residents of Russia," 3; 17 WH 702.

[24] Marguerite Oswald lived and worked in Waco at the time of her FBI interview in April 1960 (17 WH 708), but not when Lee visited her in Fort Worth in September 1959. Other false or dubious statements in this brief 1960 report (e.g. that Oswald "renounced his U.S. citizenship") are traceable to sources outside the CIA: chiefly Marguerite Oswald's interview with the FBI, and a news story about Oswald by Priscilla Johnson (CIA Doc. # 594-252D).

[25] Lopez Report, 143.

[26] DIR 74830 of October 10, 1963; 4 AH 217. The CIA's 201 file on Oswald, as submitted to the Warren Commission (WCD 692), and as released to the public in 1992, contained at least three subsequent FBI reports on Lee Harvey Oswald: the Fain Report from Dallas of August 30, 1962 (after Oswald's return to Texas), the Hosty Report from Dallas of September 13, 1963 (linking Oswald to the Communist Party and the Fair Play for Cuba Committee); and a Letterhead Memo from New Orleans (see below) of September 24, 1963 (concerning Oswald's arrest on August 9). It is difficult however to speak with confidence of the contents of Oswald's 201 file. An internal CIA memo of 20 February 1964 reported that "37 documents which should be in the 201 file are not available in it" (4 AH 208). A machine listing of the documents in the 201 file was attached to this memo, but was missing by 1978 (AR 203-04). The House Committee deposed the author of the memorandum (unidentified) and learned that, because of back-up in the CIA computer system, "physical placement of the document in the file was not always necessary" (AR 204). WCD 692, the version of the pre-assassination 201 file supplied to the Warren Commission, was available for years to the public at the National Archive under conditions of minimal security. The best we can do is take the CIA's own release of 1992 as their version of what the 201 was supposed to contain.

There is no hint in either message that, as the CIA was well informed, Oswald had been back in the United States since June of 1962. On the contrary, both messages created the impression that Oswald, when last heard of, was still in the Soviet Union. (Thus the October 10 cable to Mexico City was summarized in a later file document as "Attempts of Lee Oswald and wife to reenter U.S.")[27]

By suppressing from the cable what it knew about Oswald since May of 1962, CIA Headquarters concealed a key fact which, if transmitted, should have resulted in Oswald's case being handled much more actively, and (perhaps even more importantly) by different people inside the Agency. This key fact was Oswald's arrest in New Orleans on August 9, 1963, in connection with his Fair Play for Cuba activities on behalf of Fidel Castro.

A seven-page FBI memo on this arrest, dated September 24, 1963, had in fact been received by the Agency on October 3. It was then seen by two of the authors of the cables: Ann Egerter of the Counterintelligence/Special Investigations Group, and Jane Roman of Counterintelligence/Liaison (on October 4). It thus should have been fresh in their memories when drafting the October 10 messages a few days later. Yet they both suppressed any reference to it.[28]

3. The falsification of Oswald's 201 File

The CIA later misled the Warren Commission about its knowledge of Oswald's arrest by October 3, 1963; and individual CIA officers may have broken the law in doing so. When the CIA belatedly submitted Oswald's 201 file to the Warren Commission (as Commission Document 692), the September 24 memorandum had been relocated to a later position in the file, making it appear (falsely) that it had been received after the October 10 cables had been drafted.[29]

Here it becomes relevant that it is a felony, under Section 1001 of the US Criminal Code, knowingly and willingly to falsify, conceal, or cover up facts within the jurisdiction of any department or agency of the United States. What we have just discussed is cover-up of material facts after the assassination to the Warren Commission. This pattern of cover-up is however consistent with other concealments, prior to the assassination, within the Agency.

Another apparent sign of cover up is that the May 1962 report on Oswald, summarized in the October 10 cable, was reportedly not in the 201 file, and thus never submitted by CIA to the Warren Commission. A copy of this State Department document was indeed sent to CIA in May 1962. If it was not in the 201 file, where was it filed, and why was this file not submitted to the Warren Commission?[30]

---

[27] CIA Cable MEX1 6534 of 15 Oct 1963 (incoming 40357); file copy in WCD 692, Oswald's 201 file. To add to the mystery, the May 1962 State Department report, referred to in the October 10 cable, is not included in Oswald's 201 file as we have it, while several FBI reports following his return are included.

[28] To believe the CIA, this latest piece of information on Oswald should also have been at the top of the 201-file that was apparently consulted in the preparation of the October 10 messages. It is possible however that the 24 September memo may have been initially filed in two other files (100/300/11 and 200/300/12) that apparently dealt with the Fair Play for Cuba Committee; and that it only found its proper place in Oswald's 201 file at a later time. This delay would only make more conspiratorial the behavior of Ann Egerter, who was the first to see the memo and was also responsible for Oswald's 201 file (Lopez Report, 142; Scott, "Lopez Report," 21).

[29] The two dated pages of the September 24 memo are placed in WCD 692 after an FBI transmittal form of November 8, 1963, and an FBI memo (the so-called Kaack report) of October 31, 1963 (which had been covered by the November 8 transmittal form). However the two dated pages were originally accompanied by five undated pages of text and Appendix, on "Lee Harvey Oswald," "Fair Play for Cuba Committee," "Corliss Lamont," and "Emergency Civil Liberties Committee." In the 1992 release of the CIA's 201 file these five pages are attached, falsely, to an FBI report from James Hosty, dated September 10, 1963. They clearly do not belong there. The two-page Hosty report ends on p. 2; the Appendix likewise begins on p. 2, rather than p. 3. This elaborate dispersal and concealment of the seven-page memo of September 24 can hardly have been accidental, or by inadvertence. (In the published Rector Press edition of WCD 692, the scattered pages of the September 24 memo will be found at pp. 71-75 [five undtaed pages], 113-14 [dated memo]).

[30] The document in question is a communication of May 17, 1962 with attachment from John Noonan, Chief of the State Department's Office of Security, to FBI Director J. Edgar Hoover, "Subject: American Defectors: Status of in the U.S.S.R." This document has since been released by the FBI as part of Oswald's FBI file (WCE 834, Item 36; unrecorded copy in Oswald Headquarters FBI File 105-82555, after serial -24; original in file 100-362196-423).

4. The Falsification in the October 16 Mexico City Memo

Just as Headquarters suppressed all references to Cuba in their pre-assassination messages, so, astonishingly, did the CIA station in Mexico City. One might argue that by October 8, the date of their Oswald-Kostikov cable, they had not yet established that Oswald had also visited the Cuban Embassy. But Oswald's efforts to obtain a visa at the Cuban Consulate were certainly known by October 16, when a "counterintelligence type" in the Mexico City station (whom we shall call Ms. B) drafted a memo on Oswald.[31] This memo was given to the FBI Attache in the Embassy; and by this channel FBI Headquarters finally learned, belatedly on October 18, that Oswald had not only visited the Soviet Embassy but had allegedly spoken with the KGB Agent Kostikov.

The October 16 CIA memo was apparently compiled after comparing the voice heard on October 1 (claiming to be Lee Oswald) with an earlier voice or voices on the telephone from the Cuban Embassy inquiring about a visa. Yet the memo mentioned neither the Cuban Embassy nor the exculpating fact that the alleged conversation with Kostikov was apparently about a visa.

Instead Ms. B's memo contained the following sentence (which would later prove to be a provocative one, when matched with the alleged assassination background of Kostikov):

This officer determined that Oswald had been at the Soviet Embassy on 28 September 1963 and had talked with Valeriy Vladimirivoch [sic, i.e. Vladimirovich] Kostikov, a member of the Consular Section, in order to learn if the Soviet Embassy had received a reply from Washington concerning his request. We have no clarifying information with regard to this request.[32]

The House Committee learned from the author of this memo that she had used the word "determined" after rechecking the transcripts of the various conversations (from both embassies). By this time the station had linked to Oswald at least four apparently related transcripts between September 27 and October 1, and of these two related unambiguously to a request for a visa from Washington. Yet the station officer, who had seen these transcripts, chose to write that there was "no clarifying information."

When asked why the 10/16 memo said that there was no clarifying information on Oswald's "request" when it was known by this time that he was seeking a visa, [she] said that "They had no need to know all these other details."[33]

Another slight departure from the facts, which would also prove to be provocative after November 22, was the false statement in the memo that "Oswald" had been at the Embassy on September 28 "in order to learn if the Soviet Embassy had received a reply from Washington concerning

There are other apparent falsifications of the pre-assassination Oswald 201 file (WCD 692). A State Department Memo of Conversation of January 26, 1961 (an apparent source for the words "attempted to renounce" in the October 10 cable), is in fact a copy of an internal State Department memo that was not sent to CIA (so far as we know) until after the assassination. An FBI Report from John Fain in Dallas on July 3, 1961 was the source for the cable's reference to "an undated letter from Oswald postmarked Minsk on five Feb 1961." This FBI Report was submitted to the Warren Commission as part of Oswald's 201 file, and again to the public in 1992. We now learn from the 1993 release that this report, although charged to the 201 file, "was not in the 201," when a copy "provided us by the National Archives" was added to it after the assassination. See the note on the last page of DBF-82181 (Fain report of July 3, 1961) under the cover sheet: "DBF-82181 7-3-61 (July 3 61) is part of Commission Document (CD-692) and is available to the public in this form. (A copy of DBF-82181 was not in the 201, altho IP/Files has it charged to it. This copy was made from CD-692 provided us by the National Archives. It is also #18 on list of attachments to XAAZ-22595 [CD-692, CIA Document #509-803] which is list of documents which existed on Oswald in the file before Nov. 22, 1963.)"

[31] Lopez Report, 170-71; cf. 101.

[32] Lopez Report, 170-71.

[33] Lopez Report, 170, 171. Eventually the station had a sequence of nine apparently related transcripts between September 27 and October 3, of which five concerned a visa request. After the assassination, the CIA decided that three of the nine calls were not by Oswald: two on September 27 (in Spanish, a language Oswald was not known to speak), and one on October 3 (when Oswald, according to the FBI and Warren Commission, was already on a bus back to the United States). Cf. Lopez Report, 73-80.

his request." In fact this inquiry was made on October 2 as a follow-up to the alleged meeting of September 28. The mis-dated inquiry was later cited as evidence that Oswald had made a significant, but unclarified, request to the Soviet Embassy in Washington, *prior to* his arrival in Mexico City.[34]

How These Falsifications Prepared for the "Phase One" Hypothesis: an Oswald-KGB Plot

The effect of the memo's distorted presentation was to leave a time-delayed but potentially explosive record in CIA files. The other ingredient for the explosive mix was the allegation, suppressed in Oswald's file but already contained in other CIA files, that Kostikov was a member of the KGB's Department Thirteen, with responsibilities for sabotage and assassinations. When these two allegations were put together, as they were in a November 23 memo from yet another CIA Counterintelligence officer, Tennant "Pete" Bagley, one had apparent evidence of a KGB assassination hypothesis, or what I have called "phase one" of a dialectical cover-up. The alternative hypothesis (or what I have called "phase two") that Oswald was a lone assassin, could thus be pressed on men like Chief Justice Warren, as a necessary device to avoid an unnecessary war with the Soviet Union.

On November 23, one day after the assassination, Bagley submitted a memo describing Kostikov as "an identified KGB officer...in an operation which is evidently sponsored by the KGB's 13th Department (responsible for sabotage and assassination)." The remainder of this provocative paragraph remains redacted.[35] It may well have been explosive. Possibly drawing on either FBI or CIA information, Dallas FBI Agent James Hosty later wrote of Kostikov as the KGB "officer-in-charge for Western Hemisphere terrorist activities -- including and especially assassination... the most dangerous KGB terrorist assigned to this hemisphere."[36]

At the same time, Bagley's reference to the 13th Department was apparently ill-founded. His clarification of it in a subsequent CIA blind memo of November 27 is so tentative as to be worthless.[37]

It will be seen that many of the falsifications and distortions in the CIA's Oswald documents had the same result: creating the appearance of evidence for a "phase one" hypothesis that would however not go off prematurely, before the assassination. Consider the examples of falsification:

1) *Suppression of Kostikov from the October 10 teletype*: James Hosty, the principal FBI agent on the Oswald case, has complained that he only learned of this contact with Kostikov, who was described to him only as a "Vice-Consul," not KGB, by accident in late October. Former FBI Director Clarence Kelley, transmitting Hosty's complaint, blames the pre-assassination failure to identify Kostikov as a KGB agent as the major reason why Oswald was not put under surveillance on November 22.[38] The FBI's failure to intensify investigation of Oswald in response to the October 10 teletype in this fashion earned a reprimand for a FBI Headquarters agent.[39]

---

[34] Rocca memo ZZ

[35] Memo of 23 November 1963 from Acting Chief, SR Division, signed by Tennant Bagley, "Chief, SR/CI." CIA Document # 34-538.

[36] Clarence M. Kelley, *Kelley: The Story of an FBI Director* (Kansas City: Andrews, McMeel, & Parker, 1987), 268.

[37] Blind memo of 27 November 1963, prepared by Birch D. O'Neal, C/CI/SIG, for Mr. Papich of the FBI Liaison Office (according to O'Neal's routing slip, "Mr. Bagley of SR prepared the portion responding to the question concerning any information we have 'pinpointing' KOSTIKOV as being in the 13th Department)": "KOSTIKOV's involvement in [redacted] is our only reason to believe that he is connected with the 13th Department. KOSTIKOV was in clandestine contact with [redacted] (as definitely confirmed by [redacted]'s photo identification) and arranged [redacted]'s contact in the U.S. with a KGB colleague of Kostikov's. This colleague was identified by [redacted] from photos as Oleg BRYKIN, who has definitely been identified, by an FBI source in a position to know, as a member of the 13th Department." Hardly a very solid foundation for Bagley's "phase one" claim that had a significant impact on how the President's murder was investigated!

[38] Kelley, *Kelley: The Story of an FBI Director*, 272-74.

[39] Memorandum from FBI Inspector James H. Gale of 12/10/63; as reported in Schweiker-Hart Report, 92; cf. 3

2) *"Latest HDQS info was...report dated May 1962"*: This too suggested an inactive matter, rather than what was in fact an active FBI investigation. (This language reached the FBI via Mexico City; the falsehood might have caught someone's eyes if it had been transmitted directly to FBI Headquarters, where at least three and probably four FBI reports on Lee Harvey Oswald had been transmitted to CIA between May 1962 and October 3, 1963.)

3) *The suppression of what was known about Oswald's visa request*: One could hardly have raised the specter of nuclear war against the Soviet Union (as it was raised in the days after November 22) if it had been clearly transmitted that Oswald's "request" to the Soviet Embassy in Washington was in fact about a visa.

4) *Suppression of the links between Oswald and Cuba*: A link (via Oswald) between the FPCC and the Cuban Embassy in Mexico City could hardly have lain dormant in CIA and FBI files until after the assassination on November 22. Both the CIA and the FBI had mounted offensive operations against the FPCC, hoping precisely to prove that it was receiving its orders from abroad.

5) *"Lee Henry Oswald" and "Marina Pusakova"*: Even these apparently trivial falsifications may have had the effect of postponing an FBI response to the October 10 teletype. Before October 10, all but one of the numerous documents in the CIA's "Lee Henry Oswald" file were in fact about Lee Harvey Oswald. By supplying Oswald's vital statistics to the FBI under a falsified name, the CIA effectively delayed for two days the moment of truth when FBI agents charged with investigating Lee Harvey Oswald learned about the apparently provocative contact with Kostikov. Following receipt of an incoming FBI cable from Mexico City on October 18, Oswald's FBI file contains a fruitless name search for "Lee Henry Oswald" on October 19.[40] Even though the incoming cable was answered on October 22, FBI Assistant Director Gale later found this delay grounds for a censure of the Headquarters agent responsible.[41]

But the suppression of Cuba from the CIA's pre-assassination Oswald records (both in Langley and in Mexico City) may have been much more important for another consequence. This was to keep the responsibility for the misleading October 10 messages solidly in the hands of *Soviet* counterintelligence personnel, the chief of whom was Tennant Bagley, Chief of SR/CI (Soviet Counterintelligence). Because the FPCC was an active CIA matter, mention of Oswald's arrest in the October 10 cables would have meant expanding the small cabal of drafters to include people charged with Cuban affairs (presumably working for Desmond FitzGerald, one of the more outspoken critics in the Agency of James Angleton's Counterintelligence staff).[42]

Instead, by restricting the October 10 cables to Oswald's career in the Soviet Union, only one area section cleared the drafts of each of them. This was SR/CI, the counterintelligence staff of the Soviet Russia section, headed (as we have seen) by Tennant Bagley.[43]

One is particularly struck by the fact that in October SR/CI had nothing to say about Kostikov, and acquiesced in two messages which found Oswald more worth discussing than the KGB agent he had met. Yet on November 23, one day after the assassination, Bagley submitted a memo describing Kostikov as "an identified KGB officer...in an operation which is evidently sponsored by the KGB's 13th Department (responsible for sabotage and assassination)."[44] It is hard to pin down precisely

---

AH 518; Scott, *Deep Politics*, 63.

[40] Oswald Headquarters FBI file, 105-82555, after serial -42.

[41] Memo of December 10, 1963; 3 AH 518, 522.

[42] FitzGerald once remarked that Angleton's CI men were holed up in a small office, scrutinizing the entrails of chickens.

[43] The teletype to the FBI, Navy, and State was cleared in draft with just two sections: CI/SIG (where Ann Egerter worked and retained custody of the Oswald 201 file) and SR/CI (where Tennant Bagley was Chief). The cable to Mexico City was cleared in draft with three: SR/CI/A, CI/Liaison/Jane Roman (who was the releasing officer on the teletype), and CI/SPG (presumably the same as CI/SIG).

[44] Memo of 23 November 1963 from Acting Chief, SR Division, signed by Tennant Bagley, "Chief, SR/CI." CIA Document # 34-538.

when Bagley acquired this alleged information about Kostikov. According to Edward Jay Epstein, however, Kostikov "had been identified *for some time* [prior to October 1963] as an intelligence officer for the KGB, who specialized in handling Soviet agents operating under deep cover within the United States."[45]

Why would SR/CI withhold from the FBI the information that Oswald (whom the CIA knew to be the subject of current and extended FBI intelligence reports) had just met in Mexico City with "an identified KGB officer"? The most sinister explanation would be that they only wanted this information to become known after November 22, so that Oswald would be left free until this time and then picked up, to be identified as Kennedy's assassin. This possibility of conspiracy, however remote, is so serious that those apparently responsible for this message -- including Bagley, Egerter, and Jane Roman -- should be questioned under oath.

A far more likely explanation, for which there is some evidence, is that the Oswald-Soviet contact in Mexico City was handled anomalously, because it was part of, or somehow impinged upon, a U.S. intelligence operation.

---

[45] Edward Jay Epstein, *Legend* (New York: McGraw-Hill, 1978), 237. Epstein, though not reliable on all matters, had excellent relations with members of Angleton's CIA Counterintelligence Staff, and does not hesitate to supply restricted information about their responses and files.

IV. THE THREE OSWALD DECEPTIONS: THE OPERATION, THE COVER-UP, AND THE CONSPIRACY

April 1994 (Unfinished)

Right-Wing Conspiratorial Pressures on the CIA

In the preceding two chapters I have argued that, beginning some two or three months before the assassination, events attributed to Oswald were systematically misrepresented in CIA files. These misrepresentations appear to have been part of an intelligence operation, whether one run by the CIA or possibily some other agency.

However these misrepresentations need not necessarily have been conscious preparations for the "lone assassin" phase-two account of the Kennedy assassination. One can imagine an alternative version of events, in which some or all of the authors of the misrepresentations are not themselves part of a complex assassination conspiracy (involving a "phase one" story about Oswald and Kostikov), but the victims of such a conspiracy.

This alternative version supposes a force outside the CIA, but knowledgeable about CIA operations and procedures, and possibly represented within its ranks. In such a situation someone could embarrass the CIA into evasive procedures, delays, and even falsifications.

Let us pursue the hypothesis that the CIA had mounted a counterintelligence operation involving Oswald, or the Soviet Embassy in Mexico City, or the Cuban Embassy there. And let us return to the distinction raised by the authors of the Lopez Report, that Oswald visited the Cuban and Soviet Embassies on September 27, but that the man who identified himself as Lee Oswald on October 1 (and allegedly "spoke with consul whom he believed be... Kostikov") was someone else, an impostor.[1]

If so, the second man may well have been part of a plot, launched outside the CIA, to implicate Oswald as the patsy in the assassination. If Oswald was part of a different, authorized CIA operation, then the evasive behavior of Egerter, Roman, et al. would be understandable. The standard CIA procedure of reporting such Embassy contacts to the FBI would have put the authors of the October 10 messages in a bind; they did not want the Oswald-Kostikov link to be investigated, because in the resulting "flap" the authorized Oswald operation would be blown.

There are indications that through the immediate post-assassination period the CIA continued to be subjected to embarrassing pressures from "phase one" advocates outside, but close to, the Agency. A long CIA memorandum of 11 December 1963 welcomed the announcement by the *New York Times* one day earlier that the FBI had found Oswald to be categorically the lone assassin, and not the agent of any foreign government. The memo continued:

> These disclosures presumably eliminate the possibility of further confrontations with Mr. Robert Slusser. In the event that Mr. Slusser continues to insist that the President was murdered by the Soviet secret police, the following additional negative indications and observations may be of some value.[2]

The memo continued for three and a half single-spaced pages to argue against the KGB "phase one" hypothesis, suggesting by its thoroughness that the confrontations with Mr. Slusser had been taken seriously.

A published authority on Soviet affairs, Robert Slusser was almost put into a position to lend credibility to his hypothesis. Early FBI reports about Lee Harvey Oswald's brother Robert indicate that at one point Mr. Slusser was about to be hired to write Marina's story. Eventually, after what

---

[1] Lopez Report, 242-50; MEXI 6453 of 8 October 1963. According to the full transcript, the name of Kostikov was actually raised by "Oswald"'s interlocutor, the Soviet Embassy guard Obyedkov, rather than by Oswald (Lopez Report, 79).

[2] Memo of 11 December 1963 to Chief/Soviet Russia, from Neil Huntley, C/SRI, "Additional Notes and Comments on the Oswald Case;" CIA Document # 376-154.

looks like intrigue, the contract went instead to Priscilla Johnson (later Priscilla Johnson McMillan). Her book, long delayed in its appearance, corroborated the FBI's and Warren Commission's "phase two" finding that Oswald acted alone.[3]

Other right-wing sources, often explicitly hostile to the CIA, kept alive the phase-one specter of a link between Oswald and either Soviet or Cuban intelligence. From as early as December 1963, the CIA itself was blamed by such sources, either implicitly or explicitly, for its part in the President's murder. John Martino, an active plotter against Castro with a mob background, surfaced one such story in December 1963, blaming the President's death on Castro's response to a plot between Kennedy and the Soviets to have Castro replaced in Cuba by Huber Matos, a former Castro ally now detained in a Cuban jail.[4]

This alleged plot was a veiled allusion to the AMTRUNK plan mounted by the CIA and Robert Kennedy in 1963 to use old allies of Matos to overthrow Castro.[5] But Martino the source is perhaps more interesting than his story. In 1963 he had been receiving support for his own anti-Castro operations from Julien Sourwine, Chief Counsel for the Senate Internal Security Subcommittee.[6] It was this Committee, the reader may recall, whose phase-one interests were Johnson's reason (or pretext) for setting up the Warren Commission.

There was no shortage of such allegations, though they often came back to the same sources. In September 1963 Robert Allen, a columnist with sources in U.S. Army Intelligence, wrote of a joint U.S.-Soviet operation which planned to replace Castro by a new revolutionary coalition acceptable to both superpowers.[7] On November 14, 1963, former Cuban President Carlos Prío Socarras reported to the CIA in Miami that there was now a U.S. agreement with the Soviet Union to replace Castro with a "Tito-type government."[8] An article in the journal of the John Birch Society, whose author Revilo Oliver later cited sources among veterans of army intelligence and the FBI, also argued that Kennedy's murder "was part of a Communist plot engineered with the help of the Central Intelligence Agency," and cited the "fake 'revolt'" plotted by Kennedy and Khrushchev to replace Castro with a crypto-Communist "'agrarian reformer.'"[9]

Thus the right-wing pressures which forced the Warren Commission into being continued to play on it throughout its existence. And insofar as one can detect a common source for all these stories, that source would appear to be not only outside the CIA but extremely hostile to it.

The word "outside" here can however be misleading. Every one of the allegations here summarized drew on inside information. For example John Martino reported in his December 1963 article that Oswald had tried to penetrate the anti-Castro Cuban group JURE: this claim was not generally known at the time but it was later corroborated by Silvia Odio's account of her meeting with Oswald in September 1963. Furthermore the Kennedys and the CIA had a plan (AMTRUNK) to oust Castro, which would have used, among others, the forces of JURE. The plan was still on-going in 1964, and thus extremely sensitive. Above all it planned to install a new government which would be free from mob influence, a detail which was sufficient to incur the hostility of mob allies like John Martino.

These so-called "outsiders" knew enough about the ways of government, and specifically the CIA, to embarrass it into cover-up. It seems likely therefore that somewhere they had their spies inside government, and possibly inside the CIA.

[3] Priscilla Johnson McMillan, *Marina and Lee* (New York: Harper & Row, 1977).

[4] John Martino, "Cuba and the Kennedy Assassination," *Human Events*, December 21, 1963, 3.

[5] The chief of these allies were the JURE leaders Manuel Ray, Ramon Barquin, and Napoleon Becquer (10 AH 137; cf. *New York Times*, April 19, 1962). See pp. 47-49.

[6] Scott, *Deep Politics*, 116; 11 AH 65.

[7] *Jackson Daily News*, September 28, 1963.

[8] WAVE 8562 to DIR; cf. WAVE 7495 of 14 Nov 63 to DIR, reporting (via Bernard Barker) exile feeling of "U.S.-Soviet deal backing AMTHUG [Castro] overthrow and establishment Tito-type Commie government."

[9] Scott, *Deep Politics*, 215; Revilo Oliver, *American Opinion*, March 1964; 15 WH 710.

The Most Likely Manipulator: David Atlee Phillips

So far this discussion has focused on those "phase one" stories linking Oswald to Soviet or Cuban intelligence which at the time existed uniquely in government files, and which for a while the U.S. Government took seriously. We have not yet mentioned the veritable blizzard of similar stories which reached the FBI and CIA from external sources after the assassination. After November 24 there were still more "phase one" stories attributing a similar role to Jack Ruby. And to all these anti-Communist stories denouncing the KGB and Cuba one must add those stories with an opposite political spin, linking Oswald and/or Ruby to right-wing Texas millionaires, oilmen, anti-Castro Cubans, the mob, or the right-wing terrorist Minutemen. Most of these leads did not check out.

There were so many such false leads that one might be easily tempted to write them all off as meaningless "noise." However House Committee researcher Dan Hardway chose to look closely at all the stories that came out of Mexico City and Miami connecting Oswald with Soviet or Castro intelligence. According to his colleague Gaeton Fonzi, "Hardway's research had indicated that most of the individuals originating the reports" were assets of the Mexico City Station's Chief of Covert Action and Cuban Operations, David Phillips.[10]

Hardway had the opportunity to quiz Phillips about this at an informal Committee interview, with Fonzi present. Hardway was armed at the interview with documentation from the Agency to dispute Phillips' claim that these assets had been run by other CIA agents. After the session, Hardway told Fonzi,

I'm firmly convinced now that he ran the red-herring, disinformation aspects of the plot. The thing that got him so nervous was when I started mentioning all the anti-Castro Cubans who were in reports filed with the FBI for the Warren Commission and every one of them had a tie I could trace back to him.[11]

To date I have been unable to contact Dan Hardway, although another good source has confirmed that he did conduct this research. It is also clear that a number of the "phase one" stories linking Oswald to Cuba did come from a single milieu of anti-Castro Cubans in Miami close to, and in some cases supported by, the CIA's JM/WAVE station there. David Phillips does therefore seem a likely candidate to have co-ordinated the stories coming out of Mexico City and Miami. For in the second half of 1963 he was cross-posted to both stations, as Chief of Cuban Operations in Mexico City, and as Chief of Psychological Operations (i.e. propaganda) in Miami. (In fact it is possible that David Phillips held down three posts in 1963, and was doubling also as a member of the Special Affairs Staff Counterintelligence (SAS/CI) staff.)

A small intelligence-backed "press agency," the Agencia de Informaciones Periodisticas (A.I.P.), was a source for one recurring Oswald story, that he had worked on behalf of Cuban intelligence in the Miami area. (The A.I.P. attracted notice again during the wave of Chilean-financed Cuban terrorism of the mid-1970s, involving many Cuban exile veterans of the JM/WAVE operations, when the A.I.P. was revealed to be an agency by then financed by the Chilean intelligence service DINA.)[12] The story was traced by the FBI to Fernando Fernandez Capada of the A.I.P., who told it to Jim Buchanan, a close ally of Frank Sturgis; the story was later publicized by Frank Sturgis and John Martino.[13]

Another A.I.P. story, traced to Dr. Fernando Carrandi, spoke of Ruby's travel to Cuba. Those involved in circulating this story included Salvador Lew, p.r. agent for the CIA-backed Comandos Mambises, and Paul Bethel, described by Fonzi as "a close friend of David Atlee Phillips."[14] Yet another Oswald-Cuban intelligence story involved Miguel "Cuco" de Leon, senior adviser to Manuel

---

[10] Fonzi, 292.

[11] Fonzi, 292-93.

[12] Magnus Linklater et al., *The Nazi Legacy* (New York: Holt, Rinehart, and Winston, 1984), 278.

[13] WCD 1020.1-6,16; 26 WH 424-25; Scott, *Deep Politics*, 338.

[14] WCD 916.2-3. Bethel was also involved in another false story of hit teams dispatched by Castro to kill Kennedy: see WCD 893.1-7; 22 WH 864; Scott, *Crime and Cover-Up*, 60-61.

Artime in the JM/WAVE-backed Operation Second Naval Guerrilla.[15]

Any evidence for linking Phillips to these intelligence-tinged stories has not yet been made public. We have however Phillips' own statements that he was involved in the transmission of both of the key "phase one" allegations promoted in CIA cables, the Kostikov story of October, and the Alvarado story of November 25.

As mentioned above, it would appear that Phillips' claim to have signed off on the Kostikov cable of October 8 is simply not true. Phillips claimed this in sworn testimony, as part of his effort to rationalize the delay of one week in transmitting the intercepted conversation of October 1.[16] Phillips' admitted role in the transmission of the Alvarado story, that Oswald was paid money in the Mexico City Cuban Consulate to kill Kennedy, is however corroborated by the documentary record. Here too there is a difference between Phillips own account and the cables however. In his autobiography Phillips describes the story he heard from Alvarado's lips as a lie easily seen through, indeed as a "transparent operation."[17] In the cables sent after his interviews with Alvarado, however, the tone is quite different. There we hear that "This officer was impressed by Alvarado...wealth of detail Alvarado gives is striking."[18] One cable described Alvarado as a "quiet, very serious person, who speaks with conviction;" another, the next day, called him "completely cooperative."[19]

Most revealing was the description of Alvarado as a "well-known Nicaraguan Communist underground member," whereas in fact (as he himself revealed later the same day) he was a penetration agent of the right-wing Somoza Government of Nicaragua.[20] (This revelation was quickly confirmed by CIA cables from Managua and Headquarters.)[21]

Winston Scott, Ambassador Thomas Mann, and the Mexican DFS

Assuredly Phillips was not alone in backing the Alvarado story at the time. Ambassador Thomas Mann, together with Station Chief Win Scott and FBI Legal Attache Clark Anderson, sent a Flash cable on November 26 suggesting that Silvia Durán should be rearrested in order to corroborate it:

> We suggest that the Nicaraguan be put at the disposition of President
> Lopez Mateos on condition that Lopez Mateos will agree to order
> rearrest and interrogate again Silvia Tirado de Duran along following
> lines:
>   A. Confront Silvia Duran again with Nicaraguan and have
> Nicaraguan inform her of details of his statement to us.
>   B. Tell Silvia Duran that she is only living non-Cuban who
> knows full story and hence she is in same position as Oswald was
> prior to his assassination; her only chance for survival is to come
> clean with whole story and to cooperate completely....
>   Given apparent character of Silvia Duran there would appear to
> be good chance of her cracking when confronted with details of
> reported deal between Oswald, Azcue, Mirabal [the two Cuban consuls]

---

[15] WCD 770.7-9; Scott, *Crime and Cover-Up*, 18, 20.

[16] Lopez Report, 127-28; Fonzi, 293. After interrogating Phillips informally on this issue, Hardway told Fonzi that, "based on the research he had done tracking the routing of the cables and the lack of credible answers about them from Phillips, he believed there was a strong possibility the cables were created after the fact" (Fonzi, 293).

[17] David Phillips, *The Night Watch* (New York: Atheneum, 1977), 141-42; quoted in Scott, *Deep Politics*, 122.

[18] MEXI 7104 of 27 November 1963; CIA Document #174-616.

[19] Mexico City cable of 26 November 1963 (MEXI 7067?), retransmitted as DIR 85199 of 27 November, WCD 1000B.4; WCD 1000C.2.

[20] Memo of 26 November, WCD 1000A; MEXI 7083 of 26 November.

[21] MANAGUA cable of 26 November, 262237Z; DIR 85196 of 27 November 1963.

[22] MEXI 7072 of 26 November 1963; CIA Document #128-590.

and Duran and the unknown Cuban negro [described by Alvarado].
If she did break under interrogation -- and we suggest Mexicans
should be asked to go all out in seeing that she does -- we and
Mexicans would have needed corroboration of statement of the
Nicaraguan.[22]

Mann on his own went on to recommend the arrest of three Cuban members of the Cuban consulate, and later to argue forcefully that Castro was the "kind of person who would avenge himself" by assassination.[23]

These cables were in defiant opposition to the cooler approach in Washington. Headquarters had already tried to oppose the original arrest of Durán, rightly fearing that the arrest (and interrogation by the Mexican secret police, or DFS) "could jeopardize U.S. freedom of action on the whole question of Cuban responsibility."[24] Headquarters replied again to the new Durán cable, warning the Station Chief that the Ambassador was pushing the case too hard, and his proposals could lead to an international "flap" with the Cubans.[25]

Headquarters were absolutely right in their concern that the Mexican DFS were out to "prove" an international conspiracy involving Oswald with Cuba. Silvia Durán later confirmed that in their interrogations of her

all the time they tell me that I was a Communist...and they insisted that I was a very
important person for...the Cuban Government and that I was the link for the International
Communists -- the Cuban Communists, the Mexican Communists and the American
Communists, and that we were going to kill Kennedy, and I was the link. For them I was
very important.[26]

In its performance however, the DFS was almost certainly (as Edwin Lopez has since corroborated to me) tightly controlled by the CIA Station. The DFS was part of the Mexican Ministry of the Interior, or Gobernación; its Minister, Gustavo Díaz Ordáz, was a CIA asset, and also a close friend of Station Chief Win Scott (the best man at Scott's third wedding), as well as of Ambassador Mann -- and Lyndon Johnson.[27] Details of Durán's interrogation suggest that the DFS, seeking to prove her conspiratorial involvement, was being fed clues by the Americans.[28]

Given the predisposition of the DFS to find a communist conspiracy, a fact known even in Washington, and given the well-known brutality of DFS interrogation methods (which included torture), it is particularly revealing that Mann and Scott would recommend asking the DFS "to go all out in seeing that she [Durán]...break under interrogation." Circumstances suggest that the documentary record here is incomplete, in at least two respects:

1) Contrary to the records we now have, Durán had already been tortured, and may have already "confessed" to a sexual involvement with Oswald, since expunged from the record.

2) Mann's apparently reckless defiance of official instructions *against* the arrest of Durán was

---

[23] MEXI 7104 of 27 November 1963; MEXI cable of November 28 1963, Anthony Summers, *Conspiracy*, 441. Cf. 3 AH 569.

[24] DIR 84916 of 23 November; Lopez Report, 185-86; Schweiker-Hart Report, 25.

[25] DIR 85371 of 28 November 1963; Lopez Report, 187; Schweiker-Hart Report, 29.

[26] 3 AH 91; cf. 3 AH 86. Note that the DFS exempted the Soviets from their hypothetical conspiracy, as did Ambassador Mann (Summers, 441).

[27] Scott, *Deep Politics*, 123; Philip Agee, *Inside the Company: CIA Diary* (Harmondsworth, Middlesex: Penguin, 1975), 274-75; Dick Russell, 454, 457-58. In late 1963 Díaz Ordáz was on leave as the Presidential candidate of the ruling PRI; but his replacement as Acting Minister, Luís Echeverría, was also a CIA asset on the CIA payroll.

[28] For example, the Americans knew that Durán's name and the telephone number of the Cuban Consulate, 11-28-47, were in Oswald's address book (16 WH 54). Durán told the House committee that the DFS "asked me I don't know how many times, the way that I used to give my name and telephone number and they made me write and they take the paper out and then again, they ask me, how do you do this, and I write it down, and I give the paper. I think I do this five or six times" (3 AH 102).

probably based on unofficial guidance from a very high level in Washington.

A Suppressed "Phase One" Story: Oswald's Alleged Sexual Liaison

Alvarado introduced a sex angle into his fantastic story about seeing Oswald be paid $6,500 to kill someone. He spoke of a "pretty girl" in the Consulate (whose manners reminded him of a "prostitute") who had given Oswald an embrace and also a home address "where he could find her."[29]

In 1967, transmitting an agent's report of an interview with a source who knew Durán, Win Scott commented:

> The fact that Silvia DURAN had sexual intercourse with Lee Harvey Oswald on several occasions when the latter was in Mexico City is probably new, but adds little to the OSWALD case. The Mexican police did not report the extent of the DURAN-OSWALD relationship to this Station.[30]

Scott's choice of words ("fact," "extent") is indicative of earlier events involving Durán that have not hitherto been publicly reported.

In fact Scott had both misrepresented what the informant apparently said (reporting sexual relations with Oswald, but not "on several occasions"), and suppressed its most important revelation, that she had been tortured by the DFS until she "admitted that she had had an affair with Oswald:"

> [Long redaction] XXXX continued that Silvia Durán informed XXXX that she had first met Oswald when he applied for a visa and gone out with him several times since she liked him from the start. She admitted that she had had sexual relations with him but insisted that she had no idea of his plans. When the news of the assassination broke she stated that she was immediately taken into custody by the Mexican police and interrogated thoroughly and beaten until she admitted that she had had an affair with Oswald.[31]

It is noteworthy that Scott, far from rebutting the torture allegation, apparently accepted it as a fact, and one not worth commenting on.

The Lopez Report, in transmitting this interview, commented that "Silvia Duran admitted that the Mexican police had questioned her on this point but denied that she had had an affair with Oswald."[32] This account is confirmed by its cited source, Silvia Durán's interview of June 6, 1978.

> Cornwell: Did the officers from the Securidad Department ever suggest to you during the questioning that they had information that you and Oswald had been lovers?

> Tirado [Durán]: Yes, and also that we were Communists and that we were planning the Revolution and uh, a lot of false things.[33]

Curious as to why Ms. Durán had not been asked about the torture, I contacted Edwin Lopez, who had translated at the interview. He confirmed that, off the record, Ms. Durán had said that she was tortured badly, and that indeed in recalling this she had broken down and wept. She had however declined to say anything about the torture on the record because, as a citizen and resident of Mexico, she feared reprisal.

---

[29] MEXI 7067(?) of 26 November 1963; WCD 1000B.

[30] Dispatch HMMA-32243 of 13 June 1967 from COS, Mexico City, to Chief, Western Hemisphere Division; CIA Document # 1084-965.

[31] TX-1937 of 26 May 1967, CIA Document # 1084-965, reporting interview of informant in safehouse on 25 May, 1967. John Newman has plausibly identified the informant as Luis Alberu, a double agent turned by the CIA instead the Cuban Embassy (John Newman, *Oswald and the CIA*, 386; cf. 360). In 1964 the Station had also heard the allegation of an Oswald-Durán liaison from a dubious witness, Elena Garro, with strong DFS connections (Lopez Report, 207, 220; 3 AH 302).

[32] Lopez Report, 254.

[33] 3 AH 86.

One hesitates now to make any revelation that would put Ms. Durán at risk. The issue however is an important one. According to the account which Scott accepted as "fact," she was not only tortured on the matter of the liaison, but coerced into admitting it. If Scott's blasé comment is true (this "adds little to the OSWALD case"), then the accounts of her confession have probably been altered, to convert a suppressed "phase one" story of a sexual liaison into the innocuous "phase two" version published by the Warren Commission.[34] Lending credence to this hypothesis is the known fact that the published version was censored and rewritten (by the CIA, according to the Lopez Report) on at least one other point, Durán's original description of Oswald as "blonde and short".[35]

Were Mann and Scott Backed in Their Defiance of Official Instructions?

All this lends dramatic urgency to the question of whether or not Scott and Mann were "acting alone" in their defiant recommendation, against earlier official instructions from Headquarters, that Durán be rearrested by the DFS, and coerced into corroborating the Alvarado story.

One interpretation of the known facts is to postulate a real division within the Administration, between "phase one" enthusiasts like Scott and Mann (who wanted to ask the DFS "to go all out") and "phase two" pragmatists like Karamessines, who struggled in vain to prevent the arrest and rearrest from taking place.

The chief problem with this analysis is that Scott and Mann drew no disapprobation for their course of action. Scott remained in his post as Chief of Station until his retirement six years later. Mann, far from being rebuked, was swiftly promoted by the new President, Lyndon Johnson, on December 14, 1963, to become the new Undersecretary of State for Latin American Affairs. (Mann's promotion was the more dramatic because unexpected; he had earlier announced, under Kennedy, his plans to retire at the end of the year.)[36]

A second interpretation of the facts is that beneath the apparent contest of opposing forces, "phase one" and "phase two," a higher authority was manipulating the Alvarado story, backed as it was by Scott and Mann, towards the desired "phase two" outcome of the Warren Commission and Report. I truly do not know whether or not such a higher authority existed. If it did, however, it almost certainly involved Lyndon Johnson.

Lyndon Johnson was a close personal friend of the soon-to-be-elected Mexican President Gustavo Díaz Ordáz, who has been described as the most right-wing (and pro-American) President since Miguel Aleman in the early 1950s. Just as Díaz Ordáz maintained tight control over the DFS (along with his good friend Win Scott), so Johnson was the friend and hope of those in the CIA who thought that Kennedy had been wrong to dismiss Allen Dulles after the Bay of Pigs fiasco.

As Johnson barely spoke Spanish, he relied in his meetings with Díaz Ordáz on the translating ability of a fellow Texan, Thomas Mann. As Mann later told author Dick Russell,

> Lyndon Johnson had lines into Mexico that I knew nothing about. He was an amazing man. He didn't speak Spanish, but he was a good friend of [Gustavo] Díaz Ordáz, who became President of Mexico. He used to come down and see Johnson at the ranch several times, and Johnson would have me down to translate.[37]

(For what it is worth, former KGB Colonel Oleg Nechiporenko reports that his DFS contact told him that "many in the DFS felt that Lyndon Johnson was responsible" for the assassination.)[38]

Johnson was not particularly close to the CIA as an Agency. His lack of interest in intelligence estimates has been cited as a reason for the resignation of CIA Director John McCone in 1965, and

---

[34] 24 WH 565.

[35] Lopez Report, 190; Scott, "The Lopez Report," 6.

[36] Scott, *Deep Politics*, 94.

[37] Russell, 454.

[38] Oleg Nechiporenko, *Passport to Assassination* (New York: Birch Lane/ Carol Publishing, 1993), 181.

Johnson's replacement of him by an inept outsider, Admiral William Raborn.[39] In 1966 Johnson did however give the CIA its first Director who was also a career officer, Richard Helms, and Helms had been close to Dulles since their days together in Germany with OSS.[40] (Helms later revealed that Johnson had explained to him in 1965 that Raborn was a "temporary measure," and that Johnson would appoint Helms when he had proved himself as Deputy Director.)[41]

What remains unknown is the extent of the new President's knowledge of the "phase one" rumors which, as he informed Earl Warren, were "floating around." If he had any intimate knowledge of either the Kostikov story or the Alvarado story, he must have known that a true investigation of the case would have to be at arms length from the CIA. Instead Johnson named Allen Dulles to the Warren Commission. Dulles' strategic location was to play an important role in the CIA cover-up that ensued. If there was a conspiracy to ensure such a cover-up, then the naming of Dulles to his new post was almost certainly part of it.[42]

However important the personal connection between Johnson, Díaz Ordáz, and Thomas Mann, it could never, however, have explained the strange falsifications of CIA messages that occured at CIA Headquarters. To explain that phenomenon we must look inside the Agency itself.

Such a program of falsification and subsequent cover-up could have been co-ordinated, I shall suggest, by those who were closest to former Director Allen Dulles.

The Dulles-Angleton-Hunt-Phillips "Agency-Within-the-Agency"

In 1963 the "responsible" press, the *New York Times* and the *Washington Post* never commented critically on Johnson's choice of Allen Dulles, the most important official fired by John F. Kennedy, to serve on the Commission investigating the President's murder.

Even though one would never expect them to play this critical role, they should have, for Allen Dulles was perhaps the Kennedys' most powerful enemy in the U.S., arguably more powerful even than the new President. Dulles had resented his being made to take the blame for the Bay of Pigs fiasco: "He thought other people should be resigning before he did, and made it clear that he was thinking of one person in particular, Robert Kennedy."[43]

Before the assassination, Dulles had fought back in the media, leaking his resentment against the Kennedys to the sympathetic ears of Charles J.V. Murphy of *Fortune* magazine, part of Henry Luce's Time-Life empire. Murphy's pro-Dulles apologia, "Cuba: The Record Set Straight," was simultaneously a piece lobbying for escalated U.S. involvement in Indochina, just before Kennedy's first major Vietnam decision.[44] In this counter-attack, Dulles had Agency support. Dulles asked to have one of his CIA proteges, E. Howard Hunt, go over Murphy's article in detail; and Hunt was accordingly instructed to do so.[45]

[39] John Ranelagh, *The Agency* (New York: Simon and Schuster, 1986), 422-23. Raborn is remembered in the Agency as the man who asked "Who's this fellow Oligarchy?" and who thought that "KUWAIT" was a CIA cryptonym.

[40] Burton Hersh, *The Old Boys* (New York: Scribner's, 1992), 160-61.

[41] Ranelagh, 448.

[42] Johnson did invoke the threat of the Senate Internal Security Subcommittee as a major part of his case for a Warren Commission. As a man with years of Washington experience, he must have known of the on-going collaboration between Eastland and Sourwine of the Subcommittee with elements inside the CIA.

[43] Leonard Mosley, *Dulles* (New York: Dial Press/James Wade, 1978), 473. Although Dulles had offered to resign at the moment of failure, the offer had been refused. He declined to offer his resignation again, after being rebuked in a secret in-house CIA review. Thus he was fired, and without prior warning (ibid.).

[44] Charles J.V. Murphy, "Cuba: The Record Set Straight," *Fortune*, September 1961. Discussion in Paul W. Blackstock, *The Stategy of Subversion* (Chicago: Quadrangle, 1964), 250; Peter Dale Scott, *The War Conspiracy* (New York: Bobbs Merrill, 1972), 19-20.

[45] Tad Szulc, *Compulsive Spy: The Strange Career of E. Howard Hunt* (New York: Viking, 1974), 95; E. Howard Hunt, *Under Cover* (New York: Berkley, 1974), 216.

If Hunt was close to Dulles, he was even closer to his own protege, David Atlee Phillips. In fact it was probably through Hunt that Phillips became "an active player in a small clique within the CIA hierarchy who were almost autonomous in their operational capabilities," an OSS brotherhood of whom Allen Dulles, inside the Agency or out, was the acknowledged leader.[46] What merits further investigation is that members of this brotherhood played key roles on both sides of the Oswald "phase one"-"phase two" dialectic.

The key to Dulles' "agency-within-the-Agency," as Aarons and Loftus have called it, was the power Dulles had conferred on his close friend Jim Angleton.[47] As Counterintelligence Chief Angleton was authorized to spy on the rest of the CIA, and maintain a CI network of assets in other branches. The close connection between Dulles and Angleton endured well beyond Dulles' departure from the Agency.[48]

One sign of in-house CIA intrigue over the assassination is that those responsible for falsifying the Oswald-Kostikov story were not punished, or even distanced from the investigation of Kennedy's murder. On the contrary, John "Scelso" of WH/3, the Mexico desk, and Birch D. O'Neal, the head of CI/SIG, both involved in the falsified October messages from Headquarters, were assigned after the assassination to key roles in the CIA investigation and resulting liaison with the FBI.[49]

The man responsible for these assignments was Deputy Director of Plans Richard Helms, another Dulles loyalist and OSS brother. It is not clear that Helms' role was conspiratorial. On the contrary, while "Scelso" may have encouraged the proliferation of "phase one" Oswald stories, Helms appears to have constrained them.[50] What remains to be explored is whether these two apparently opposing efforts were actually part of a single co-ordinated scenario.

Helms's assignment of "Scelso" and O'Neal to the investigation made the same kind of sense as Johnson's putting Dulles on the Warren Commission. On the Commission, it is generally conceded, Dulles actively covered up the CIA involvement in the CIA-Mafia plots against Castro.[51] The House Committee, in an Appendix to its Report, concluded that Helms himself, "though the main contact with the Commission, apparently did not inform it of the CIA plots to assassinate Castro," and found a further "indication that his testimony before the Commission was misleading."[52]

Helms and Angleton designated Angleton's Chief of Research and Analysis, Ray Rocca, to be the CIA's point of contact with the Commission.[53] Angleton clearly hoped by doing so to prevent a number of highly relevant counterintelligence operations from being exposed, such as the CIA's illegal HT/LINGUAL mail-opening program (overseen by Birch D. O'Neal), and the photographic and electronic surveillance of the Soviet and Cuban Embassies in Mexico City.[54]

Angleton also visited Dulles on instructions from Helms, in order to learn and prepare for the questions which Dulles thought the Commission might put to the CIA.[55] Angleton's consistent approach was, in Rocca's words, "to wait out the Commission."[56] One might have expected as much

---

[46] Fonzi 331, 346n. Cf. Scott, *Deep Politics*, 54, 67, 322. Phillips had not served in OSS; his mentor Hunt had.

[47] Mark Aarons and John Loftus, *Unholy Trinity* (New York: St. Martin's Press, 1991), 260.

[48] David Wise, *Molehunt* (New York: Random House, 1992), 39; Scott, *Deep Politics*, 67.

[49] 11 AH 57, 476, 485.

[50] "Scelso"'s role is hard to assess. On November 23, 1963, when ordered by Assistant Deputy Director of Plans Karamessines to tell the Mexico City CIA Station to stop the arrest of Silvia Durán, "Scelso" entered a memo for the record, which said in part, "We phoned as ordered, *against my wishes*, and also wrote a FLASH cable which we did not then send" (TX-1240 of 23 November 1963; C/WH/3 memo for record; emphasis added). On the other hand, he soon afterward prepared a summary report for Helms which was transmitted to President Johnson. "This report stated that Oswald probably was a lone assassin who had no visible ties to Soviet or Cuban intelligence though such ties could not be excluded from consideration" (11 AH 477).

[51] Mosley, 477-78; Arthur M. Schlesinger, *Robert Kennedy and His Times*, 536, 663.

[52] 11 AH 58.

[53] 11 AH 47, 477-79.

[54] 4 AH 215; 11 AH 476, 479, 491; AR 205.

[55] 4 AH 232-35.

[56] 4 AH 215, 232.

from the man who would later tell the Church Committee, "It is inconceivable that a secret intelligence arm of the Government has to comply with all the overt orders of the Government."[57]

Having observed how closely the Dulles-Helms-Angleton network controlled the Warren Commission after the assassination, one is moved to ask about certain pre-assassination personnel movements, presumably authorized by Helms, which affected the Oswald-Kostikov story. One crucial move was the recall in 1963 of Tennant Bagley from Berne to Langley, where he was rapidly promoted to chief of the Counterintelligence Branch of the Soviet Division" (C/SR/CI).[58] This promotion came in time for him to suppress mention of Kostikov in the October messages, and then sound the assassination alarm about Kostikov on November 23.

Another move at this time was the temporary duty assignment of David Phillips, the Chief of Cuban Operations and Covert Action at the Mexico City Station, to Washington and Miami, "from at least late September to October 9, 1963."[59] In view of allegations about Hunt's Counterintelligence activities at this time (see below), it is relevant that while in Washington Phillips appears to have been attached to the Counterintelligence Staff of the Fitzgerald's Special Activities Staff devoted to anti-Castro operations.

Then there is the much disputed question of whether, as Tad Szulc has alleged, Howard Hunt was assigned to temporary duty in Mexico City for the period of August and September 1963, at the time of Oswald's alleged visit there.[60] Both Hunt and the CIA have strongly denied this claim. It is however supported by the sworn testimony of David Phillips in a libel suit, that he had seen Hunt in Mexico City at the time Hunt denied being there.[61] In a 1973 House Watergate Hearing, Hunt testified how a retired CIA agent "had during the Cuban operation been my inside man in the Embassy when I was outside in Mexico operating as part of the Cuban task force.[62]

An even more dramatic allegation, also strongly disputed, is that Hunt was in Dallas on November 22, 1963, at the time of the assassination. According to reporter Joseph Trento, a secret CIA memo of 1966, said to have been initialed by Angleton and Helms, emphasized the importance of keeping Hunt's presence there a secret, and suggested a cover story to provide Hunt with an alibi.[63] According to author Dick Russell, Trento later told him that Angleton himself was the source of the story, and arranged for a copy of the internal CIA memo to be delivered to him, as well as the House Committee.[64] If this is true, Angleton's role is sinister, and apparently part of a cover-up, whether the memo is real (and Hunt was in Dallas), or whether it was disinformation (and Hunt was not).

Trento told Russell he understood from Angleton that Hunt was in Dallas because "of a serious counterintelligence problem with the [CIA] Cubans," some of whom were known to be "penetrated by Castro's intelligence."[65] Far-fetched as an explanation to justify Hunt's presence in Dallas, it would make sense of his temporary detachment to Mexico City, where a number of JURE Cubans, suspected by Hunt and Angleton for their left-leaning politics, were preparing to take part in a Bobby Kennedy-backed operation against Castro. It would indeed have been characteristic of Angleton to

[57] Hersh, *Old Boys*, 317; citing Seymour Hersh, *New York Times Magazine*, June 25, 1978.

[58] Mangold, 170.

[59] Lopez Report, 128.

[60] Szulc, *Compulsive Spy*, 96, 99.

[61] Mark Lane, *Plausible Denial* (New York: Thunder's Mouth, 1991), 193. Hunt had made the sworn statement, "I was not in Mexico between the years 1961 and 1970." Phillips testified under oath that he had seen Hunt in Mexico City "sometime between September of 1961 and March of 1965," adding that he "must have seen him once or twice" somewhere in Mexico prior to November 22, 1963.

[62] Nedzi Hearing, 518 (June 28, 1973).

[63] *Wilmington Sunday News Journal*, August 20, 1978; reprinted in Lane, *Plausible Denial*, 152-55; Dick Russell, 474-75. In his book Lane claims that former CIA official Victor Marchetti had told him about this memo prior to the Trento story, citing Marine intelligence Colonel William Corson as his source (Lane, 134-35). Corson was close to Trento; the two eventually were co-authors of the book *Widows*.

[64] Ibid.

[65] Ibid.

use a CIA officer like Hunt, not nominally part of the Counterintelligence Staff, to spy on left-leaning CIA-sanctioned operations. And Hunt's animosity against the Cuban Manuel Ray of JURE, conceded by Hunt himself in his memoir *Give Us This Day*, was well-known throughout the Agency.

The CIA itself has said that Hunt's title at this time was Chief of Covert Operations for the Domestic Operations Division headed by Dulles' old friend Tracy Barnes.[66] Szulc however has written that Hunt was asked to assist Dulles in writing a book, *The Craft of Intelligence*, that Dulles wrote following his involuntary retirement in 1961.[67] Just how long it took to complete the book is not clear; it was however published in 1963. Certainly the book would have given Hunt the opportunity to spend many long hours (presumably on Company time) with Dulles, his former boss.

A third person who would presumably have been present would have been Howard E. Roman, Dulles' close friend and alleged collaborator on the book.[68] Another member of the OSS "Old Boy" brotherhood in the CIA, Roman resigned in 1962 before taking up the book-writing job with Dulles (and possibly Hunt). Roman went on to write a total of two books (and two more edited volumes) with Dulles. In that capacity he was with Dulles at the moment, on November 22, 1963, when Dulles heard of the President's murder.[69]

Roman's post-war career had been with Soviet matters, but I know nothing to connect him officially with the Lee Harvey Oswald files. The same cannot however be said of his wife, Jane Roman. A CIA official herself, it was Jane Roman who, as noted earlier, was the releasing officer on the falsified CIA cable to Mexico City on October 10, 1963.

Conclusion: The "Phase One" Stories Affected History

Assuredly the new President was not prevaricating, or being over-cautious, when he spoke to Chief Justice Warren of the risk of war. "Phase one stories" were not just street rumors, they were being promoted energetically, and almost conspiratorially, on at least the Ambassadorial level.

We need to insist that the promotion of such stories, per se, does nothing to link the proponents to the assassination. It is hardly surprising that opponents of Castro within the Government, along with anti-Castro Cubans in Miami, should seize this opportunity to reverse what they saw, rightly or wrongly, as the Kennedy policy of prolonged inaction.

With the pre-assassination Kostikov story, on the other hand, we can be more specific. Unlike the Alvarado and other false stories, the Kostikov story was never exploited to achieve a policy change. It remained a secret in government files, and those who spoke publicly of KGB involvement never referred to it.

To say that the falsifications of the October 1963 CIA messages had something to do with the plot to kill the President does not tell us anything about the motives of those falsifying the cables. As said above, they may have been illegal conspirators, or they may have been responding to a potential embarrassment created for them by these conspirators.

One can reach one simple conclusion about these two alternative ways of reading the facts: The public has both the right and the need to know which of these alternatives is the true one.

The first person one would have wanted to interrogate under oath about these falsifications, and about other falsehoods in his own earlier testimony, would have been David Atlee Phillips. Mr. Phillips unfortunately has since died, as have Win Scott and other relevant witnesses. This only adds to the urgency of securing testimony under oath from those who survive.

---

[66] *San Francisco Chronicle*, December 31, 1974, 1.

[67] Szulc, 95.

[68] Mosley, 475-77.

[69] Mosley, 477.

V. THE KENNEDY-CIA DIVERGENCE OVER CUBA

July 1994

In all the hundreds of thousands of words of official documentation about the John F. Kennedy assassination, one of the major gaps has been the full range of Kennedy's policies in 1963 towards Cuba. It is clear however that he was simultaneously pursuing more than one "track" in 1963, and that in one of these tracks -- the exploration of a possible accommodation with Castro through direct contacts -- the President pointedly excluded the CIA.[1]

The carrot of accommodation was not the only track. We shall see that by June the Kennedys were also applying the stick of sabotage operations (in conjunction with the CIA). But there were powerful reasons prompting the Kennedys towards accommodation and even direct contacts with Castro representatives, reasons pointing beyond Cuba to the President's larger hopes for accommodation and improved relations with the Soviet Union.

In 1963 both strategies of accommodation, with Cuba and with the Soviet Union, developed increasingly hostile opposition, in the country, in Congress, and within the Administration. Particularly within the CIA, those elements still smarting from the Bay of Pigs defeat went beyond their policy directives to frustrate the accommodation track.

I shall argue that senior officials within the CIA, notably Richard Helms and Desmond FitzGerald, knew of the Kennedy brothers' secret moves to initiate direct communications with Castro, disapproved of them, and took steps to poison them. Their most flagrant action was to initiate a new series of secret meetings with a known assassin and suspected double agent, Rolando Cubela Secades (code-named AMLASH), at which a major topic of discussion was the assassination of Fidel Castro. Helms, without consulting the Attorney General, authorized a contact plan whereby in October 1963 (and possibly again on November 22) FitzGerald met with Cubela, and promised him material assistance in assassinating Castro, while posing (falsely) as a "personal representative of Robert F. Kennedy."[2]

This meeting seems to have been designed to poison the informal Kennedy-Castro contacts already under way. For there was already anxiety within the Agency that Cubela, who had refused to be polygraphed in 1962, was reporting the substance of these contacts to Castro. We shall see that FitzGerald's own Counterintelligence Chief, Joseph Langosch, recommended with another CIA officer that FitzGerald not meet with Cubela.[3]

There were good reasons for their advice. On September 7, 1963, within hours of the first new CIA meeting with Cubela in Brazil, Castro had turned up at the Brazilian Embassy in Havana, and warned "U.S. leaders" that "if they are aiding U.S. terrorist plans to eliminate Cuban leaders, they themselves will not be safe."[4] At the time, and thereafter, "nervous CIA men wondered whether Castro had chosen the Brazilian Embassy to make his threat in order to signal his knowledge of the Sao Paolo meeting."[5]

It cannot be conclusively proven that these secret assassination rendez-vous with Cubela from September to November 1963 were *designed* to frustrate the President's accommodation track. (One clear factor here is that once again there has been much lying in high places; we can name some of those who have engaged in possibly felonious cover-up.) But even to entertain this hypothesis of a perverse design is to raise a serious question about the recurring stories we shall consider in Chapter VIII, that Oswald either offered information about a CIA plot to kill Castro, or alternatively offered, within the Cuban Consulate, to kill Kennedy (a move allegedly interpreted by the Cubans as a crude

---

[1] Hinckle and Turner, 195-96. The 1994 CIA releases have partially filled this gap, but only with respect to Agency operations.

[2] Assassination Report, 87; I.G. Report, 89.

[3] Schweiker-Hart Report, 17n; Schorr, 165.

[4] Michael Beschloss, *The Crisis Years*, 639-40.

[5] Beschloss, 640; citing *Baltimore Sun*, September 9, 1963.

but official CIA provocation). Either of these two initiatives, while too clumsy and indeed bizarre to gain Cuban interest and "assistance," could nonetheless have had the immediate effect of further poisoning any trust that was beginning to develop, outside the CIA, between representatives of Castro and the President.

It is not gratuitous to link Oswald's provocative talk of assassination with FitzGerald's. For as we shall see, Oswald in Mexico was being watched and reported on by Ann Goodpasture, a member of the same small conspiratorial FI/D Staff (or Staff D), which at the same time was engaged on the tightly held secret task of preparing exotic poison devices for delivery to Cubela, possibly by FitzGerald himself, on November 22, 1963.[6]

The "Separate Track" of Accommodation and Direct Contacts With Castro

On March 30, 1963, the U.S. State and Justice Departments (the latter of course headed by Robert Kennedy) jointly announced that they would take "every step necessary" to ensure that raids by Cuban exiles against Cuba were "not launched, manned, or equipped from U.S. territory." Surveillance of the exiles and their bases was immediately intensified.[7]

The primary concern behind this policy shift was not Cuba but the Soviet Union. For some weeks the Cuban exile group Alpha 66, and its spin-off, Comandos L, had been targeting Soviet ships in Cuban waters, hoping to wreck the U.S.-Soviet agreement over Cuba that had been reached after the Cuban Missile Crisis. (The terms of that agreement had never been fully disclosed, but were generally understood to include a U.S. promise not to invade Cuba if the Soviet Union proceeded to withdraw its missiles and most of its troops.)[8] As we shall see, these anti-Soviet raids had the blessing and financial backing of Henry Luce and his Time-Life empire, a determined opponent of accommodation with the Soviets over Cuba or any other part of the world.[9] Some also believe that the Soviet-targeted raids may have been masterminded by the CIA, possibly by an operative with the pseudonym "Maurice Bishop."[10]

Behind the Kennedy decision to curb the exile raids may have been the desire to bolster Khrushchev's waning status in Moscow against the rising hardliners, headed by Frol Kozlov, who sought reconciliation with Beijing at the expense of U.S.-Soviet reconciliation.[11]

Nevertheless the March 30 announcement had the important spin-off for Kennedy's Cuba policy of reviving what McGeorge Bundy called the "separate track" of accommodation with Castro, as documented by the Assassination Report of the Church Committee:

> As early as January 4, 1963, Bundy proposed to President Kennedy that the possibility of communicating with Castro be explored. (Memorandum, Bundy to the President, 1/4/63). Bundy's memorandum on "Cuba Alternatives" of April 23 [sic, i.e. April 21], 1963, also listed the "gradual development of some form of accommodation with Castro" among policy alternatives. (Bundy memorandum, 4/21/63) At a meeting on June 3, 1963, the Special Group agreed it would be a "useful endeavour" to explore "various possibilities of establishing channels of communication to Castro." (Memorandum of Special Group meeting, 6/6/63)[12]

---

[6] Newman, *Oswald and the CIA*, 374-75.

[7] U.S. Department of State, *Bulletin*, April 22, 1963; Stebbins, 279-80; and sources therein cited. Although the *New York Times* did not immediately carry this announcement, it reported on April 1 that fifteen exiles had been curbed by the Justice Department.

[8] Arthur M. Schlesinger, *Robert Kennedy*, 582; Fonzi, 121-22; Hinckle and Turner, 135, 155-56.

[9] Hinckle and Turner, 164-67.

[10] Arthur M. Schlesinger, *Robert Kennedy*, 586 (CIA); Hinckle and Turner, 154-56 (Bishop).

[11] Beschloss, 583-84.

[12] Assassinations Report, 173.

The date of the April memo, April 21, is an interesting one. That very morning the *New York Times* had reported Castro's charge that the U.S. had abandoned a plan for a second invasion of Cuba in favor of a plot to assassinate Cuban leaders. The charge, as reported, may have been in error. Bundy's memo actually called for the National Security Council's Standing Group (successor to the Ex Com of the Cuban Missile crisis) to assess the consequences to the U.S. of Castro's dying independently. As might have been expected, in May the Group agreed with the CIA's Board of National Estimates that the consequences would probably be unfavorable. Castro's probable successors, Raul Castro and Che Guevara, were long-time overt Marxist-Leninists, deemed to be even more anti-U.S. than Fidel.[13]

Soon after the Bundy memo and NSC Group meeting of April 23, Averell Harriman made a quick trip to Khrushchev in Moscow as the President's personal emissary. Harriman's view was that Khrushchev and his bureaucracy were divided over the issue of a hard line or accommodation towards America, much as Kennedy and the CIA were rumored to be.[14] Harriman had three major agenda items to discuss which threatened to block an improvement in U.S.-Soviet relations: violations of the 1962 Laotian Accords, the problem of Cuba, and continued atomic testing.[15]

On April 3 and April 11 Khrushchev and Kennedy had exchanged secret letters, still not declassified, that concerned Cuba.[16] At the same time a highly-publicized meeting of eight Presidium members without Khrushchev prompted rumors that Khrushchev would soon be ousted. Then on April 11 the leading hard-liner, Frol Kozlov, suffered a near-fatal seizure; and disappeared forever from Soviet politics. Khrushchev met the next day with Norman Cousins, editor of the *Saturday Review*, and passed the informal message that he was ready for a "fresh start" with Kennedy.[17] Kennedy received Cousins at the White House on April 22, and Harriman left for Moscow soon after to meet Khrushchev. Fidel Castro also left on April 26 for the Soviet Union at Khrushchev's invitation.

On April 21 and again on April 24, shortly before he left, Castro told Lisa Howard of ABC that the "U.S. limitations on exile raids" were "a proper step toward accommodation."[18] On her return to the United States, Lisa Howard told CIA officials that Castro

> was "looking for a way to reach a rapprochement," probably for economic reasons. She thought Guevara and Raúl Castro would oppose an accommodation, but both [René] Vallejo [Castro's doctor] and [Raúl] Roa [the Foreign Minister] favored negotiations. Castro gave her the impression that he was ready to talk with "proper progressive spokesmen," though Kennedy would probably have to make the first move.[19]

An edited version of Howard's report appeared on ABC on May 10.

The simultaneous convergence on Moscow of Harriman and Castro was thus preceded by hopeful signals that progress in accommodation between them could be brokered by Khrushchev (who had every motive vis-a-vis his own hard-liners to be successful in this respect). Soon afterwards the right-wing journalists Robert Allen and Paul Scott, who had excellent sources in military intelligence, wrote a column under the provocative title, "Did Harriman Meet Castro in Russia?" They reported that the Senate Preparedness Subcommittee, chaired by the pro-military Senator John Stennis, was investigating the allegation that the two men had met "around April 28, in either Moscow or Murmansk" (where both were visiting). Castro allegedly was seeking diplomatic recognition in exchange

---

[13] Assassinations Report, 170-71; Beschloss, 96.

[14] Beschloss, *The Crisis Years*, 584-88 (Khrushchev); Summers, 421 (Kennedy).

[15] Beschloss, 592-93; Rudy Abramson, *Spanning the Century: The Life of W. Averell Harriman, 1891-1986* (New York: William Morrow, 1992), 594.

[16] Beschloss, 584-85, 777. It has been suggested that Kennedy's "Peace Speech" at American University on June 10, 1963, was based partly on ideas agreed to in this secret correspondence (*U.S. News and World Report*, July 22, 1963).

[17] Beschloss, *The Crisis Years*, 586-87.

[18] CIA debriefing of Lisa Howard, May 1, 1963; in RFK Papers; Arthur M. Schlesinger, Jr., *Robert Kennedy and His Times* (New York: Ballentine, 1978), 584, Robert E. Quirk, *Fidel Castro* (New York: W.W. Norton, 1993), 458; Beschloss, *The Crisis Years*, 594-95.

[19] Quirk, 458.

for a reduction in Soviet troop levels. The article was placed by a right-wing Congressman in the *Congressional Record*.[20]

Though inadequate to demonstrate that such a face-to-face meeting occurred, the article (together with the reprinting of it in the *Congressional Record*) is an important symptom of the political opposition developing in Washington to the process of accommodation.

The Track of Overthrow From Within

In fact, though not all of the Kennedys' opponents knew it, the accommodation track was not the only one being explored by the Kennedy brothers. On March 14, Robert had sent his brother a memo urging a combined program to stop Cuban subversion abroad and to appeal within Cuba to elements of the Cuban military:

> John McCone spoke at the meeting today about revolt amongst the Cuban military. He described the possibilities in rather optimistic terms....Do we have evidence of any break amongst the top Cuban leaders and if so, is the CIA or USIA attempting to cultivate that feeling? I would not like it said a year from now that we could have had this internal breakup in Cuba but we just did not set the stage for it.[21]

The Bundy memo of April 21 envisaged a total of three possible options: a) forcing "a non-Communist solution in Cuba by all necessary means," b) insisting on "major but limited ends," c) moving "in the direction of a gradual development of some form of accommodation with Castro."[22]

There are abundant indications in the newly released CIA documents that the CIA, along with other agencies, became part of a new U.S. strategy aimed at promoting revolt from within Cuba, particularly among the Cuban military. This inter-agency plan was called AMTRUNK inside the CIA, and "Operation Leonardo" by its original authors, George Volsky of USIA, the Cuban exile Nestor Moreno, and Tad Szulc of the *New York Times*. Szulc, who had excellent connections inside the Kennedy White House, presented the plan to the State Department Cuban Coordinator, Robert Hurwitch in early 1963, when the State Department and the White House pressured the CIA "to consider a proposal for an on-island operation to split the Castro regime."[23]

The CIA's own documents make it abundantly clear how distasteful this White House-backed plan was to them. Old disagreements from the Bay of Pigs operation were revived: the White House preference was to use participants in the original Castro revolution, notably men close to Manolo Ray and Huber Matos; and such men were anathema to the more right-wing Cubans who had defected earlier and been championed by the CIA. By 1963 Ray and Nestor Moreno, both close to Szulc, had formed the anti-CIA and anti-Castro group JURE, which not only rejected CIA influence but was suspected by CIA of trying to penetrate its JMWAVE operations. The links of Moreno and Volsky to JURE became key arguments in the CIA's case for disliking AMTRUNK.[24]

By April 5, 1963, JMWAVE Station Chief Theodore Shackley was ready to recommend that the whole AMTRUNK operation "be terminated at the earliest possible moment:"

> The AMTRUNKers admit to being anti-KUBARK [CIA] and to be working "with" KUBARK now only because there was no alternative if they were to accomplish their mission....[Redacted, a key AMTRUNK member] believes he is receiving special attention because of his [Washington] connections, and he will not hesitate to go behind KUBARK's back to AMTRUNK-1 [Volsky]...or higher authority, if the operation or KUBARK handling of AMTRUNK does not progress to his liking.[25]

---

[20] *Washington World*; placed by Congressman Bruce Alger in *Congressional Record*, June 12, 1963, A3785-86.

[21] Schlesinger, *Robert Kennedy*, 580.

[22] William Attwood, *The Twilight Struggle* (New York: Harper and Row, 1987), 254.

[23] CIA Memo of 14 Feb 1977, "AMTRUNK Operation, Interim Working Draft," 1.

[24] CIA Memo of 14 Feb 1977, "Tadeusz (Tad) Witold Szulc," 6; WAVE Dispatch 17410 of 20 Aug 1964, 9-11.

[25] WAVE Dispatch 8351 of 5 April 1963.

This recommendation to terminate was supported at Headquarters, whose return cable to JMWAVE on April 10 "concurred that the AMTRUNK operation should be terminated for a number of reasons, including the fact that CIA could not at that time be certain that hostile elements [these, in CIA's view, included Volsky and Szulc] were unaware of the plan."[26]

Nevertheless, after the decision recorded in the April 21 Bundy memo, the CIA continued to support the AMTRUNK operation until March 1964.[27] In the Johnson era, however, the purpose of AMTRUNK appears to have changed completely. Instead of infiltrating agents to woo Cuban military leaders, AMTRUNK operations in early 1964 had become the depositing inside Cuba of Belgian FAL rifles for the assassination of Castro.[28] Along with this change in AMTRUNK's purpose, the CIA JMWAVE Station terminated the involvement of Nestor Moreno, the plan's original author "in the sensitive aspects of AMTRUNK in November 1963."[29] AMTRUNK in other words was by this time subordinated to the Cubela/AMLASH operation, which had become similarly diverted from politics to assassination (see Chapter VI).

The CIA's continued support of AMTRUNK appears to have been unwilling; and Headquarters soon implemented Shackley's alternative recommendation of giving AMTRUNKers cash to mount their own independent operations.[30] In June the Standing Group approved a sabotage program of raids by exiles, "to nourish a spirit of resistance and disaffection which could lead to significant defections and other byproducts of unrest."[31] It was hoped that the pressures on the economy would contribute to "internal discontent that would take appropriate political and military forms."[32] This "track two" concept of "autonomous operations," as distinguished to the "track one" of CIA's support of Artime, was proposed by Walt Rostow of the State Department (a political ally of Lyndon Johnson). A principal beneficiary proved to be JURE, the group which CIA suspected of being behind AMTRUNK.[33] Because "track two" supplied resources to JURE for military operations, it had the effect of de-emphasizing the political objectives of the original Plan Leonardo.

Both the plans for an internal military-based coup and the supporting infiltration and sabotage missions were hereafter given the CIA code name AMTRUNK. The renewed CIA sabotage operations became operational in August 1963. As part of this program, a new exile group, with U.S. Army training and advisers, launched raids on August 18 and October 21 as "Comandos Mambises," from the CIA ship "Rex," a former subchaser.[34]

Rolando Cubela, himself an Army Major, was by CIA accounts approached in 1963 because of his contacts in the Cuban military. His case officers were also part of an operation (which can only be AMTRUNK)

> to penetrate the Cuban military to encourage either defections or an attempt to produce information from dissidents, or perhaps even to forming a group which would be capable of replacing the then government in Cuba.[35]

As mentioned above, in 1964 AMTRUNK teams were used by the CIA to supply assassination rifles with long-distance scopes to Cubela (AMLASH).[36]

---

[26] CIA Memo of 14 Feb 1977, "AMTRUNK Operation, Interim Working Draft," 2, 4.

[27] Ibid.

[28] CIA Inspector General's Report on Plots to Assassinate Fidel Castro, 23 May 1967, 95, 96; cf. 79, 101.

[29] CIA Memo of 14 Feb 1977, "Nestor Antonio Moreno Lopez," 3; NARA ID number 1993.07.21.18:28:44:840470, Box JFK36, F16.

[30] David Corn, *Blond Ghost*, 102. David Corn, a *Nation* editor, volunteers that "Shackley's instincts were right" about AMTRUNK and "other harebrained projects."

[31] Assassination Report, 173.

[32] Morris Morley, *Imperial State and Revolution* (Cambridge: Cambridge UP, 1987), 153.

[33] 10 AH 77, 140.

[34] Morley, 153; Hinckle and Turner, 137-44.

[35] Assassination Report, 86n; citing AM/LASH Case Officer #1, 8/11/75.

[36] I.G. Report, 95, 96; cf. 101.

The CIA's redirection of AMTRUNK exemplified their long-term disagreement with the Kennedy White House over policy objectives. Arthur Schlesinger has argued that, since 1961:

> The CIA wished to organize Castro's overthrow from *outside* Cuba, as against the White House, the Attorney General's office and State who wished to support an anti-Castro movement *inside* Cuba. The CIA's idea was to fight a war; the others hoped to promote a revolution. Any successful anti-Castro movement inside Cuba would have to draw on disenchanted Castroites and aim to rescue the revolution from the Communists. This approach, stigmatized as *Fidelismo sin Fidel*, was opposed by businessmen, both Cuban and American, who dreamed of the restoration of nationalized properties. But the CIA alternative was probably dictated less by business interests than by the agency's preference for operations it could completely control -- especially strong in this case because of the Cuban reputation for total inability to keep anything secret.[37]

To this preference for control can be added another one. The CIA, despite its fiasco at the Bay of Pigs, was still hoping to reassert itself as the preferred agency for paramilitary operations, which had accounted for the biggest item in its annual budget. In this respect AMTRUNK, an inter-agency operation, was not one to its liking: for by all accounts the key co-ordinating role was given, not to the CIA, but to the Department of the Army under Cyrus Vance and his aides Joseph Califano and Alexander Haig.[38]

Given the normal CIA penchant for secrecy, it is the more remarkable that the CIA, at the Brazil meeting in September, took the suspected blabbermouth Cubela into its AMTRUNK planning. According to the CIA's IG Report of 1967,

> Cubela discussed a group of Cuban military officers known to him, and possible ways of approaching them. The problem was, he explained, that although many of them were anti-Communist, they were either loyal to Fidel or so afraid of him that they were reluctant to discuss any conspiracies for fear they might be provocations. Cubela said that he thought highly of [redacted, apparently Major Ramon Guin Diaz] (AMTRUNK-[short redaction]) who was hiding [redacted, identified by the Cubans as the infiltrated CIA agent "Miguel Diaz"]. ["Diaz"] had been sent to Cuba to recruit [Guin] in place, and had done so. Cubela said he planned to use [Guin] but was concerned about [Guin's] "nervous condition" and the fact that he drank heavily. Cubela was told to assist [Guin] in [Guin's] intelligence assignments, but not to help [Guin] leave Cuba -- as Cubela proposed.[39]

According to a later memo from Helms to Rusk, Ramon Guin "was recruited by a CIA agent in August 1963 inside Cuba as a Principal Agent to recruit high-level military leaders."[40] By all accounts the October 29 meeting of FitzGerald with Cubela continued to focus on what Richard Helms, the senior CIA official cognizant of the AMLASH meetings, later called in testimony "the political action part of it...have a group to replace Castro."[41]

Excluding the CIA: The Secret Attwood Initiative

Robert Kennedy's penchant for pro-active operations, even if rationalized as a "stick" to encourage Castro to behave reasonably, was clearly unhelpful to unblocking the accommodation

---

[37] Schlesinger, *Robert Kennedy*, 510-11; cf. 514. *Fidelismo sin Fidel* was originally Manolo Ray's phrase to describe his own political program (Hugh Thomas, *The Cuban Revolution*, 508). See Chapter VI.

[38] Hinckle and Turner, 153, 342. (Haig was appointed to his position under Vance on June 28, 1963.) The CIA lost this bureaucratic battle to the U.S. Army, which in 1964 took over the CIA's Special Operations Group (SOG) in Vietnam, along with its Green Berets.

[39] I.G. Report, 86.

[40] Memo of Richard Helms, Deputy Director of Central Intelligence, for Secretary of State Dean Rusk, "CIA Involvement in Counter-Revolutionary Activities," 7 Mar 1966, para. 2.

[41] Assassination Report, 173; quoting Helms testimony to Church Committee, 6/13/75, 131, 117.

track. Sabotage missions in particular had been denounced in September, not only by Castro, but also the Soviet Union.[42]

Nevertheless the accommodations track, even if interrupted from time to time, seems never to have died under Kennedy. On June 3 the Special Group agreed that it would be a "useful endeavor" to explore "various possibilities of establishing channels of communication to Castro."[43]

Shortly afterwards a public suggestion by Castro that Cuba might consider normalization of relations was rebuffed by John Kennedy at a press conference. The President attacked Cuba as a Soviet satellite. It is possible however that another cause for concern was the fear of some experts, apparently unfounded at this time, that Castro might be tilting towards Beijing in the increasingly evident Sino-Soviet split.[44]

Despite this public rebuff, in September the President approved secret contacts at the UN in New York between a Special Advisor to the U.S. Delegation, William Attwood, and the Cuban Ambassador to the U.N., Carlos Lechuga. On September 5 Lisa Howard told Attwood she was convinced that Castro wanted to restore communications with the United States, and she offered to arrange a social gathering in her apartment so that Attwood could meet informally with Lechuga. (It is not clear if Howard was simply reacting to her Castro interview, or whether the Cubans had proposed talks on September 5. as suggested by the Schweiker-Hart Report.)[45] (Note that September 5 was two days before the CIA resumed contact with Cubela in Brazil; Attwood comments laconically that "the CIA must have had an inkling of what was happening from phone taps and surveillance of Lechuga.")[46]

A week later Attwood went to Washington and saw Harriman, a man with whom he had traveled to India in 1959. Harriman was interested in the proposed approach to Lechuga; and he requested a memo which Attwood submitted to him on September 19. Attwood's memo transmitted information from Guinea's U.N. Ambassador that Castro was unhappy about his dependence on the Soviet Union "and would go to some length to obtain normalization of relations" with the U.S. It proposed a discreet inquiry to achieve three objectives: "a. The evacuation of all Soviet bloc military personnel. b. An end to subversive activities by Cuba in Latin America. c. Adoption by Cuba of a policy of non-alignment."[47] The President gave his approval via Ambassador Adlai Stevenson at the U.N., but it was understood that Attwood would report directly to McGeorge Bundy in the White House. The CIA and the State Department were to be excluded. (Stevenson's response to Attwood's memo was that "Unfortunately the CIA is still in charge of Cuba.")[48]

In addition to knowing Harriman, Attwood had interviewed Castro in 1959 as an editor of *Look* magazine.[49] On becoming Kennedy's Ambassador to Guinea, he was exposed to the neutralist initiatives of Guinea's President Sekou Touré and Ghana's President Kwame Nkrumah, both of whom were on good terms with Castro. Attwood monitored Cuba as an Advisor to the U.S. Delegation at the 1962 Session of the UN General Assembly.[50] It was the Ghanaian Ambassador to the UN who in March of 1963 had obtained a Cuban visa for Lisa Howard; and it was the Guinean Ambassador to Cuba who in September told Attwood that Castro, dissatisfied with his Soviet relationship, was looking for a way to escape.[51]

[42] *New York Times*, September 9, 1963; Quirk, 480.

[43] Assassination Report, 173.

[44] Quirk, 473-75, 477. In 1965 Guevara traveled to China, before returning to by-pass Soviet line Communist parties in Latin America with guerrilla groups using Maoist tactics (Quirk, 518, 523).

[45] Attwood, *The Twilight Struggle*, 258; Schweiker-Hart Report, 20; citing William Attwood testimony, 7/10/75.

[46] Attwood, *The Twilight Struggle*, 264.

[47] Attwood, *The Twilight Struggle*, 258-59.

[48] Attwood, *The Twilight Struggle*, 258-59; Assassinations Report, 173-74; Hinckle and Turner, 196.

[49] Attwood, *The Twilight Struggle*, 248-51.

[50] Quirk, 445.

[51] Quirk, 457 (Howard); Schlesinger, *Robert Kennedy*, 594 (Attwood).

The first meeting between Attwood and Lechuga took place on September 23, 1963, at a cocktail party hosted for this very purpose by Lisa Howard.[52] (Note that this meeting occurs just four days before Oswald, in Mexico City, is supposed to have made contact with Silvia Duran, whom the CIA had reported in early 1963 to be Carlos Lechuga's mistress.)[53] The meeting was productive, and produced a series of informal contacts broken only by Kennedy's death on November 22.

Attwood saw Robert Kennedy the day after his rendezvous with Lechuga. Robert told Attwood that a Havana visit would be too risky. It was bound to leak....But the general idea was worth pursuing. He told Attwood to stay in touch with Bundy and his staff man on Cuban affairs, Gordon Chase. The Attorney General consulted his brother, who declared himself willing to normalize relations if Castro ended the Soviet bloc military presence on his island, broke ties with the Cuban Communists, and stopped the subversion of Latin America.[54]

Robert Kennedy proposed that direct U.S. contacts with a special Castro emissary, as proposed by Attwood, should take place at a neutral site in Mexico, with Lisa Howard serving as a go-between.[55] We do not yet know if Thomas Mann, the U.S. Ambassador in Mexico, or Win Scott, the CIA Station Chief, were in any way consulted about, or alerted to, the projected meeting.

UN Ambassador Adlai Stevenson contributed to Attwood's initiative with a speech suggesting "that if Castro wanted peace with his neighbors, he could have it if he stopped trying to subvert other nations, stopped taking orders from Moscow and started carrying out the original democratic pledges of his revolution.[56]

The Conflict Between the AMLASH and Attwood Initiatives

On October 24, at Attwood's urging, the President saw the French journalist Jean Daniel, who was about to interview Castro in Havana. (Note that this is just five days before the meeting with AMLASH in which FitzGerald presented himself, falsely, as a representative of Robert Kennedy.)

The President is not known to have mentioned the problem of the Cuban Communists to Daniel, but complained that Castro had "agreed to be a Soviet agent in Latin America." "'The continuation of the blockade,' Kennedy said, 'depends on the continuation of subversive activities.' Then: 'Come and see me on your return from Cuba. Castro's reactions interest me.'"[57] Daniel went on to wait three frustrating weeks in Havana before seeing Castro.

On October 11, and again six days later, Cubela in Europe had asked to meet a high-level U.S. government official, "preferably Robert F. Kennedy," for "assurances that the U.S. Government would support him if his enterprise were successful."[58] On October 29, five days after the President's meeting with Daniel, Desmond FitzGerald met with Cubela in Paris, using the AMLASH case officer Nestor Sanchez as an interpreter.[59] According to the CIA's I.G. Report, the contact plan for the meeting, a copy of which was in the AMLASH file, had this to say on its cover: "Fitzgerald will present self as personal representative of Robert F. Kennedy who traveled Paris for specific purpose meeting Cubela and giving him assurances of full U.S. support if there is change of the present

[52] Beschloss, 638.

[53] John Newman, *Oswald and the CIA*, 279-82; cf. Chapter III.

[54] Beschloss, 638-39. These three conditions were roughly those outlined as policy objectives in Attwood's original memo which he submitted to Harriman on September 18.

[55] Quirk, 481; William Attwood, *The Reds and the Blacks* (New York: 1967), 142-43.

[56] Attwood, *The Reds and the Blacks*, 143. In his second book Attwood revealed that "Stevenson had asked me for a draft of a reply" (Attwood, *The Twilight Struggle*, 260). He did not mention that in the speech Stevenson demanded that Castro let the people "exercise the right of self-determination through free elections" (Quirk, 480).

[57] Schlesinger, *Robert Kennedy*, 596-97.

[58] I.G. Report, 87-88

[59] I.G. Report, 88-89.

government in Cuba." FitzGerald claimed he discussed the planned meeting with the DD/P (Helms) who decided it was not necessary to seek approval from Robert Kennedy for FitzGerald to speak in his name.[60] Helms, for whom the I.G. Report was prepared, later confirmed that he had not consulted the Attorney General.[61]

Sanchez' report of the meeting does not mention assassination. It says that FitzGerald told Cubela U.S. support "will be forthcoming only after a real coup has been effected and the group involved is in a position to request U.S....recognition and support."[62] Nevertheless both FitzGerald and Cubela agree that assassination was discussed. FitzGerald recalled that Cubela wanted "a high-powered rifle with telescopic sights."[63] Cubela, conversely, told his interviewer Tony Summers that "it was the CIA who brought up the idea of assassination in the first place -- and he who resisted."[64]

Even if assassination was not the purpose, this meeting between a high-level CIA official and a known assassin was extraordinary, perhaps unprecedented. Normally the CIA uses covers and (when assassins are involved) intermediaries or cut-outs. In the well-studied case of the Giancana- Roselli-CIA plots against Castro, the CIA even used one cut-out (Maheu) to contact another (Giancana). Cubela's inability to keep a secret had become known to the CIA a year earlier; and two CIA officials (Shackley and Langosch) later testified that they had warned FitzGerald against this meeting.[65] Their fears were well-grounded. Earlier that same month the FBI had learned of the renewed CIA-Cubela contact (in a report that was not transmitted to the CIA).[66]

There is perhaps one other case where the CIA in 1963 prepared to abandon its normal guidelines of plausible deniability, and it too raises questions of the CIA's loyalty to the Kennedys. In 1962 Robert Kennedy's representative James Donovan, a New York attorney, along with John Nolan of Kennedy's staff, had negotiated the release of the Bay of Pigs prisoners. In April 1963 Donovan and Nolan returned to Cuba, to conclude their negotiations with Castro personally. Their mission concerned a few prisoners, including some CIA men, who remained to be released. But the occasion led predictably to the possibility of normalizing the relations between the two countries. Arthur Schlesinger links the success of the Donovan-Nolan mission to the important interview given by Castro to Lisa Howard in late April.[67]

Desmond FitzGerald of the SAS staff does not appear to have looked favorably towards this step on the accommodation track. In early 1963 the staff arranged for the CIA's Technical Services Division to purchase a wet suit, and contaminate it with tuberculosis bacilli and the spores for a disabling skin disease. The plan was for Donovan (who was not informed of the plot) to give the suit to Castro, his companion in scuba diving.[68]

FitzGerald's assistant Samuel Halpern, an important witness to whom we shall return, later told the authors of the I.G. Report that the plan was abandoned as "impracticable" and "overtaken by events."[69] Significantly he did not apparently mention to them what critics called

> the most elementary considerations -- for example that it [i.e. the suit] was in effect a gift from the United States, while the idea was to *keep it secret*; or, then again, Donovan's feelings about being the gift-giver in this plot. If he wasn't let in on the plot, after all, he might try on the suit himself.[70]

---

[60] I.G. Report. 89.

[61] Assassination Report, 87.

[62] I.G. Report, 89.

[63] I.G. Report, 90.

[64] Summers, 351.

[65] I.G. Report, 84 (inability); Schweiker-Hart Report, 17n (warnings).

[66] Ibid.

[67] Schlesinger, *Robert Kennedy*, 583-84.

[68] Assassination Report, 85-86; I.G. Report, 75. FitzGerald told the I.G. Report authors that the plot began after he took over the SAS staff in January 1963. The Church Committee considered it "likely that the activity took place earlier, since Donovan had completed his his negotiations by the middle of January 1963" (Assassination Report, 86). But the premise for this conclusion was obviously incorrect

[69] I.G. Report, 75.

We can see the same CIA antipathy to the accommodation track in October 1963: Helms and FitzGerald offered FitzGerald as a personal representative of Robert Kennedy, at a time when Robert had authorized an accommodation initiative from which the CIA was being excluded. More crudely put, they chose unilaterally to represent him, precisely at a time when they could not know what he wanted, or was up to; a time when there was a distinction and potential divergence between CIA and Kennedy interests.

That the CIA was well aware of this distinction is unconsciously revealed in 1976 by Samuel Halpern. In testimony to the Schweiker-Hart Subcommittee, Halpern discounted the danger that the Fitzgerald-Cubela meeting "exposed the CIA to possible embarrassment, because Fitzgerald had not used his real name and, therefore, AMLASH would have been unable to identify Fitzgerald *as a CIA officer.*"[71]

Only Robert Kennedy would be embarrassed, in other words. This indeed would seem to be the most rational intention of such an unprofessional and disloyal meeting. Both Kennedys were lending support to explorations which promised (or alternatively, threatened) to lead to an accommodation with Castro. Those initiatives could only be harmed by FitzGerald's discussion of assassinating Castro with a suspected leaker or double-agent, while pretending, falsely, to be a representative of Robert Kennedy.

The same Samuel Halpern has argued that the CIA, far from being disloyal to Robert Kennedy in this operation, had in fact gained his explicit approval informally. In the words of John Davis,

Since Kennedy and FitzGerald often met socially and at work, there was no need for formal authorization. The attorney general's approval could just as easily have been conveyed informally and be far less risky for all concerned. This opinion was confirmed by former CIA official, Samuel Halpern, who in 1963 had been executive assistant to the Task Force on Cuba and one of the four men directly involved in the AM/LASH operation. In an interview on November 18, 1983, Mr. Halpern told me that he was absolutely certain that "Des" FitzGerald "had full authorization from Attorney General Kennedy and President Kennedy to proceed with the AM/LASH plot against Castro," adding that he always felt that since they often met socially, Bobby Kennedy and "Des" FitzGerald conducted most of their business together at Washington cocktail parties and receptions, rather than in their respective offices.[72]

But Halpern and Davis seem to have missed the point. It is indeed clear that the CIA had authorization to proceed with the political initiative. But that it had authorization to involve Robert Kennedy's name and authority in an assassination plot, at a time when the Kennedys were attempting to open discussions with Castro, is virtually unimaginable. Both FitzGerald and Helms later denied that the AMLASH operation contemplated assassination.[73] In this case Kennedy's authorization for AMLASH would have been limited to what they described it as, an attempt to find a group to replace Castro.

From this point on the AMLASH initiative had the looks of an anti-Kennedy provocation. This was Attwood's retrospective evaluation of the FitzGerald/AMLASH meetings: "One thing was clear: Stevenson was right when he told me back in September that 'the CIA is in charge of Cuba'; or anyway, acted as if it thought it was, and to hell with the president it was pledged to serve."[74] It would

---

[70] Thomas Powers, *The Man Who Kept the Secrets* (New York: Knopf, 1979), 150. The fact that Donovan and Castro planned to dive together may possibly have inspired FitzGerald's famous plan to kill Castro with an exploding sea-shell (Assassination Report, 87, I.G. Report, 77). Samuel Halpern told Thomas Powers that he "protested the seashell plan....Castro blowing up on the ocean floor would point a finger directly at the United States" (Powers, 150). Once again, there is no trace of such protest in the I.G. Report, which has this to say: "FitzGerald states that he, Sam Halpern, and [redacted] had several sessions at which they explored this possibility, but that no one else was ever brought in on the talks. Halpern believes that he had conversations with TSD on feasibility...." (I.G. Report, 77). Halpern's protest was first recorded after FitzGerald had died in July 1967.

[71] Schweiker-Hart Report, 17n; citing Executive Officer testimony, 4/22/76, 55); emphasis added.

[72] John Davis, *The Kennedys* (New York: McGraw-Hill, 1985), 495.

[73] Assassination Report, 87

[74] Attwood, *The Twilight Struggle*, 263.

get worse.

Economics Versus the Larger Agenda of Accommodation

But the CIA was not necessarily acting as a rogue elephant. In these diverging paths of accommodation and provocation, Attwood, the Kennedys, and Harriman may have been much more isolated than the CIA. Bundy told Attwood on November 5 that the President was more interested than the State Department in exploring the Cuban overtures.[75] A State Department memo two days later seemed to confirm this: in contrast to the President's three conditions for accommodation, it called on Cuba to "renounce Marxism-Leninism as its ideology, remove Communists from positions of influence, provide compensation for expropriated properties and restore private enterprise in manufacturing, mining, oil and distribution."[76] This detailed list made it clear that at least the oil and mining interests in Cuba (Exxon, Freeport Sulphur, etc.) continued to enjoy their usual influence on the formation of State Department foreign policy.

They were of course powerful in Congress as well. In 1963 the President, according to Ted Sorensen, "opposed an effort in the Congress to impose as the first condition to our dealing with a new Cuba its compensation of those Americans whose property had been expropriated by Castro."[77]

The President's policy was dictated by geopolitics, not economics. A White House memo from Bundy for Attwood on November 12 reiterated that the only "flatly unacceptable" points in Castro's policy were Cuba's submission to external Communist influence and his subversion directed at the rest of Latin America.[78] It is obvious that, in this inattention to economic compensation, it was the White House that threatened to diverge from traditional foreign policy priorities.

It is possible that the President, and Harriman, had a larger agenda that dictated this divergence. They sought accommodation, not just with Cuba, but above all with the Soviet Union; and a possible formula for achieving this was a reduction of troop levels, not just by the Soviet Union in Cuba, but also by the Americans in Vietnam.[79]

It is not clear to what extent Khrushchev had agreed to his part in such an agenda. In October Joseph Alsop reported that Khrushchev had assured Harriman in Moscow all Soviet troops would eventually leave Cuba. At his October 31 press conference, Kennedy said that "the numbers have steadily been reduced." A week later he reportedly said that he expected "nearly all of them to be out by the end of the year."[80] No commentator seems to have observed that the usual American estimate of these numbers, 17,500 troops, roughly equalled the number of troops introduced by Kennedy into Vietnam. (Half of them had arrived in 1963, since the Cuban Missile Crisis, at a time when the Vietnam War was officially said to be going well.)[81] The makings of a quid-pro-quo were certainly there.

In his pursuit of this larger agenda of accommodation, the President may have had a slightly different agenda from even his own brother. Schlesinger's generally insightful account of these final months of the Kennedy Presidency has one striking omission: it fails to note the October escalation of sabotage operations:

> On October 3, 1963, the Special Group approved nine operations in Cuba, several of which involved sabotage. On October 24, 1963, thirteen major sabotage operations, including the sabotage of an electric power plant, an oil refinery, and a sugar mill, were approved for the period from November 1963 through January 1964. (Memorandum,

---

[75] Attwood, *The Twilight Struggle*, 261; Schlesinger, *Robert Kennedy*, 597.

[76] Schlesinger, *Robert Kennedy*, 597.

[77] Theodore C. Sorensen, *Kennedy* (New York: Harper and Row, 1965), 723.

[78] Schlesinger, *Robert Kennedy*, 597.

[79] Cf. Scott, *Deep Politics*, 225.

[80] Beschloss, 657.

[81] Scott (1972), 227-28.

7/11/75, CIA Review Staff to Select Committee, on "Approved CIA Covert Operations into Cuba")[82]

If the aim of these raids was to balance carrots with sticks, the results were counterproductive. The Comandos Mambises raid of October 21, 1963, almost certainly contributed to Castro's long delay in meeting Jean Daniel.[83]

The President's IAPA Speech and Its Twofold Consequences

After three weeks of impasse on both the Attwood and Daniel fronts, the President went public with his conditions for accommodation. Flying to Miami on November 18, he delivered to the Inter-American Press Association a speech which, in the Kennedy style, offered something to both the hawks and doves in his audience. As such, it divided aides then, as it still continues to divide scholars. Thomas G. Paterson has recently characterized it as a "tough-minded speech:" "The president, according to his aide McGeorge Bundy, sought to 'encourage anti-Castro elements within Cuba to revolt' and to 'indicate that we would not permit another Cuba in the hemisphere."[84] Michael Beschloss, citing Kennedy's top speech-writer Ted Sorensen, presents it as "a speech that would open a door to the Cuban leader."[85]

The speech itself seems to have been carefully drafted to justify both of these conflicting contentions. Its appeal to reject forces from outside the hemisphere could be responded to by either Castro or his CIA-supported opposition. Thus the language was deliberately ambiguous to the point of duplicity. The President noted that the Alliance for Progress did "not dictate to any nation how to organize its economic life." But

> It is important to restate what now divides Cuba from my country and from the other countries of the hemisphere. It is the fact that a small band of conspirators has stripped the Cuban people of their freedom and handed over the independence and sovereignty of the Cuban nation to forces beyond the hemisphere. They have made Cuba a victim of foreign imperialism, an instrument of the policy of others, a weapon in an effort dictated by external powers to subvert the other American republics. This, and this alone, divides us. As long as this is true, nothing is possible. Without it, everything is possible....Once Cuban sovereignty has been restored we will extend the hand of friendship and assistance to a Cuba whose political and economic institutions have been shaped by the whole Cuban people.[86]

Quite clearly the President, unlike his own State Department, required no economic concessions for normalization. Instead "Cuban sovereignty" had to be "restored." This agenda could be accomplished by Castro himself, as the President had indicated to Daniel. Alternatively, Castro and the other "conspirators" could be ousted by the non-Communist AMTRUNK opposition.

The speech's double message immediately energized both conflicting policy initiatives, the Attwood-Daniel accommodation track and the AMLASH provocation track. On November 19, the day after the President's speech, Castro finally talked to Daniel, from 10 PM at night until four in the morning. He expressed great interest in what Daniel reported of his meeting with Kennedy, and asked for key phrases to be repeated. While refusing to retract past criticisms of Kennedy, Castro

---

[82] Assassinations Report, 173. (Note however the late date and addressee of the cited memo.)

[83] Hinckle and Turner, 139 (raid).

[84] Thomas G. Paterson, *Containing Castro* (New York: Oxford UP, 1994), 261; citing Bundy, "Meeting With the President," Dec. 19, 1963, Box 19, Aides Files-Bundy, NSF, LBJL. An internal CIA memo of December 9 appears to have interpreted the President's speech the same way (Schweiker-Hart Report, 20n).

[85] Beschloss, 659; citing Sorensen, *Kennedy*, 723. Sorensen's actual characterization of the speech, though balanced and ambiguous like the speech itself, seems to tilt rather towards the Bundy reading. According to Sorensen, the speech reminded the "Cuban people" of "the freedoms...and the American aid which would be forthcoming once they broke with Moscow."

[86] *Public Papers of the Presidents, Kennedy, 1963*, 876.

said that the Cubans could live with him, and that "anyone else would be worse." Castro added that he found "positive elements" in what Daniel had reported, and asked Daniel to prolong his stay so they could continue their discussions.[87] Meanwhile, on November 18, Bundy told Attwood by telephone that the President wanted to see him, and instruct him on what to say to Castro, as soon as he returned from a "brief trip" to Texas.[88]

The CIA, at the same time, used the speech to urge on AMLASH, in a manner which, although unclear, seems quite conspiratorial.

The IAPA Speech, AMLASH, and Assassination

In 1975 Nestor Sanchez, the AMLASH case officer, told the Schweiker-Hart Subcommittee that he

> met with AMLASH on November 22, 1963. At that meeting, the case officer referred to the President's November 18 speech in Miami as an indication that the President supported a coup. That speech described the Castro government as a "small band of conspirators" which formed a "barrier" which "once removed" would ensure United States support for progressive goals in Cuba. The case officer told AMLASH that Fitzgerald had helped write the speech. The case officer also told AMLASH that explosives and rifles with telescopic sights would be provided. The case officer showed AMLASH [a] a poison pen and suggested he use the commercial poison, Black-Leaf 40 in it....As AMLASH and the case officer broke up their meeting, they were told the President had been assassinated.[89]

Arthur M. Schlesinger, who himself had a hand in writing the speech, strongly denies that it was a green light for a coup, and doubts that FitzGerald helped write it. He writes that the speech "was meant in short as assistance to Attwood, not to FitzGerald;" but he fails to consider the very Kennedyesque probability that the speech was meant to assist both.[90]

The I.G. Report of 1967, discussing FitzGerald and the AMLASH operation, says nothing about the IAPA speech or FitzGerald's alleged role in writing it. Richard N. Goodwin, the alleged principal author, is likewise silent in his memoir, *Remembering America*, which sums up Kennedy's Cuba policy by referring to the Attwood initiative.[91]

On the other hand, FitzGerald's interpretation of the speech was not only reasonable, it was the prevailing one at the time. The Associated Press called the speech "an appeal to the Cuban people to overthrow the Castro regime." The *Ithaca Journal* ran the story under the front-page banner headline, "KENNEDY URGES OVERTHROW OF CASTRO."[92] Particularly significant, though less objective, was the informed comment of Hal Hendrix, a journalist whose CIA connections, later admitted to,

---

[87] The two men met again on November 22, and heard together of the President's murder. *Es una mala noticia,* Castro muttered over and over: "This is bad news." Jean Daniel, *New Republic,* December 7,14, 1963; Schlesinger, *Robert Kennedy,* 598-99; Quirk, 482-83.

[88] Attwood, *The Twilight Struggle,* 262; Beschloss, 659, Quirk, 183.

[89] Schweiker-Hart Report, 19-20. Nestor Sanchez' name, generally redacted out of the declassified I.G. Report, was allowed to remain on pages 77a and 100.

[90] Schlesinger, *Robert Kennedy,* 598n: "On its face the passage was obviously directed against Castro's extracontinental ties and signaled that, if these were ended, normalization was possible; it was meant in short as assistance to Attwood, not to FitzGerald. This was the signal that Richard Goodwin, the chief author of the speech, meant to convey. A search of the JFK Papers shows that Goodwin, Ralph Dungan, Bundy, Gordon Chase of Bundy's staff and I were involved in discussions about the speech. No evidence was uncovered of any contribution from FitzGerald and the CIA (W.W. Moss to author, March 30, 1978)."

[91] Richard N. Goodwin, *Remembering America* ZZ: "By the end of 1963, Kennedy would begin secret discussions with officials of the Cuban government, hoping to lay the foundation for a meeting with Castro and a peaceful solution to the 'Cuban problem.'" It is surprising that Goodwin should be recorded as the principal author of the IAPA Speech, since by his own account he moved after the 1962 Missile Crisis from State to the Peace Corps.

[92] *Ithaca Journal,* November 19, 1963; Hurt, *Reasonable Doubt,* 343.

have drawn critics' attention for his suppressed role in the Oswald story.[93] Inspired no doubt by his usual sources in the JM/WAVE station, Hendrix wrote that the crucial paragraph of the IAPA Speech "may have been meant for potential dissident elements in Castro's armed forces [i.e. Cubela's contacts] as well as for resistance groups in Cuba."[94]

In short those books are wrong which treat the IAPA Speech unilaterally as an olive branch to aid Attwood and Daniel.[95] Equally wrong are those who see it as evidence of a unified Kennedy-CIA advocacy of rebellion.[96] Like other speeches from late 1963, especially on Cuba, the Soviet Union and Vietnam, the speech is an example of calculated Kennedy doubletalk.

The Kennedy habit of speaking out of both sides of the mouth at once, like the larger Kennedy habit of trying to please both hawks and doves simultaneously, can be criticized as a defect of leadership, even of character.[97] The weakness that led to such ambiguity may well have contributed to the Kennedys' downfall, for it maximized frustration and mistrust within a divided Administration.

But the political schizophrenia expressed by such doubletalk was not just personal, it was national. If the Kennedys failed to speak or to pursue a single policy on Cuba, we must take into account the hurricane of dissenting voices in Congress, and manipulators inside the Administration, that made it virtually impossible to do so.

The CIA, reinforced by powerful forces in the media and corporate world, was becoming particularly manipulative in its massaging of the AMLASH operation into an assassination initiative. As we shall see in the next chapter, there is a deep CIA secret surrounding the November 22 meeting with AMLASH, which the I.G. Report of 1967 does more to conceal than reveal.

We must also consider the claim that the Kennedys had their own conspiratorial connection to the Giancana-Roselli-CIA plots against Castro, a connection the family and their friends still strive to conceal.[98] We must look at E. Howard Hunt, a man whose known role in the AMLASH story may have played a key role in the Watergate intrigue.[99] And above all we must look at a man whose behavior, and whose CIA watchers, were intertwined with the already complex Attwood-AMLASH-Hunt story. This man was Lee Harvey Oswald.

[93] For Hendrix and Oswald, see below, p. 96; Seth Kantor, *The Ruby Cover-Up* (New York: Zebra, 1978), 373-82. Hendrix himself played a part in what may have been the key 1963 assassination plot against Castro, the AMTILT Bayo-Pawley raid (Scott, *Deep Politics*, 114-17; cf. Hinckle and Turner, 169).

[94] Hal Hendrix, *Miami Herald*, November 20, 1963; reprinted by Cong. Bob Wilson in *Congressional Record*, November 20, 1963, A7190.

[95] Schlesinger, *Robert Kennedy*, 598n; Beschloss, 659. Cf. Daniel Schorr, 166: "At the November 22 meeting Fitzgerald [i.e. Sanchez] called attention to [the IAPA speech]. That, he told Cubela, was the signal of the President's support for a coup. It was a gross distortion of a speech in which Kennedy had actually extended a hand of friendship to Castro on condition the Cuban regime cease subversive efforts in other West Hemisphere countries."

[96] Paterson, 261; Hurt, 343.

[97] Richard Reeves, *A Question of Character* (Rocklin, CA: Prima, 1992), 278.

[98] Davis, *The Kennedys*, 348-53; Reeves, 262.

[99] Hinckle and Turner, 240, 299-306.

VI. AMLASH, THE I.G. REPORT, AND OSWALD

(THE INSPECTOR GENERAL'S REPORT: AN INTRODUCTION)

August 1994

The Inspector General's Report of 1967 on CIA Plots to Assassinate Fidel Castro is probably the most important CIA document ever released by the Agency. The document that neither Johnson nor (apparently) Nixon was allowed to see in its entirety, despite their asserted interest, the document so tightly held that only a single ribbon copy was retained even within the CIA, is now available to everyone.

Many of the IG Report's most important revelations have been known for two decades, but the release of the full text is nonetheless important. Although many of its key statements were transmitted by Congressional Committees in the 1970s, the document as a whole tells us far more than any of its parts. It is informative in what it chooses to tell us about the CIA's conscious collaboration with (its phrase) the "criminal underworld" (p. 15). But it is also informative in the facts which it strives to disguise or suppress. These include key events in the immediate context of President Kennedy's assassination.

The IG Report was the result of an investigation ordered in 1967 by President Johnson, after a Drew Pearson-Jack Anderson column of March 7, 1967, had published for the first time details of "a reported CIA plan in 1963 to assassinate Cuba's Fidel Castro."[1] However Johnson never got to see the actual report: Helms merely spoke to him from a set of notes which excluded the key events of late 1963. President Nixon never got to see it either, although it would appear that he had his aide John Ehrlichman try over many months to pry it out of CIA Director Richard Helms.[2]

The Report's story of CIA-underworld assassination murder plots will startle no one in the 1990s. In 1967 it was so explosive as to be virtually unmentionable in the public arena for another eight years. Even the Anderson column, which told only a small part of what Anderson would eventually reveal, was published four days late by the *Washington Post*, by which time the column's references to the recruitment of "underworld figures" had been edited out, presumably after checking with the CIA. We shall see that a follow-up column by Jack Anderson in 1971 was likewise edited. Not until the 1975 reports from the Rockefeller Commission and the Senate Church Committee did the press treat the story of CIA-mafia murder plots as more than a wild left-wing allegation.

And if that story is by now familiar, there is still plenty more in the IG Report to engage and even shock ordinary readers in the 1990s. I shall focus on four major issues:

---

[1] Church Committee, *Assassination Plots Report*, 179 (Johnson); *Washington Post*, March 7, 1967, p. C13 (column). The IG Report refers to "Drew Pearson's column of 7 March 1967" (p. 6); the column itself made it clear that it was written by Pearson's associate Jack Anderson. I shall refer to it hereafter as the Anderson column, as I consider the distinction to be important.

[2] H.R. Haldeman, Nixon's other top aide, wrote that in 1969, immediately after he came to office, Nixon charged Ehrlichman to obtain from the CIA a "document," described by the President as a complete report on the Bay of Pigs, that Richard Helms refused to deliver to the President. (H.R. Haldeman, with Joseph DiMona, *The Ends of Power*, 25-26). In Ehrlichman's *roman-à-clé*, *The Company*, the document requested by President "Monckton" was a document dealing with CIA sponsored assassinations in the Caribbean. Ehrlichman's notes of a meeting on September 18, 1971, record that the President instructed him to tell CIA to turn over "the *full* file [on the Bay of Pigs] *or else* (House Judiciary Committee, Impeachment Hearings, Appendix Three; see also Arthur M. Schlesinger, *Robert Kennedy and His Times*, 523-24). It remains unclear if Nixon's intent was to obtain the IG Report or the earlier in-house Kirkpatrick Report on the Bay of Pigs failure, which also existed in just one copy (Ranelagh, *The Agency*, 381; cf. 531), or both. The "full file," in theory, should have delivered both. (In the Watergate "smoking gun" tape of June 23, 1972, Nixon predicted that Hunt "will uncover a lot of things," including "the whole Bay of Pigs thing;" and Haldeman's book later surmised that "in all those Nixon references to the Bay of Pigs, he was actually referring to the Kennedy assassination" [Haldeman, *The Ends of Power*, 39]. Haldeman backed away from this speculation before his death, but it was a reasonable one: we now learn that E. Howard Hunt's name is almost certainly included in the IG Report, at pp. 99 and 101 [14-letter redactions; cf. below at footnote 6; Warren Hinckle and William Turner, *The Fish Is Red*, 240]).

1) The CIA's conscious efforts to restore organized crime elements, including drug traffickers, to their traditional position of influence in Cuba.

2) The CIA's pronounced hostility to presidential policy directives and controls, including its willingness to act controversially without consultation in the Kennedys' name.

3) The indications that the CIA's AMLASH assassination project in 1963 was designed to frustrate a presidentially authorized exploration of accommodation with Castro, in a project from which the CIA had been excluded.

4) The IG Report's total and suspicious evasion of the major question raised by the unedited Anderson column: that the CIA's plots against Castro had possibly "backfired" in such a way as to cause the president's murder.

In the interests of expanding the boundaries of what we now know, I shall focus on some of the limitations of the Report. This is not meant to discredit it as a significant source of historical information. Even when I talk below of misrepresentations in the IG Report, one can assume that much of this came from key witnesses (such as Sheffield Edwards) who had clearly something to hide, rather than originating with the Report's authors. But on the fourth topic (the murder of JFK) we find more continuous evasion and false logic, enough to raise questions about the purpose of the Report itself.

CIA-Underworld Plots and the Restoration of Organized Crime to Power in Cuba

Perhaps the most astonishing section of the IG Report tells the story of how the CIA allied itself with those whose motives (the FBI had warned them) were to re-establish the pre-Castro Cuban drug traffic. More specifically, the CIA was guided by the advice of mafia leader Santos Trafficante, and entrusted the assassination plot to Tony Varona, the Cuban leader of their own political creation for the Bay of Pigs, the Democratic Revolutionary Front:

> Varona was the head of the Democratic Revolutionary Front, [redacted] part of the larger Cuban operation. [CIA officer Jim] O'Connell understood that Varona was dissatisfied [redacted].
>
> (Comment [by CIA]: Reports from the FBI suggest how Trafficante may have known of Varona. On 21 December 1960 the Bureau forwarded to the Agency a memorandum reporting that efforts were being made by U.S. racketeers to finance anti-Castro activities in hopes of securing the gambling, prostitution, and dope monopolies in Cuba in the event Castro was overthrown. A later report of 18 January 1961 associates Varona with those schemes. Varona had hired Edward K. Moss, a Washington public relations counselor, as a fund raiser and public relations adviser. The Bureau report alleged that Moss' mistress was one Julia Cellini, whose brothers represented two of the largest gambling casinos in Cuba.) (29-30)

Comment by PDS: one of these was Meyer Lansky's Tropicana, where the manager was first Dino Cellini and then his and Jack Ruby's mutual friend Lewis McWillie, who arranged Ruby's mysterious trips to Cuba in 1959.[3] Then Dino and Eddie Cellini (with a third brother, Goffredo or Girodino Cellini) managed the casino at Lansky's $14 million dream palace, the Riviera, which opened in 1957. Thanks to the presence of top international couriers like Giuseppe de Giorgio, Havana casinos served as way-stations in the transfer of large heroin shipments from Europe to the United States.[4]

---

[3] 5 AH 20, 109-20; Scott, *Deep Politics*, 179-80.

[4] Scott, *Deep Politics*, 180-81; 5 AH 163. De Giorgio was both a gambler and a dealer at the Capri, where Lansky's associate Charles Tourine was the lead mob owner, and Ruby's friend McWillie was manager (5 AH 163). Twenty years later, when Tourine and his crime associate Joe Nesline were active in Amsterdam and Hamburg

According to the IG Report,

The Cellini brothers were believed to be in touch with Varona through Moss and were reported to have offered Varona large sums of money for his operations against Castro, with the understanding that they would receive privileged treatment 'in the Cuba of the future.' Attempts to verify these reports were unsuccessful.[5] (There is a record of CIA interest in Moss, but there is no indication that the Agency had any involvement with him in connection with Cuba. [Long redaction]...). (29-30)

I shall argue later that the most sustained misrepresentation in the IG Report is this pretense that the CIA did not understand (or could not "verify" reports on) the complex crime world others (like the FBI) were telling it about. However, even taken at face value, it is a shock to see the IG Report's lack of hypocritical surprise or concern about an FBI report that the CIA's efforts to install Varona in the place of Castro would serve the purposes of those mobsters who had "hopes of securing the gambling, prostitution, and dope monopolies in Cuba." Apparently it was accepted that the CIA's efforts would have the effect of restoring the tyranny of the U.S. mob in Cuba, whose presence had been one of the chief factors mobilizing Cuban middle-class revulsion against Batista.

On reflection, this should appear brazen, but not surprising. The mob had functioned as enforcers of U.S. interests in Cuba since the repeal in 1934 of the Platt Amendment which had "legalized" U.S. interventions in Cuba. Their corruption of Cuban politicians like Carlos Prio Socarras (Varona's patron), or Fulgencio Batista helped reduce these men (whatever their original ambitions) to the role of docile feeders at the U.S. capitalistic trough.

There may have been politics behind the March 1961 decision of the CIA's Office of Security to follow Trafficante's guidance and give a murder role to Varona. At the time Varona's influence in the Frente had been undercut by the incoming Kennedy Administration's stated preference for younger and less reactionary political leaders, notably the young engineer Manolo Ray, who had served briefly as a Minister under Castro. Bowing to the inevitable, senior CIA officials like Richard Bissell had made this leftward adjustment. After removing the right-wing Howard Hunt as the Frente's political liaison, on March 22 they appointed the more neutral Miro Cardona to be head of the CIA's "provisional government," with Ray and Varona as his lieutenants.[6]

The political difference between Varona and Ray was significant, at least from the point of view of the CIA. Varona was explicitly in favor of restoring the land, banks, and industries that had been nationalized under Castro to their original owners; Ray (whose political slogan was *Fidelismo sin Fidel*) accepted this part of the Castro revolution.[7]

Trafficante as well as Varona could correctly interpret the Kennedys' leftward move towards Ray as a threat to their influence in a post-Castro Cuba. Varona's and Trafficante's interests were not identical -- indeed Varona had once denounced mob influence in Cuba -- but Varona in exile depended on the funds and other resources of the mob-tainted Prio. The even more right-wing ideologue Hunt preferred the young Catholic leader Manuel Artime over Varona; and in January took steps to counter a leftward shift of the Frente by increasing the status of Artime (who by now was a Varona ally) in the CIA invasion force.[8] All three men, Varona, Trafficante, and Hunt, had reasons to

---

criminal activities, the Cellini brothers and Giuseppe de Giorgio were again present. See Alan Block, *Perspectives on Organizing Crime*, 234-36.

[5] HSCA investigator Michael Ewing told Warren Hinckle and Bill Turner that Varona "was dealing with Lansky, who offered to back him;" and that it was actually Lansky who turned Varona over to Trafficante (Hinckle and Turner, *The Fish Is Red*, 75). This appears to be the source for Charles Rappleye's claim that "Varona had met with Meyer Lansky to secure financing for his nascent Frente" (Rappleye and Becker, *All-American Mafioso*, 192).

[6] Szulc and Meyer, *The Cuban Invasion*, 107; Wyden, *Bay of Pigs*, 116; cf. Hunt, *Give Us This Day*, passim. Bissell replaced Hunt with James Noel (called "Jim Noble" in Wyden's account, and "Jim" in Hunt's). Noel and Hunt disliked each other intensely, but would later supervise the 1965 assassination meeting between Rolando Cubela (AMLASH) and Artime (when Noel acted as Cubela's case officer, and Hunt as Artime's). See IG Report, 99-101; Hinckle and Turner, *The Fish Is Red*, 240.

[7] *Time*, January 27, 1961, April 28, 1961 (Varona); Hugh Thomas, *The Cuban Revolution*, 508 (Ray). The new CIA releases contain a letter of 3/3/61 from U.S. businessman William D. Pawley, warning of the dire dangers if either Ray or Miro Cardona were given important positions in a new post-Castro government.

[8] Szulc and Meyer, 92-94. This book does not name Hunt; but cf. Szulc, *Compulsive Spy*, 84-85, 91-93; Hunt,

oppose the Kennedy-backed forces of social democracy.

O'Connell's decision to involve Varona in a sensitive and central murder operation, at a time when his status and influence in the Bay of Pigs Operation was diminishing, reflects at a minimum the kind of bureaucratic inertia that has made the CIA such a reactionary force throughout the Third World. But what are we to make of his decision to do so without seeking guidance from Bissell or higher authority? Other considerations suggest that his decision, like Hunt's promotion of Artime, and indeed the whole CIA-mafia collaboration to kill Castro, was not just insensitive to the Kennedys' political directives but consciously and actively opposed to them.

The CIA's Hostility to the Policies and Directives of the Kennedys

Under the guidance of Kennedy aides Richard Goodwin and Arthur Schlesinger, the New Frontier was a perceived threat to those like Varona and Hunt (and presumably O'Connell) who wished to return Cuban politics to the status quo ante. Also threatening was Robert Kennedy's avowed opposition to mob political influence, whether in Cuba or in the United States.

It is important to understand that CIA-underworld collaboration was an established and continuing mode of operation going back to the suppression of Sicilian and French Communism after World War II.[9] The Kennedy family had their own well-established mob connections, dating back to Joseph Kennedy's liquor operations during and after prohibition.[10] Almost certainly the mob helped elect Kennedy in 1960, as it has frequently helped to elect Presidents (and more importantly advance them through the primaries) before and since.[11]

And yet Bobby Kennedy was undeniably (and dangerously) committed to the goal of reducing the power of organized crime in America. Both in his years with the McClellan Rackets Committee and then in his book *The Enemy Within*, published in February 1960, Kennedy specifically targeted both Santos Trafficante and Sam Giancana along with Jimmy Hoffa (almost certainly another CIA asset, and possibly involved in the murder plot, although unnamed in the IG Report).[12] And when as Attorney General Bobby drew up a list of the hoods he wanted to go after, "heading the list was none other than Sam Giancana."[13] In fact the *Parade* article and photographs which allegedly revealed to O'Connell he was dealing with Giancana and Trafficante (IG Report, 19) were later recalled by O'Connell as describing "Bobby Kennedy's ten most wanted individuals" (5 AH 249).[14]

The truth is that in 1960 Trafficante and Giancana were relatively little known, apart from Robert Kennedy's pursuit of them. It can hardly be a coincidence that in August 1960, shortly after John Kennedy secured the Democratic nomination, Bissell and Edwards took steps to create (via Roselli, Giancana's subordinate) a CIA connection to these two men, effectively conferring on them a CIA immunity, or "get-out-of-jail free" card, that Giancana, in particular, would use dramatically on two occasions when his nemesis was Attorney General (IG Report, 57-60, 67-70).

Both Trafficante and Maheu, along with Maheu's mentor Edward Bennett Williams (through whom Maheu had met Roselli), were allied to Bobby Kennedy's arch-enemy, Jimmy Hoffa.[15] Using

157-64.

[9] See Scott, *Deep Politics*, 166-69, 173-75.

[10] Scott, *Deep Politics*, 356; John H. Davis, *The Kennedys*, 56-57, 75-77, 485-86.

[11] Davis, *Kennedys*, 289-90 (Kennedy in 1960).

[12] Robert F. Kennedy, *The Enemy Within*, 228, 240-41; Scott, *Deep Politics*, 173; Moldea, *The Hoffa Wars*, 131, 277, 387.

[13] Brashler, *The Don*, 196.

[14] Cf. Assassination Plots Report, 77. Maheu also claims that he learned that Giancana and Trafficante "were among the ten most powerful Mafia members...after seeing their pictures in a magazine soon after meeting them" (Maheu, *Next to Hughes*, 141). But the Church Committee was unable to locate the article, and other investigators have questioned its existence.

[15] Maheu's questionable investigative activities for Williams and Hoffa had come under Robert Kennedy's hostile scrutiny during the Rackets Committee Hearings (pp. 15247-49, 19672-74).

Maheu as his investigator, Williams had performed a number of favors for the CIA in the past, as well as Hoffa. So, according to his biographers, had John Roselli.[16] It is thus understandable, and hardly treasonable, that the CIA should have taken these steps to protect their underworld assets, before the Kennedys came to power.

By contrast, the revival of the plan with Varona, probably in March 1961 (IG Report, 29; Assassination Plots Report, 82), set the CIA in clear and witting alliance with the underworld, in opposition to the policy priorities of the new Attorney General, backed by the President of the United States

What was really being protected by the CIA here was not so much the underworld per se, but the political life of Washington in which the underworld, with its lobbyists and call girls and cash, was an integrated part.[17] Perhaps the most revealing clue to this is the Report's startling digression (IG Report, 30) on the Cellini brothers (who were top Lansky lieutenants) and the Washington p.r. man Edward K. Moss, a man so powerful (especially among Democrats) that all reference to him has been deleted in the Church Committee's extended (and Democratic) Assassination Plots Report.

Whether or not Moss actively represented the Cellinis, he did for years represent a number of far more famous people who were simultaneously CIA assets. One of these in the 1970s was Adnan Khashoggi, then known as "the richest man in the world." (Khashoggi's kickbacks on lucrative defense contracts with Saudi Arabia generated a slush fund for such intelligence-driven operations as the Iran-Contra affair.) We learn from Khashoggi's biography that in 1954 Moss, a Yale man and former assistant to the president of the American Management Association, "started Moss International Inc., which has advised nineteen countries, helped the Democratic National Committee organize conventions, and represented the National Coffee Association and the Bank of America."[18]

It is striking that one of Moss's acts for Khashoggi was to secure for him the legal services of Edward P. Morgan, the attorney whom Maheu had previously hired for Howard Hughes (another source of funds for CIA operations) and who turns up in the IG Report (p. 36) as attorney for John Roselli. As Ron Kessler remarks in his Khashoggi biography, Morgan was the kind of man who "knew that clients and issues come and go, but the powers in Washington remain largely unchanged."[19]

The chief result of the so-called assassination plot of 1960-61 was not to threaten Castro. It was to preserve the dubious underpinnings of the world that made men like Maheu and Moss and Morgan (and their friends in the CIA) enduringly powerful.

One can indeed surmise that this was not only the result, but for some, and above all Maheu himself, the conscious aim of the operation. For the CIA gained no protection whatsoever by introducing such sinister cut-outs as Roselli, Giancana and Trafficante. Far from suppressing the involvement of the CIA, these men advertised it whenever it suited them, as even the IG Report is aware.[20] Even riskier, from the point of view of the CIA's security, was the fact that by 1961 Trafficante was widely suspected of being a double agent, reporting to Castro's DGI as well as the CIA.[21]

The plot makes much more sense, however, if one imagines that the initiative for it came from below; and that the purpose was to protect, not the CIA, but the mob and its allies. This is quite possible, for Edwards, O'Connell, Maheu, and Roselli were more clannish than the IG Report lets on. The sentence "Edwards consulted Robert A. Maheu...to see if Maheu had any underworld contacts" (IG Report, 15) is particularly misleading. Edwards, O'Connell, Maheu, and Roselli had already dined together in Maheu's home the previous spring.[22] Maheu claims that Edwards and O'Connell

---

[16] Rappleye and Becker, *All-American Mafioso*, 152-55.

[17] Scott, *Deep Politics*, 217-41.

[18] Kessler, *The Richest Man in the World*, 183.

[19] Kessler, *The Richest Man in the World*, 165.

[20] IG Report, 67-69, 125. Trafficante testified to the HSCA that Roselli "told me that the CIA and the United States Government was involved in eliminating Castro" (5 AH 357). So much for generating cover and deniability!

[21] George Crile, *Washington Post*, May 16, 1976; reprinted at 5 AH 309; see also Arthur M. Schlesinger, *Robert Kennedy and His Times*, 520.

[22] Rappleye, *All-American Mafioso*, 184-85; Assassination Plots Report, 75.

originally met and talked with Roselli at a party Maheu threw for an ex-FBI agent, Scott McLeod, when he left the State Department's Office of Security in 1957.[23]

Nor did Maheu open his office with a CIA subsidy in 1956, as the IG Report claims (15); he opened it in 1954.[24] In the next six years he had done a number of jobs for the CIA, and O'Connell in particular. In this time period the Maheu office, which Jim Hougan characterizes as one of the CIA's "deniable proprietaries," had been involved in the 1956 kidnap-murder of a leading intellectual from the Dominican Republic, Jesus de Galindez, in collaboration with the mob figure Bayonne Joe Zicarelli.[25]

Could the four men who dined together at Maheu's house have dreamed up this escapade to reinforce their alliance against Bobby's house-cleaning? It is striking that (according to the IG Report, 16-18) Edwards took this risky step on his own initiative, merely informing his superiors of a *fait accompli*. What increases the possibility of that Edwards was using the CIA to help the mob (rather than vice versa) is the fact that so many of those involved (O'Connell, Maheu, Morgan, and others) were, as the IG Report notes (15) former FBI men. For the mob had been receiving the same privileged treatment from some high officials in the FBI, and from J. Edgar Hoover in particular, for many years.[26]

Another possibility, not inconsistent, is that the plot was intended to fail, and that Trafficante, the suspected double agent, was in fact supposed under CIA direction to leak some of the details to the Cuban DGI. This would have the effect of increasing Trafficante's credibility and utility to the Castro intelligence forces, and thus help open a window for the CIA inside Cuba. One of the IG Report's authors, Scott Breckenridge, later maintained to a Senate staff member "that Trafficante had been providing Castro with details of the plot all along".[27]

The AMLASH 1963 Project as a CIA Revolt Against Presidential Policy

Much has been written (albeit inconclusively) about Robert Kennedy's angry reaction on learning that the CIA had used Giancana in an operation, how he ordered CIA in May 1962 to clear such operations in future with the Justice Department, and how the CIA failed to do so.[28] The Democratically-controlled Church Committee assembled much evidence on the question of Bobby Kennedy's knowledge, but was inconclusive. We shall soon see that the issue is an important one. From my own reading of the evidence I would conclude:

1) Robert Kennedy (and probably his brother John) had known of these plots from as early as May 22, 1961, if not earlier.[29]

---

[23] Robert Maheu and Richard Hack, *Next to Hughes* (New York: HarperPaperbacks, 1992), 136-38.

[24] Maheu, *Next to Hughes*, 47. Maheu adds the intriguing detail that Edwards and the CIA Office of Security disliked Bobby Kennedy from as early as 1954, when they tried in vain to get Maheu to cease sharing an office with the Kennedys' accountant and trouble-shooter, Carmine Bellino: "Because of Bobby, the CIA told me that if I were to work with the Agency, I would have to move away from Carmine and any possible Kennedy connection. I said I couldn't afford to move out. So the company put me on a monthly retainer of $500, thereby becoming my first steady client and enabling me to move into an office of my own."

[25] Assassination Plots Report, 74-75; Hougan, *Secret Agenda*, 12 ("proprietaries"); Alan A. Block, *Perspectives on Organizing Crime*, 168-71.

[26] Curt Gentry, *Hoover*, 531-32; Anthony Summers, *Official and Confidential*, 242-45; Scott, *Deep Politics*, 144-46, etc.

[27] *Washington Post*, May 16, 1976, C1; reprinted at 5 AH 309.

[28] IG Report, 62a-65; Assassination Plots Report, 132-35; Schlesinger, *Robert Kennedy*, 531 ("Plainly Kennedy had known nothing about assassination plots"); Powers, *The Man Who Kept the Secrets*, 155 ("The record is clear, then, that Kennedy was thoroughly briefed about the details"); Hinckle and Turner, *The Fish Is Red*, 124 ("Kennedy was hopping mad that he had not been told"); Ranelagh, *The Agency*, 384n ("Robert Kennedy had known about this involvement for at least a year"); John H. Davis, *The Kennedys*, 743 ("I do not...believe that Kennedy learned that Giancana had been hired by the CIA until the spring of 1962").

[29] Assassination Plots Report, 123-31. The question of Kennedy knowledge of course raises the role of Judith Campbell Exner, who in the period 1960-62 became the simultaneous friend of John Kennedy and of Sam Gianca-

2) It is possible, if not certain, that both Kennedys, although not officially informed of these assassination plots, continued by their non-intervention to tolerate them, up to March 1963.[30]

3) After March 1963, and particularly after a new Cuban policy memorandum of April 21, 1963, the Kennedys neither knew nor sanctioned by silence such plots. On the contrary, Bobby's Justice Department warned on March 30 it would crack down hard on Cuban exile activities launched from U.S. territory. And a new set of Presidential policy options explored in April and May led to the reasonable finding, by a committee of the National Security Council that U.S. interests were not likely to be served by Castro's death.[31]

This does not seem to have deterred the CIA. On the contrary, the CIA's conduct of the Cubela (AMLASH) operation in late 1963, unambiguously, has the earmarks of a hostile revolt against Presidential authority and policy.

Not mentioned in the IG Report, but crucial to understanding the AMLASH operation, are the secret contacts in 1963 between representatives of the Kennedys and of Castro. The CIA, now deeply distrusted by the White House, was pointedly excluded from these secret negotiations; but almost certainly it had knowledge of them. The CIA's assassination initiatives in 1963 seem completely bizarre, and irrational, unless we consider that they were designed to prevent these secret contacts from succeeding.

Normal to any CIA illegal operation, and indeed dictated by the CIA's charter, is the condition that it must be plausibly deniable. In 1963 the CIA flagrantly violated this elementary rule, as if deliberately. Whereas in 1960 it had brought in the mob as a means of concealing government responsibility, in 1963 it repeatedly sought to establish a convincing trail of responsibility leading into the Kennedy White House.

In 1962, for example, New York attorney James Donovan, accompanied by John Nolan of Robert Kennedy's staff, had negotiated with Castro the return of the Bay of Pigs prisoners. In April 1963 the two men returned to Cuba for more negotiations which, even if not conclusive, were fruitful in opening a doorway for further talks towards possible normalization.[32] The CIA was informed of this mission but did not take part in it.

Desmond FitzGerald of the CIA's SAS staff does not appear to have looked favorably towards this step on the accommodation track. In early 1963 the staff arranged for the CIA's Technical Services Division to purchase a wet suit, and contaminate it with tuberculosis bacilli and the spores for a disabling skin disease. The plan was for Donovan (who was not informed of the plot) to give the suit to Castro, his companion in scuba diving.[33]

It is not hard to see that this wild proposal violated "the most elementary considerations -- for example that it [i.e. the suit] was in effect a gift from the United States, while the idea was to *keep it secret*; or, then again, Donovan's feelings about being the gift-giver in this plot. If he wasn't let in on the plot, after all, he might try on the suit himself."[34]

---

na. Originally Exner claimed to have no knowledge of the CIA-mafia plots (Davis, *The Kennedys*, 739-43). By 1991 she was claiming, somewhat implausibly, that she had been part of an April 1961 hotel-room meeting where John Kennedy and Giancana plotted the death of Castro together (*Sunday Times* [London], October 6, 1991).

[30] Assassination Plots Report, 139-70.

[31] Assassination Plots Report, 170-73.

[32] Arthur Schlesinger links the success of the Donovan-Nolan mission to the important interview given by Castro to Lisa Howard in late April, which in turn helped set up the secret Attwood-Lechuga discussions of Fall 1963 (Schlesinger, *Robert Kennedy*, 583-84).

[33] Assassination Report, 85-86; IG Report, 75. FitzGerald told the IG Report authors that the plot began after he took over the SAS staff in January 1963. The Church Committee considered it "likely that the activity took place earlier, since Donovan had completed his his negotiations by the middle of January 1963" (Assassination Plots Report, 86). But the premise for this conclusion was obviously incorrect.

[34] Thomas Powers, *The Man Who Kept the Secrets*, 150. The fact that Donovan and Castro planned to dive together may possibly have inspired FitzGerald's famous plan to kill Castro with an exploding sea-shell (Assassination Report, 87, IG Report, 77). FitzGerald's assistant Samuel Halpern told Thomas Powers that he "protested the seashell plan....Castro blowing up on the ocean floor would point a finger directly at the United States" (Powers,

We can see the same CIA antipathy to the accommodation track in October 1963. By this time (thanks in part to the Donovan-Nolan mission) there had been presidentially authorized meetings at the UN between William Attwood, a Special Advisor to the U.S. Delegation, and the Cuban UN Ambassador, Carlos Lechuga. The President's authorization specified that Attwood would report directly to McGeorge Bundy in the White House; the CIA and the State Department were to be excluded. The talks began in September and soon involved others, including the French journalist Jean Daniel. On November 18 Attwood finally reported to Bundy that Castro would be sending Lechuga instructions for the agenda of a meeting with Attwood in Havana. Bundy replied that the President would see Attwood after a brief trip to Dallas. With the President's death, the project for normalization lapsed.[35]

The time frame of the short-lived Attwood initiative fits closely with the 1963 Cubela assassination plot. The go-between who arranged for Attwood to meet Lechuga (the American journalist Lisa Howard) told Attwood of her intentions on September 5. Two days later, on September 7, the CIA resumed contact with Rolando Cubela, a member of Castro's entourage whom the CIA had first contacted in 1961, and then dropped in 1962, after proof of his notorious inability to keep a secret.[36] Attwood himself comments that the CIA must have had an inkling of what he was up to, from their phone taps and surveillance of Lechuga.[37]

This first coincidence of dates may have been fortuitous. Less excusable is the unauthorized decision of Richard Helms and Desmond FitzGerald to have FitzGerald present himself to Cubela on October 29 as a personal representative of Robert Kennedy, especially since FitzGerald proceeded to discuss an assassination plot against Castro which the Kennedys almost certainly knew nothing about. October 29 was just five days after the President had met personally with Jean Daniel, and given him a personal message to transmit to Fidel Castro. Robert Kennedy had just authorized the Attwood accommodation initiative from which the CIA was being excluded. Crudely put, Helms and FitzGerald chose unilaterally to represent Robert Kennedy, precisely at a time when they could not know what he wanted, or was up to: a time when there was a distinction and potential divergence between CIA and Kennedy interests.

That the CIA was well aware of this distinction was unconsciously revealed in 1976 by FitzGerald's assistant Samuel Halpern. Halpern was deposed by the Schweiker-Hart Subcommittee, who had learned that two senior CIA officers had counseled FitzGerald against the security risk of a personal meeting with Cubela. Halpern discounted the danger that the Fitzgerald-Cubela meeting "exposed the CIA to possible embarrassment. because Fitzgerald had not used his real name and, therefore, AMLASH would have been unable to identify Fitzgerald *as a CIA officer*."[38]

Only Robert Kennedy would be embarrassed, in other words. This indeed would seem to be the most rational intention of such an unprofessional and disloyal meeting. Both Kennedys were lending support to explorations which promised (or alternatively, threatened) to lead to an accommodation with Castro. Those initiatives could only be harmed by FitzGerald's discussion of assassinating Castro with a suspected leaker or double-agent, while claiming to be a representative of Robert Kennedy.

---

150). But there is no trace of such protest in the IG Report, which has this to say: "FitzGerald states that he, Sam Halpern, and [redacted] had several sessions at which they explored this possibility, but that no one else was ever brought in on the talks. Halpern believes that he had conversations with TSD on feasibility...." (IG Report, 77). Halpern's protest was first recorded after FitzGerald had died suddenly in July 1967, three months after the preparation of the IG Report.

[35] William Attwood, *The Twilight Struggle*, 257-62.

[36] William Attwood, *The Twilight Struggle*, 258; Schweiker-Hart Report, 20 (September 5); IG Report, 84-86; Schweiker-Hart Report 13-14 (September 7).

[37] William Attwood, *The Twilight Struggle*, 264.

[38] Schweiker-Hart Report, 17n (citing Executive Officer testimony, 4/22/76, p. 55); emphasis added. The two senior dissenting officers were Joseph "Langosch," chief of SAS/CI, and Theodore Shackley, the chief of the Miami JMWAVE station (Schweiker-Hart Report, 74-75). The Church Committee, finding written evidence of which the IG Report was unaware (IG Report, 92), concluded that FitzGerald had attended the November 22 meeting with Cubela as well (Assassination Plots Report, 89, Daniel Schorr, *Clearing the Air*, 166). Thomas Powers, relying on an anonymous CIA source (Halpern?) disputes this (p. 343n).

The same Samuel Halpern has argued that the CIA, far from being disloyal to Robert Kennedy in this operation, had in fact gained his explicit approval informally. In the words of John Davis,

> Since Kennedy and FitzGerald often met socially and at work, there was no need for formal authorization. The attorney general's approval could just as easily have been conveyed informally and be far less risky for all concerned. This opinion was confirmed by former CIA official, Samuel Halpern, who in 1963 had been executive assistant to the Task Force on Cuba and one of the four men directly involved in the AM/LASH operation. In an interview on November 18, 1983, Mr. Halpern told me that he was absolutely certain that "Des" FitzGerald "had full authorization from Attorney General Kennedy and President Kennedy to proceed with the AM/LASH plot against Castro," adding that he always felt that since they often met socially, Bobby Kennedy and "Des" FitzGerald conducted most of their business together at Washington cocktail parties and receptions, rather than in their respective offices.[39]

There is a germ of truth underlying this false allegation. Robert Kennedy had indeed authorized the AMTRUNK political operation which the IG Report relates to the AMLASH (Cubela) initiative. AMTRUNK was an ambitious attempt to promote a military coup within Cuba, using assets such as Major Ramon Guin whom Cubela contacted (IG Report, 86). As Helms rightly testified to the Church Committee in 1975, he "had pre-existing authority to deal with AM/LASH regarding 'a change of government' (as opposed to assassination)."[40]

But Halpern and Davis seem to have missed the point: namely, that FitzGerald and Helms never presented the Cubela initiative to their superiors as an assassination operation. It is indeed likely, almost certain, that the CIA had authorization to proceed with the political initiative. But that it had authorization to involve Robert Kennedy's name and authority in an assassination plot with a notorious leaker, at a time when the Kennedys were attempting to open discussions with Castro, is virtually unimaginable. Both FitzGerald and Helms later denied that the AMLASH operation contemplated assassination.[41] It seems clear that Kennedy's authorization for AMLASH would have been limited to what they described it as, an attempt to find a group to replace Castro.

From this point on the AMLASH initiative had the looks of an anti-Kennedy provocation. This was Attwood's retrospective evaluation of the FitzGerald/AMLASH meetings: "One thing was clear: Stevenson was right when he told me back in September that 'the CIA is in charge of Cuba'; or anyway, acted as if it thought it was, and to hell with the president it was pledged to serve."[42] Indeed the conduct of the AMLASH episode, as much as of the Attwood initiative, is symptomatic of the mistrust and hostility which divided the CIA from the Kennedys over Cuba in late 1963.

The Evasiveness of the IG Report With Respect to the Murder of JFK

In light of this hostility, it is striking how unresponsive the IG Report is to the central charge in the Pearson-Anderson column which it was supposed to investigate. As the IG Report itself admits (p. 6), "Drew Pearson's column of 7 March 1967 refers to a reported CIA plan in 1963 to assassinate Cuba's Fidel Castro." Yet in the Report's 133 pages, only ten and a half (pp. 86-95) refer to a 1963 plot at all, and that one (the Cubela plot) is (we shall see) not the one Anderson was writing about.

But the principal evasiveness of the IG Report is much more striking. In the entire report, less than a dozen lines (pp. 118, 127) are devoted to what Anderson himself called the "political H-bomb" in the second and more important clause of the quoted sentence, under the heading, "Castro Counterplot:"

---

[39] John Davis, *The Kennedys*, 495.
[40] Assassination Plots Report, 175; citing Helms testimony of 6/13/75.
[41] Assassination Plots Report, 87.
[42] Attwood, *The Twilight Struggle*, 263.

The publicity over New Orleans District Attorney Jim Garrison's investigation of a 'Kennedy assassination plot' has focussed attention in Washington on a reported CIA plan in 1963 to assassinate Cuba's Fidel Castro, which according to some sources *may have resulted in a counterplot by Castro to assassinate President Kennedy.*[43]

Even this version of the Anderson "counterplot" story, as published belatedly in the *Washington Post*, was a bowdlerized one. Four days earlier Anderson's column, as originally published, contained a much stronger story, not just that Castro had "cooked up a counterplot," but that this counterplot had possibly been executed:

> President Johnson is sitting on a political H-bomb -- an unconfirmed report that Senator Robert Kennedy (Dem.-N.Y.) may have approved an assassination plot which then possibly backfired against his late brother....One version claims that underworld figures actually were recruited to carry out the plot. Another rumor has it that three hired assassins were caught in Havana....For weeks after the tragedy, this column was told, Bobby was morose and refused to see people. Could he have been plagued by the terrible thought that he had helped put into motion forces that indirectly may have brought about his brother's martyrdom? Some insiders think so.[44]

Note that p. 118 of the IG Report quotes many of these specific details: "underworld figures," "three hired assassins," "Castro...cooked up a counterplot". Yet the Report wholly fails to investigate, just like the *Washington Post*, the central thesis that the Robert Kennedy authorized a CIA plot which then "possibly backfired" against Kennedy.

There was a lot of politics to the timing of Anderson's charge, and it involved among other matters the worsening war scene in Vietnam.[45] Both Pearson and Anderson were close to Johnson, who by 1967 was convinced that Bobby Kennedy was the leader of those forces opposing his Vietnam policies from the left.[46] Johnson's almost paranoid obsession with Bobby could only have been enhanced on March 2, 1967, the day before the Pearson-Anderson column appeared, when Robert Kennedy came forward with a controversial proposal for the suspension of bombing against North Vietnam. By this time Johnson's paranoia had also come to embrace the CIA, whose initial support of the escalated war had become much more critical in late 1966.[47]

Hence the Anderson column must have struck Johnson as a convenient opening to gather ammunition against Robert Kennedy and the CIA at the same time. His request to Helms for the facts must have struck Helms too as part of a political strategy against Robert Kennedy, in which the CIA, even if not the primary target, would also get mauled. Assuredly Helms' sense of loyalty to the CIA would have justified in his eyes a refusal to become part of this game.[48] But Helms's refusal to execute Johnson's request for information about this sensitive area only makes sense if we accept that there was indeed something to the Anderson story.

Before proceeding, I should also make it clear that I do not believe (as Jack Anderson apparently still does) that Castro killed Kennedy. Nevertheless I now believe that the March 3

---

[43] *Washington Post*, March 7, 1967, p. C13 (column). Note that the only reference to this "counterplot" in the IG Report (p. 118: "Castro...is reported to have cooked up a counterplot against President Kennedy") is actually language taken, along with other details, from the much stronger Anderson column of March 3 (see below).

[44] *San Francisco Chronicle*, March 3, 1967, p. 41.

[45] I have argued that the timing of Anderson's charge involved other political issues as well, notably the unfolding Garrison investigation in New Orleans (Clay Shaw had just been indicted on March 1) and the inter-related matter of the conviction of Jimmy Hoffa (whose petition for relief had been denied by the Supreme Court on February 27, 1967) which depended on the testimony of an early Garrison target, Edward Grady Partin. See Peter Dale Scott, *Crime and Cover-Up*, 25-29; cf. Scott, *Deep Politics*, 187-90.

[46] Schlesinger, *Robert Kennedy and His Times*, 799; Doris Kearns, *Lyndon Johnson and the American Dream*, 331.

[47] Powers, 174-75; Ranelagh, 154-55, cf. 443. In 1969 Johnson had Connally tell Nixon that one of Nixon's three main problems would be "disloyal people in State and CIA" (Haldeman, *Haldeman Diaries*, 102).

[48] See Powers, 156-58, and passim. The redaction of the story by the *Post* likewise had the effect of protecting Kennedy and the CIA, both of whom the *Post* was probably closer to in 1967 than to the Johnson White House. The war was a factor here as well.

allegation, that the CIA plot "possibly backfired," was suppressed in the *Post* and the IG Report because it had hit a nerve. That is, it contained an element of truth and people (probably in the CIA) knew it.

The extreme sensitivity of this allegation was demonstrated again in January 1971, when Anderson repeated it. This time Anderson outlined the CIA-underworld plots in some detail, naming Maheu, Harvey, O'Connell, Roselli, the CIA poison pills, and "Cuban assassination teams equipped with high-powered rifles."[49] Once again Anderson asked the forbidden question: "Could the plot against Castro have backfired against President Kennedy?" Once again, predictably, this part of his column was suppressed, not just by the newspapers publishing it, but by the Senate Watergate Committee which found it relevant.[50]

By this time, of course, Robert Kennedy was dead. However most accounts of Watergate agree that by early 1971 Richard Nixon's "abiding nightmare" was that his nemesis Larry O'Brien "would somehow rebuild Teddy Kennedy to be [Nixon's] opponent for the presidency in 1972."[51] Once again Jack Anderson appeared to threatening a Kennedy-Helms area of vulnerability, at a time when the Nixon White House (with a more hard-line Vietnam policy) was hostile to both men.[52]

Not until September 1976, after Roselli had testified and been murdered, did Jack Anderson spell out the "political H-bomb" that he had merely hinted at in 1967. The full Rosselli allegation was not just about a "counterplot" or a "retaliation," but an actual turnaround of mob killers from their original target (Castro) to President Kennedy. This time the *Washington Post* finally ran the full story:

> Before he died, Roselli hinted to associates that he knew who had arranged President Kennedy's murder. It was the same conspirators, he suggested, whom he had recruited earlier to kill Cuban Premier Fidel Castro....Snipers were dispatched to a Havana rooftop. They were caught. The word reached Roselli that some of the plotters had been tortured and that Castro had learned about the whole operation....

PDS Comment: This would appear to be the three-man team who on March 13, 1963 set up a sniper's nest at the University of Havana and were discovered by security police just before Castro arrived for a scheduled appearance.[53] The location suggests that the men may have been drawn from the university milieu of the old anti-Batista Directorio Revolucionario that produced both Juan Orta (the associate of Trafficante and Varona who was central to the 1960-61 plots) and the 1963 plotter Rolando Cubela, a former DR leader and friend of Orta (IG Report, 80).[54]

> According to Roselli, Castro enlisted the same underworld elements who he had caught plotting against him. They supposedly were Cubans from the old Trafficante organization. Working with Cuban intelligence, they allegedly lined up an ex-Marine sharpshooter, Lee Harvey Oswald, who had been active in the pro-Castro movement. According to

---

[49] *Forum*, January 18, 1971.

[50] *Miami Herald*, January 19, 1971; Watergate Hearings, 9913; cf. 9723, 9755. Columns reprinted with discussion in Peter Dale Scott, Paul L. Hoch, and Russell Stetler, *The Assassinations: Dallas and Beyond*, 375-80.

[51] Fred Emery, *Watergate*, 33. Cf. H.R. Haldeman, *Haldeman Diaries*, 134, 297, etc.; J. Anthony Lukas, *Nightmare*, 16-17, 81, etc. As in 1967, the timing of the column can be related to Hoffa's legal difficulties as well: his petition for review of his Chicago Pension Fund conviction had just been denied by the U.S. Supreme Court, on January 11, 1971.

[52] J. Anthony Lukas, *Nightmare*, 26-27; Emery, 22 (Nixon on Helms). Of course Anderson was never as close to Nixon as he and Pearson had been to Johnson, but it was not until 1972 that Anderson also would be attacked by the Nixon White House as an enemy. In late March of 1972 Liddy and Hunt discussed drugs for "neutralizing" Anderson with Dr. Edward Gunn (Fred Emery, *Watergate*, 98), the former CIA doctor, now also in business with McCord (Hougan, 95n), who had earlier supplied the CIA lethal poisons for first Edwards and then Cubela (IG Report, 21, 93). Hunt and Liddy paid Gunn with a $100 bill from CRP intelligence funds (Liddy, *Will*, 407-08), thus possibly laying yet another trail back to the 1960-63 "Bay of Pigs thing."

[53] Hinckle and Turner, *The Fish Is Red*, 174.

[54] The Cuban Government gave to Senator McGovern and later to the HSCA the name of one of the three men, Samuel Carballo Moreno (5 AH 264, 298); according to an earlier witness, Harry Dean, a Sam Moreno had been involved in a 1962 plot against President Kennedy in Mexico (AARC Archives, interview of Harry Dean).

Roselli's version, Oswald may have shot Kennedy or may have acted as a decoy while others ambushed him from closer range.[55]

Almost certainly the CIA knew of the three-man plot against Castro in March 1963, whether or not it was itself involved. As I have written elsewhere, there was at least one other three-man assassination team that was sent, this time with CIA support, against Castro in 1963. These three men were Eddie "Bayo" Perez and the other two survivors of the so-called Bayo-Pawley mission, sent in the summer of 1963 by Roselli's close friend and room-mate John Martino.[56] The recently released CIA documents confirm "the large amount of assistance from JMWAVE" (the CIA's Miami station) for this mission, and also the efforts of John Martino to exfiltrate Angel Luis Castillo Cabrera, "Bayo"'s brother-in-law, to join them.[57]

This Luis Castillo is the "Castillo" cited by the IG Report on p. 118 as corroboration of the "counterplot." Martino himself claimed before his death to have had special knowledge concerning the Kennedy assassination, to have known Ruby in Cuba, and even to have watched Oswald passing out his pro-Castro leaflets in New Orleans.[58] Above all, Martino had already given to the Warren Commission and to the FBI an early version of the Roselli-Anderson story, that the Kennedy assassination "had been an act of retaliation for an anti-Castro plot."[59]

The Anderson column was explicitly about "a reported CIA plan *in 1963.*" Thus it is most disingenuous of the IG Report to focus on the reported "rumor" of a three-man team, and conclude that this must refer to an assassination plot *in 1962.*[60] Not only is such an inference impossible, it is dishonest. Such dishonesty suggests that at least some of the sources and/or authors of the IG Report were suffering from a guilty conscience: they knew there was something to hide.

Whether or not one believes Castro's intelligence networks to have been involved, one can entertain the hypothesis that a shooter team, in effect licensed by the CIA to kill Castro, might then have returned from Cuba and killed the President instead. Such an idea, floated by Martino and later Roselli, would have exerted pressure on the CIA whether true or untrue. The mere appearance that a CIA team had been "turned around," while other killers took care of the actual job, would have been enough to coerce the CIA and its friends into the ranks of those claiming to be true believers in a lone assassin.

Such a possibility is by no means proven. But one is more inclined to take it seriously, once one has been exposed to the evasiveness and false logic of the IG Report. We must add to this the indications we have seen, that the mob and their in-house allies did not merely execute the CIA's assassination plans, but helped originate them to serve their own ends.

Given these signs of a mob influence within the CIA (as within the FBI), it seems at least possible that the mob could have helped secure CIA authorization for a plot against Castro, which it then exploited to murder the President of the United States.

---

[55] *Washington Post,* September 7, 1976, C19. Reprinted at 5 AH 365; 10 AH 159-60.

[56] Hinckle and Turner, *The Fish Is Red,* 171-73, 349-50; Scott, *Deep Politics,* 113-17.

[57] Dispatch of 7/26/63 from COS, JMWAVE to Chief, SAS (FitzGerald), concerning JMWAVE Relationship to Pawley ("assistance");

[58] Anthony Summers, *Conspiracy,* 452; Scott, *Deep Politics,* 117-20 (Ruby); Gaeton Fonzi, *The Last Investigation,* 325 (Oswald)

[59] G. Robert Blakey and Richard Billings. *The Plot to Kill the President,* 80; citing memo of April 1, 1964 from Warren Commission counsel David Slawson to J. Lee Rankin. Scott, *Deep Politics,* 111-13, 338.

[60] IG Report, 118, 133.

VII. OSWALD, HARVEY LEE OSWALD, AND OSWALD'S COMMUNIST PARTY CARD

"OSWALD, HARVEY LEE...CARD CARRYING MEMBER OF COMMUNIST PARTY"[1]

September 1994

Prologue

One cannot understand the assassination and related cover-up without analyzing the interlocking secrets about Oswald in government files, ranging from the CIA in Mexico City to the FBI, military intelligence, and local police in Dallas. The secrets which concern this paper are those reports, predating the assassination, that Oswald was a Communist, a KGB or Castro agent, a potential assassin, or all of the above. I have called such pre-assassination reports "phase-one" reports, because they generated the initial response to the assassination of some individuals in the CIA, FBI, military intelligence, and Dallas Police Department.

Particularly interesting are those false reports which passed from one agency to another, and which may indicate communication, or even collusion, between sources as far afield as Mexico City and Dallas. The falsity of these phase-one reports does not make them unimportant to the case, or to U.S. history. On the contrary, it is known that they became the pressing justification for creating the Warren Commission, which from the outset promoted what I have called the "phase-two" hypothesis: that Oswald acted alone. This hypothesis was equally unproven, but politically less disruptive and less dangerous to world peace.

Some of the false phase-one reports, on analysis, appear to be shallow and virtually groundless. Others, in contrast, may derive from other government secrets, quite possibly involving legitimate, if covert, government operations. Some may have been partly true.

This latter group includes two separate allegations, which sounded more sinister when reported together. One was that weeks before the assassination someone identifying himself as Oswald entered the Cuban Consulate in Mexico City and, in pursuit of a visa, presented documentation to establish his membership in the U.S. Communist Party. The other was that this person also offered to kill President Kennedy.

These two allegations helped engender the Warren Commission and subsequent cover-up. That they did so does not prove them to be part of the preliminary planning for the assassination. There may well be some other explanation for why the stories were floated. Even if relevant to the assassination, the stories may have been exploited by those responsible for it, not planted by them. At this point, one cannot say.

However the true relationship of Oswald to U.S. government agencies (and hence of these agencies to the assassination) can never be understood until these phase-one reports have been properly analyzed. Hence documentation of such phase-one allegations, even if known to be false, should be construed by the Review Board as "assassination-related."

The False Story of Oswald and an "International Communist Conspiracy"

The early rebuttal to the Warren Commission case of Oswald as a loner was the superabundance of extended government files showing continuous interest in him. With the newly released documents we realize more and more clearly that these files also contained alleged information (or disinformation) about Oswald that were potentially embarrassing to the agencies concerned. Prominent among these early allegations were the claims that he was a self-professed Communist, and that

---

[1] U.S. Army Cable 480587 from Fort Sam Houston, Texas, to U.S. Strike Command, McDill AFB, Florida, 230405Z (Nov. 22, 10:05 CST).

while in Mexico City he had talked of assassinating Kennedy in the Cuban Embassy.

These and other early claims about Oswald were not just eventually forgotten, they were systematically suppressed. The historical record of this suppression supplies a framework or structure for understanding more fully the dialectical process by which this nation arrived at its tenet of political orthodoxy: the belief that Oswald was a lone assassin. For each of these secrets has little meaning considered by itself. Put together, we see how those in power suppressed false evidence that Oswald was a Communist, or a KGB or Cuban agent, in order to arrive at the least disturbing alternative: that he acted alone.

Let us begin with the Dallas authorities: the Dallas Police Department, Sheriffs, and District Attorney's office. The first secret here is that, the day of the arrest, the Dallas authorities made known their intentions to charge Oswald as part of an international Communist conspiracy. This of course was no secret at the time, but it has become one since. We must look at it in the light of the simultaneous high-level efforts (to prove Oswald part of an international Communist conspiracy) that took place down in Mexico City.

The Dallas secret was officially covered up by Wade's testimony to the Warren Commission, that "the rumor...we were getting ready to file a charge of Oswald being part of an international conspiracy" was scotched by him as baseless on the night of November 22 (5 WH 229; cf. 218, 240). Wade conceded that the FBI on the night of November 24 phoned from Washington "to have me quit talking about it," and "may have" asked him not to say that a foreign government was involved (5 WH 236-37). But Wade testified he had already made clear to State Attorney General Waggoner Carr on November 22 that the "Russian conspiracy" idea "was silly because I don't know where the rumor started" (5 WH 240).

Gerald Posner, in *Case Closed*, discusses this crucial matter in a footnote. He spoke to Wade's assistant, William Alexander, who actually drafted the Kennedy murder indictment for Wade's signature (23 WH 321, cf. 319). Posner writes that, on the night of November 22,

Alexander decided to "shake things up a bit" and spoke to a friend at the *Philadelphia Inquirer*, Joe Goulden, and told him that he intended to indict Oswald for killing the President "in furtherance of a Communist conspiracy."[2]

This was not (as Posner's language might imply) a trivial matter, nor was Goulden the only man Alexander spoke to. In fact the story Alexander now admits spreading had activated alarmed responses that night all the way up to the White House, where someone ("around 8 or 9 o'clock at night on November 22") telephoned State Attorney General Waggoner Carr about it (5 WH 259). The content of that call was reportedly the same message repeated by federal officials for the next week, and used by Johnson to justify creating the Warren Commission: "This would be a bad situation, if you allege it as part of a Russian, the Russian conspiracy, and it may affect [the] international relations...of the country" (5 WH 240).

Declassified White House and FBI documents make it clear that "Dallas police...statements on the Communist conspiracy theory" were a principal reason why the Justice Department was determined by November 25 that "the public must be satisfied that Oswald was the assassin" (an "objective" which "may be satisfied" by "the appointment of a Presidential Commission").[3]

On November 29 Lyndon Johnson announced the formation of the Warren Commission. Lyndon Johnson's conversation with Congressman Charles Halleck the same day gives the clearest picture of the role played by false "phase one" allegations: "This thing is getting pretty serious and our folks are worried about it...it has some foreign implications...CIA and other things...and I'm going to try to get the Chief Justice on it." Johnson added that "we can't have Congress, FBI and others

---

[2] Gerald Posner, *Case Closed*, 348n; citing Alexander interview of March 6, 1992.

[3] Memo to Moyers from Deputy Attorney General Nicholas Katzenbach, 11/25/63, 3 AH 567-68; cf. Walter Jenkins memo of 11/24/63 reporting phone call by J. Edgar Hoover, 3 AH 472: "Fritz... is giving much information to the press. Since we now think it involves a conspiracy charge...we want them to shut up....The thing I am concerned about, and so is Mr. Katzenbach, is having something issued so we can convince the public that Oswald is the real assassin."

saying that Khrushchev or Castro ordered the assassination:" "This thing is so touchy from an international standpoint....This is a question that could involve our losing 39 million people."[4]

Johnson drew particular attention to the plans which Senator Eastland had revealed to him the previous day, of holding hearings before his Senate Internal Security Subcommittee. Speaking to House Speaker John McCormack, Johnson explained that he had to announce the Warren Commission quickly: "I better get him [Senator Eastland] to call off his investigation." He added that some Dallas official would testify that Khrushchev planned the assassination.[5]

But the Eastland Committee may have got wind of the still secret allegation that in Mexico City someone identifying himself as Oswald had offered to kill President Kennedy. Their staff person Al Tarabochia, a Cuban exile, claimed to "know someone who has access to confidential information about the Cuban Embassy in Mexico City."[6] Although Committee Counsel Julien Sourwine refused to reveal the identity of this informant, the thrust of the Eastland inquiry would seem to suggest that he was someone conversant with the alleged assassination offer.[7]

We know from FBI files that on November 24, 1963, the Eastland Subcommittee had already received testimony in executive session from Edward Scannell Butler, whose right-wing propaganda organization INCA managed the Oswald radio debate in New Orleans. According to an FBI summary of that testimony Butler spoke to the Subcommittee of Communist responsibility for the assassination:

> Butler stated his impression of Oswald was he was a rational and wholly indoctrinated procommunist individual who...exhibited a tremendous capacity to repeat by rote communist propaganda.... Butler stated it seemed to him that the fact that many of the materials that Oswald had available to him were originally sponsored by official communist sources, placed the blame for Oswald's actions on the authors or the disseminators of that material.[8]

As late as May 1964 Hoover affirmed to the Warren Commission, as he had earlier to LBJ and others, his opinion that Oswald "was a dedicated Communist."[9]

The Communist conspiracy theory that Butler and Hoover merely hinted at was voiced much more energetically in Dallas. Wade heard on November 22 from Carr and U.S. Attorney Barefoot Sanders, one of whom told him that "Alexander had said something about it" (5 WH 218, 240). A second source reportedly was David Johnston (5 WH 240), the Justice of the Peace who arraigned Oswald on the indictments Alexander prepared (15 WH 506-08), and who earlier that day had taken part along with Alexander in the search of Oswald's apartment at 1026 North Beckley (15 WH 507).[10] Wade testified that he asked both Alexander and Johnston about this, and they denied it (5 WH 240, cf. 218). That was enough for the Warren Commission, who did not query Johnston about the allegation (15 WH 503-13), and who, remarkably, did not interview Alexander at all.[11]

---

[4] LBJ telephonic transcripts: conversation at 18:30 11/29/63.

[5] LBJ telephonic transcripts: conversation at 16:55 11/29/63.

[6] Warren Commission staff memorandum of March 27, 1964 from W. David Slawson to J. Lee Rankin, reproduced at 11 AH 176; cf. 11 AH 65, 175, WCD 351. Warren Commission Document 351, which discussed this matter, also revealed that the Staff of the Senate Internal Security Subcommittee had been in touch with Ed Butler (see below).

[7] Julien Sourwine was involved in other CIA-supported covert operations that may have had a bearing on the Kennedy assassination and cover-up. See Scott, *Deep Politics*, 116; cf. 215-16, 260, 262, 264-66.

[8] FBI memo from DeLoach to Mohr, 11/26/63, furnishing copy of Butler's Executive Session testimony; FBI memo from W.R. Wannall to W.C Sullivan. Cf. Peter Dale Scott, *Crime and Cover-Up* (Santa Barbara: Prevailing Winds Research, 1993), 53.

[9] 5 WH 104. Earlier, Hoover had hinted at an Oswald conspiracy. Filing a friend's opinion that "the whole situation becomes logical when you fit it into the ACLU viewpoint," Hoover added that "Oswald...had a very bad background; and that the first lawyer he wanted was John Abt who appears in all the communist cases we have" (Hoover Memo of 11/29/63, FBI HQ 105-82555-93).

[10] Wade testified that on November 22 he heard from both State Attorney General Waggoner Carr and U.S. Attorney Barefoot Sanders: "one said, 'Well, David Johnston, the J.P. has said this,' and the other has said, 'Bill Alexander...said it'" (5 WH 240).

[11] The HSCA, alerted to Bill Alexander's importance in the events of November 22, did not investigate him. It

In November 1993 the PBS news show "Frontline" aired an interview in which former Dallas FBI agent James Hosty charged that the original indictment prepared by Alexander had charged Oswald in almost exactly the language admitted to by Alexander in his interview with Posner: murder "in furtherance of an international [rather than "Communist"] conspiracy." Lyndon Johnson himself, the show charged, had obtained the suppression of this phrase (20 WH 321, cf. 24 WH 830).[12]

Something like this phase-one/phase-two dialectic (the advancement of the Communist conspiracy allegation, followed by suppression of public reference to it) clearly did happen on November 22. Most of Wade's Commission testimony (as well as Carr's) concerned this matter, and Wade made it clear that "the calls from Washington and somewhere else" were "what prompted me to go down and take the complaint, otherwise I would never have gone down to the police station" (5 WH 229).[13] The institutionalized forgetting of this episode must have begun by November 24, when Wade assured the press that he had called a press conference strictly on his own in response to newsmen "from all over the world....I have heard nothing...from Washington or any of the officials in this country on this matter."[14]

However, in his various press conferences, Wade never ruled out the possibility that, whatever the indictment said, Oswald might be prosecuted as part of a conspiracy. Asked repeatedly on the night of November 22-23 if "this was an organized plot," Wade's consistent answer was that "we don't know" (24 WH 840; cf. 24 WH 836). The issue of Oswald's "Communist" record (to which we shall return) drew the same agnostic answer: "Does he have a Communist record? WADE. I don't know" (24 WH 840). Asked again, "Are you willing to say whether you think this man was inspired as a Communist or whether he is simply a nut or a middleman?" Wade answered, suggestively, "I'll put it this way: I don't think he's a nut" (24 WH 840).

The FBI may have shifted from a phase-one to a phase-two mode as early as mid-afternoon. Around 2:30 PM (Central Standard Time) Dallas FBI Agent James Hosty, the man in charge of the Oswald file was ordered to join the Dallas Police Department in interviewing Oswald. At 4:05 PM he was ordered to desist from interrogating Oswald, and forbidden "to divulge anything to the Dallas police."[15]

Both the order to cooperate with the Dallas police, and the order to cease doing so, came from FBI Headquarters in Washington. The man who revealed this publicly, former FBI Director Clarence Kelley, explained that the author of the second order, FBI Assistant Director William Sullivan, read information on Oswald in the Headquarters file, "reviewed CIA surveillance data on the Soviet Embassy in Mexico City, studied FBI wiretaps involving Oswald and Kostikov" (a KGB officer in that Embassy), then read the provocative follow-up letter of November 9 which Oswald had just sent about "comrade Kostin" (Kostikov) to the Soviet Embassy in Washington.

---

even suppressed the well-witnessed meeting of Alexander with Jack Ruby on November 21 from its extensive chronology of Jack Ruby's movements and contacts (9 AH 1099). Thus it is not yet known if Alexander did deny saying this (making him a liar either then or to Posner), or did not deny it (making Wade an apparent liar). Carr spoke briefly about the White House telephone call (5 WH 259-60), but not about what had given rise to it.

[12] In 1967 author William Manchester wrote that Alexander "prepared to charge Oswald with murdering the President 'as part of an international Communist conspiracy'" (Manchester, *The Death of a President*, [New York: Harper and Row, 1967], 326). This I suspect is close to the truth. Alexander's intended move would explain the conflicts in testimony with respect to Oswald's alleged arraignment on the charge of murdering the President. These conflicts led Sylvia Meagher to raise the possibility in 1967, with good reason, that the murder indictment we now have is a "retroactive completion." See Sylvia Meagher, *Accessories After the Fact* (New York: Random House, 1976), 305-09. Other documents, which Meagher never saw, corroborate her charge that there was no second arraignment at all (e.g. Mexico City FBI serial 105-3702-170).

[13] "I never go up there....I have been in that building probably once every two years" (5 WH 241).

[14] 24 WH 827. Under oath, Wade told the Warren Commission that "there was an inspector of the FBI [i.e. in Washington] who called me two or three times" (5 WH 226), in addition to the calls from Washington to Carr, Sanders, and Wade's assistant Jim Bowie (5 WH 229).

[15] Kelley, *Kelley*, 288-89, 293. Cf. FBI HQ serial 105-82555-50L.

FBI Director Kelley is not alone in speculating that this information was used to silence Hosty, possibly with the approval of the new Johnson White House:

> This information, it would surely have struck him [Sullivan], had such dire international implications that the White House must be informed immediately. Sullivan probably went straight to Hoover and then hastened to the National Security Council at the White House. No doubt, President Johnson [at that time still returning from Dallas on Air Force One] was then apprised....So, it seems, the silence imposed on Jim Hosty originated at the highest level -- the White House.[16]

But in his brief hour at the Dallas Police Department, Hosty had helped feed the phase-one fever in Dallas, by telling a police lieutenant, Jack Revill, that Oswald was a Communist.[17] He had good grounds for saying this, but for thirty years America would not hear them. FBI Headquarters had already taken steps to suppress all stories at odds with its phase-two agenda, both those which were false and also those which were true.

The Revised Oswald Legend: Not a Communist, But a Marxist

The phase-two agenda of the FBI was clearly spelled out in an internal memo from Alan Belmont on November 24, 1963, outlining how an FBI memorandum to the Attorney General would

> set out the evidence showing that Oswald is responsible for the shooting that killed the President. We will show that Oswald was an avowed Marxist, a former defector to the Soviet Union, and an active member of the FPCC, which has been financed by Castro.[18]

Not spelled out, but known to FBI Headquarters, was that this task would require the erasure of the phase-one story circulating on November 22: that Oswald was not just a Marxist, but a card-carrying Communist. As we shall see, FBI Agent Hosty in Dallas had called Oswald a Communist in an exchange with Dallas Police Detective Jack Revill. That same day, in Washington, Hoover had called Oswald a "Communist" in telephone calls to both Lyndon Johnson and Richard Nixon.[19] Both men had reasons to say what they did.

Throughout the country that first week-end, but especially in Dallas, New Orleans, and Miami, witnesses came forward who spoke of Oswald's Communism. Most of them were swiftly brought within days into conformity with Belmont's guideline ("Oswald was an avowed Marxist"). As will be seen from Appendix I, some of these witnesses were associated with organizations (such as military intelligence and Cuban anti-Castro groups like the DRE) from which other bellicose phase-one stories proliferated.

A second category, much more important, were witnesses like Ruth and Michael Paine who were close to Oswald in 1963. As will be seen from Appendix I, these witnesses are consistent both in their initial claims, that Oswald said "I'm a Communist," and in their later corrections of them: when addressed as a Communist, Oswald said, "I am a Marxist."[20]

---

[16] Kelley, *Kelley*, 293-94. Both Henry Wade (5 WH 251, 254) and Waggoner Carr (5 WH 259) talked about their phone calls from the White House, the former specifying that he thought it was from Johnson's staff aide Cliff Carter. [ZZ cite from Alan Rogers]

[17] Kelley, *Kelley*, 290.

[18] Memo of November 24, 1963 from Belmont to Tolson, 3 AH 666; cf. Schweiker-Hart Report, 33.

[19] Hoover-Johnson telephone call, November 22, 1963 (LBJ Library); Nixon, *Memoirs*, (New York: Grosset and Dunlap, 1978), 252; quoted in Curt Gentry, *J. Edgar Hoover: The Man and His Secrets* (New York: Penguin, 1992), 542. Revill later told the Warren Commission Hosty said that "a Communist killed President Kennedy" (5 WH 34). Hoover's response to Nixon's question ("What happened?") was similar: "It was a Communist."

[20] See Appendix I. Both these quotations are from Michael Paine's friend Frank Krystinik, the first to the FBI on November 25 (SAC Dallas to DIR, 12/3/63, FBI HQ 105-82555-158), and the second to the Warren Commission (9 WH 466).

Ruth Paine is the most important such witness. It seems clear that she told James Hosty before the assassination that Oswald "admitted to her being a 'Trotskyite Communist'" (23 WH 508, 17 WH 777, 23 WH 459, etc.). Oswald probably did so; Ruth's brother, a doctor in Cincinnati, later told the FBI that the husband of the Russian woman staying with his sister "was a Communist."[21] Yet Ruth Paine assured the Warren Commission in March 1964 that "He always corrected anyone who called him a Communist and said he was a Marxist" (3 WH 108).

No less than five credible witnesses in Dallas -- Ruth and Michael Paine, Frank Krystinik, Florence ("Betty") McDonald, and Richard Pierce -- described Oswald as a self-professed Communist. Three of these witnesses later corrected themselves; the last two were not followed up on by the Warren Commission.[22] Even more interesting is that, in the passionately anti-Communist circle of emigre Russians among whom the Oswalds moved, none ever said they heard Oswald call himself a Communist. This suggests that in Dallas as in New Orleans, Oswald played different roles to different audiences, and that his professed Communism was in fact a fiction for another agenda.

Oswald's self-description as a Communist could of course have indicated a different identity, not as a Communist but as a potential penetration agent for the FBI or some other agency. The FBI's zeal in "correcting" or suppressing this story by itself proves nothing. It is however interesting that Ruth Paine was asked by the Warren Commission if she had ever told anyone "that Lee Harvey Oswald in your opinion was doing underground work" (3 WH 108).[23] This certainly was the opinion of Oswald's mother (1 WH 162, 316, 325, etc.).

It may also have been the opinion of Michael Paine. Without invitation, he recalled for the Warren Commission

> thinking to myself for a person who has a business to do he [Oswald] certainly can waste the time. By business I mean some kind of activity and keeping track of right-wing causes and left-wing causes or something. I supposed that he spent his time...trying to sense the pulse of various groups in the Dallas area. (2 WH 412)

What else could Michael Paine have supposed? He himself had gone with Oswald to a meeting of the liberal ACLU, which Oswald told him "he couldn't join" (2 WH 409), and heard Oswald describe to the ACLU an earlier right-wing meeting where General Walker had spoken (2 WH 403).[24] Clearly Oswald could not have attended both meetings out of inner convictions, any more than in New Orleans he could have been sincerely both a pro-Castro and anti-Castro partisan.[25]

By November 23 there were two types of phase-one stories for the FBI to eradicate: 1) those linking Oswald to Moscow or Havana or Peking (risking war), and 2) those linking Oswald to the FBI itself, which was said by Police Chief Curry to have been in contact with Oswald shortly before the assassination. For whatever reason, the FBI appears to have approached all the stories that Oswald was a Communist, or said he was a Communist, as high on its agenda of eradication.

To implement this agenda, the number two man in the FBI's Criminal Investigative Division, James R. Malley, was dispatched urgently on November 24 to Dallas. He was followed within hours by two of his Supervisors, Richard Rogge and Fletcher Thompson (3 AH 464-65, 666). In 1978 Malley told the House Committee that his instructions from Alan Belmont (reflecting the new President's comments to Hoover) were to contact District Attorney Wade, Chief of Police Curry, and the office of Sheriff Decker, "and see if I couldn't put a stop to miscellaneous statements they were making" (3 AH 464; cf. 3 AH 171-73). Another Headquarters FBI Agent, Larry Keenan, was soon dispatched to Mexico City with a similar mission.

---

[21] SAC Cincinnati to DIR, 12/3/63, FBI HQ 105-82555-146.

[22] See Appendix I.

[23] Ruth Paine, a veritable font of phase-two correctness, denied vigorously that she had.

[24] What adds to the intrigue is that Paine himself had been to both meetings, a revelation about which both he and the Warren Commission were somewhat evasive (2 WH 388, 403; WR 463).

[25] For this double role of Oswald in New Orleans, see Scott, *Deep Politics*, 80-86, 248-53.

This phase-two blitz was successful. Today it is hard to learn, at least from the otherwise exhaustive Warren volumes, what the offending statements from Wade and Curry were. A number of Wade's and Curry's televised interviews are transcribed; interestingly, as we have already seen, these largely contain soothing rebuttals of earlier phase-one rumors. For example, the Warren Commission did not reprint the front-page news story on November 24 (leaked by Curry) that the FBI had interviewed Oswald on November 16.[26] Instead it reprinted the transcript of a late November 23 TV interview, where Curry, abjectly, said repeatedly he wanted to correct an earlier story "that the FBI did know this man was in the city and had interviewed him."[27] Almost certainly the Commission never received the FBI account of how FBI SAC Shanklin and reporter Jeremiah O'Leary, one of the Hoover-approved "close friends of the Bureau," got Curry to retract the statement that the FBI had recently interviewed Oswald.[28] In a later article I shall argue that the swiftly retracted statement was probably true, as a recent article about Ruby and gun-running would suggest.[29]

Even the Dallas Police Report printed in the Warren volumes (Warren Commission Exhibit 2003) appears to have been edited, if not falsified, to conform closely to the Belmont guidelines.[30] To judge from the DPD pagination, eight pages of the original Report are now missing.[31]

In its section addressing the possibility of a Communist conspiracy, the published DPD Report includes two letters to Oswald from V.T. Lee of the Fair Play for Cuba Committee, and two from Arnold Johnson, Information Director of the Communist Party (24 WH 274-76).[32] However the two letters from Arnold Johnson are both entirely innocuous and without interest. They do not fit the description of the letters "on Communist Party of America letterheads" which Bill Alexander told the press on November 26 "showed a 'working friendly relationship' between Oswald and the party."[33] Still less do they fit the account apparently leaked by Alexander and the Dallas Police Department and reported by UPI and the *New York World Telegram and Sun* on November 26. According to the UPI account of Alexander's remarks, these letters, found "in Oswald's personal belongings...were written on official Communist...stationary [sic]." One "offered advice on how to set up a Dallas chapter of the Communist-inspired 'Fair Play for Cuba Committee....Another told him how to 'keep nosy neighbors away.'"[34] As described by Alexander, the leaked letters implied CP direction of both Oswald and the Fair Play for Cuba Committee, an impression entirely at odds with the two letters published later by the DPD and Warren Commission.[35]

---

[26] *Dallas Morning News*, November 24, 1963.

[27] 24 WH 754-55. As if reading from a piece of paper, Curry repeated no less than five times versions of the statement, "I do not know if and when the FBI has interviewed this man." See also the TV interview of November 24, where Wade said (falsely), "I have heard nothing from any of the -- from Washington or any of the officials in this country on this matter" (24 WH 827).

[28] FBI HQ 62-109060-211, 217 (O'Leary-Curry); Anthony Summers, *Official and Confidential: The Secret Life of J. Edgar Hoover*, 100 (O'Leary-FBI): "When O'Leary wrote a 'hard-hitting review' of a book by an author Edgar regarded as an enemy, the FBI distributed thousands of copies around the country. For his part, according to the file, O'Leary once even helped the FBI when it was trying to identify another reporter's sources. He also submitted an article for review, and according to the file, 'any changes we desired.'"

[29] *Washington Post*, August 7, 1994.

[30] 24 WH 195-404; originally submitted as WCD 81b.

[31] DPD pages 159-60, 173-76, 255-56; at 24 WH 284, 290, 329.

[32] Significantly, the evidence does not include Oswald's two membership cards in the FPCC, one issued by V.T. Lee, and the other signed "A.J.Hidell" -- i.e. by himself, even though these are supposed to have been found in Oswald's wallet by the police at the time of his arrest, and then given by Homicide Detective Fritz to the FBI on November 22 (24 WH 17). We shall return to these cards, one of which played a major role in Oswald's visit to the Cuban Consulate in Mexico City.

[33] *New York Times*, November 27, 1963.

[34] UPI story from Seth Kantor of *Fort Worth Press*, 11/26/63; FBI HQ 105-82555-261; cf. SAC New York to DIR FBI, 11/26/63; FBI HQ 105-82555- 17th no. 50.

[35] What is intriguing about Alexander's characterization of the letters is that it is quite consistent with Oswald's letters to the Communist Party (20 WH 262-63, 22 WH 168). But Alexander could not have seen these out-going letters, unless Oswald had (as an undercover agent) supplied copies to Dallas law enforcement.

There is no trace of these phantom leaked letters in the Dallas Police and Warren Commission records, and it is likely that they existed only in the fertile imagination of leakers like Bill Alexander.[36] My point is rather that the DPD Report, as published, is at odds with what was leaked from Dallas in the first four days; and it reflects the more sober DPD view of Oswald-Communist relations taken after the FBI had got to Curry. Indeed the focus of the Oswald-Communist Party section is a belated right-wing column in December by Fulton Lewis, Jr. (one of Hoover's press favorites), noting that "while the Johnson letters indicate Oswald was not under Communist discipline, they do show he was a dedicated Marxist."[37]

Conversely, the DPD's best documentary "evidence" that Oswald was a Communist is not to be found in the published DPD Report. Astonishingly, there is no mention of the *Daily Worker* or *The Militant* in the photograph showing Oswald with a rifle (WR 404, 16 WH 510, 17 WH 498), even though Police Chief Curry had on at least three different occasions drawn attention to the names of these two newspapers in his press conferences on November 23.[38] Though Captain Fritz was one of those talking conspiracy on November 22, his published report of his interrogation of Oswald (written "several days later," 4 WH 209) is as anti-conspiratorial as the Warren Report. Noting that Oswald was shown a picture of himself "holding a rifle" (ignoring the newspapers, 24 WH 268), Fritz later erases the Communist issue by saying Oswald "repeated two or three times, 'I am a Marxist, but not a Leninist-Marxist'" (24 WH 270). Although the newspapers are prominent in the enlarged version of the photo, the DPD Report never mentions *The Daily Worker*'s presence in the photo.[39]

Indeed the whole of Fritz's belated report seems designed to allay the phase-one rumors that may have provoked Malley's visit to Dallas.

> I asked him what his political beliefs were, and he said he had none but that he belonged to the Fair Play for Cuba Committee....I asked him if he owned a rifle in Russia, and he said, 'You know you can't buy a rifle in Russia, you can only buy shotguns.' 'I had a shotgun in Russia and hunted some while there.'...I asked him if he belonged to the Communist Party, but he said that he never had a card, but repeated that he belonged to the Fair Play for Cuba organization. (24 WH 265-67)

---

[36] One can however ask why the two FPCC letters were reproduced by the DPD directly, while the two CP letters were copied from a microfilm prepared when the exhibits were turned over to the FBI on November 26 (24 WH 274-76). It would appear that the FPCC letters were reproduced before this date, the published CP letters afterwards (which is to say, after the phase-one leaks to the press).

[37] 24 WH 273; column by Fulton Lewis, Jr., in *Dallas Morning News* (?), December 12 (or 19), 1963. From the index to the DPD report, as well as the interpolated page numbers, it appears that the "Letters to Oswald from Johnson and Lee," as well as the Fulton Lewis column, are a belated insertion into the report after it had been compiled (24 WH 197). The interpolated page numbers appear to run from 143A to 143G, though there is some confusion (24 WH 273-76).

[38] 24 WH 760, 778; cf. WR 233. In one supposedly complete inventory of photos, the rifle photo is omitted (24 WH 278). We are asked to believe that the photo was included by Detective Stovall under the rubric "miscellaneous photographs and maps" (24 WH 348; cf. 21 WH 598, 7 WH 194).

[39] 24 WH 250 ("picture of defendant holding a rifle"); 24 WH 290 ("two snapshots and negatives showing Oswald holding the rifle"); 24 WH 348 ("miscellaneous photographs"). Fritz's reticent description of the photograph ("the picture...of him holding a rifle," 24 WH 268, WR 607), can be contrasted with Secret Service Inspector Thomas Kelley's account of the same Oswald interview ("photographs taken of Oswald holding a rifle in one hand and holding up a copy of a paper called the *Militant* and 'The Worker' in the other," WR 628), which is the version one might have expected. Nor does the DPD Report refer to much more sinister, but false, "evidence" that Oswald was a Soviet spy -- notably a book in Russian from which certain letters had been excised, suggesting a codebook (16 WH 481-82). One can believe the ultimate finding of the National Security Agency, that it is "most unlikely that this process of letter removal has any cryptographic implication" (26 WH 155). However it is hard to believe Marina's attempt at an innocent explanation, that Oswald had cut the letters "to form her name, MARINA NIKOLAEVNA OSWALD...to place over the bell at the Elsbeth Street address" (23 WH 519). (The letter , which had been excised, does not appear in Marina's Russian name.) The book is *prima facie* evidence of a conspiracy: not a conspiracy involving Oswald, but one targeting him. The published DPD Report, thankfully, ignored it, referring to it only as "Book, 'Sofia' dated 1962" (24 WH 277; cf. 23 WH 519).

So much for the stories, false but circulating and already spuriously documented, that Oswald was a card-carrying Communist who had brought his murder weapon with him from Russia.[40]

Suppressed Official Evidence (Whether True or False) that Oswald Was a Communist

Missing from the published DPD Report was clear (though later disputed) documentary evidence that Oswald *was* a Communist, not just a Marxist. This was a November 22 memo from Dallas Police Lieutenant Jack Revill, which only came to light after a misleading article about it by Hugh Aynesworth in the *Dallas Morning News* of April 24, 1964.[41] Revill's memo told his superior, Captain W.P. Gannaway of the DPD Special Service Bureau, that at about 2:50 PM on November 22, he had met FBI Agent Hosty in the Dallas police basement, where Hosty told him that Oswald "was a member of the Communist Party."[42] About 30 minutes later, at "approximately 3:30, 3:35" (5 WH 40), Revill prepared a memo containing these words, for his superior to take to Police Chief Curry (5 WH 39). Thus it is more than likely that Revill's memo contributed to the conspiracy flap generated the same day by Fritz, Curry, and Alexander.

Hosty for some years has conceded that he did say Oswald was a Communist; he has since admitted it both to interviewers and in the book by his friend and superior, former FBI Director Clarence Kelley.[43] Kelley's book tells us that "Jim based his statement" ("His name is Lee Harvey Oswald...and he's a Communist") "on information he learned from 12:30 to 3:00 [on November 22], not on what he knew from Oswald's file."[44] Malley later told the House Committee that Hosty had been reprimanded for "some loose, unnecessary statements he made the day of the assassination" (3 AH 491). He did *not* say that Hosty's statements had been untrue.

Unfortunately Hosty's admission that he called Oswald a Communist is not consistent with the rigorously "phase-two" denial of Revill's claim which Hosty prepared and swore to in an affidavit for the Warren Commission (WCE 831, 17 WH 780-84). That affidavit is silent on the question of Oswald's alleged Communist status. Instead it mentions that Hosty told Revill of Oswald's defection to Russia and return, of his employment at the Texas School Book Depository, and that he "was the main suspect in the assassination of President Kennedy." "The above," Hosty then stated, "constitutes the entire contents of my conversation with Lieutenant Revill" (17 WH 782).

One has to have some sympathy for the situation Hosty was in, both on November 22 when he called Oswald a Communist, and on April 24 when he implicitly denied having done so. His April affidavit was in response to Aynesworth's news story, which had Hosty saying "we knew he was capable of assassinating the president" (17 WH 779). This had infuriated Hoover, and moved him to have his aides "tell Dallas to tell Hosty to keep his big mouth shut. He has already done irreparable harm."[45]

His situation on November 22 was even less enviable. Twenty minutes before encountering Revill, Hosty had had just enough time at the office to call up the Oswald file. There he learnt for the first time that two new items had reached Dallas. One was a change of origin notice from New Orleans, making him again responsible for the Oswald file.[46] The other was an Airtel from the

---

[40] For the document of November 22, falsely claiming that Marina "presumed" that her husband's rifle in Texas was one "that Lee Harvey Oswald...used in Russia about two years ago" (23 WH 383), see discussion in Scott, *Deep Politics*, 267-70. This document is an FBI paraphrase of Marina's police affidavit of November 22 (24 WH 219). But in the published DPD affidavit the offensive identification of the two weapons is missing.

[41] 24 WH 778-79.

[42] WCE 709, 24 WH 495.

[43] Clarence Kelley, *Kelley* (Kansas City: Andrews, McMeel, and Parker, 1987), 290.

[44] Kelley, 290. If this is true, one has to ask if the information was part of the telephone call in which Alan Belmont, special assistant to FBI Director J. Edgar Hoover, instructed Dallas FBI Chief Gordon Shanklin to have Hosty interview Oswald. (It was this phone call, at about 2:00 PM, which explained Hosty's presence in the Dallas police station; Kelley, 288-89.)

[45] Curt Gentry, *J. Edgar Hoover*, 549n.

[46] 4 WH 462 (Hosty testimony): "It apparently arrived on the afternoon of the 21st. I got it for the first time

Washington Field Office, summarizing the content of Oswald's November 9 letter to the Soviet Embassy.[47] In that Airtel there were provocative and unexplained statements about "time to complete his business" in Havana, and "that he could not request a new visa unless he used his real name."[48] Still to come was the actual text of the letter, much worse than the FBI's bowdlerized summary of it. Oswald had actually written to the Soviet Embassy about "time to complete *our* business" in Havana. And there was an equally provocative reference to a meeting on November 1, not documented elsewhere, between Oswald and FBI "Agent James P. Hasty" (16 WH 33).

Hosty might well have felt that he himself was being made something of a patsy.[49] Indeed Hoover might well have suspected a concerted and cunning effort to embarrass the whole FBI, and coerce it into cover-up. If Oswald, as some alleged, were actually a self-professed Communist, then the FBI should have pursued a whole schedule of statutory and administrative requirements which it took most seriously, and which had not been followed in this case.

It would appear, moreover, that Kelley's source for Hosty's statement ("he's a Communist") is not the whole truth. Hosty himself reported, and later testified to, the November 5 statement by Marina Oswald's host, Ruth Paine, that Oswald had "admitted to her being a 'Trotskyite Communist.'"[50] Hosty's report of November 24, 1963, to FBI Bureau Chief Gordon Shanklin, incorporated Ruth Paine's statement that "he admitted to being a 'Trotskyite Communist.'"[51] We have already seen that in all probability Oswald had said something like this to the Paines.[52]

The Commission's lack of interest in the "Communist" charge is clear from their silence about it, when interrogating Curry and Hosty about the Revill memo (4 WH 194, 464, 474). With Curry and Hosty the loaded word "Communist" was not once asked about or mentioned. It did come up with Revill, in a leading question which gave Revill a chance to deny his own affidavit.[53]

> Mr. RANKIN. Now, you say here that you were told that the subject
> was a member of the Communist Party. Is that right?
>
> Mr. REVILL. This might be my interpretation of Mr. Hosty saying a Communist
> killed the President....He did not say that he was a member"
> (5 WH 41-42).

after the assassination."

[47] Kelley, *Kelley*, 288-89.

[48] SAC WFO to DIR FBI, 11-19-63; FBI HQ serial 105-8255-78, apparently filed December 5, 1963.

[49] The Warren Report tells us that on November 1 and 5 Hosty had driven out to the Paine residence where Marina was staying, but "on neither occasion was Oswald present" (WR 739).

[50] WCE 830, 17 WH 777 (a redacted version of Hosty's Report of 12/11/63 on Ruth Paine, WCD 208, pages 10-11, 23 WH 508-09). Cf. 4 WH 454 (Hosty testimony); Kelley, 277. The date of the FBI memo published as WCE 830 is not given in Volume 17; but Hosty had already written up the contents in his memo to Shanklin of November 24, 1963 (Dallas FBI 100-10461-72), which was not seen by the Warren Commission. The FBI seems to have been evasive about WCE 830. Alan Belmont, the number three man in the FBI, told the Warren Commission that "we checked with our Dallas office, and they do not have a specific record of when that information was recorded" (5 WH 26). (WCE 830 is obviously not, as the Table of Contents describes it [17 WH xxii], "Two pages from an F.B.I. Report by Special Agent Fain [sic!], dated September 10, 1963.)

[51] Hosty to SAC, 11-24-63, DL FBI 100-10461-72.

[52] Ruth's estranged husband Michael, who spent time alone with Oswald, allegedly told Deputy Sheriff Eddy Walthers on November 22 that Oswald was "a Communist" (7 WH 549). And Dallas Police Captain Westbrook reportedly told Sergeant Gerald Hill on the afternoon of November 22 that "our suspect had admitted being a Communist" (7 WH 59). All three of the alleged sources were questioned by the Warren Commission and its staff; none were asked if Oswald had ever made such an admission. Ruth Paine was asked a different question, if she had said this to Agent Hosty (3 WH 104). Her first answer was "Oh, I doubt seriously I said Trotskyite Communist. I would think Leninist Communist, but I am not certain." Her questioner, Albert Jenner, was not tempted by this to ask what Oswald had said. Nor did Assistant Commission Counsel Liebeler run to ground Michael Paine's statement: "It was mentioned could he be connected with a Communist plot and there I thought of Russian Communists and that didn't seem to ring a bell" (2 WH 414; cf. 408: "I thought to myself if that is the way he has to meet his Communists, he has not yet found the Communist group in Dallas"). Westbrook's closest testimony was that he "had nothing to do with Oswald after he got to City Hall" (7 WH 114).

This erasure of Hosty's admitted statement ("He's a Communist") suited the Commission's "phase-two" agenda in 1964, but in 1994 we can afford to be more curious. No nuclear war now threatens if we point out that Oswald may very well have told the Paines he was a "Communist," who in turn told Hosty. We shall see that in Mexico Oswald (or someone calling himself Oswald) did tell others this.

We should also pursue the matter of Oswald's alleged membership in the Communist Party. Regardless of what Hosty actually said, it is possible that Revill actually heard this (either from Hosty or someone else). Don Stringfellow of Revill's Criminal Intelligence Section (the DPD subversive or Red squad) reported at 5:05 PM CST to Fourth Army Intelligence, Region II

> that Oswald had confessed to the shooting of President Kennedy and Police Officer Tibbets. The only additional information they have obtained from Oswald at this time is that he defected to Cuba in 1959 and that he is a card carrying member of the Communist Party.[54]

Army Intelligence was clearly receptive to this phase-one story, however improbable.[55] At 10:05 that night a provocative cable, with the kind of message the White House had been concerned about, was sent from Fort Sam Houston in Texas to the U.S. Strike Command at McDill Air Force Base in Florida, the base that had both the capacity and the location for a swift retaliatory attack against Cuba.

This cable read, in part:

> Following is additional information on Oswald, Harvey Lee.... Don Stringfellow, Intelligence Section, Dallas Police Dept., notified 112th Intc Gp, this HQ, that information obtained from Oswald revealed he had defected to Cuba in 1959 and is card carrying member of Communist Party.[56]

Stringfellow, in spreading this story, was not acting alone. Dallas Police Captain Westbrook reported on the afternoon of November 22 that "our suspect had admitted being a Communist" (7 WH 59). The memo from Stringfellow's superior, Jack Revill ("the Subject was a member of the Communist Party") would have struck the phase-one audience as further corroboration. All these documents are assassination-related, not in the sense that their content is true, but that they are part of the phase-one case which was used to justify the phase-two Warren Commission.

The best corroboration of all for Stringfellow and Revill came from Mexico City. It was there in September, not in Dallas on November 22, that we have persuasive documentary evidence Oswald (to quote the Warren Report) "apparently also stated that he was a member of the Communist Party and displayed documents which he claimed to be evidence of his membership" (WR 734).

Oswald in Mexico: He Did *Present Himself as a Card-Carrying Communist*

The document in question is the visa application which Oswald submitted to the Cuban consulate in Mexico City. Unambiguously, that application has the following "Observations" typed on it in Spanish:

> The applicant states that he is a member of the American Communist Party and Secretary in New Orleans of the Fair Play for Cuba Committee....He displayed documents in proof of his membership in the two aforementioned organizations and a marriage certificate."

[54] 112th Army Intelligence Group Region II Spot Report 417, 1715 hrs, Nov.22 (Dallas FBI serial 89-43-2381C). (Note: this Spot Report refers to an earlier one, #415, that is not known to have been released.)

[55] Stringfellow's information seems of course to be wildly wrong. Oswald told the press at 6:37 PM that "I never killed anybody" (20 WH 362), and at his midnight press conference Oswald said the first he had heard about killing the President "was when the newspaper reporters in the hall asked me that question" (WR 201, 24 WH 817; cf. 20 WH 373).

[56] U.S. Army Cable 480587 from Fort Sam Houston, Texas, to U.S. Strike Command, McDill AFB, Florida, 230405Z (Nov. 22, 10:05 CST). Discussion in Scott, *Deep Politics*, 275, etc.

(WR 303; WCE 2564, 25 WH 814-15; cf. 3 AH 137, 142)

This application was supplied by the Cubans in late August 1964, too late for the Warren Commission to investigate it further. Fourteen years later the House Committee confirmed from the man who signed the "Observations", Cuban consul Alfredo Mirabal, that Oswald actually "presented a card or credentials as belonging to the Communist Party of the United States" (3 AH 176).

Consul Mirabal also shared with the Committee his suspicions about this card:

> I was surprised by the fact the card seemed to be a new card. I must say that I also have been a Communist for a number of years and that generally we do not use credentials or a card to identify ourselves as members of the party. Rather we are identified to ourselves as Communists by our own behavior and by our own ideas. I was surprised by his unusual interest in using identification as a Communist. I think it would be interesting to know how he obtained the card. It did have his name, and it did coincide with the same name that appeared in the other document. (3 AH 176)

Silvia Durán also communicated her suspicions:

> When he said he was a member of the Party, of the Communist Party, the American, I said why don't they arrange, the Party, your Party with the Cuban Party, and he said that he didn't have the time to do it....It was strange. I mean because if you are a Communist and you're coming from a country where the Communist Party is not very well seen, and in Mexico City that the Communist Party was not legal at that moment -- crossing the border with all of his paper, it was not logical. I mean, if you're really Communist, you go with *anything*, I mean just nothing, just your passport, that's all.... it was strange, travelling with all of his documents just to prove one thing....He said that he was a Communist. That was strange. Because it would be really easy for him to get the visa through the Communist Party. (3 AH 34, 35, 57)

However Silvia Durán's published testimony, while recalling that Oswald said he was a member of the Communist Party, incongruously omits the Communist Party card from the list of political documents which Oswald submitted to her:

> He show me letters to [sic: from?] the Communist Party, the American Communist Party, his labor card...from Russia, his [uh] marriage pact....And a card saying that he was a member of the Fair Play for Cuba in New Orleans. (3 AH 33)

This list of political documents (the FPCC card, the Soviet work permit, the Soviet marriage license) is roughly consistent with the Warren Commission version (significantly revised, as we shall see) of her statement in November 1963 to the Mexican Security Police, or DFS (25 WH 588). (However the Warren version of the list contains nothing pertinent to the Communist Party -- a significant omission we shall return to). The list is also consistent with Oswald's noted attachments to the political document in his handwriting (WCE 93) which the Warren Report connected to his visits to the Mexican consulates.[57] This document also formed part of Commission Document 81, the Dallas Police Department Report, as published by the Warren Commission (24 WH 279-83).

However Durán's apparent silence about the Communist Party card, however consistent with her past statement in the Warren volumes of 1964, is totally at odds with her typed "Observations" at the time, as corroborated by Azcue, Mirabal, and herself in 1978. The Committee, having ascertained (3 AH 38, 40) that she typed the "Observations" about his "proof of membership," did not pursue the matter of the card.[58]

---

[57] 16 WH 343 ("FPCC membership card"), 16 WH 346 ("letters commending photo work by the Party"). Cf. WR 734, fn. 1157 ("connected"); also Priscilla McMillan, *Marina and Lee* [New York: Harper and Row, 1967], 364).

[58] The Committee heard from outgoing Cuban consul Eusebio Azcue that the "Observations" had been typed by consulate employee Silvia Durán, for the signature of the incoming consul Alfredo Mirabal (3 AH 142). Mirabal stated that Durán and Azcue "provided me with all the information" in the "Observations" (3 AH 176). Durán confirmed typing the words (3 AH 38, 40).

In other words, the House Committee in 1978 failed to press Silvia Durán on the matter of the Communist Party card, just as the Warren Commission in 1964 failed to ask Hosty about his claim that Oswald was a Communist (or Communist Party member). I should make it clear that in this instance I approve of the Committee's reticence, for in Durán's case it is fairly easy to understand good reasons for it, and also what was really going on.

Azcue and Mirabal were Cuban citizens deposed by the Committee in Cuba. Durán in contrast was a Mexican citizen deposed in Mexico, and not for the first time. On November 23, 1963, she had been interviewed by the Mexican Security Police, the Dirección Federal de Seguridad (DFS), a crude organization known to obtain information through torture. In 1978 Durán, still in Mexico, was still a witness at risk; and the House Committee appears to have acted in such a way as to protect both her and her prior interrogators.

From recently declassified documents, above all the so-called Lopez Report, an HSCA staff study on "Lee Harvey Oswald, the CIA and Mexico City," we learn that the American versions of what is called Durán's "signed statement" of November 23 have been altered over time.[59] Specifically the 1964 version of her statement printed by the Warren Commission was a redacted version, different from an earlier one received by the CIA on November 26, 1963.[60]

But even the November 26 version has been redacted, if we can credit the earliest account of the November 23 statement. This is a CIA cable from Mexico City the same night, reporting what the Mexican Minister of Gobernacion (Luis Echeverria) told the CIA Chief of Station (Winston Scott):

> Echeverria told COS Duran completely cooperative and gave written statement attesting to two visits by Oswald. Could not remember exact dates but said latter part Sept. Oswald showed her U.S. passport showing long stay in USSR. Said he Communist and admirer of Castro.[61]

The Communist characterization of Oswald was even stronger in the variant of Durán's story leaked by the DFS to the Mexico City journal *Excelsior*: "He supported his petition by the fact that his wife was a Soviet citizen, that he was a militant Communist and had lived three years in Russia."[62] The FBI, normally eager to run down all allegations of Communism and militant Communism, was on this occasion the dog that did not bark. An internal FBI memo, repeating that Durán was said to be completely cooperative, deleted all reference to Oswald's Communism.[63] The statement

---

[59] 24 WH 587, 25 WH 634 ("signed statement"). No version that we have is actually signed by Durán, and all are in the third person. CIA Cable MEXI 43699 of January 27, 1978 quotes from a blind FBI memo dated May 5, 1964, as follows: "SA [FBI Special Agent] Joe B. Garcia... handled liaison with the Mexican Federal Security Police [DFS] and arranged for delivery of a copy of the signed statement of Silvia Tirado de Duran by Captain Fernando Gutierrez Barrios" (NR19-263). The "Duran" statement in the Warren volumes at 25 WH 634-37 is in fact signed by Gutierrez, not by her. Did the CIA know this, and draft a misleading cable accordingly? Or was a statement signed by Duran actually delivered to the FBI? If the latter, where is it? One person whom the Review Board might ask about this is SA Joe B. Garcia; another is Fernando Gutiérrez Barrios, who later became President Salinas' Mexican Minister of Gobernación.

[60] Lopez Report, 186-91. In the Warren Volumes, the later version, CE 2120, appears to have reached the Commission via the State Department and Mexican Foreign Ministry on May 28, 1964 (25 WH 562). In the Warren version, Durán's description of Oswald as "blonde" -- the description supplied by Azcue in 1978 -- had been deleted, presumably because it did not appear to fit the man arrested in Dallas. (Lopez Report, 186). Although the Dallas Oswald was clearly not blonde, the Spanish word used by Durán ("rubio") could cover brown hair like Oswald's, as opposed to black. The issue here is not the murky one of who called himself Oswald in Mexico, but the simple fact that what is called Durán's "signed statement" of November 23 (24 WH 587, 25 WH 634), had changed between November 26 and May 1964.

[61] MEXI 7046 to DIR[ector], 240419Z, CIA Document # 66-567.

[62] *Excelsior*, November 25, 1963, 1A; in Mexico City Oswald FBI file at serial 105-3702-30. Contextually it would appear that Oswald said this in the Soviet Embassy. Durán told the House Committee in 1978 that it was the police who gave her story to "*Excelsior*...the first government paper" (3 AH 87). Cf. CIA MEXI 7055 (251721Z) on *Excelsior* story: "Cannot eliminate Gobernacion [Ministry of DFS] as source." Cf. *New York Times*, December 3, 1963, reprinted at 24 WH 585: "A Mexican official said Oswald told the Cubans and the Russians he was a Communist who had lived two years in the Soviet Union and had married a Russian woman."

[63] Branigan to Rosen, 11-27-63 (Serial 105-82555-122). The FBI cable on Durán's statement of November 23 is likewise silent on the issue of Oswald's political status and documentation; it mentions only his U.S. passport and

that he was a "militant Communist" went into a file without comment.

What then happened to this very simple phase-one statement ("Said he Communist") is what we might expect from what happened in Dallas: it disappeared. On November 26 the CIA received from one of her interrogators a written account in Spanish of Durán's interview, which was then forwarded under a memo, still redacted, signed by a "JKB." This JKB version was then hand-carried to Washington on November 27 by a Headquarters CIA officer, John Horton.[64] On the question of Oswald's Communist status, so clear in the November 24 cable and the statement typed by Durán in October, the November 26 version of her November 23 statement is silent: her only reference to his politics was that "he was married to a Russian and said he belonged to the 'Fair Play for Cuba.'"[65] The May 1964 version of the same statement (CE 2120) now supplied the extended list of documents with respect to Russia and the FPCC, which ignored the Communist Party. It also had Durán say that Oswald insisted on a visa

> in view of his background and his loyalty and his activities on behalf of the Cuban movement. The declarant [Ms. Durán] was unable to recall accurately whether or not the applicant told her he was a member of the Communist Party.[66]

Note that what has been reversed here is not attributable to a change in Durán herself: the successive reports (of November 24, November 26, and May) are of the same written statement.[67]

It is most unlikely that Durán could not remember in November what she had written so clearly one month before. Oswald's claim to be a Communist was prominent in her first American press interview, in 1976 ("he claimed to be a member of the American Communist Party"); and again in her testimony to the House Committee in 1978 ("he said he was a member of the Party, of the Communist Party").[68] It is more probable that the JKB version and CE 2120 have been not only redacted but expanded, to reinforce the notion, necessary to the "phase-two" hypothesis, that there was only one Oswald, not a Communist, and certainly not a card-carrying Communist, who acted alone.

Faced with Durán's embarrassing typed statement of October 1963, the Warren Report came unglued. One section of it, as we have seen, believed it; and repeated that "He [Oswald] apparently also stated that he was a member of the Communist Party and displayed documents which he claimed to be evidence of his membership" (WR 734). Another section disbelieved it ("Senora Duran's notation was probably inaccurate"), relying in part on Commission Exhibit 93, which it described as Oswald's "prepared statement of his qualifications as a 'Marxist'" (WR 288-89). A third section used credited the altered May version of her November 23 statement, because of the close fit between CE 93 and that statement's "description...of the documents Oswald had shown her" (WR 304).[69] To

---

Soviet wife (Legat to DIR, 11/25/63; 105-82555-967, p. 3).

[64] Washington was alerted to its and Horton's arrival by MEXI 7105 of November 27 (cf. CIA memo, "Response to HSCA Request of 28 August 1978," ND 6-32; Win Scott letter of November 27, 1963, to J.C. King, CIA Document # 1380-1073-A).

[65] JKB memo and Attachment of 26 November, 1963, CIA Doc. #131-593; translated in DIR 85758 of 29 November 1963, CIA Doc. #223-647. The JKB cover memo is clearly an assassination-related document which should be reviewed.

[66] WR 302. Compare the FBI translation of the same passage: "because of his background and his partisanship and personal activities in favor of the Cuban movement, the declarant [Ms. Durán]'s not being able to specify because she does not remember whether or not he said that he was a member of the Communist party" (24 WH 565; as translated at 24 WH 589, 25 WH 636).

[67] According to the Lopez Report, the CIA told the House Committee that the Mexico City Station had no personality file on Durán. This was untrue: the Station's personality file on Durán was "P-7969," which to judge from its number was probably opened some time before the assassination (MEXI 7065 of 25 November 1963, CIA Document #96-372). The Review Board should obtain it. All documentation on Durán should be considered assassination-related.

[68] *Washington Post*, November 26, 1976, A7; 3 AH 34 (1978).

[69] Evidence that the May version of the November 23 statement has been altered alerts us to the possibility of alterations in CE 93 as well. As published by the Warren Commission (16 WH 337-46), and in the bowdlerized DPD Report (24 WH 279-83), Oswald's "qualifications as a 'Marxist'" consist of ten lined notebook pages on seven sheets. However, when turned over in early December to the FBI by the Dallas police, the same notes (according to an FBI report) consisted of seven pages (FBI HQ serial 105-82555, 2nd no. 89; 62-109060-1835: "7 page background on lined notebook paper found by Adamcik Stovall Rose Moore Nov. 23, turned over 12/2 to Bookhout and

complete the disarray, the footnotes to the two phase two sections of the Warren Report (doubting that Oswald said he was a Communist) refer us to Appendix XIII, where the statement is accepted.

Furthermore, if Edwin Lopez can be believed, the version published by the House Committee of her 1978 statement -- "He show me letters to the Communist Party, the American Communist Party" -- has been redacted as well. His summary of the same page of her testimony, before it had been published, refers unambiguously to the missing card, as we would expect from her October 1963 "Observations" and the 1978 testimony of Azcue and Mirabal:

> As identification, Oswald showed her documents he had brought: his Russian labor card, marriage certificate with the name of his Russian wife, his American Communist Party membership card and his "Fair Play for Cuba" membership card.[70]

Reviewing all this evidence, we can conclude:

1) Oswald (or someone identifying himself as Oswald) did present himself to Durán as a Communist Party member, and he did supply documentation for this claim. Even in the Warren version of Oswald's career, it is not hard to imagine that he carried a forged CP card, just as he carried a forged FPCC card which he also presented. After all, Oswald was said to have been carrying two or three forged cards (his New Orleans FPCC card, the Hidell Selective Service card, his Marine Reserve card) at the time of his arrest.[71] Why not one more?

2) This phase-one fact of Oswald's alleged Communist membership and documentation was systematically effaced from the official record, beginning with the JKB memo dated November 26.

3) While this erasure in 1963 might be explained by fear of war with Cuba or the Soviet Union, the effacement continued in 1978, when such a risk had presumably subsided.

One other important conclusion can be reached. Not only did Oswald present himself as a documented Communist Party member, *the CIA probably knew this*, at least by November 23, when the Mexican DFS arrested Silvia Durán. There is really no better explanation for the intense reaction in Washington to the news that day about Durán's arrest, as reported years ago by the Church Committee:

> At 5:00 p.m. [sic; probably 3:47 p.m.] CIA Headquarters received a cable from the Mexico Station stating that the Mexican police were going to arrest Sylvia Duran....Headquarters personnel [John Scelso] telephoned the Mexico Station and asked them to stop the planned arrest. The Mexico Station said that the arrest could not be stopped. After learning the arrest could not be stopped, [Assistant Deputy Director for Plans] Karamessines cabled the Mexico Station that the arrest "could jeopardize [sic; the released cable says "prejudice"] U.S. freedom of action on the whole question of Cuban responsibility."[72]

George W.H. Carlson"). Quite possibly the FBI report meant to say "seven sheets," rather than "pages." However the discrepancy makes us aware that the famous self-description as a "Marxist" ("I first read the communist manifesto and 1st volume of capital in 1954 when I was 15") is on the reverse side of one of the sheets signed into evidence, and is possibly an addition.

[70] Lopez Report, 192; citing p. 28 of Durán's testimony (i.e. 3 AH 33).

[71] 24 WH 17. For the problematic story of the Marine Corps Reserve Card, see Ray and Mary La Fontaine, *Houston Post*, November 22, 1992, A-1; Scott, *Deep Politics*, 372.

[72] Schweiker-Hart Report, 25. We now know that the cited documents are MEXI 7029 of 23 November, not yet released (see Lopez Report, 185, A49), Scelso's memo of 23 November (TX-1240 of 23 Nov 1963, CIA Document #36-540), and DIR 84916 of 23 November (232319Z; CIA Document # 37-529). I have proposed the time of 3:47 PM EST (8:47 GMT, or 232047Z) for MEXI 7029, because MEXI 7028 has a Zulu time group of 232045Z, and MEXI 7030 of 232049Z.

It is hard to explain from the available documentary record why the CIA should have been so alarmed by news of Durán's arrest at 3:47 PM on November 23. According to this record Langley had heard of Durán for the first time at 11:59 EST, in a cable which was also the first true report that Oswald had visited the Cuban Embassy at all.[73] Just minutes before the arrest cable, Langley had received the full transcript of the September 28 phone conversation involving Durán, Oswald, and the Soviet Embassy. This message is intriguing, even suspicious (Oswald talks about having to ask the Cuban Embassy "for my address because they have it"). There is nothing in it to link Oswald's business to as simple a matter as a visa application.[74] But neither does it justify the CIA's urgent desire to interfere in the arrest procedures of a foreign government.

One is left with the impression that the CIA already knew about the CP card and the problems this could raise. There are of course two ways that they could have known.

1) By intelligence reports or surveillance of Oswald's activities, in either the Cuban or the Soviet Embassy. (He is said to have presented documentation in both consulates.) The "FBI wiretaps involving Oswald and Kostikov," cited by former FBI Director Kelley as a reason why Washington called Hosty away from the interviews of Oswald in Dallas, are one such possible source: Oswald would hardly have concealed his Communist documentation from the Soviets.[75]

2) Because Oswald presented the CP and FPCC cards as part of a penetration mission organized by a U.S. intelligence agency.

Conceivably, both of the foregoing could be true. A U.S. agency could have picked up traces of its own mission, or one U.S. agency could have eavesdropped on the operation of another.

There is other evidence, some of which I shall not go into here, that the CIA knew more of Oswald's activities in Mexico than has been revealed in the available record. The Warren Report itself reported that "the Commission has been advised by the CIA and FBI that secret and reliable sources corroborate the statements of Senora Duran [i.e. in the May 1964 version of her November 23 "signed statement"] in all material respects" (WR 309). Inasmuch as the May 1964 Durán statement appears to have been falsified, the Review Board should obtain the original signed statement, as well as the documents in which the CIA and FBI gave the Warren Commission this advice.

In 1967 an internal high-level FBI memorandum also referred to "reliable sources" as to what went on in the Cuban Embassy:

> Sensitive and reliable sources of the Bureau and CIA reported Oswald was unknown to Cuban government officials when he visited the Cuban Consulate in Mexico City on 9/27/63, and attempted, without success, to get a visa for travel to Cuba.[76]

These reports did not end up in the CIA's 201 file on Oswald, nor the FBI Headquarters file. There is no sign that they ever reached the House Committee. The new Review Board should review them and their subsequent history; and hopefully release them, for they are surely assassination-related.

The Missing Card: Was It Harvey Lee Oswald's?

We now see a similar pattern of development with respect to Oswald's alleged politics as reported in both Dallas and Mexico City. In the first stage, or phase one, he was either presented, or

---

[73] MEXI 7023 of 23 November, 231659Z; CIA Document # 49-545.

[74] MEXI 7025 of 23 November, 232034Z; CIA Document # 60-550.

[75] Kelley, *Kelley*, 293. See above.

[76] Memo from Rosen to DeLoach, 2/15/67; quoted in Schweiker-Hart Report, 81. The memo was in response to an inquiry from the Secret Service, prompted by columnist Drew Pearson's report to Chief Justice Warren that Castro had decided in 1963 to retaliate against U.S. government attempts to assassinate him.

presented himself, as a card-carrying Communist. Both in Dallas on November 22, and again in Mexico City a day later, this provokes a high-level intervention from Washington. Then in the second stage, or phase two, reports reports of Oswald's Communism and credentials were systematically expunged or rewritten. Many years later, starting in 1978, we see a third stage, or phase three, where the original sources again present Oswald as a Communist, but not a card-carrying member.

These parallels can be expressed schematically, as follows:

Phase One: Oswald is called "member of the Communist Party" (in Revill memo) and "card carrying member of the Communist Party" (in Army cable).

Phase One: Durán documents before assassination that Oswald stated "he is a member of American Communist Party" and "displayed documents in proof." On November 23 her written statement to DFS reportedly "said he Communist and admirer of Castro" (MEXI 7046)

Intervention by Washington: FBI and White House exert pressure on Dallas District Attorney Wade and others to silence Hosty and Dallas Police. Malley and two supervisors dispatched from FBI Headquarters to Dallas

Intervention by Washington: CIA phone call to prevent arrest, followed by high-level CIA cable warning arrest "could prejudice U.S. freedom of action on the whole question of Cuban responsibility." John Horton dispatched from CIA HQ to Mexico City; brings back second version of Durán's November 23 statement.

Phase Two: Allegation that Oswald is called "member of the Communist Party" is denied under oath by both Revill and his alleged source (Hosty). Army cable is suppressed, surviving by accident in an ONI copy.

Phase Two: Durán statement of November 23 is progressively revised until it allegedly says she "does not remember whether or not [Oswald] said that he was a member of the Communist Party" (24 WH 589).

Phase Three: Kelley's book (1987) concedes Hosty said "He's a Communist."

Phase Three: Durán tells HSCA in 1978 "he said he was a member of the Party" (3 AH 34).

In one respect the situations in Dallas and in Mexico City appear to be profoundly different. The allegations in Dallas that Oswald was a card-carrying Communist are by themselves barely credible, and indeed surrounded by falsehoods. The evidence that Oswald in Mexico *presented himself* as a card-carrying Communist is however hardly contestable, and is indeed strengthened by the later spurious efforts to cover it up. Of course this does not make Oswald's professed Communism and Castroism any more genuine than his expressed willingness in New Orleans "to join the fight...against Castro" (WR 728). Oswald himself was a recurring player of roles, and in Mexico he may have been impersonated.

It is unlikely that there is no relationship at all between the dubious allegations in Dallas and the fact, probably known to U.S. intelligence, that Oswald did present himself in Mexico as a card-carrying Communist. It is much more likely that Oswald's September performance as a Communist in Mexico led to confused echoes of it in Dallas. We know that there was inter-communication between the two cities: the Dallas Police brought in a Jose Rodriguez Molina for questioning on November 23, 1963, and the Mexican Minister of Gobernación, the same man responsible for arresting and interrogating Durán, was asking the CIA for information about him that same afternoon.[77]

Military Intelligence in Dallas on November 22, 1963

′ There are two reasons to believe that a U.S. intelligence source (probably in military intelligence) fed the dangerous phase-one rumors in Dallas that in turn were fed back to the U.S. Strike Command, basing the false picture in Dallas on the true picture in Mexico City.

The first reason is the recurring proximity of military intelligence figures to the real and alleged sources of the Dallas phase-one story. James Hosty had spent almost three hours on the morning of November 22 with an Army Intelligence or CIC Agent called Edward J. Coyle; and Coyle, it has just been revealed, was perhaps no stranger to the activities of Lee Harvey Oswald. For Coyle and Hosty had worked together on an arms case involving a Cuban anti-Castro group called the DRE, with which Oswald had been involved in New Orleans; and there are grounds to suspect that Oswald may have been an informant for Hosty on the Dallas arms case.[78] The DRE Headquarters in Miami, furthermore, was named as the source of a number of phase-one stories about both Oswald and later Ruby. The DRE Intelligence Officer in Miami, Jose Antonio Lanusa, reportedly "described Oswald [as] definitely a Communist and supporter of Castro."[79] A rebuttal memo in the Miami FBI files has the DRE chief Manuel Salvat talking, like the 112th Military Intelligence Group, about "Harvey Lee Oswald."[80]

Other military intelligence agencies may also have been involved. One day earlier, on November 21, Hosty and Coyle had met with Jack Revill, author of the memo claiming Hosty called Oswald a "member of the Communist Party." On November 22, according to his colleague V.J. Brian, Revill arrived at his meeting with Hosty in the Dallas Police basement in a car which had also carried "some type of...Army intelligence man," whether "a CIC agent or a CID or OSI" (5 WH 57). Revill has since identified him as an agent of OSI, the Office of Special Investigations of the U.S. Air Force.

Like Army Intelligence and ONI (Navy), OSI had maintained a continuous dossier on Oswald (though probably not under his name), since Oswald's defection in 1959. Their official ground for concern was that Oswald's half-brother, John Edward Pic, was a member of the USAF.[81] In fact OSI is the only military intelligence agency known to have consulted Oswald's Office of Security Confidential file in the Washington Headquarters of the State Department.[82]

As I have shown elsewhere, Army Intelligence Reserve also played a role in generating one other piece of evidence that Oswald acted in furtherance of an international Communist conspiracy: Marina's affidavit suggesting that Oswald's rifle in Dallas was one "which he used in Russia."[83] Army Intelligence knew of Marina's affidavit by 10:35 PM on November 22, 1963, before it was public knowledge.[84] Finally there is the unexplained knowledge of Army Intelligence in San Antonio, as early as 3:15 CST on November 22, that Oswald was arrested "carrying a Selective Service card bearing the name of Alex Hidell."[85] This was the FBI's first knowledge of the card, indeed the first documented source from any agency.

---

[77] MEXI 7026 of 23 November (232024Z); cf. WR 237-38.

[78] Ray and Mary La Fontaine, *Washington Post*, August 7, 1994, C1, C6; Scott, *Deep Politics*, 255-56; cf. WCD 853A.2.

[79] SAC Washington Field Office to FBI DIR, 11/23/63; FBI HQ 62-109060-1570.

[80] SA Paul Scranton to SAC Miami; Miami FBI 105-8342-29.

[81] For a schedule of OSI documents on Oswald through 1961, see Appendix C.

[82] U.S. State Dept. Passport File for Lee Harvey Oswald, Document X-67, OSI Review sheet, 3/8/60; NARA RG 59 Lot File 85D275, Box 2, Record Number 119-10004-10083.

[83] 23 WH 383-84, FBI version (written by James Bookhout) of affidavit taken from Marina Oswald on November 22; discussion above at footnote 41, also in Scott, *Deep Politics*, 267-72. The DPD account of this affidavit in the DPD Report (24 WH 219) lacks this provocative language.

[84] 112th Army Intelligence Group Region II Spot Report 419, 2235 hrs, Nov. 22 (Dallas FBI serial 89-43-2381B).

[85] San Antonio FBI Letterhead Memorandum of November 22, 1963; FBI HQ serial 102-82555-49D.

The second reason for suspecting military intelligence is the recurrence, otherwise unexplained, of the name "Harvey Lee Oswald," in Mexico City as in Dallas. Earlier I failed to mention one other respect in which the November 26 version of Durán's statement, or JKB Memo attachment, was apparently rewritten. The ten-page attachment is a Report from a source (still redacted in the released version) who personally interviewed Durán and seven of her personal associates.[86] In that report Oswald is mentioned by name a total of thirteen times. In the first half of the report, the important interviews of Durán and her husband, we find "Oswald" once, "Lee Oswald" once, and "Lee Harvey Oswald" a total of six times. But in the second half, the interviews of five minor witnesses, beginning with Durán's brother-in-law, all end with variations of the same sentence: each person asserted that he did not know "Harvey Lee Oswald."[87]

In the English translation of this Report, as we might expect, the anomaly has been corrected; and we hear only of "Lee Harvey Oswald."[88] It seems likely that this rationalization of the text completes a task that in the Spanish text was done only for Durán and her husband, and not for the minor witnesses. In other words, whoever deleted the earlier reference to "Communist" (or "militant Communist") may have deleted references there to "Harvey Lee Oswald" as well. Thus there is a good chance that, as originally transcribed, Durán's November 23 statement reported that Harvey Lee Oswald was a Communist (with or without a card).

We are thus faced with an anomaly. In Mexico City as in Dallas and Miami, when we dig back to the root statement that Oswald was a Communist, we encounter another name: Harvey Lee Oswald. In fact the name "Harvey Lee Oswald" was used in many early assassination documents, from many different agencies. This anomaly suggests that there must be a hidden common source.

This hidden source, or archetype, may have had to do with military intelligence. Relatively deep in the Mexico City FBI Oswald file is a cover sheet, dated 1-22-64, from an otherwise unidentified source called "Wesley." The document interests us not for its enclosure, which is not yet released, but for its file data. It now resides in the FBI Mexico City file, 105-3702, which was opened on October 18, 1963. But it was originally typed for a lower-numbered file (presumably opened some time earlier): "105-2137 (Harvey Lee Oswald)."[89] Wesley has not been identified, but there are grounds for suspecting that he was a part of military intelligence.[90]

Other sources on Oswald who actually or reportedly used the name "Harvey Lee Oswald" (such as New Orleans Police Lieutenant Francis Martello) are also figures in touch with military intelligence.[91] The key example here is Jack Revill, who spent both November 21 and November 22 in the company of military intelligence agents. His phase-one memo about Hosty, as reproduced by the Warren Commission, gives Oswald's normal name to an address where in fact he had never lived: "Lee Harvey Oswald 605 Elsbeth Street" (17 WH 509). However the list of employees compiled at

---

[86] This is the "JKB" statement hand-carried to Washington on November 27 by a Headquarters CIA officer, John Horton. See above at footnote 65.

[87] JKB memo and Attachment of 26 November, 1963, CIA Doc. #131-593; pp. 7 (twice), 8, 9, 10.

[88] DIR 85758 of 291945Z (CIA HQ to White House, State Dept., and FBI), CIA Document # 223-647.

[89] FBI serial MC 105-3702-254 [redacted]; NARA # 124-10029-10270. This enclosure, this earlier file, and indeed all government documents which deal with Harvey Lee Oswald, should be considered assassination-related. There are many such documents. I have appended a schedule showing that they emanate from Mexico City, from Dallas, and many other places, and from such diverse agencies as Army Intelligence, the Secret Service, FBI, CIA, and the Dallas Police Department. See Appendix II, "Harvey Lee Oswald."

[90] Other documents, once described as referring to "Harvey Lee Oswald," may have been re-labeled. One example is the File of the Dallas County Sheriff on Oswald, entered into evidence on April 16, 1964, as follows: "Mr. HUBERT. Let me mark this document, then -- I am marking it...as Exhibit 5323, Deposition of Sheriff J.E. Decker....It is called Acco Press on the inside and bears the label on the outside, 'Harvey Lee Oswald, WM 24, Murder--11-22-63 of John Fitzgerald Kennedy'" (12 WH 51). However the File as reproduced in the Warren volumes bears a different title: "OSWALD, Lee Harvey W/M 24 MURDER 11-22-63 of JOHN FITZGERALD KENNEDY" (19 WH 54).

[91] 4 WH 432 (see Appendix C, "Harvey Lee Oswald"); Scott, *Deep Politics*, 258. At least one of the policemen who reportedly asked for "Harvey Lee Oswald" at the Beckley St. rooming house (6 WH 438), was B.L. Senkel, who had just driven in the pilot car of the presidential parade with a local army reserve commander (discussion in Scott, *Deep Politics*, 273).

the same time by and for Jack Revill at the School Book Depository (5 WH 34) has a different name at the head of the list: "HARVEY LEE OSWALD 605 ELSBETH" (24 WH 259).[92]

If we are correct in our analysis of the evidence from Mexico, there is a good chance that the documented reports from there of a Harvey Lee Oswald had included the information that Oswald had presented himself as a card-carrying Communist, and that members of the Dallas police, including Revill, had in some way learned of this. If so the two federal interventions, in Dallas and in Mexico, may have been targeting the same problem.

The vehemence of the Washington response is even more credible if we credit the *Excelsior* version of Oswald's self-presentation: that he was a "militant Communist." That clue is supported by the backyard photograph of Oswald, holding a rifle in one hand, and in the other copies of the "Worker" and the "Militant".[93]

If we credit for the moment that Oswald arranged for this photo and had it in his possession, three questions present themselves. First, what purpose could the photo have served, other than precisely to present himself as a "militant Communist?" Second, what viewership did he have in mind for this photo, if not the consulates of Cuba and the Soviet Union in Mexico City? Third, given his desire to demonstrate his Communist affiliations to the Cuban consulate, why would he not have availed himself of this photograph, whatever its original purpose?

But if Oswald, or Harvey Lee Oswald, did present himself as a militant Communist, the relevance of his Mexico performance to the assassination becomes even greater. It leads us to look again at old but authoritative allegations, from high levels in the FBI and the CIA, that Oswald in the Cuban embassy actually offered to assassinate President Kennedy.[94]

[92] Cf. Scott, *Deep Politics*, 277.

[93] WR 404, 16 WH 510, 17 WH 498. Many critics have noted the incongruity of Oswald holding the newspapers of two parties, the Communist Party and the Socialist Workers' Party, that detested each other. It may be pertinent that, according to the army intelligence cable about Harvey Lee Oswald as a card-carrying Communist, the Fair Play for Cuba Committee was described as "primarily controlled by the SWP with CPUSA influences present" (U.S. Army Cable 480587 from Fort Sam Houston, Texas, to U.S. Strike Command, McDill AFB, Florida, 230405Z).

[94] See for example Kelley, *Kelley*, 269. Discussion in Chapter VIII, 90-109.

VIII. "I'M GOING TO KILL KENNEDY FOR THIS:"

DID OSWALD SAY THIS IN THE CUBAN EMBASSY? OR WAS THE STORY PLANTED?

Updated Revision of Paper Presented at COPA Conference, October 7-10, 1994

The CIA's On-Going Oswald Secret

Did Lee Harvey Oswald remark during his visit to the Cuban Embassy in September 1963 that he was going to kill Kennedy? In October 1994 I presented a tentative argument that Lee Harvey Oswald (or someone else using this name) might have made such remarks, and that the CIA may have had (and since concealed) knowledge of them that pre-dated the Kennedy assassination. I called for the release of the key documents that could corroborate this claim, notably Warren Commission Document 1359 of June 17, 1964, the *only* top-secret document transmitted to the Commission by the FBI, and the FBI's "Solo" assassination records that gave rise to it.

Since my initial presentation of this material in October 1994 CD 1359 and the "Solo" records have been released. These confirm that one of the FBI's top Communist Party informants, Jack Childs ("Solo"), reported in June 1964 to the Party (and simultaneously to the FBI) that Castro told him a version of this story: namely that Oswald, angry and frustrated at the Cuban refusal to issue him a visa, "headed out saying, 'I'm going to kill Kennedy for this.'"[1]

That CD 1359 contains this allegation does not mean that it happened. As we shall see, Castro himself denied a corrupted version of this story (attributed falsely to an alleged interview with the British journalist Comer Clark). Knowledgeable Cuban officials have continued to deny corrupted accounts, falsely used to link Cuba to the assassination. CIA officials have promoted similar stories, obviously false.

On the other hand it is clear that the CIA did have something in its pre-assassination files that it hid from the FBI in 1963 and still wishes to hide: a secret so sensitive that it is still willing, not just to suppress documents, but even to dissemble about them. This key suppression has to do with Oswald's visit to the Cuban Embassy in Mexico City, which the CIA initially kept secret from the FBI, and CIA Headquarters' knowledge in October 1963 of Oswald's Cuban activities (both in New Orleans and in Mexico City), when the CIA affected ignorance of them in a misleading cable to the FBI.[2] Some of this dissembling has verged on the criminal, as when the CIA falsified an FBI transmittal form in order to conceal their knowledge in October of Oswald's Cuban activities from the Warren Commission.[3]

---

[1] Warren Commission Document 1359; FBI HQ 62-109090-63rd nr 172; NARA Record Number 124-10103-10138.

[2] Peter Dale Scott, "The Lopez Report and the CIA's Oswald Counterintelligence Secrets," published in *Oswald in Mexico: Book Three: The Lopez Report* (Evanston, IL: Rogra Research, 1993), 5-6, etc. (i.e. Chapter II, 5-6); Peter Dale Scott, "CIA Files and the Pre-Assassination Framing of Lee Harvey Oswald" (i.e. Chapter III). The misleading cable is also discussed in John Newman, *Oswald and the CIA* (New York: Carroll and Graf, 1995), 403-05.

[3] See above, 11, 28.. The falsified transmittal form was received from the FBI with the date stamp "November 8, 1963" together with a copy of the October 31 report on Oswald prepared by FBI Agent Kaack. Someone in the CIA then wrote on a copy of this form the inscription "DBA-52355," i.e. the serial number for an FBI Letterhead Memorandum of September 24, 1963, which discussed Oswald's leafleting for the Fair Play for Cuba Committee, and his arrest on August 9. In fact this September 24 LHM had been received by the CIA on October 3, and read by CIA Liaison officer Jane Roman on October 4. In other words Jane Roman had seen this LHM six days before the CIA cable (which she had signed off on) saying "latest HDQS info was [State] report dated May 1962." The falsified transmittal slip covered up this embarrassing fact by its implication that the LHM had been received later. At some point (presumably after the assassination) the LHM, together with the falsified transmittal form, were placed in Oswald's 201 file after the misleading October 10 cable; and a copy of this altered 201 file, as transmitted to the Warren Commission, can now be read in the National Archives as Warren Commission CD 692. The CIA then declassified the 201 file in 1992, and this 1992 release contained a copy of the falsified transmittal form. This is published in Lewis B. Sckolnick, ed., *Lee Harvey Oswald: CIA Pre-Assassination File* (Leverett MA: Rector

That the CIA sent a misleading cable about Oswald in October 1963 became itself a secret. It appears however to be a secondary secret, protecting another secret, that was both prior and more important. In this paper I shall argue what that prior secret may have been: a pre-assassination report (true or false) that in September 1963 someone in the Cuban Embassy identified himself as Lee Oswald and threatened to kill President Kennedy. The available evidence would suggest, furthermore, that despite contrary evidence in the Warren Report that person may not have been the Lee Oswald arrested in Dallas.[4]

It is important before proceeding to contextualize this threat. First we must forestall the easy but erroneous suggestion, once made by the *New York Times*, that it would constitute "evidence... that Mr. Oswald had had Cuban backing in his assassination attempt."[5]

A similar word must be said in defense of the now beleaguered CIA. I myself suspect that the CIA possibly knew by October of Oswald's assassination remarks, took steps to cover them up, and may even have played the major role in making the remarks happen. Even if true, these facts would not by themselves prove CIA involvement in the assassination, although they would seem to implicate one or more individuals who had knowledge of what was going on.

I myself shall argue, as I have before, that there may be a quite different explanation for the CIA's systematic falsification of information about Oswald, including the story of the assassination remarks. This is that information about Oswald was being disseminated in different forms through different channels, as part of what the counterintelligence world calls a "barium meal," to trace and define a possible leak of information to the Soviets.[6] John Newman's new book, *Oswald and the CIA*, has thoroughly documented the recurring anomaly in Oswald files of both the CIA and FBI: the splitting or compartmentalization of Oswald information in ways that are not cross-referenced.[7] The fact that Oswald's 201 file was opened and maintained by CI/SIG, the CIA's mole-hunting unit, strengthens the hypothesis that Oswald's provocative behavior in embassies, in 1959 and again in 1963, was grist for a counterintelligence operation, and intended to provoke a leak.

Of course, if this provocative behavior involved an assassination threat, or (as Oleg Nechiporenko has claimed) the display of a gun, other covert operations, such as an authorized propaganda operation or an unauthorized assassination plot, could have been piggy-backed upon the original counterintelligence operation.[8] Manufactured evidence that Oswald was a Soviet-controlled potential assassin could be rationalized as part of the propaganda offensive which we know was being mounted against the FPCC by both the CIA and FBI.[9] It could also mean that some of those officers controlling the authorized propaganda operation were simultaneously involved in a criminal assassination plot.

Rector Press, 1993), 112, and also by Newman (p. 503). As if aware of its vulnerability for this deception, the CIA re-released the 201 file in 1993, with the original, unaltered transmittal form. This form (in its innocent, 1993 version) is also reproduced without discussion in Newman, *Oswald and the CIA*, after p. 300. But what should concern us is the falsified transmittal form, not the innocent one. The JFK Act Review Board should interview the CIA officers responsible for Warren CD 692 and for the 1993 release, to begin to learn what missing records about Oswald underlie the CIA's deceptive falsification of its records to mislead the Warren Commission.

[4] The CIA initially distributed photos, said to be of the man who identified himself as Oswald, who was clearly not Oswald; in addition an early FBI memo to the Secret Service stated that a recording of the man who identified himself as Oswald had been listened to by FBI agents in Dallas, in whose opinion the "individual was not Lee Harvey Oswald" (AR 249-50). Subsequent efforts by the CIA, FBI and House Committee to rationalize the false photos and the FBI memo are in my opinion (and that of House Committee investigator Edwin Lopez) more provocative than convincing (cf. Scott, *Deep Politics*, 41-44; Lopez Report Introduction, 8-14).

[5] Nicholas Horrock, *New York Times*, November 14, 1976, 30. See discussion below.

[6] Scott, Lopez Report Introduction, 5-6, 20-22. For the counterintelligence concept of a "barium meal," see William R. Corson, Susan B. Trento, Joseph J. Trento, *Widows* (New York: Crown, 1989), 60; Peter Wright, *Spycatcher* (New York: Viking, 1987), 303.

[7] Newman, 57, 140-41, 152-53, 319, 392-419, etc.

[8] Col. Oleg Maximovich Nechiporenko, *Passport to Assassination* (New York: Carol/Birch Lane, 1993), 77-81.

[9] Newman, 236-44; Schweiker-Hart Report, 65-67; Scott, *Deep Politics*, 261.

We shall see that the notorious David Phillips, and others in his milieu, were important in the dissemination of the assassination-threat story. I shall argue that undoubtedly Phillips lied on the matter of Oswald's assassination remarks. Phillips however was not necessarily lying because he was (in the usual sense) a co-conspirator. We must consider that he may have been no more than a good soldier, lying, as so many CIA officers have felt themselves duty-bound to do, to protect what he believed was an unrelated intelligence operation.

To state the situation from the Agency's own perspective, we should not necessarily impart "sinister motives to the Agency's desire to uphold the law relative to the protection of sources and methods."[10]

The CIA's Oswald Secret: Was It a Threat in Mexico to Assassinate Kennedy?

In my book *Deep Politics* I presented a two-phase dialectic behind the Warren Commission finding that Oswald was a "lone assassin." I argued that in pre-assassination CIA and FBI files a false legend about Oswald was planted, which after the assassination made him falsely appear to be a possible Soviet assassination agent. This "phase-one" story was then supplemented by a false second post-assassination story that he might have been a Castro assassination agent. The two "phase-one" stories created a "case" for the risk of a nuclear war; the new President, Lyndon Johnson, used this risk to justify the creation of the Warren Commission, which moved to validate the "phase-two" story that Oswald acted alone.

The pre-assassination Oswald-KGB legend I focused on was not pure fiction; it was based on real, if deceptive, events in Mexico City, linking Oswald to an alleged KGB assassination expert by the name of Valeriy Kostikov. On October 1, 1963, someone telephoned the Soviet Consulate in Mexico City, identified himself as Lee Oswald, and indicated that he had talked earlier to someone by the name of Kostikov (identified in FBI and CIA files as a KGB agent and possible expert on assassination).

Further pre-assassination investigation established that Oswald had also visited the Cuban consulate in connection with a visa application. The CIA Station in Mexico notified Headquarters about the visit to the Soviet Consulate.[11] According to the available record, the visit to the Cuban consulate was not communicated until after the assassination. That record however may not be complete.[12]

The recently declassified documents have helped clarify some issues of fact about the CIA performance here. It is now clear that CIA Headquarters' response to the alleged Soviet visit, in a cable sent to the FBI and State Department, was falsified by CIA Counterintelligence personnel. (By "falsified," I do not mean wholly invented, but deliberately contaminated with error, possibly as part of the search then current for a KGB mole inside the CIA. For the purpose of this falsification may have been to create a tracer, or "barium meal," to determine if the falsified information from this unique source was passing back to the Soviets.)[13] Oswald's name was falsified (as "Lee Henry Oswald"), the important detail about Kostikov was initially suppressed, as was information already known to the CIA about Lee Harvey Oswald's interest in Cuba, as exemplified by his arrest with two Cubans on August 9.[14]

The result of this biased reporting, or Big October Lie, was to focus the Oswald pre-assassination 201 file on his Soviet connections, to the exclusion of his Cuban ones. This exclusion was persistent, and probably deliberate. We find it again in a Mexico City CIA memo of October 16,

---

[10] CIA undated document, ca. 1978, "Comments upon HSCA Study: CIA's Performance in Its Role of Support to the Warren Commission" [Staff Report, 11 AH 471-504], p. 3.

[11] MEXI 6453 of 8 October 1963, CIA Document #5-1A; 4 AH 212.

[12] Cf. Lopez Report, 175-76; Newman, 413-18, etc.

[13] Scott, Lopez Report Introduction, 5-6, 20-22.

[14] Newman, *Oswald and the CIA*, 401-05, 512-13.

1963, whose author knew by this time of Oswald's visits to the Cuban Embassy.[15] We find it in the first post-assassination cables which we have from the CIA station in Mexico City.

What was Oswald doing in the Cuban Embassy? Here the recently declassified documents do very little to resolve the issue. On the contrary, they reinforce the sense that more went on during the Oswald visits than the Warren Report was allowed to record. One can say only that the documents, including the declassified Lopez Report and FBI Solo records, strongly corroborate an old but explosive allegation, suggested earlier by FBI Director J. Edgar Hoover, in Warren Commission Document 1359 (Hoover's letter of June 17, 1964 to the Warren Commission), and corroborated in 1987 by his successor Clarence Kelley. This is that Oswald (or someone who identified himself as Oswald) talked in the Cuban Embassy (according to Kelley, in both the Soviet and Cuban Embassies) about assassination, even about assassinating President Kennedy.[16]

A preliminary word about the degree of resistance that has surrounded this entire topic. It is not, on the face of it, proof that we have found an important clue to the Kennedy assassination. On the contrary, Warren CD 1359 carried the national security classification of Top Secret for the obvious reason that the report came from a highly-placed intelligence source. FBI Director Kelley correctly identified that source as "Solo," i.e. the Communist Party double-agents Morris and Jack Childs.[17] The Childs brothers have been described as possibly "the most successful double agents in American history;" they became the crucial link by which about one million dollars a year from Soviet funds reached the American Communist Party.[18]

In 1995 the release of the FBI's "Solo" assassination records, including CD 1359, confirmed that the FBI's source was indeed Jack Childs. These records also made it clear that what Castro attributed to Oswald in the Cuban Embassy was not an offer to kill Kennedy (as reported by Kelley), but an angry threat, in response to being denied a visa. This was clear even in the account of Jack Childs' interview of Castro transmitted by Hoover in CD 1359:

> According to our source [Childs], Castro recently is reported to have said, "Our people in Mexico gave us the details in a full report of how he (Oswald) acted when he came to Mexico to their embassy (uncertain whether he means Cuban or Russian Embassy)." Castro further related, "First of all, nobody ever goes that way for a visa. Second, it costs money to go that distance. He (Oswald) stormed into the embassy, demanded the visa, and when it was refused to him, headed out saying, 'I'm going to kill Kennedy for this.'" Castro is alleged to have continued and asked, "What is your government doing to catch the other assassins?" and speculated, "It took about three people."[19]

When we compare Childs' actual report of Castro's comments to his discussion of it with the FBI, we see that in fact it was unambiguously the Cuban Embassy where the meeting took place. We see also that Oswald's assassination remark was apparently a spontaneous one, and not (as later reported) a considered "offer" or "plan." Jack Childs' ("Solo"'s) own written statement supplied the initial account of what Castro had to say to him about Oswald, which occupied one paragraph in a report of eight pages:

---

[15] Memo of October 16, 1963 for the Ambassador (CIA Document #9-5); reprinted in Sckolnick, 122. This memo says that "This officer determined that Oswald had been at the Soviet Embassy on 28 September 1963." The author told the HSCA that this determination "must have been because she had rechecked the transcripts by this time as otherwise she would not have used such certain language" (Lopez Report, 171; cf. Newman, 367). The September 28 transcript spoke unambiguously of an "American citizen at the Cuban Embassy" (MEXI 7023 of 23 November 1963; cf. Lopez Report, 76). Yet there is no reference to the Cuban Embassy visit in the October 16 memo. The Review Board should interview the author of this memo, to ascertain what other records, if any, are being covered up by this misrepresentation.

[16] Clarence Kelley, *Kelley: The Story of an FBI Director* (Kansas City: Andrews, McMeel and Parker, 1987), 268-69.

[17] Kelley, *Kelley*, 269; Curt Gentry, *J. Edgar Hoover*, 502 (Childs).

[18] David J. Garrow, *The FBI and Martin Luther King* [Harmondsworth: Penguin, 1981], 35-37.

[19] Warren Commission Document 1359; FBI HQ 62-109090-63rd nr 172; NARA Record Number 124-10103-10138.

His next question was do you think that Oswald killed President Kennedy? Before I could answer, he said he could not have been in it alone. I'm sure of that. It was at least 2 or 3 men who did it. Most likely 3. He said soon after the President was assassinated, he and a number of his sharp shooters got similar rifles with telescopic sights and shot at the target under the same conditions, same distance, same height and after this shooting, he came to the conclusion it was impossible for one man to have shot the President....He said Oswald was involved. Our people in Mexico gave us a full report of how he acted when he came to Mexico to their embassy. He said first of all nobody ever goes that way for a visa. Second, it costs money to go that distance. He stormed into the embassy, demanded the visa and when it was refused to him headed out saying I'm going to kill Kennedy for this.[20]

At the time Childs also told the FBI in New York that Castro was sober when he spoke. Moreover, he "treated the question as a very serious matter and indicated that this was something he must have asked about and talked about with many people."

Although Castro spoke to NY 694-S* [Childs' informant number] in broken English, without benefit of translation, there is no question as to the accuracy of what he said for the informant indicated that he had made notes at the time Castro was talking.... NY 694-S* is of the opinion that the Cuban Embassy people must have told Oswald something to the effect that they were sorry they did not let Americans into Cuba because the U.S. Government stopped Cuba from letting them in and that is when Oswald shouted out the statement about killing President Kennedy.

Childs and another witness present concluded that the Embassy personnel who dealt with Oswald "apparently had made a full, detailed report to Castro after President Kennedy was assassinated."[21]

Castro's general remarks about Oswald's stormy behavior are consistent with the later testimony of Consular officials Silvia Duran and Eusebio Azcue, about Oswald getting "angry" (3 AH 47) and slamming the door (3 AH 133). Azcue further confirmed talking to his Ministry in Havana after the assassination (3 AH 157).

One must approach this topic with methodical caution. In the first place the allegation of an assassination remark has been made recurrently from other sources (such as the Nicaraguan intelligence agent Gilberto Alvarado) who were almost certainly lying. Furthermore, even if shown to be true, the allegation that Oswald (or someone who identified himself as Oswald) talked of killing the President would by itself prove almost nothing, either about Oswald's actual involvement, or (even less) about Cuba's. The reported reaction of Fidel Castro to these alleged remarks -- that it was nothing more than a CIA provocation -- can be shown to be plausible, at least as plausible as the alternative that the threat was a sincere one from an arrogant and frustrated lone nut.

The fact is that, even if we dispense with debatable sources like Alvarado, there remain a number of authoritative sources which collectively corroborate the idea of an Oswald assassination threat, or offer. As reported in his memoirs by FBI Director Clarence Kelley, this assassination story had four separate elements:

1) an offer of "*information* on a CIA plot to assassinate Fidel Castro."

2) this offer in exchange for *assistance* from the Soviet and Cuban consulates, in obtaining "Soviet and Cuban visas" (other sources speak of travel assistance, or cash).

3) additional *remarks about killing* President Kennedy, which Kelley characterized as an "offer."

---

[20] SAC New York to Director Airtel 6/11/64, Subject: Solo, IS- C, FBI HQ File 100-428091-3930; NARA Record 124-10274-10339, p. 19.

[21] SAC New York to Director Airtel 6/12/64, Subject: Solo, IS- C, FBI HQ File 100-428091-3911; NARA Record 124-10274-10338, pp. 1-2.

4) *Castro "verified"* the remarks about killing Kennedy and shared this knowledge after the assassination with "Solo," one of the FBI's top Communist informants.[22]

There is also a fifth ingredient to the full account of the alleged Oswald assassination remark. The fifth ingredient is that the Cubans, including Castro, treated the remark as a *"deliberate provocation."* This fifth ingredient, not mentioned by Kelley, is erroneously attributed by the journalist Daniel Schorr to CD 1359.[23] It is however consistent with what Jack Childs told the FBI about Castro's alleged account of Oswald's assassination threat: that "Castro was trying to imply that the assassination was a deliberate and conscientious plot to involve Cuba as well as the Soviet Union."[24] Despite their bizarre and implausible character, there exists recurring corroboration for all five of these distinct ingredients to the alleged Oswald assassination threat story.

Let me at the outset point out the importance of the story, whether true or false. Paradoxically, one can argue that the greater the number of falsehoods in the story, the greater the potential evidentiary importance.

1) If the threat was made sincerely by Marina's husband, this would immediately become the best available evidence for the latter's murderous intent to kill Kennedy.

2) If the threat were made by the same person, but insincerely as an organized provocation, it would increase the chances of organized involvement in the murder of the President.

3) If the threat were made by someone who identified himself as Lee Oswald, who was demonstrably not the man we know as the husband of Marina, we would have *prima facie* proof of conspiracy.

4) If the Oswald assassination threat was in fact never made at all, but merely reported by a well-placed source to the Cuban and American authorities, that source is implicated in a conspiratorial act. This could be part of a cover-up or some other irrelevant conspiracy, if the report (like that of the Nicaraguan intelligence agent Gilberto Alvarado) post-dates the assassination.

5) If there are (or were) documented *pre-assassination* reports of an Oswald assassination threat, that in fact was never made, we have isolated a central ingredient in a dialectical conspiracy to assassinate the President.

---

[22] "It appeared that Oswald confided to the Soviets and the Cubans that he had information on a CIA plot to assassinate Fidel Castro. He would, he promised, provide all of this highly classified information in exchange for Soviet and Cuban visas for his family and himself respectively. It is possible to assume that at the Soviet Embassy he offered to kill President Kennedy....Oswald...told the Cuban Embassy officials much the same. But here he definitely offered to kill President Kennedy....[O]ur informant "Solo," a double-agent, met with Castro after the assassination. Castro himself verified that Oswald had offered to kill the American president and that the offer was made by Oswald directly to Cuban officials at their embassy in Mexico City" (Clarence Kelley, *Kelley*, 268, 269).

[23] Daniel Schorr, *Clearing the Air* (Boston: Houghton Mifflin, 1977), 176-77: "On June 17, 1964, J. Edgar Hoover sent, by special courier, a top-secret letter to Counsel Rankin. It said that 'through a confidential source which has furnished reliable information in the past, we have been advised of some statements made by Fidel Castro, Cuban Prime Minister, concerning the assassination of President Kennedy.' The paragraph containing what Castro said was deleted from the letter as released in 1976 [to the public]. It stated, I have since learned, that Oswald, on his visit to the consulate, had talked of assassinating President Kennedy. The consul had taken this as a deliberate provocation. The Cuban ambassador in Mexico City had reported the incident to Havana. It had not been taken seriously at the time, but after the Kennedy assassination, Castro had come to suspect that the effort to get Oswald into Cuba was part of a right-wing conspiracy. Oswald would return from Cuba, then assassinate the President, and it would look as though Castro had been responsible."

[24] SAC New York to Director Airtel 6/12/64, Subject: Solo, IS-C, FBI HQ File 100-428091-3911; NARA Record 124-10274-10338, p. 2.

There are still other possibilities. We should consider, for example, whether Jack Childs was lying, and (if so) for what reason. It seems unlikely that Childs would have invented this story on behalf of the FBI, which was committed to the portrait of Oswald as a lone assassin, and (as we shall see) had already helped suppress the version of Oswald's assassination remarks floated by the admitted liar Gilberto Alvarado. It is easier to imagine that Childs might have lied in this way on behalf of the CIA, but no one to date has suggested that either of the Childs brothers was a CIA asset. If they were, it would be important to learn who controlled them (see below).

Whatever the facts, it is incumbent upon the Review Board to review, and if possible release, all of the documentation dealing with the five ingredients of the alleged Oswald assassination threat.

We should note that the "Solo" records partially discredit, as well as partially confirm, what Kelley had to say about them. Childs clearly reported a spontaneous threat, where Kelley wrote that Oswald "definitely offered to kill President Kennedy, speculating that Oswald "may...have been influenced by Castro's public threat on September 9 [sic, i.e. 7] against American leaders."[25] This last speculation, repeated in many places, cannot be based on what we are told Jack Childs reported.[26]

There are other reasons to be skeptical of Kelley's claims. Not only is his account of the "Solo" report fallible, he must have come late to knowledge of it: in 1963 he was chief of the Kansas City Police Department, where he remained until returning to the FBI as Director in 1973. For at least some of his information he appears to have relied on his friend James Hosty, who clearly would not be a good source for what happened in Mexico City. FBI sources have since allegedly claimed that the entire chapter is written by Hosty, which if true would weaken the chapter's authority on material at FBI Headquarters.[27]

On the other hand, the newly released account of Jack Childs' interview with Castro makes it more rather than less likely that Oswald (or someone claiming to be him) did talk in the Cuban Embassy of killing President Kennedy. (It also makes us look again at the claim of former KGB colonel Oleg Nechiporenko that Oswald, the next day, showed great agitation in the Soviet Embassy, displayed a revolver, and said that if "they" didn't leave him alone on his return to the U.S., he was going to "defend" himself.)[28]

The Childs report raises the question of whether this information was picked up by U.S. HUMINT or electronic sources at the time. Director Kelley himself claimed that "some very highly placed [CIA] informants within the [Soviet] embassy," whose existence has not yet been officially confirmed, contributed to his knowledge of Oswald's activities there.[29] House Committee investigator Edwin Lopez has since revealed that the CIA had two or more well-placed informants (or what the trade calls HUMINT sources) in the Cuban Embassy as well.[30] The presence of at least one such informant, identified by John Newman as Luis Alberu Soto, is further corroborated by contemporary cables.[31]

---

[25] Kelley, 269.

[26] See for example Daniel Schorr, *Clearing the Air*, 177-78; cf. Posner, 168. One of the first to suggest that Oswald was influenced by Castro's remarks was the CIA-linked journalist Hal Hendrix, in a story datelined November 23, 1963. See *Rocky Mountain News*, November 24, 1963.

[27] Cf. Kelley, 317: Hosty "devoted considerable time and energy to assisting us with data on the Kennedy assassination."

[28] Oleg Nechiporenko, *Passport to Assassination*, 77-81.

[29] "The information that Oswald talked to Kostikov at the Russian Embassy was obtained variously. One method was through CIA wiretaps of the embassy's phone in Mexico City. Oswald's call from the Cuban to the Russian Embassy, for instance, was tapped by our government. The Soviet Embassy was also being watched by ultrasensitive CIA surveillance cameras. What's more, the agency had some very highly placed informants within the embassy itself. Thus, the fact that Oswald met with this particularly dangerous KGB official is certain." (Kelley, *Kelley*, 268)

[30] Edwin Lopez, "Commentary," in *Lopez Report*, 3; Lopez Report [1996], 223. See below.

[31] MEXI 7115 of 28 November 1963, CIA Doc. # 196-626; MEXI 7613, 7615, and 7625 of December 1963; memorandum for record of 6 January 1964 (Document NR15-232); Newman, 360, 386-90, 602.

Normally one would accede to maintaining the highest degree of protection to such HUMINT sources, whose safety and perhaps life would otherwise be placed at risk. However such protection should not be automatically extended to a HUMINT source if it can be shown they transmitted a false or misleading story of an Oswald assassination threat, prior to the assassination.

Authoritative Corroboration of the Oswald Assassination Threat

There is repeated authoritative corroboration for all four ingredients of the Oswald assassination remark as reported by Kelley, as well as for the fifth ingredient (that the Cubans interpreted the remark as a "deliberate provocation," or "deliberate and conscientious plot to involve Cuba").

In brief, the claim that Oswald offered "unspecified information" to the Soviet Consulate in exchange for assistance or pay (elements #1 and #2 of the Kelley story) was attributed to three sources in the Mexico City CIA station by the *Washington Post* in 1976. These included David Phillips, who in 1963 was simultaneously the CIA Station's Chief of Cuban Operations and of Covert Action (including propaganda), and an unnamed "typist" who was said to have typed the transcript of the message on which this offer was made. (If this transcript ever existed, there is no public record of it today.)[32]

Phillips apparently repeated the story about Oswald's request for *assistance* (but not the offer of *information*) in his testimony under oath to the Committee (and not yet released) the next day.[33] Nor did Phillips mention the information offer in his book written the same year. On the contrary, Phillips wrote categorically that "I know of no evidence to suggest that...any aspect of the Mexico City trip was any more ominous than reported by the Warren Commission."[34] This was a remarkable turnaround for a man who (we shall soon see) had in 1963 been a vigorous supporter of the story that Oswald had threatened in the Cuban Embassy to kill Kennedy, and also been paid to do so.[35]

The House Committee later learned that the story of Oswald's assistance request (from both Embassies) had been told earlier by Winston Scott, the Chief of the Mexico City CIA Station, in a letter which Scott wrote in 1970, after his retirement from the CIA:

> During my thirteen years in Mexico, I had many experiences, some of which I can write in detail. One of these pertains to Lee Harvey Oswald and what I *know* [emphasis in original] of his activities from the moment he arrived in Mexico, his contacts by telephone and his visits to both the Soviet and Cuban Embassies *and his requests for assistance from these two Embassies in trying to get to the Crimea with his wife and baby* [emphasis added]. During his conversations he cited a promise from the Soviet Embassy in Washington that they would notify their Embassy in Mexico of Oswald's plan to ask them for assistance.[36]

---

[32] As reported to the *Washington Post* in 1976 by David Phillips, Oswald had been overheard saying words "to the effect, 'I have information you would be interested in, and I know you can pay my way [to Russia].'" According to Ron Kessler, the author of the news story, Phillips' claim was supported by two other CIA employees, the translator and the typist of the message: "'He said he had some information to tell them,' the typist said in an interview in Mexico. 'His main concern was in getting to one of the two countries [Russia or Cuba] and he wanted them to pay for it'" (story by Ron Kessler, *Washington Post*, November 26, 1976; cf. Anthony Summers, *Conspiracy* [New York: McGraw-Hill, 1980], 388-89; Fonzi, *The Last Investigation* [New York: Thunder's Mouth, 1993], 285.)

[33] Lopez Report, 87, at footnote 348, citing Phillips testimony to HSCA, November 27, 1976, 52-53. Two staff members of the Committee in 1976, Bob Tanenbaum and Gaeton Fonzi, agree that Phillips neither volunteered nor was asked about the alleged information offer in this testimony, largely because questioning focused on Phillips' recent false claim that the tape of "Oswald"'s voice in Mexico City had been destroyed.

[34] David Atlee Phillips, *The Night Watch* (New York: Ballantine, 1987), 181. Phillips' book was written in 1976 and originally published by Atheneum in 1977. Phillips' book is in other details at odds with his accounts elsewhere of the Oswald affair (Phillips, *The Night Watch*, 179; Lopez Report, 127). The book contains additional errors. It claims for example that the false name "Lee Henry Oswald" originated in Mexico City.

[35] Discussion of Phillips' turnaround also in Scott, *Deep Politics*, 121-22; Newman, 376.

[36] Lopez Report, 88; draft of letter from Winston Scott to John Barron, November 25, 1970; cf. 11 AH 488 ("November 28 telegram that Oswald intended to settle down in Odessa"). This draft letter was among the materi-

The House Committee received further corroboration of the assistance request from Mrs. Tarasoff, the translator-typist who had been reported in Ronald Kessler's article as a source for the information offer.

> According to my recollection, I myself, have made a transcript, an English transcript, of Lee Oswald talking to the Russian Consulate or whoever he was at that time, asking for financial aid. Now, that particular transcript does not appear here and whatever happened to it, I do not know, but it was a lengthy transcript and I personally did that transcript. It was a lengthy conversation between him and someone at the Russian Embassy.[37]

As for Oswald's alleged threat to kill Kennedy, the verification of this by Castro, and the Cuban view of this as a provocation (elements #3, #4, and #5), the most authoritative available source (since their release in 1995) are the FBI Solo records. Similar accounts, all mentioning the assassination remarks, and between them adding the verification by Castro to an FBI informant, appeared in the *Washington Post*, the *New York Times*, and the *Los Angeles Times*.[38]

Finally the authors of the House Committee Report confirmed that the substance of these allegations (as discussed in an unofficial, much less reputable version, a tabloid article by the British author Comer Clark) was "supported by highly confidential but reliable sources available to the U.S. Government" (a possible reference to the Solo records and CD 1359).[39] Clark's story had mentioned items #3, #4, and #5: the threat to kill, the verification by Castro, and Castro's determination that this was a CIA provocation.[40]

Unfortunately the so-called Comer Clark version is almost completely lacking in credibility. No one now defends the article's claim to be based on an actual interview with Castro, or disputes Tony Summers' account that it was instead ghosted by Clark's assistant Nina Gadd, allegedly on the basis of a report from a Latin American foreign minister.[41] We shall see that the actual words attributed to Oswald by the falsified "Clark" story -- "Someone ought to shoot that President Kennedy....Maybe I'll try to do it" -- are suspiciously like those attributed to Oswald by another source, the admitted liar Gilberto Alvarado, a Mexico City CIA asset.[42] They are however quite different in tone from the version attributed to Castro in CD 1359 -- "I'm going to kill Kennedy for this."

I now suspect that all of these early stories were deliberate leaks, perhaps by the CIA. What they all have in common is a tendency to misrepresent the remark reported in CD 1359 ("I'm going to kill Kennedy for this") as a "plan," or an "offer," or "intentions," rather than what the transmitter of the remarks took them to be, the stormy response of "a real madman" to an unexpected frustration.[43] This distortion fit the *Washington Post*'s gratuitous innuendos "about a possible involvement of the Castro government in the murder of Kennedy," the *New York Times*'s absurd allegation that, if true, Castro's knowledge of Oswald's "plan...would be the strongest evidence yet found that Mr. Oswald had had Cuban backing in his assassination attempt."[44]

---

als which James Angleton retrieved from Scott's personal safe in Mexico City, at the time of Scott's death. Cf. also Winston Scott's unpublished manuscript, "Foul Foe," quoted in Newman, 369.

[37] A. Tarasoff Testimony, 4/28/78, 6; in Lopez Report, 83; cf. Newman, 370-75. There are no lengthy transcripts in the current official record.

[38] John Goshko, *Washington Post*, November 13, 1976; Nicholas Horrock, *New York Times*, November 14, 1976, 30 (FBI informant, Castro); Norman Kempster, *Los Angeles Times*, November 17, 1976 (FBI informant). For these articles, and for much else in this essay, I am again indebted to Paul Hoch.

[39] AR 122; cf. 3 AH 283; Blakey and Billings, 145-47.

[40] *National Enquirer*, October 15, 1967. Cf. Summers, *Conspiracy*, 389; 3 AH 282-83; AR 122.

[41] *National Enquirer*, October 15, 1967; Summers, *Conspiracy*, 389; 3 AH 282-83; AR 122; Gerald Posner, *Case Closed* (New York: Random House, 1993), 193. For the record, the British author whose name was falsely used on the *Enquirer* story actually spells his name, "Comer Clarke."

[42] "You're not man enough [to kill Kennedy] -- I can do it" (Summers, 440); cf. below.

[43] "Plan:" *New York Times*, November 14, 1976; Comer Clark, *National Enquirer*, October 15, 1967. "Offer;" AP story in *Washington Post*, May 27, 1982; cf. Kelley, *Kelley*, above. "Intentions:" *Washington Post*, November 13, 1976.

[44] *Washington Post*, November 13, 1976; *New York Times*, November 14, 1976.

This survey of the "authorities" behind the Oswald assassination threat forces us to reflect on what we mean by "authority." The dictionary distinguishes between authority which is "conclusive" or "evidentiary," because of its proximity to the claims being made, and authority which is "official" or "governmental." (To the latter category of "authority" we might also add the *Washington Post* and the *New York Times*.)

If we now look at the authoritative sources for the Oswald assassination threat, we see that nearly all are authorities in the second sense. But only those who corroborated the offer of information and request for assistance (items #1 and #2) can be called authorities because of their proximity to the evidence. There is in the public record no such authority for the threat to kill, and only the unsupported word of "Solo" (Jack Childs) for the verification of the threat by Castro.

Of all the various sources for the five elements of the Oswald assassination threat, the closest witness so far mentioned, and also the most interesting, is the Russian translator-typist for the Mexico City CIA station, Mrs. Tarasoff. Taken by itself, her detailed account of the phantom assistance transcript that we do not have is persuasive but not very illuminating. In the context of former FBI Director Kelley's four startling allegations, it is most striking to learn from the sworn testimony of Mrs. Tarasoff (confirming the allegations of three other station members, including Win Scott and David Phillips) that one of them, the request for assistance, was known *and documented* before the assassination. If that document ever existed, it has now for some reason been systematically suppressed.

Did that document exist, and if so where is it now? Perhaps the Review Board can resolve these questions. At a minimum they can give us all the House Committee testimony of David Phillips, Mrs. Tarasoff, and her husband. Mr. Tarasoff added the important and possibly relevant detail that the name of Lee Oswald was known to the CIA station ("they were very hot about the whole thing") *before* he transcribed the October 1 telephone conversation of "someone who identified himself as Lee Oswald."[45]

Assessment of the Oswald Assassination Threat: Evidence and Counter-Evidence

Before assessing whether there ever was in fact anything like the alleged Oswald assassination threat, we must acknowledge the many different levels at which "it" might have happened. Normally an allegation presents a maximum of two levels of verification: a) did the source allege it? and b) did the alleged event occur? Like other aspects of Oswald's alleged career, the story of the assassination threat presents many more levels at which issues of verification occur. For this reason we should perhaps refer to it as a meta-allegation (an allegation where issues of verification occur at more than two levels).

A high percentage of the apparent data about Oswald in the Warren Report dissolve on analysis to meta-allegations. We read for example in the Warren Report that "Marina said that the officials at the Soviet Embassy [in Mexico City] 'refused to have anything to do with [her husband]."[46] In fact Marina Oswald claimed to have heard this from Lee (1 WH 28). Thus we need to verify this meta-allegation on three levels: 1) Did Marina say this? 2) Did Lee say this? 3) Was Lee telling the truth?

An extreme instance is perhaps CD 1359, as originally reconstructed by Daniel Schorr. Schorr's meta-allegation had more layers than an onion: he claimed that Hoover told the Warren Commission that a reliable FBI informant had said that Castro had heard from the Cuban Ambassador in Mexico that Oswald had threatened to kill President Kennedy. As Paul Hoch wrote some years ago, "This issue gets very complicated very fast. If the source says Fidel said it, did Fidel say it? If Fidel said it, did Oswald say it? If Oswald said it, what does that imply -- premeditation, a provocation, or what?"[47] To which we can add one more issue: if someone calling himself Oswald said it,

---

[45] Lopez Report, p. 85; Newman, 371.

[46] WR 734.

[47] Paul Hoch, 4 EOC 3 (1982), 5.

was this person the man arrested in Dallas?

The abundance of corroboration suggests the same conclusion reached by Robert Blakey and Richard Billings, the two authors of the House Committee Report: that there was indeed a pre-assassination event, in the environment of the Cuban Consulate, that gave rise to the story of the Oswald assassination threat. For what it is worth, I suspect that both Castro and the Cuban Ambassador may have heard this report, though what gave rise to it is of course unclear and perhaps unverifiable. As I argued earlier, this is an important issue, and one purpose of this paper is to persuade the Review Board of its importance.

Such a conclusion is a tenuous one. There is counter-evidence, and the affirmative corroboration, though authoritative, is also shaky.

The strongest rebuttal evidence to the story of the assassination threat, as reported through CD 1359, is that Castro himself denied a falsified variant of the story (the Daniel Schorr account of the alleged Comer Clark interview) to the House Committee: "I didn't say that.... It has been invented from the beginning until the end."[48] But as we have seen the alleged assassination remarks in the "Clark" story ("Someone ought to shoot that President Kennedy") are quite different from the "Solo" report. There were obvious political considerations constraining both Castro and his questioners. Castro, as the Committee noted, was clearly concerned that failure to have reported what the "Clark" story spoke of (an intention or "plan to kill President Kennedy") might be taken to "implicate" Cuba in the assassination.[49] Such an implication, however debatable logically, was a legitimate Cuban political concern, based on their reading of the contemporary U.S. press.[50]

But political considerations constrained the House Committee also. Blakey at least knew of CD 1359 and believed it; his book (despite the Castro interview) argued later that "the threat probably did occur."[51] Yet, even though armed with Daniel Schorr's book *Clearing the Air*, the Committee interviewer steered away from Schorr's summary of CD 1359 in his questioning of Castro. Instead he asked Castro to respond to Schorr's summary of the falsified "Comer Clark" tabloid article, fatally misrepresented as a Castro-Clark interview which we now know never occurred.

Thus, when Castro answered, "I didn't say that," he was clearly saying, truly, that he never the words attributed to his interview with Comer Clark.[52] What Castro might have responded to the CD 1359 meta-allegation (that he said something to an FBI informant) is not yet known. Castro might well have denied this also, but so far as we know he was not asked.

I know of no other comparable counter-evidence. The silence of other Consulate witnesses such as Silvia Duran tells us nothing, for we do not know to what audience the threat was allegedly made.

The closest to independent authoritative corroboration is Kelley's carefully worded suggestion that "It is possible to assume that *at the Soviet Embassy* he [Oswald] offered to kill President Kennedy." To my knowledge, no other authoritative source has made this claim; it stands alone. (We shall deal with other, discreditable sources later.)

As stated above, we can be skeptical of Kelley's claims. The fact remains that Kelley is now partially corroborated by the recent release of CD 1359. Furthermore Kelley alleges that the curious claim to know what happened inside both Consulates is based on information "gathered through

---

[48] 3 AH 273; cf. AR 122; 3 AH 273-75; 3 AH 282-84; Blakey and Billings, 145-47.

[49] 3 AH 284; Blakey and Billings, 148.

[50] As noted earlier, Nicholas Horrock's article in the *New York Times* had twisted the story of CD 1359 to precisely this implication: "The informant, according to the memorandum, said that he had learned of Mr. Oswald's plan from Fidel Castro, the Cuban premier. If this were true, it would be the strongest evidence yet found that Mr. Oswald had had Cuban backing in his assassination attempt" (Nicholas Horrock, *New York Times*, November 14, 1976, 30).

[51] Blakey and Billings, 147. Cf. p. 148: "we were inclined to believe that Oswald had uttered the threat attributed to him in the Cuban Consulate." To their credit, Blakey and Billings talk throughout of a "threat," rather than of a "plan" (Horrock) or "offer" (Kelley). The question remains whether Blakey and Billings knew of any other evidence other than CD 1359 and the "Solo" assassination records. The Review Board should ask them about this.

[52] Thus Castro continued: "But how could they interview me in a pizzeria [in Clark's article]. I never go to public restaurants and that man invented that" (3 AH 274).

informants, wiretaps, surveillance cameras, and other types of foreign intelligence techniques" (presumably bugs planted within the embassies).[53]

> The information that Oswald talked to Kostikov at the Russian Embassy was obtained variously. One method was through CIA wiretaps of the embassy's phone in Mexico City. Oswald's call from the Cuban to the Russian Embassy, for instance, was tapped by our government. The Soviet Embassy was also being watched by ultrasensitive CIA surveillance cameras. What's more, the agency had some very highly placed informants within the embassy itself. Thus, the fact that Oswald met with this particularly dangerous KGB official is certain.... It appeared that Oswald confided to the Soviets and the Cubans that he had information on a CIA plot to assassinate Fidel Castro. He would, he promised, provide all of this highly classified information in exchange for Soviet and Cuban visas for his family and himself respectively. It is possible to assume that at the Soviet Embassy he offered to kill President Kennedy....Oswald...told the Cuban Embassy officials much the same. But here he definitely offered to kill President Kennedy.[54]

In other words the FBI Director told the world in 1987 of far more credible sources than "Solo;" CIA HUMINT sources inside the Soviet Embassy, along with unspecified "other types of foreign intelligence techniques." This resolves to a much simpler meta-allegation than Solo's in CD 1359, with the following issues: a) Were there such informants and other sources? b) Did they report an Oswald assassination remark? c) Was the report honest? d) If so, were the remarks genuine or a provocation? e) Last but not least, was this Oswald the man arrested in Dallas?[55]

Kelley's account refers to HUMINT sources (double agents) at the Soviet Embassy only, evading the question of whether they were also at the Cuban Consulate, where he is so much more definite about Oswald's assassination remarks. But in 1967 an internal high-level FBI memorandum also acknowledged special knowledge of what went on in the Cuban Embassy:

> Sensitive and reliable sources of the Bureau and CIA reported Oswald was unknown to Cuban government officials when he visited the Cuban Consulate in Mexico City on 9/27/63, and attempted, without success, to get a visa for travel to Cuba.[56]

These reports themselves are not to be found in the CIA's pre-assassination 201 file on Oswald, nor the FBI Headquarters file. There is no sign that they ever reached either the Warren Commission or the House Committee. The Review Board should search for them, since they are surely assassination-related.

In 1994 we learned from HSCA investigator Edwin Lopez that there were at least two CIA HUMINT sources in the Cuban Embassy, and he himself has pointed to the importance of what they could tell with respect to what they saw and heard about Oswald there, both before and after the assassination.[57]

Edwin Lopez chose his words carefully. Apparently he himself spoke to two of these double agents in Mexico City in 1978, without CIA approval. From them he learned that in the opinion of embassy officials after the assassination, the "Oswald" who visited the Cuban Consulate was not the Oswald arrested in Dallas. The double agents told Lopez

---

[53] Kelley, *Kelley*, 267.

[54] Kelley, *Kelley*, 268-69.

[55] HUMINT sources and/or bugs in the Soviet Embassy would explain the otherwise inexplicable and suspicious claim of a CIA Station officer on October 16, 1963, that she "determined that Oswald had been at the Soviet Embassy" (Memo of 16 October 1963; Lopez Report, 170-72; Scott, *Deep Politics*, 41; Lopez Report Introduction, 12.)

[56] Memo from Rosen to DeLoach, 2/15/67; quoted in Schweiker-Hart Report, 81. The memo was in response to an inquiry from the Secret Service, prompted by columnist Drew Pearson's claim to Chief Justice Warren that Castro had decided in 1963 to retaliate against U.S. government attempts to assassinate him.

[57] Edwin Lopez, "Commentary," in *Lopez Report* (Rogra), 3: "Dan Hardway and I determined that the CIA had some double agents planted in the Cuban Embassy, maybe more. These agents could tell us so much. Did they see Oswald at the Embassy? Did they hear the discussions among the embassy staff after the assassination? What was said? Would it anger you as it did myself to learn that the CIA would not permit us to interview these double agents?"

that the consensus among employees within the Cuban Consulate after the Kennedy assassination was that it wasn't Oswald who had been there. The assets said that they reported that to the Agency but there were no documents in the CIA file noting that fact.[58]

If it is true that the CIA suppressed this report, it is only one more indication that the "Oswald" visit to the Cuban Embassy involved a sensitive Agency secret.

It will not be easy for the Review Board to resolve questions about HUMINT resources. If the informants performed honestly, their cover will not and perhaps should not be broken. But if by any chance we were to learn that the informants invented or transmitted a false report about Oswald, then considerations of national security would seem to demand their interrogation.

This possibility remains hypothetical, and problematic. Even if informants in the Cuban Embassy transmitted the assassination threat story, this still would not explain the "Solo" report in CD 1359. For this they would have had to report the assassination remarks, not just to the Americans, but to the Cubans as well.

But we have now to consider that, in addition to the authoritative sources for the Oswald assassination offer or threat, there are other sources, much less credible. Of these discreditable sources, one at least (Gilberto Alvarado) soon confessed he was lying.

Even lies, when we know their sources, can tell us something. We shall see that there is a common denominator to the discreditable sources: their common links to the Mexico City CIA station, and above all to the propaganda networks of David Phillips.

Was the story of the Oswald assassination remark (whether or not Oswald actually made it) a propaganda operation from the outset? If it were, then we cannot rule out that CIA resources in the two Consulates were part of that operation.

Discreditable Sources: The Oswald Assassination Remark and the Network of David Phillips

Kelley was not the first to claim publicly that Oswald made remarks about assassinating Kennedy in the Cuban Embassy. We have seen that a similar claim appeared in the *National Enquirer* in 1967, under the name of Comer Clark, but actually ghosted by his assistant Nina Gadd on the basis of a report from a Latin American foreign minister.[59]

A similar claim was put forward in 1975 by a prominent anti-Castro Cuban, Ernesto Rodriguez, who said he was a former CIA contract agent in Mexico City. According to a 1975 news account of Rodriguez' story, "'Oswald' told both the Soviets and Cubans that he had information on a new CIA attempt to kill Fidel Castro. Oswald offered more information, said Rodriguez, in exchange for a Cuban entry visa."[60] Rodriguez' account, however, was implausible: he claimed that Oswald had talked about this on the telephone, to local reporters, and even with Fair Play for Cuba Committee members in Mexico City.[61]

---

[58] Fonzi, *The Last Investigation*, 293-94. The presence of HUMINT assets and/or bugs inside the Cuban Consulate would appear to explain some of the extensive redactions in the released Lopez Report. It may also help explain the astonishing footnote 319 to the Report, on page A-23. This refers to a call between "a woman named Silvia" and a Consulate employee named Guillermo Ruiz (the cousin of Alpha 66 leader Antonio Veciana, another CIA asset). Silvia asks Ruiz for the Consul's telephone number, and "Ruiz says that the number is 11-28-47." This number, which critics had hitherto assumed to be the publicly available one, is the number for the Cuban Consulate entered with Duran's name in Oswald's address book (16 WH 54). If it was publicly available, it is hard to understand why Silvia Duran would have had to telephone Ruiz to obtain it.

[59] *National Enquirer*, October 15, 1967; Summers, *Conspiracy*, 389; 3 AH 282-83; AR 122; Gerald Posner, *Case Closed* (New York: Random House, 1993), 193.

[60] Summers, *Conspiracy*, 389; citing *Dallas Morning News*, September 24, 1975 (reprinting a *Los Angeles Times* story by Charles Ashman).

[61] Ibid.

We learn less from the content of this story than from its sources. If Ernesto Rodriguez was truly a former CIA contract agent in Mexico City, then he presumably worked under the Mexico City Station's Chief of Cuban Operations, who in 1963 was the noted propaganda expert David Phillips. Meanwhile the author who broke the Rodriguez story was Charles Ashman, who before being disbarred had been the lawyer and publicist for the anti-Castro activities of Sam Benton and Gerry Patrick Hemming.[62] Thus Ashman was not at arm's length from the strange narrative of Oswald's life: both Hemming and Benton were associated with the Lake Pontchartrain arms cache and training camp which Oswald apparently attempted to penetrate in August 1963.[63]

Ashman's story, at best a dubious one, does not stand alone. At noon on November 25, 1963, three days after the assassination, a full and detailed account of an offer by Oswald in the Cuban Consulate to assassinate Kennedy was provided to the U.S. Embassy in Mexico City by an alleged eyewitness. (The timing is important, since Oswald's visit to Mexico did not become public knowledge before the evening edition of the Mexican newspaper *Excelsior* on November 24. If the story was a spur-of-the-moment low-level fabrication, as is often assumed, the fabricator must have acted swiftly.)

The alleged eyewitness was a Nicaraguan, Gilberto Alvarado, who was later identified in a belatedly published Warren Commission memorandum as "a 23-year-old Nicaraguan secret agent."[64] (Contemporary FBI documents refer to Alvarado as a "source of CIA's" or "CIA source.")[65] Chronologically Alvarado is in fact the first known published source for two of the ingredients of the Oswald assassination offer as narrated by Kelley: he offered to kill Kennedy inside the Cuban Consulate, and he did so in exchange for something: not visas (as Kelley claimed) but cash. In Alvarado's account, a Cuban in the consulate passed some money to "a tall, this Negro with reddish hair....The Negro then allegedly said to Oswald in English, 'I want to kill the man.' Oswald replied, 'You're not man enough, I can do it.'...The Negro then gave Oswald $6,500 in large-denomination American bills."[66]

David Phillips admitted in his book that he was one of the two CIA agents assigned to interrogate Alvarado, and he added, deceptively, that "It was soon apparent that he was lying."[67] It was certainly not apparent in the CIA Station cables that we have (some are still withheld) and that David Phillips presumably drafted (the other interviewer, Eldridge Snight, was the Embassy Security Officer). One cable described Alvarado as a "well-known Nicaraguan Communist underground member" (when in fact he was anti-Communist).[68] A second cable on November 27, by which time Alvarado had "admitted he really on penetration mission for Nicaraguan secret service," still described Alvarado as a "quiet, very serious person, who speaks with conviction."[69] A third cable called him "completely cooperative."[70] A fourth cable reported that the CIA officer interviewing Alvarado "was impressed...wealth of detail Alvarado gives is striking."[71] As late as November 29, a station officer, described by his chief as "very intelligent," was inclined to believe "Alvarado telling truth in general outline," but "mixed up on dates."[72]

---

[62] Hinckle and Turner, *The Fish Is Red*, 163-64, 212.

[63] Scott, *Deep Politics*, 88-89; Newman, 319 (Hemming).

[64] 11 AH 162; Coleman-Slawson memorandum (published by the House Committee in 1978).

[65] 3 AH 595 (FBI memo of December 12, 1963); Mexico City FBI serial MC 105-3702-22 (Legat Cable to HQ of November 26, 1963).

[66] WR 307-08.

[67] David Phillips, *The Night Watch*, 182.

[68] WCD 1000A. In his book Phillips claimed a CIA cable from Managua said that "the Nicaraguan intelligence service had identified the walk-in as a prominent Nicaraguan Communist" (p. 182). The Managua cable we have says the opposite, that he was an informant of the Nicaraguan security service (MANAGUA cable of 26 November, 262237Z; cf. DIR 85196 of 27 November 1963).

[69] WCD 1000B.4; CIA-52 of 26 November 1963; retransmitted as DIR 85199 of 27 November 1963, CIA Doc. # 136-55.

[70] WCD 1000C.2.

[71] MEXI 7104 of 27 November, CIA Doc. #174-616.

[72] MEXI 7156 of 29 November 1963, CIA Doc. #260-670. The name of the station officer is redacted. It should now be released.

Alvarado's wealth of detail *was* striking. Far more fully than has ever been publicly acknowledged, some of this young man's elaborate particulars ("a tall thin Negro with reddish hair," a blonde-haired hippie with a Canadian passport, a girl called "Maria Luisa" with the address Calle Juarez 407 who gave Oswald an embrace) were corroborated by what other communications intelligence or COMINT sources (i.e. intercepts) and human intelligence or HUMINT sources told the Mexico City CIA station.[73] These complex, recurring details are less interesting than their sources, to which we shall return.

There were however two problems with Alvarado's story. The first was the date, September 17 or 18, on which he claimed to have seen Oswald at the Cuban consulate. Fairly soon the FBI had established Oswald's entry into Mexico on September 26, which would have implied two separate trips by Oswald to Mexico City.[74] But for some time after that, the FBI had no information on the date of Oswald's departure from New Orleans.[75] By the time of the Warren Report, that date had been fixed at September 25, with many witnesses. These witnesses are however far more problematic than the Report let on. For example it stated that a neighbor saw Oswald leave his apartment "on the evening of September 24."[76] In fact the neighbor, Eric Rogers, gave no precise date in September. And when shown a famous photograph of Oswald handing out one of his FPCC leaflets (20 WH 4), Rogers answered, "I never saw this man" (11 WH 464).[77]

But by November 30 there was a much better reason for disbelieving Alvarado: on that day he himself "admitted in writing that his whole narrative about Oswald was false."[78] Not that that ended the matter. Alvarado's recantation was made to the FBI, who by then were firmly committed to the phase-two theory of Oswald as a lone assassin. On December 3 Alvarado (now in the hands of the pro-conspiratorialist Mexican Gobernación) recanted his recantation, "asserting that it had been extorted from him under pressure."[79] On December 5, Alvarado was re-interviewed yet again and polygraphed under the guidance of an officer from CIA Headquarters (over-riding the local CIA station), with the FBI Legal Attache acting as interpreter. Told that he had failed the polygraph, the hapless Alvarado "stated that he had heard of the polygraph and respected its accuracy. He added that if the polygraph indicated he was lying, then it must be so."[80]

In short, we have from Alvarado a bizarre story, scripted with precise gothic details (such as the red-haired negro and blonde-haired hippie) that are so weird they sound as if they had been deliberately crafted for what they soon received -- corroboration. And yet the Alvarado story was given the highest level of attention by the U.S. Ambassador in Mexico (Thomas Mann), the Station Chief (Win Scott) and even the FBI Legal Attache (Clark Anderson). Anderson's support is the most eloquent, since by this time his boss, J. Edgar Hoover, was already irrevocably committed to the phase-two lone assassin theory.

---

[73] DIR 85199 of 27 November 1963; Memo of 25 November 1963 from CIA Station employee (CIA-40); Memo of 29 November 1963 from CIA Station to Legal Attache (CIA 491); Coleman-Slawson memo, 11 AH 162-63 (details); 3 AH 297, 300; Lopez Report, 213, etc. (corroboration).

[74] Eventually there were reports, from as high as Ambassador Mann, that Oswald *had* made two trips to Mexico (Russell, 370-71). But these reports may indicate nothing more than their sources continued belief in the Alvarado story.

[75] WCD 205, 23 WH 302.

[76] WR 730 at footnote 1107, citing 11 WH 460-64 (Eric Rogers). Rogers was the penultimate alleged witness of Oswald in New Orleans; the last, a busdriver, was "uncertain of the exact date" (WR 730).

[77] In all Rogers was shown three pictures of Oswald leafleting in New Orleans, and denied seeing Oswald in any of them. There are other alleged witnesses, and still other problems with them.

[78] WR 308. Cf. MEXI 7168 of 30 Nov 1963; CIA Doc. #261-99.

[79] Helms letter of 4 June 1964 to Rankin of Warren Commission, 26 WH 858; Birch D. O'Neal Memo for the Record of 3 December 1963, CIA Doc. #287-690 (Info via Papich from the FBI).

[80] WCD 78.5; cf. MEXI 7324 of 10 Dec 1963. On December 3 the CIA in Mexico City, who earlier had vigorously promoted Alvarado's story of an assassination offer, requested authority to re-interview him, but was told to defer to the officer arriving from Headquarters (MEXI 7229 of 3 Dec 63, CIA Doc. #284-688; DIR 86659 of 4 Dec 63, CIA Doc. #291-695).

A cable from the three men on November 26 shows how far they were willing to go in support of the Alvarado story:

> We suggest that the Nicaraguan be put at the disposition of President Lopez Mateos on condition that Lopez Mateos will agree to order rearrest and interrogate again Silvia Tirado de Duran along following lines:
>
> A. Confront Silvia Duran again with Nicaraguan and have Nicaraguan inform her of details of his statement to us.
>
> B. Tell Silvia Duran that she is only living non-Cuban who knows full story and hence she is in same position as Oswald was prior to his assassination; her only chance for survival is to come clean with whole story and to cooperate completely....
>
> Given apparent character of Silvia Duran there would appear to be good chance of her cracking when confronted with details of reported deal between Oswald, Azcue, Mirabal [the two Cuban consuls mentioned by Alvarado] and Duran and the unknown Cuban negro [described by Alvarado]. If she did break under interrogation -- and we suggest Mexicans should be asked to go all out in seeing that she does -- we and Mexicans would have needed corroboration of statement of the Nicaraguan.[81]

Mann on his own went on to recommend the arrest of three Cuban members of the Cuban consulate, and later to argue forcefully that Castro was the "kind of person who would avenge himself" by assassination.[82]

These cables were in defiant opposition to the cooler approach in Washington. Headquarters had already tried to oppose the original arrest of Duran, rightly fearing that the arrest (and interrogation by the Mexican secret police, or DFS) "could jeopardize U.S. freedom of action on the whole question of Cuban responsibility."[83] Headquarters replied again to the new Duran cable, warning the Station Chief that the Ambassador was pushing the case too hard, and his proposals could lead to an international "flap" with the Cubans.[84]

Yet on the basis of the Alvarado story, Silvia Duran was rearrested, against clear orders, twice repeated, from CIA Headquarters.[85] In analyzing this strong and provocative response, we must mention that two details of the Alvarado story (the money, and the contact with "Maria Luisa," whom he identified from a photograph as Embassy official Luisa Calderon) appeared to have superficial corroboration from telephonic intercepts at the time.[86] That corroboration was however so weak (and soon demolished) that we must ask if there was not some other, unmentionable reason why the three men believed so strongly in the reality of the Oswald assassination offer.

Especially so, because the CIA interest in the Alvarado story escalated, even after Alvarado recanted it on November 30. Around December 5 CIA Director McCone told Gerald Ford, newly appointed to the Warren Commission, "that CIA had uncovered some 'startling information'...a source of CIA's in Mexico had seen money exchange hands between Oswald and an unknown Cuban Negro."[87] Also on December 5 Senator Russell wrote a memo about his discussion with Earl Warren

---

[81] MEXI 7072 of 26 November 1963, CIA Document #128-590. The CIA Station Chief, two months earlier, had signed off on a description of the Federal Security Police (DFS) who interviewed Duran, "as being dishonest, cruel, and abusive" (Appendix to HMMA 22267 of October 8, 1963; Project Report for September 1963). In effect the three men were proposing that Duran be tortured to obtain the story of the assassination offer. My understanding is that she was tortured.

[82] MEXI 7104 of 27 November 1963; MEXI cable of November 28 1963, Anthony Summers, *Conspiracy*, 441. Cf. 3 AH 569.

[83] DIR 84916 of 23 November; Lopez Report, 185-86; Schweiker-Hart Report, 25.

[84] DIR 85371 of 28 November 1963; Lopez Report, 187; Schweiker-Hart Report, 29.

[85] Win Scott claimed to Headquarters that the second arrest was made on a Mexican Government initiative "without prior consultation with Station" (MEXI 7118 of 28 November 1963). Informed observers find this extremely unlikely.

[86] Luisa Calderon talked of the assassination as if she might (by one controversial interpretation) have had foreknowledge (AR 254, 4 AH 181, 11 AH 494); the Cuban Ambassador had spoken to Cuban President Dorticos about money (MEXI 7068 of 26 November 1963; cf. MEXI 7072 of 26 November, MEXI 7104 of 27 November, 11 AH 489).

[87] FBI Memo of December 12, 1963, 3 AH 595; Scott, *Deep Politics*, 122. Alvarado retracted his story on No-

("I told of Mexico & Nicaraguan *NOT mentioning sums*") based on information from McCone which made Russell characterize Warren's push for a lone assassin as an "untenable position."[88]

By December 5 the Alvarado story, already well recanted, had gathered additional corroboration. On December 2, before any of Alvarado's story had gone outside intelligence circles, another informant, Pedro Gutierrez, repeated the detail of seeing Oswald receive money at the Cuban Consulate from someone "almost of 'negroid' type kinky hair."[89]

Belated corroboration continued to drift in. In April 1964 an important defector from the Cuban DGI, AMMUG-1, told the CIA that Oswald "might have had contact" (i.e. "been involved") with Luisa Calderon, previously identified by Alvarado as Oswald's familiar and possibly sexual companion.[90] A different version of Oswald's alleged sexual liaison, as reported in 1965, linked Oswald to the same two striking companions as did Alvarado: "a Latin American negro man with red hair" and someone with "long blond hair."[91] (It would be important to ascertain whether these details were part of the Oswald sex story originally reported to the CIA station in 1964 by an important "witting" source, June Cobb.)[92]

The corroboration we have mentioned so far is all post-assassination. There is no pre-assassination corroboration, unless we believe the second and belated version of Silvia Odio's problematic story in Dallas. In mid-December 1963 Silvia Odio told the FBI that on September 26, 1963, one day before the official date of Oswald's first visit to the Cuban Consulate, she had heard that the "Leon Oswald" who had visited her in Dallas the evening before had said, "[Cubans] don't have any guts....President Kennedy should have been assassinated after the Bay of Pigs, and some Cubans should have done that, because he was the one that was holding the freedom of Cuba."[93] (This second version of the Odio story, reproduced in the Warren Report, supplanted an earlier and quite different one: "that she knew Oswald, and that he had made some talks to small groups of Cuban refugees in Dallas in the past.)"[94]

The language of Odio's second Oswald story -- where Oswald allegedly said Cubans "don't have any guts" -- is arrestingly similar to what Alvarado claimed Oswald said in the Cuban Consulate, on September 18, 1963: "You're not man enough -- I can do it [kill the man]."[95] It is also close to the words later attributed to Oswald in the falsified "Comer Clark" story -- "Someone ought to shoot that President Kennedy....Maybe I'll try to do it" -- that may have been planted by the CIA.

There are two opposing ways to interpret this similarity between the Odio story and the two other Oswald stories. One can see it as corroboration of all three stories, because the sources are so

---

vember 30. We do not yet know if CIA Director McCone told President Johnson this when he discussed Alvarado with him on November 30 and December 1 (Schweiker-Hart Report, 103. An LBJ-McCone telephone transcript at 3:14 PM November 30 is withheld on grounds of national security). No matter: by November 29 Lyndon Johnson had announced the formation of the Warren Commission.

[88] Sen. Richard Russell, Memorandum of 5 December 1963, Russell Memorial Library, University of Georgia; quoted in Dick Russell, *The Man Who Knew Too Much*, 500.

[89] WCD 566.6-7; cf. 24 WH 634.

[90] CIA-295; CIA Doc. #687-295; 11 AH 496 (AMMUG-1). Alvarado reportedly both identified a photograph of Calderon and heard her name as "Maria Luisa" (MEXI dispatch of 5 December 1963, CIA Doc. #310-702; CIA memo of 13 December 1963; CIA Doc. #399-747).

[91] 3 AH 300, Memo of conversation with Elena Garro de Paz; cf. Lopez Report, 217.

[92] Lopez Report, 207-09; citing CIA memo of 10/12/64; 3 AH 286-87 ("Miss Y"); CIA-393. Because June Cobb was an early CIA source corroborating Oswald's alleged sexual activity in Mexico City, this memo and perhaps any government document concerning her should probably be considered "assassination-related" under the terms of the JFK Act. These documents would include 1) her work in penetrating and discrediting the Fair Play for Cuba Committee, 2) her successful penetration of Fidel Castro's entourage in 1959, allegedly at the same time as Marita Lorenz (see Cobb's testimony on March 30, 1962, before the Senate Internal Security Subcommittee, published in 1966; cf. Marita Lorenz, *Marita* [New York: Thunder's Mouth, 1994], 17-18); Newman, 106-12, 237-44, 301-02, 378-84.

[93] Blakey and Billings, 163; cf. WR 321-24.

[94] 26 WH 738; Scott, *Deep Politics*, 118.

[95] Summers (1980), 440; citing 25 WH 647. The similarity between WCD 1359 and the Alvarado story is noticed by Epstein, *Legend*, 325 (cf. 238).

widely scattered and probably did not know each other. Alternatively, one can see the Odio story of mid-December 1963, followed by the Solo story of June 1964, as belated efforts to revive the phase-one Alvarado disinformation, after the hapless Alvarado had himself recanted it.

Two Alternative Hypotheses

Why did the bizarre Alvarado story, so swiftly recanted, dominate the responses of the U.S. Embassy in Mexico to the Kennedy assassination? And why was it accompanied and followed by so much detailed corroboration? If these two questions could be resolved, it would tell us much about the relationship of the CIA to the assassination.

Coincidence will not account for all of these events. It might appear that we are forced to choose between one of the two following alternatives, each of which is awkward to the notion of Oswald as a lone assassin:

1) There was never any Oswald assassination remark. In this case the only non-conspiratorial explanation is that all the allegations of such a remark are totally but separately false, and no more than individual propaganda efforts to implicate, not just Oswald, but Cuba and/or the Soviet Union in the assassination. PROBLEM: If the story was false, why did the Embassy back it so strongly, to the point (as Washington recognized) of risking war against Cuba?

2) There was in fact an Oswald assassination threat. In this case CD 1359 may be true, and it is imperative to establish whether the threat was made from personal motives, or as part of a CIA provocation. PROBLEM: If Oswald's motivation was personal, why did the FBI suppress the only known instance where Oswald, described by others as an admirer of Kennedy, in fact proposed to kill him?[96]

These two alternatives (that there was, or was not, an assassination remark) might seem to exhaust the factual possibilities. I would like however to propose a different perspective, looking at the reported allegation, rather than the alleged event, as the key issue. This is based on the hint in Kelley's book, that the story of the Oswald assassination assassination remark in Mexico was based on HUMINT and other hitherto unrevealed intelligence resources (presumably bugs) in the Embassies.

From this perspective, we come up with two different alternative hypotheses, either of which would be highly pertinent to the assassination conspiracy.

3) Whatever the facts, the *appearance* of an Oswald assassination remark had been created prior to the assassination, had become a part of CIA records, and was believed by U.S. authorities. This appearance could have been created

    a) by Oswald himself (the man arrested in Dallas), OR
    b) by someone else, not Oswald, who identified himself as Oswald, OR
    c) by HUMINT or other sources, reporting such a remark to both their Cuban (or Soviet) and American superiors.

This possibility, I submit, is no more bizarre than the facts it is trying to explain. It has the merit of rationalizing the response of the U.S. Embassy to the outlandish Alvarado: they attributed to the implausible Alvarado a story which they in fact believed to be true, from other sources, which they were not able to name even in secret cable traffic.

---

[96] Those who spoke of Oswald's admiration for Kennedy included his wife Marina, other relatives, and even the New Orleans policeman who interviewed him after his arrest: WR 627, 2 AH 209, 217, 252 (Marina), 10 WH 60 (Martello), 12 AH 361, 413; Summers (1980), 129-30.

This would be, it appears, a standard intelligence procedure. It is now conceded that the court record of the Rosenberg treason trial was a substitute for the intercepted Soviet cable traffic which actually led to their conviction.[97] The CIA itself sought to establish from the testimony of Silvia Duran allegations which it had first learned from (what it did not wish to mention) the intercepts of Cuban and Soviet telephone conversations.[98] And the House Committee Report, in dealing with the important but sensitive matter of the Oswald assassination threat, completely ignored CD 1359 (of which the Committee had knowledge). Instead (even in the important Castro deposition) they discussed the almost worthless Comer Clark tabloid article, based on an alleged "interview" which never occurred. Alvarado may have been a similar stand-in for the true source of the Oswald assassination remarks: the Embassy knew that the man was not credible, but had reason to believe that the remarks had occurred.

But the publication of the Solo records has encouraged me on reflection to take more seriously a fourth possibility:

4) Solo was used after the assassination to create the appearance of an Oswald remark, in order to rationalize the CIA Station's incongruous backing of the Alvarado story. The belated timing of the Solo story (June 1964) encourages this interpretation. By then Warren Commission counsels Coleman and Slawson had compiled an extensive memorandum on the possibility of a foreign conspiracy, in which the glaring problems with Alvarado's story were thoroughly examined.[99] It is unlikely that the FBI would have asked Solo to corroborate Alvarado. But the CIA may have used Solo to make their brief backing of the Alvarado story look less unprofessional. Here again the moving force may have been David Phillips, who appears to have been both Alvarado's strongest CIA backer and (as we have seen), a probable source for other false and/or unsupported stories about Oswald in Mexico City. If this version is correct, then the CIA may have been the source behind the "foreign minister" to whom the Comer Clark version of the Solo story was attributed. If a CIA connection to Solo is ever established, this fourth possibility will have been corroborated. And this would increase the chances that the CIA (perhaps even Phillips) had been behind the December revision of Odio's story as well.

What is important here is that both of these alternative hypotheses suggest substantive misrepresentations by of the CIA of the truth concerning Oswald. And either the third or the fourth hypothesis would help to explain the ever-industrious, ever-shifting representations and misrepresentations of David Phillips. One can imagine that his constant purpose underlying his many shifting positions was to protect what was, in his view, a legitimate CIA secret, whether or not it was related to the assassination.

Consider the various phases of Phillips' activity:

1) His early promotion of the Alvarado story (understandable, if he considered Alvarado to be no more than a substitute source for an earlier story he believed true).

2) His claim to the *Washington Post* in 1976 that Oswald offered information to the *Soviet* Embassy (thus deflecting attention away from the first news stories, less than two weeks earlier, about the alleged Cuban assassination threat in CD 1359).[100]

3) Both his news story and his quite different book account of Oswald in Mexico can be seen as propaganda efforts to steer the House Committee, then just constituted, away from the

[97] David Martin, *Wilderness of Mirrors*, 42; Scott, *Deep Politics*, 66, 324.

[98] DIR 85245 of 27 November 1963; cf. DIR 90466 of 20 December 1963; Lopez Report, 188; 11 AH 485-87. We have already seen that Win Scott and Thomas Mann hoped to have Duran provide the substance of the Alvarado version of the assassination offer as well (MEXI 7072 of 26 November 1963).

[99] 11 AH 162-63.

[100] To recapitulate the dates given above: the stories of Oswald's Cuban assassination threat appeared on November 13, 14, and 17, 1976; Phillips' story appeared on November 26, 1976.

sensitive area of the Alvarado and Solo stories.[101]

Finally the third alternative hypothesis has the merit of rationalizing the CIA Station's extraordinary and provocative performance with respect to photos they have failed to supply of Oswald at the two Consulates, as well as the misleading photos they supplied of someone else (the alleged "mystery man," who in fact may have had little or nothing to do with the case). This is just what we might expect from the CIA, if there had been an Oswald assassination "offer," or "threat," made or reported as part of an intelligence operation by someone who was not Oswald.[102] In like fashion it would rationalize the extensive misreporting by the CIA with respect to the missing tapes of "Oswald"'s voice.[103]

I will conclude by repeating that an Oswald assassination threat, even if not sincere but part of an intelligence operation, may have had some quite different goal in mind than the assassination of the President. As suggested at the outset, the alleged assassination threat may have been a spurious event, falsely reported, as part of an intelligence propaganda operation (against the FPCC) or counterintelligence operation (to trace if this false report was transmitted by a mole). In this case the operation may conceivably have been no more than a convenient event exploited by others with more sinister motives.

Thus to establish the origin and nature of that pre-assassination operation would not necessarily supply us with the names of conspirators against Kennedy. It would however be an important step in establishing how that conspiracy was constructed.

Alternatively, if the Solo story was a post-assassination disinformation product, the authors of that disinformation would appear to have been involved in a possibly criminal obstruction of justice.

---

[101] The HSCA Report (AR 103-29), and for that matter even the Lopez Report, are totally silent about the Alvarado and Solo stories, even though both reports purport to focus on Oswald's dealings with the Cuban Consulate in Mexico City. The HSCA Report does not even mention Kostikov when discussing the KGB (AR 99-103).

[102] For the now hoary question of the "mystery man" photos, see Lopez Report, 12-52, 91-115, 137-42; Scott, *Deep Politics*, 42-44; Lopez Report Introduction, 5, 8-11; Summers, *Conspiracy* (1980), 366-92, etc.

[103] Lopez Report, 162-70; Scott, *Deep Politics*, 42-44; Lopez Report Introduction, 5, 11-14; Summers, *Conspiracy* (1980), 366-92.

IX. OSWALD, HOSTY AND MASEN: WAS OSWALD AN FBI INFORMANT?

(November 1994)

Most people now recognize that, in the public response to the Kennedy assassination (or what I have called the dialectical cover-up), a number of false or misleading leads linking Oswald to Moscow or Cuba (what I have called phase-one stories) were effaced and replaced by a new phase-two story: that Oswald was a lone assassin. The record shows that this story was preferred by those in power, not because it was true, but because it was less likely to lead this country into a groundless war.

In my discussion of this phase-one/phase-two dialectic in *Deep Politics*, I failed to address the complicating detail that not all of the phase-one stories were wholly false; some of them, even if misleading, were in a limited sense true. Since then I have analysed some of these true phase-one stories, which collectively suggest that Oswald was indeed an agent operating under a hidden agenda. More likely, however, he was an agent or informant working, not for Moscow, Havana, or Peking, but for some U.S. agency.

I wish here to discuss three linked allegations, possibly true, that were lost sight of because discussion was pre-empted by later similar but false stories emanating from disinformation sources. These allegations are that Oswald knew Ruby, that he had had contact with the Dallas FBI shortly before the assassination, and that he was an FBI informant.

Clearly baseless versions of all three stories circulated vigorously a few days after the assassination. Effective refutation of the false stories (e.g., that Oswald was Ruby's illegitimate son)[1] prevented the public from learning, or remembering, earlier versions of these three claims that deserved to be taken seriously, and have never been properly refuted.

A very early, credible, and corroborated story that Oswald knew Ruby was finally published in August 1994 by Ray and Mary La Fontaine in the *Washington Post*. According to the story, a cellmate of Oswald's on November 22, John Elrod, had told the Memphis Sheriff's office in August 1964 that he had information on Oswald's murder. Oswald, he said, had told him of a business meeting in a motel room some days earlier with four men, one of whom had been Jack Ruby. Elrod's story was ignored after the FBI supplied the Sheriff's Office with his FBI arrest record, which "showed Elrod had been arrested five times -- but not on Nov. 22, 1963." It remained in limbo until the release of Dallas Police Department files in 1992, which "confirmed that Elrod *was* in the Dallas City Jail on the day of the assassination."[2]

Why might officials (in either the FBI or possibly the Dallas Police Department) have misrepresented Elrod's arrest record? The answer may lie in Elrod's claim that in the jail he and Oswald had seen another of the men from the business meeting with Ruby: a man with an injured face, who had driven a Thunderbird loaded with guns. The La Fontaines noted that these details dovetailed neatly with a Dallas story of two arrests on stolen gun charges four nights before the assassination. In the course of these arrests, made after a tip-off from an unknown informant, Dallas police retrieved high-powered rifles from a blue Thunderbird that had crashed after a high-speed chase which injured the car's occupants. One of the two injured men, Lawrence Miller, was indeed in the Dallas jail when Elrod claimed to have seen him.

The La Fontaines in their article asked, "Is it possible that Lee Oswald was the informant who tipped off the FBI about the gun deal of Nov. 18, 1963?" In support of this possibility, they note that the FBI file on one of the suspects in the case, John Thomas Masen, was charged to the same FBI agent, James P. Hosty, who was also responsible for investigating Lee Harvey Oswald. Hosty's name, phone number and license plate appeared in Oswald's address book under the date of "Nov. 1, 1963," the day of an internal FBI memo in which Hosty was charged to investigate Masen. Hosty

[1] 25 WH 166.

[2] *Washington Post*, August 7, 1994, C6.

spent the morning of November 22, 1963, discussing the case with an ATF Agent, Frank Ellsworth, who later gave information to the Warren Commission staff about the Kennedy assassination.[3] Shortly after Oswald was murdered by Ruby on November 24, Hosty, acting on orders from his superiors, destroyed a note that Oswald had left him in the FBI office one or two weeks earlier.

On a different level, the La Fontaines noted that there was only one gun store in Dallas where Oswald could have purchased the specially loaded Mannlicher-Carcano ammunition which allegedly killed the President -- the gun shop of John Thomas Masen.

The public record adds two further large reasons for suspecting that Oswald may have been the informant on the Masen case. One is the anti-Castro Cuban connection. Masen, a gun dealer, was amassing weapons to sell to anti-Castro Cubans in Dallas; and he supplied the names of two of his Cuban buyers to Frank Ellsworth, who later transmitted them to the Secret Service and the Warren Commission. Of the two Cubans, one, Manuel Rodriguez Orcarberro, was the leader of the local chapter of one of the most anti-Kennedy Cuban exile terrorist groups, Alpha 66.[4]

The FBI subsequently learned from Rodriguez that SNFE-Alpha 66 meetings took place in Dallas at the address 3126 Hollandale, an address that has been confirmed by researchers in Dallas such as Mary Ferrell.[5] This address, slightly garbled, had been linked to Oswald's activities in Dallas by a Deputy Sheriff, E.R. "Buddy" Walthers, the day after the assassination. In a memo of that date, Walthers reported:

> About 8:00 am this morning, while in the presents of [deputy sheriff] Allen Sweatt, I talked to Sorrels the head of the Dallas Secreat [sic] Service. I advised him that for the past few months at a house at 3128 Harlendale some Cubans had been having meetings on the weekends and were possibly connected with the 'Freedom For Cuba Party' of which Oswald was a member.[6]

Three days later, Walthers reported that he had learned the Cubans had just moved, adding that "My informant stated that Oswald had been to this house before."[7]

This intriguing allegation about Oswald must be added to the many that were never refuted, thanks to everyone else's striking lack of interest. Sorrels attended Oswald's final interview on November 24, but by all accounts failed to bring up anything about the alleged "Freedom for Cuba Party." Both Sorrels and Walthers were interviewed extensively by the Warren Commission, the former twice, but their alleged encounter on November 23 was not explored with either man.[8]

The claim that Oswald had joined the "Freedom for Cuba Party" is certainly plausible, for Oswald was an inveterate joiner, or would-be joiner, of widely dispersed and indeed incompatible political movements. In New Orleans Oswald not only joined the Fair Play for Cuba Committee (FPCC), he even organized his own one-member chapter.[9] In 1956, just before his 17th birthday and only three weeks before enlisting in the Marines, Oswald had written to the (democratic) Socialist Party of America, enquiring how to join.[10] After his return in 1962 from the Soviet Union, Oswald initiated correspondence with the Communist Party (CPUSA), its antagonist the Trotskyite Socialist Workers' Party (SWP), and the splinter Socialist Labor Party (SLP).[11]

Oswald's interest in all these groups can hardly have been sympathetic: it is more likely that he was a pawn in some larger investigative project. In the end his courtship of these groups brought them nothing but embarrassment; and Oswald's embrace of the FPCC in particular proved deadly.

---

[3] Also at the meeting was an Army counterintelligence officer, Edward J. Coyle.

[4] WCD 853a; WCD 1085 U.4.

[5] WCD 1085 U.4.

[6] 19 WH 534.

[7] Ibid.

[8] Allen Sweatt, the third man reportedly present, was not interviewed at all.

[9] WR 407-08.

[10] WR 681; 25 WH 140-41.

[11] WR 287-89. The CPUSA and the SWP were the two groups which the FBI suspected of controlling the FPCC at one point (17 WH 774).

Because of Oswald the group dissolved after the assassination, but from the outset Oswald's behavior was demonstrably hostile. In New Orleans, soliciting members for the FPCC, some of Oswald's handbills encouraged them to write to 544 Camp Street, the address of the anti-Communist private investigator and FBI contact Guy Banister.[12]

Oswald planned to play the same dubious role of self-appointed political organizer in Dallas as well. Although the SWP declined to accept his application in October 1962 to join the party, Oswald proceeded to act as if he represented it.[13] Having obtained for himself a Dallas P.O. Box, # 2915, he prepared to invite SWP potential members to write to it, the stratagem he employed later with the FPCC in New Orleans. He drew up the following statement: "Join the Socialist Workers Party. Fight for a Better World! Write Box 2915, Dallas, Texas."[14] It is not known whether Oswald actually published this appeal.

In New Orleans Oswald prepared a similar membership appeal for the FPCC ("Join the Fair Play for Cuba Committee"), and directed applicants at different times to three different addresses: the 544 Camp Street address of Guy Banister, his home address of 4907 Magazine Street, and "P.O. Box 30016, New Orleans" (his actual P.O. Box was 30061).[15]

Back in Dallas, Oswald was apparently appointing himself to act in similar fashion on behalf of the American Civil Liberties Union (ACLU), a group he visited precisely once and then left, telling his companion Michael Paine that "it wasn't political" and he couldn't join it.[16] Before even joining the ACLU, Oswald applied for yet another P.O. Box in Dallas on November 1, 1963, telling the Post Office the box would be for the use of the Fair Play for Cuba Committee (which had no Dallas chapter) and the American Civil Liberties Union (which had as yet no knowledge of his interest in them).[17] Oswald also sent a membership check to the New York Headquarters office of the ACLU which apparently arrived there on November 4, 1963.[18]

All of Oswald's political targets (including the ACLU) were also targets of the security squads of the local police and the FBI. It seems likely indeed that Oswald's incipient penetration of the ACLU was conducted with the knowledge and at the direction of the FBI. For somehow Hoover knew on November 29 of Oswald's membership application, whereas the ACLU itself did not learn of it for another two weeks.[19] Hoover's personal antipathy for the ACLU was strong. It led him to place on record in Oswald's file the recommendation in a telephone call from his friend Judge Milton Kronheim that the FBI report on the assassination should focus, not on Castro or Khrushchev, but on the ACLU itself.[20] It is thus reasonable to speculate that the FBI knew of Oswald's membership application, not from the unlikely and cumbrous procedure of an illegal surveillance of the ACLU mails, but because the FBI knew from the outset that Oswald, as an informant, had been directed to apply.

All of this adds to the likelihood that Oswald was being used by some agency to conduct surveillance on Cuban groups in Dallas such as the one on Hollandale. To be sure, a "Freedom for Cuba Party" would have been of opposite political inclination to the left-wing Fair Play for Cuba Committee. But Oswald's political interests spanned both ends of the political spectrum. His visit in August to the New Orleans delegate of the anti-Castro Directorio Revolucionario Estudiantil (DRE) strongly

[12] Scott, *Deep Politics*, 84-88.

[13] "In October of 1962 he attempted to join the [Socialist Workers] party, but his application was not accepted since there was no chapter in the Dallas area" (WR 289; 19 WH 578).

[14] Letter of J. Lee Rankin to Hoover, May 1964; filed at FBI HQ 62-109090-32nd after serial 136; NARA # 180-10056-10152.

[15] 22 WH 824-25.

[16] 2 WH 209.

[17] 20 WH 172 (Holmes DE 1).

[18] 7 WH 325, 17 WH 671.

[19] J. Edgar Hoover memo for Tolson et al., 11/29/63, FBI HQ 105-82555-93; 7 WH 325 (ACLU knowledge). Oswald's application is listed in the physical evidence as "D-46": it should be possible to learn the date of this classification (17 WH 671).

[20] Ibid.

suggests, both by its timing and Oswald's privileged information, that it was a visit on behalf of the FBI. (As I have written elsewhere, Oswald seemed interested in "La Cosa Nostra" as well as in training Cubans; the mob's interest in a nearby anti-Castro arms cache and training installation was known at the time to the FBI, but not to the general public.)[21]

In Dallas in October, Oswald's visit to the left-wing ACLU followed by only two days his attendance at a right-wing "U.S. Day" rally where a featured speaker was General Walker. Only a week earlier, Oswald reportedly attended a DRE meeting in Dallas, along with the same General Walker.[22] There was also an independent report that Oswald "had made some talks to small groups of Cuban refugees in Dallas in the past," and that he was suspected of acting as a "double agent."[23]

There are other good reasons why the Warren Commission should have been interested in Oswald and the alleged "Freedom for Cuba Party." One is that, on the night of November 22, District Attorney Wade had said at a press conference that "Oswald was a member of the movement -- the Free Cuba movement --" (24 WH 830). This of course was at odds with earlier published stories that Oswald was part of the pro-Castro Fair Play for Cuba Committee. It would seem to support an unknown Oswald-Ruby involvement that Wade's surprising remark on November 22 was immediately corrected, and by none other than Jack Ruby.[24]

Though there is almost no trace of it in Warren Commission records, there actually was a Free Cuba Movement, or Free Cuba Patriotic Movement, whose Cuban name was Cuba Libre.[25] Cuba Libre moreover was active in Dallas, though the name of the Dallas leader (Delfin Leyva Avila) will not be found among the ostensibly wide-ranging interviews of Cubans conducted for the Warren Commission by the FBI.

Walthers, both at the time and to the Warren Commission, reported physical corroboration for his story. He claimed to have discovered out at Ruth Paine's residence "a big pasteboard barrel and it had a lot of these little leaflets in it, 'Freedom for Cuba.'"[26] We shall see that Walthers, although an important witness, is not by himself a very credible one.[27] He was however corroborated by another deputy sheriff at the scene, Harry Weatherford, who also reported that they "found some literature on Cuban Freedom affairs" (19 WH 503). More significantly, all three deputy sheriffs there reported at the time finding six or seven metal cabinets which, according to Walthers, contained "records that appeared to be names and activities of Cuban sympathizers."[28] They all reported handing this evidence over to Captain Fritz in the Dallas Police Department. In the DPD records, however, the only Cuban literature found in Irving was some "Fair Play for Cuba papers in an envelope," while the six or seven cabinets now contained "letters" and "phonograph records."[29] This is consistent with Ruth Paine's own claim that the police and sheriffs carried off "my filing cases of old

---

[21] Scott, *Deep Politics*, 250-52.

[22] WCD 205.846.

[23] 26 WH 738. This was the original story about Oswald from Silvia Odio, as transmitted to the FBI on November 29 by her social worker Lucille Connell Odio herself denied this story some months later (26 WH 837), but it is likely that the many changes in Odio's story over the months were the result of pressures on her to change it. Cf. Scott, *Deep Politics*, 118-19.

[24] 24 WH 830; WR 342; 5 WH 189, 223-24; 25 WH 229. The Warren Report, as if to make Wade's statement sound like a simple slip of the tongue, misquotes what he said, as "Free Cuba Committee" (WR 342, citing, though not by page or exhibit number, 24 WH 830). In that interview Wade later distinguished between "Free Cuba" and "Fair Play for Cuba" as "two different organizations" (24 WH 839).

[25] The leader of the Free Cuba Patriotic Movement was Dr. Carlos Marquez Sterling, the registered foreign lobbyist for Cuba Libre (22 WH 864).

[26] 7 WH 548; cf. 19 WH 503, 520, 530.

[27] 19 WH 520; 7 WH 550.

[28] 19 WH 520; cf. 7 WH 548: "we found some little metal file cabinets." Weatherford reported "some literature on Cuban Freedom affairs and some small files" (19 WH 503). J.L. Oxford reported "about 7 metal boxes which contained pamphlets and literature from abroad" (19 WH 530).

[29] 21 WH 596 (Stovall Exhibit A); cf. 24 WH 337-40. Warren Commission Counsel Liebeler secured retractions from Walthers by a series of leading questions, substituting "Fair Play for Cuba" (7 WH 550) where Walthers had said "Freedom for Cuba" (7 WH 548), and turning his written report of November 22 about the names of sympathizers (19 WH 518-21) into "some story that has developed" (7 WH 549).

correspondence and 78 rpm phonograph records."[30]

I would not confidently prefer the Deputy Sheriff's testimony, linking Oswald to anti-Castro Cubans like Manuel Rodriguez, over the conflicting testimony of the Dallas police and Ruth Paine. On the contrary, I will argue that there was a pre-assassination disinformation campaign to implicate all those Cuban groups who were being secretly backed (outside the CIA) by Robert Kennedy, through the Cuban exiles Harry Ruiz-Williams and Paulino Sierra Martinez.[31] The SNFE-Alpha 66 alliance, of which Manuel Rodriguez Orcarberro was the local leader in Dallas, was the largest such group.[32]

CIA officers and their Cuban exile clients seem to have helped target the SNFE and Manuel Rodriguez. On November 24, 1963, a CIA source in Miami reported that "one Manuel Rodriguez...living Dallas was known be violently anti-Kennedy;" and the CIA cable reporting the rumor noted that a Manuel Rodriguez was "organizer of SFNE in Dallas."[33] Theodore Shackley, the CIA's JMWAVE Station Chief in Miami, repeated this rumor in his weekly report (or "Shackley-gram").[34] But, as we shall see, there were many such rumors. This disinformation campaign may have successfully taken in Robert Kennedy himself, who received a call from Ruiz-Williams on the afternoon of the assassination, and then said (to journalist Haynes Johnson), "One of your boys did it."[35]

Even if claims of an Oswald-Alpha 66 connection were to prove part of a malevolent disinformation campaign, this would not diminish our interest in learning the sources for Walthers' story. Moreover the notion that Oswald in Dallas cultivated anti-Castro Cubans associated with Minutemen and suspected of illegal gun activities would be entirely in keeping with Oswald's behavior a few months earlier in New Orleans. There too he approached such a group, the DRE, two members of whom had been arrested shortly before in connection with an illegal arms cache at Lake Pontchartrain. Rich Lauchli, a co-founder of the Minutemen, had been arrested with them.[36]

On the base of this recurring behavior in Dallas and in New Orleans, I speculated a year ago, without ever having heard of John Elrod, that "Oswald's unexplained approaches to anti-Castro Cubans could have been (as [one of them] suspected), as an informant for the U.S. government, perhaps to investigate illegal arms trafficking."[37]

For whatever reason, the Warren Commission conspicuously failed to explore Frank Ellsworth's suggestion to its Assistant Counsel Burt Griffin that the Minutemen organization, with links to General Edwin Walker and oil millionaire H.L. Hunt, was "the right-wing group most likely to have been associated with any effort to assassinate the president."[38] The Commission even withdrew two Commission Exhibits that had already been placed into evidence: Commission Exhibit 1053, a handbill attacking Krushchev as "Wanted for Murder," and signed "The Minutemen," and Commission Exhibit 710, transmitting DPD reports on right-wing extremists in Dallas.[39]

---

[30] 17 WH 194.

[31] Cf. Scott, *Deep Politics*, 89-90, 329-30.

[32] 10 AH 100; cf. AR 134.

[33] WAVE 8130 of 24 Nov 1963, CIA #88-27, HSCA #10732.

[34] The term "Shackleygram" appears to have been invented later, after Shackley became Chief of Station in Saigon in December 1968 (David Corn, *Blond Ghost: Ted Shackley and the CIA's Crusades* [New York: Simon and Schuster, 1994], 179-81. But Shackley's habit of sending weekly situation reports to Headquarters dated back to his stint as COS in Miami.

[35] Summers, *Vanity Fair*, 109.

[36] The two arrested DRE members were Carlos Eduardo "Batea" Hernandez Sanchez and John Koch Gene.

[37] Scott, *Deep Politics*, 254; 248-57.

[38] Scott, *Deep Politics*, 255.

[39] For "CE 1053" see 5 WH 545; cf. CD 320, *Dallas Times Herald*, September 1, 1963. For "CE 710," see 4 WH 194, also the missing exhibits CE 706-08 at 4 WH 202. These exhibits, introduced and then withdrawn, constitute another example of what I have called a "negative template," denoting evidence to which our attention is drawn by its disappearance (Scott, *Deep Politics*, 60-61, 69).

The "Wanted for Murder" Minutemen handbill was initially investigated by the Commission for its similarity to the anti-Kennedy "Wanted for Treason" handbill distributed at the time of the President's visit. The latter was traced by the Commission to General Walker's aide Robert Surrey (WR 298-99), but Surrey was not asked about the companion Minutemen publication, an apparent example of the Minutemen-Walker connection Ellsworth had warned about.

This lack of interest in the Masen-Minutemen-Walker-Ellsworth story was sustained.[40] Frank Ellsworth should by any account have been an important witness for the Warren Commission, yet his name will not be found at all in the first fifteen volumes, and only once or twice in the next eleven. He had been present in the School Book Depository when the rifle was found (24 WH 320). He had been investigating the Cuban exile group, the SNFE-Alpha 66 alliance, to which Oswald had been linked by Walthers' informant. Last but not least, Frank Ellsworth, as he revealed to reporter Dick Russell in 1976, was one of the federal agents who first interviewed Oswald after the President's murder.[41] Ellsworth's interrogation with Oswald is remarkable from a bureaucratic viewpoint: alone of all the known interrogations of Oswald in those last two days of his life, Ellsworth's was for years effaced from the available bureaucratic record.

What Ellsworth chiefly recalled about his interview with Oswald was also striking. Oswald and Masen, he recalled, "were like identical twins; they could've passed for each other."[42] Ellsworth's account of an Oswald look-alike in the Dallas Cuban community was only one of many such leads. In fact the FBI, tracking down a report that Oswald had been sighted in Oklahoma, concluded that in fact the mistakenly identified individual was none other than Manuel Rodriguez Orcarberro.[43] It is probable that at a nearby firing range an Oswald look-alike had been firing Mannlicher-Carcano ammunition (available at Masen's and only one other store).[44] Sylvia Meagher concluded from Secret Service interviews that, as a witness reported, Robert Surrey, author of the Minutemen handbill, also "closely resembled" Oswald.[45]

Whether or not Oswald did frequent and/or inform on right-wing anti-Castro Cubans, it is clear that in Dallas he pursued other political interests as well. We have see that in addition to a possible right-wing interest he also visited a meeting of the American Civil Liberties Union in Dallas, considered so liberal that it was under investigation by the Dallas Police Department.[46] Oswald's ACLU visit on October 25, 1963, in fact followed by only two days his attendance at a "U.S. Day" rally at which a featured speaker was General Edwin Walker.

This ability to switch politically appears to have impressed Michael Paine. Without invitation, Paine recalled for the Warren Commission

> thinking to myself for a person who has a business to do he [Oswald] certainly can waste the time. By business I mean some kind of activity and keeping track of right-wing causes and left-wing causes or something. I supposed that he spent his time as I would be inclined to spend more of my time if I had it, trying to sense the pulse of various groups in the Dallas area.[47]

What else could Michael Paine have supposed? He himself had gone with Oswald to a meeting of the liberal ACLU, which Oswald told him "he couldn't join" (2 WH 409), and heard Oswald describe to the ACLU an earlier right-wing meeting where General Walker had spoken (2 WH 403).[48] Clearly

---

[40] Neither Masen nor his associate Manuel Rodriguez Orcarberro will be encountered in the Warren volumes, even though accusing fingers had been pointed at Rodriguez and his associates from as early as November 24, 1963 (WAVE Cable 8130 of 24 November 1963, 242027Z, CIA Doc. #88-27).

[41] Dick Russell, *The Man Who Knew Too Much*, 542.

[42] Russell, 543.

[43] WCD 23.4; Scott, *Deep Politics*, 371.

[44] Scott, *Deep Politics*, 391 (look-alike).

[45] Meagher, *Accessories After the Fact*, 385, citing 25 WH 658; cf. 23 WH 515-16.

[46] "CE 710."

[47] 2 WH 412. Oswald's landlady in New Orleans, Mrs. Jesse Garner, also recalled that Oswald "was always home," to the extent that she had doubted Oswald worked at the Reily Coffee Company "as long as he did...unless he worked at night" (10 WH 271).

[48] What adds to the intrigue is that Paine himself had been on October 24 and 25 to a John Birch Society meet-

Oswald could not have attended both meetings out of inner convictions, any more than in New Orleans he could have been sincerely both a pro-Castro and anti-Castro partisan.

Neither can Oswald's political tourism be attributed to mere intellectual curiosity; his behavior can only be called manipulative. On November 1, one week after he told Paine he couldn't join the ACLU, Oswald opened a P.O. Box in Dallas to receive mail from the FPCC and the ACLU (WR 739).[49] Oswald apparently told the FPCC he had done this (20 WH 532); but there is no sign he told the ACLU, which he did not get around to joining (with a $2.00 check) until November 4 (7 WH 325). Had he lived, one suspects, Oswald might have proceeded to implicate the ACLU by association with his own deviant Marxism, just as he did the FPCC.

In his two-fold political behavior, switching swiftly from right to left-wing, Oswald's performance in Dallas again echoed his performance in New Orleans. There he had posed as an anti-Castro activist on August 5, 1963, and as a pro-Castro activist only four days later. I speculated in *Deep Politics* that this two-fold behavior was motivated by his informant status: Oswald posed as an FPCC activist in order to discredit them and thus gain an entree into their designated political opponents the DRE.[50]

In Dallas however, in the proximity of the assassination, this second-level agenda, of which Oswald was presumably aware, may have been inspired by a still deeper third-level agenda, of whcih Oswald was almost certainly ignorant. This is that he was being supplied with an untraceable legend that was politically ambiguous, indeed inscrutable, precisely to confound rational analysis of his motivations.

Whether or not this third-level agenda inspired his activity in New Orleans, or conceivably even in the Soviet Union, I propose that it motivated Oswald's unknown handlers during his last weeks in Dallas.

Ruby too, at the last minute, wrapped himself in the inscrutable mystery of a political polarity, simultaneously liberal and anti-liberal. On the one hand, he had in his notebook the names of Thomas Hill, at the head office of the John Birch Society, and Lamar Hunt, son of H.L. Hunt, whose office he visited on November 21.[51] On the other hand he is supposed to have been "enraged" at the Birchite radio scripts (funded by H.L. Hunt) which he had in his possession; and to have taken time, late at night, to take a picture of a billboard, which he found offensive, saying "Impeach Earl Warren."[52]

Ruby, in other words, both approached the right-wing Hunts and also acted as if he was opposed to them: behavior intriguingly analogous to Oswald's. The main difference here is that this possible third-level agenda appears to have been an idea of the last moment, whereas Oswald's legend had been built over several months, if not longer.

---

ing and the same ACLU meeting, a revelation about which both he and the Warren Commission were somewhat evasive (2 WH 388, 403; WR 463).

[49] 20 WH 172; cf. WR 634.

[50] For this double role of Oswald in New Orleans, see Scott, *Deep Politics*, 80-86, 248-53. In theory, of course, Oswald could have posed as a DRE sympathizer in order to investigate their friend Guy Banister, rather than on Banister's behalf.

[51] 26 WH 472-73; 25 WH 381; WR 367-68.

[52] WR 367-68; 15 WH 259-61.

X. THE DFS, SILVIA DURAN, AND THE CIA-MAFIA CONNECTION:

DID STAFF D FEED THE OSWALD-KOSTIKOV LIE TO THE CIA?

Abstract: There exist at least four successive versions (or falsifications) of Silvia Durán's so-called statement of November 23, 1963, to the Mexican DFS (Dirección Federal de Seguridad), about her interviews of Oswald in the Cuban Consulate. The successive changes mirror the shift in the Mexico City CIA Station's view of Oswald, from a "phase-one" position (Oswald was part of a Cuban Communist conspiracy) to a more standard "phase-two" position (Oswald was a lone nut). From other sources we learn that the DFS itself, as well as the CIA Station, pushed the "conspiracy" story hard in their November 23 interview. Revisions to the Durán statement seem also designed to bring her story into line with an alleged telephone intercept of "Oswald" at the Cuban Consulate on September 28, 1963, when in fact he was not there. In protecting this falsified intercept from exposure, the DFS was probably protecting itself as well as the CIA; for the DFS was involved in the LIENVOY intercept project and probably manned the listening posts.

The DFS may have been assisted in this LIENVOY project by Richard Cain, an expert telephone tapper and adjunct to the CIA-Giancana assassination connection, when he was in Mexico City in 1962 as a consultant to a Mexican Government agency. Richard Cain at the time was also part of that Dave Yaras-Lennie Patrick-Sam Giancana element of the Chicago mob with demonstrable links to Ruby in 1963, and the HSCA speculated that Cain may have been part of the 1960-61 CIA-Mafia plots against Castro.

Unmistakably Staff D, the small secretive part of CIA in which the CIA-Mafia plots were housed, controlled the LIENVOY intercept intake inside the Mexico City CIA station (Ann Goodpasture, the responsible officer, was a member of Staff D). If Richard Cain trained and possibly helped recruit the Mexican LIENVOY monitors, then the CIA-DFS LIENVOY collaboration would present a matrix for connecting the CIA's internal mishandling of Oswald information to the behavior of Ruby and other criminal elements in Dallas. It would also put the CIA-Mafia connection, through Staff D, in a position to feed to the CIA the false intercept linking a false Oswald to a suspected Soviet assassination expert (Kostikov), which became a major pretext for creating a Warren Commission to reach the less dangerous conclusion of a lone assassin.

There are contextual corroborations of this matrix. Both Ruby and the DFS had links to the Mexico-Chicago drug traffic, dating back to the 1940s. The DFS and the Mexican drug traffic became increasingly intertwined after 1963; the last two DFS Chiefs were indicted, for smuggling and for murder; and the DFS itself was nominally closed down in the midst of Mexico's 1985 drug scandals. (José Antonio Zorrilla, the ex-DFS chief arrested and indicted in 1989 for murder, was in 1963 private secretary to Fernando Gutiérrez Barrios, the DFS agent whose signature attested to the validity of the most radically altered version of Durán's statement.) At least two ex-DFS officers who were also former CIA agents have been named by the *New York Times* in connection with the Colosio assassination of 1994; and one of these, ex-DFS Chief Miguel Nazar Haro, was also involved in the investigation of the John F. Kennedy assassination.

What should most concern us in this deep political interaction between the CIA and a criminal DFS is the CIA's protection of at least one guilty DFS leader (Miguel Nazar Haro) from deserved prosecution in U.S. courts. This protection should be evaluated in the light of the CIA immunity granted to Sam Giancana in 1961 (in which Cain may have played a role) and the Warren Commission's false isolation of Ruby from the Giancana-Yaras-Patrick Chicago mob in 1964.

Thus it is important that the ARRB recognize the substantive relevance of the DFS to the case. It should press for the release of the Mexican Government documentation of its investigation. It should also release information about the DFS in CIA records that is relevant to anomalies in the handling of the case.

The Four Versions of Silvia Durán's November 23 DFS Statement

With the release of the new documents, it is now abundantly clear that the visit of Oswald to the Cuban and Soviet consulates in Mexico City became for some reason too sensitive to be handled normally by the CIA and FBI. CIA officials, both before and after the assassination, misreported what happened, falsified documentary records, and concealed the surviving tapes of Oswald's alleged telephone conversations.[1] In this collusion the CIA had the support of a sister Mexican agency which it had helped to create, the Mexican Dirección Federal de Seguridad (Federal Security Police), or DFS.

The DFS, before it was abolished because of its deep involvement in Mexico's drug traffic, was a key agency in the Mexican Gobernación (Ministry of the Interior).[2] It also had close links with the FBI as well as the CIA, being part of a tradition of binational intelligence cooperation dating back to the turn of the century.[3]

Three different operations involving Oswald can be distinguished in Mexico. The most obvious is the post-assassination cover-up. As I have written elsewhere, a falsified bus manifest, supplied by the Gobernación to establish Oswald's return to the U.S. on October 3, was probably altered in the office of the Mexican President.[4] But post-assassination cover-up activity should be distinguished from pre-assassination operations involving Oswald, and both of these from the assassination plot. I shall suggest that the DFS, if only by its involvement in the CIA's LIENVOY telephone intercept program, became enmeshed in pre-assassination Oswald operations, and possibly the plot as well.

As for the pre-assassination operations, one clue as to what is being concealed is the suppressed content in successive alterations of a single key document, the DFS account of Silvia Durán's statement when arrested on November 23, 1963. There are at least four successive versions of this single document; and if we focus on what is being suppressed by these successive alterations, we arrive at a working hypothesis of what actually may have happened and has since been hidden.

Later in this chapter I shall argue that the anomalies help us to distinguish between two different pre-assassination operations involving Oswald. The first was an authorized intelligence operation (involving Oswald's request for a visa), which aimed to discredit the Fair Play for Cuba Committee by linking Oswald to the American Communist Party. The second, which may have been part of the assassination plot, involved a simulated meeting between an Oswald impostor and Vladimir Kostikov, an alleged KGB assassination expert.[5] It appears that the DFS, through its role in wire-tapping the Soviet and Cuban embassies for the CIA, played an important role in both operations, but especially the second.

One of the suppressed facts is that the DFS, in its first versions of the testimony gathered from Durán and her friends about Oswald, used the name "Harvey Lee Oswald." Those familiar with the

---

[1] See Chapter II, also Chapter VIII. The CIA station in Mexico misled even others in government about the man who allegedly identified himself as Oswald in Mexico City. We are still just beginning to learn how great the misrepresentations may have been. For example, in the latest CIA release there is a penciled note from 1976, reporting inside hearsay that the "caller (who called himself Oswald) had difficulty making himself understood both (as I recall) in English and Russian" (Handwritten comment on Memo of 12/3/76 for the Record from Scott D. Breckinridge, OLC; NARA # 104-10095-10001; CIA File # 80T01357A). The Review Board should pursue this claim to its source. If the "caller (who called himself Oswald)" was not a native English speaker, those in U.S. service who knew this should have to explain any delays in the transmission of this information.

[2] For the DFS and drug trafficking, see Peter Dale Scott, *Deep Politics and the Death of JFK*, 104-05, 142. Writing before the release of the Lopez Report, I did not then know that Miguel Nazar Haro, the DFS Chief and CIA agent indicted for smuggling stolen cars, had also overseen the 1978 visit of HSCA staff to Mexico City, when they were denied access to the important DFS witness Manuel Calvillo (Lopez Report, 270-81).

[3] W. Dirk Raat, *Mexico and the United States: Ambivalent Vistas*, 97, 122, 130, 151; W. Dirk Raat, "U.S. Intelligence Operations and Covert Action in Mexico, 1900-1947," *Journal of Contemporary History* 22 (1987), 618ss. The evolution of both the FBI and U.S. Army Intelligence have been affected by their deep involvement in Mexico.

[4] 24 WH 673, 621; WR 736; Scott, *Deep Politics*, 105.

[5] As I shall make clear, I am indebted for this distinction to John Newman; cf. Newman, *Oswald and the CIA*, 364-68.

Oswald documentation will be aware that this anomalous variant of his name is not unique to the DFS. We find more than twenty such references widely dispersed through the records of at least six government agencies in the U.S.: the FBI, the CIA, the Secret Service, Army Intelligence, Naval Intelligence, the State Department, and the Dallas Police. They are supplemented by still other references to Oswald as "Harvey Lee Oswald," in the oral testimony of a wide range of witnesses to the Warren Commission and elsewhere.

All of the documentary references we now have to "Harvey Lee Oswald" are post-assassination. I will speculate however that there are pre-assassination archetypes for some of these references, and that the reason these archetypes have not surfaced is because of their relevance to operations involving Oswald, specifically in Mexico City. In the first version we have of the DFS record of the interrogation of Silvia Durán, the name "Harvey Lee Oswald" occurs no less than five times.[6]

Not surprisingly, these anomalous references are suppressed in the CIA translation of the same document, and standardized to become "Lee Harvey Oswald."[7] For this reason I shall refer to "Harvey Lee Oswald" as the suppressed name, and "Lee Harvey Oswald" as the public one.[8] We find the same conversion or suppression of the name "Harvey Lee Oswald", and its replacement by "Lee Harvey Oswald," in a cable of November 29, 1963, from the FBI Legat in Bern, Switzerland,[9] and again in documents from the Secret Service.[10] So many scattered and unexplained references to "Harvey Lee Oswald" attest to at least one suppressed archetypal document we do not have. The FBI's first question to Robert Oswald on November 22 was, "Is your brother's name Lee Harvey Oswald or Harvey Lee Oswald?... We have it here as Harvey Lee."[11] This suggests that one might begin to search for this lost archetype by interviewing Robert's FBI interrogators.

The important fact here is that the suppression of the name "Harvey Lee Oswald" in the early version of the DFS documentation was paralleled by the simultaneous suppression of the name "Harvey Lee Oswald" across the border, in documents of the United States government. The same suppression happened to the one of the first details reported by the DFS about Durán's version of Oswald's visit to the Cuban Consulate: that Oswald said he was a Communist.[12] As I have shown elsewhere, there were other witnesses, above all in Dallas, who first claimed Oswald had said he was a Communist, and then denied this allegation.[13] It would appear, therefore, that suppressions in the content of Durán's DFS statement were part of a wider suppression of evidence.

---

[6] CIA Doc. #131-593; JKB memo of 11/26/63 and 10-page attachment: Summary of first Mexican interview of Silvia Durán et al, pp. 7 (twice), 8, 9, 10 "Aseveró no conocer a Harvey Lee Oswald." Versions of this sentence are used five times in all in this document, in the minor supporting statements of Ruben Durán, Betsy Serratos, Agata Roseno, Barbara Ann Bliss, and Charles Bentley. In the statement of Silvia Durán, the variant recorded is "Lee Harvey Oswald." In this JKB memo the standardized name "Lee Harvey Oswald" has apparently been corrected from an earlier "Harvey Lee Oswald " (See Chapter VII, "Oswald...and Oswald's Party Card.")

[7] CIA Headquarters Cable 85758 of 29 November 1963 to the White House, State Department, and FBI, CIA Doc #223-647, pp. 8, 9 11.

[8] One purpose for the alternative name may have been to hide sensitive file documents on Oswald. It is striking that when the FBI and CIA searched (as is customary) for name variants of Oswald, "Harvey Lee Oswald" was never among the variants searched, even though the name "Harvey Lee Oswald" occurs in widely dispersed FBI and CIA records. (Cf. the search slips in the HQ Oswald file 105-82555 after serial -42; and in the Dallas Oswald file DL 100-10461 right after the assassination.)

[9] FBI HQ File 105-82555-88, Cable # 241 from Legat Bern to DIR: [Title] "Changed. Lee Harvey Oswald, aka Harvey Lee Oswald, Internal Security - R and Cuba. Title changed to show correct sequence of first and middle names." Cf. Mexico City FBI File 105-3702-254; see below.

[10] 16 WH 721; CE 270: Transcript of Secret Service Agent J.M. Howard interview 11/25/63 with "Mrs. Marguerite Oswald, mother of Harvey Lee (crossed out, replaced by "Lee Harvey") Oswald:" "This is an interview with Mrs. Marguerite Oswald, mother of Harvey Lee Oswald;" 16 WH 749; CE 270: Transcript of Secret Service Agent J.M. Howard interview 11/25/63 with "Robert Lee Oswald, brother of Harvey Lee (crossed out, replaced by "Lee Harvey") Oswald:" "This is an interview with Robert Lee Oswald, brother of Lee Harvey Oswald." (Both interviews refer to LHO as "Lee" [Marguerite] or "Lee Harvey" [Robert]).

[11] Robert Oswald, *Lee: A Portrait of Lee Harvey Oswald* (New York: Coward-McCann, 1967), 18.

[12] MEXI 7046 to DIR[ector], 240419Z, CIA Document # 66-567.

[13] See Chapter V, "Oswald, Harvey Lee Oswald, and Oswald's Communist Party Card."

There were at least four successive versions of this single important piece of evidence, the original Mexican DFS report of Durán's statement:

DFS-1) The "written statement" first given by the Mexicans to the CIA Station Chief on the night of November 23, and summarized in the Station's cable MEXI 7046 of November 24, 1963. We do not have this statement. A CIA cable summarizing it reported that Oswald said he was a "Communist and admirer of Castro."[14] This information was then incorporated in Headquarters' November 24 summary of its information about Oswald.[15] As we shall see, what Headquarters knew on November 24 about Oswald's self-professed Communism was soon effaced from memory.[16]

DFS-2) The Spanish-language version of Durán's interview received on November 26 by the CIA from one of her DFS interrogators, and forwarded under a memo, still redacted, signed by a "JKB."[17] This "JKB version" was then hand-carried to Washington on November 27 by a Headquarters CIA officer, John Horton.[18] In it there is no reference to Oswald's saying he was a Communist. In the reported statements of Durán's friends, but not in her own, Oswald is referred to (five times in all) as "Harvey Lee Oswald."

DFS-3) The CIA's English-language translation of DFS-2, in which the five references to "Harvey Lee Oswald" are replaced by the now standard "Lee Harvey Oswald."[19] We shall also discuss another point on which this "translation" differs from its Spanish original: an unsupported reference to the Cuban Consul phoning the Soviet Consulate.

DFS-4) The Warren Commission version of Durán's statement, dated "November 23," and attested to and signed by Captain Fernando Gutiérrez Barrios, then Deputy Federal Director of Security.[20] A photostat of this Spanish-language version, certified on May 7, 1964, was transmitted by the Mexican Government to the State Department in a note of June 9, 1964.[21] As we shall see, the several minor changes introduced into the DFS-4 version all have the effect of eliminating conflicts between the earlier versions and the body of evidence which by May 1964 supported the "phase two" official story of Oswald as a lone assassin. I would tentatively date the DFS-4 version from about May 1964.[22]

---

[14] MEXI 7046 to DIR[ector], 240419Z, CIA Document # 66-567.

[15] XAAZ-35907, "Summary of Relevant Information on Lee Harvey Oswald at 0700 24 November 1963." CIA Document # 130-592, NARA #104-10015-10359.

[16] See also Chapter VII, "Oswald, Harvey Lee Oswald, and Oswald's Communist Party Card."

[17] JKB Memo and attachment of 26 November, 1963, CIA Document #131-593.

[18] MEXI 7105 of November 27, 1963.

[19] DIR 85758 of 29 November 1963, CIA Document #223-647. A different translation of part of DFS-2 will be found in the Lopez Report, pp. 186-87, citing a Blind Memo of 26 November 1963, CIA #473. I have decided to relegate this version to a footnote as DFS-2A, because I can find no significant differences in content from DFS-2. Both DFS-2A and DFS-3 contain minor translation errors. Contrary to what the Lopez Report implies (p. 190), the text of DIR 85738 was transmitted by the CIA to the Warren Commission under cover of a memo of February 21, 1994.

[20] Warren Commission CE 2123, 24 WH 669-72. The Lopez Report, without supporting evidence, attributes the significant alterations in DFS-4 to the CIA (p. 190).

[21] 24 WH 663-64.

[22] A long extract from this version (24 WH 565-66) had already been transmitted in a Mexican note of May 14 (24 WH 563-64); and three xerox copies of the full text had been given on May 22 to the Mexico City office of the FBI (FBI MC 105-3702-1A.80). This version (DFS-4A) was translated into English twice, by the State Department, and the FBI. See 24 WH 686-89 (State); 24 WH 587-90 = 25 WH 634-37 (FBI). There are differences of content between the translations, but I have found no serious ones. (The age of Durán is given correctly as "26" in the State version, as "25" by the FBI.) The interviews of the other witnesses in DFS-2, where the name "Harvey Lee Oswald" was given, follow the FBI version of DFS-4A, using the name "Lee Harvey Oswald" (24 WH 591-93). The FBI claims to have received these subsidiary interviews in a report of November 25, 1963, which its source T-17 received on November 29 (24 WH 591). The latter date is that of CIA Cable 85758 to the FBI; but the JKB version it translated (DFS-2) was dated November 26.

Clearly it is time to request from the Mexican Government all surviving documentation which the DFS collected on the Kennedy assassination. In the case of the Durán interview, it is possible that they still have a copy of the contemporary stenographic record which (according to Durán) was made of her DFS interrogation.[23]

The Mexican government records on the JFK assassination case may help us understand what the CIA and FBI were hiding in this matter. The FBI, for example, appears to have understood completely that the three earlier DFS versions of Durán's statement (which it had received either directly or through the CIA) were for some reason to be replaced by the spuriously altered DFS-4 of May 1964. Thus, when on May 18, 1964, it finally transmitted to the Warren Commission the results of the DFS interviews of the eight Mexicans arrested with Silvia Durán, the seven other interviews were taken from the JKB memo attachment of November 26, 1963, which originally included the DFS-2 version of Silvia Durán's statement. Instead of the DFS-2 version, however, the FBI provided the more convenient ("phase two") DFS-4 version of Silvia's alleged interview "on November 23." This artificially contrived amalgam, Commission Document 1084(e) of 5/18/64, was then published as Commission Exhibit 2121 by the Warren Commission (24 WH 587-93).[24]

What Were the Rewrites of the Durán DFS Statement Trying To Hide?

The suppression of "Harvey Lee Oswald" is not the only change made to the first available version (DFS-2) of the Durán statement. Her description of him as *"rubio, bajo, vestido no elegante"* was transmitted in the initial CIA translation ("blond, short, poorly dressed"); but this anomalous characterization of Oswald was suppressed in the final version of her statement (DFS-4) published by the Warren Commission.[25] The JKB version (DFS-2) and original CIA translation (DFS-3) contain the significant statement that Oswald "never called again" after Durán gave him her telephone number on Friday, September 27 (which as John Newman has shown appears to invalidate an alleged telephone call made by Durán and Oswald together on the next day).[26] In the Warren Commission version of the same statement (DFS-4) this important clue has been robbed of its significance: "she does not recall whether Oswald subsequently called her or not."[27]

There were further revisions of the original DFS version of Durán's statement. According to the first summary report by the Mexico City CIA Station of the DFS version of Durán's statement about Oswald, she reportedly "said he Communist and admirer of Castro."[28] This is what we would expect from Durán's testimony in 1978 to the House Committee ("He said he was a member of the Party, of the Communist Party"), and above all from Durán's observation typed on Oswald's visa application, according to which Oswald stated "he is a member of the American Communist Party," and "displayed documents in proof."[29] But the significant statement, "said he Communist," is missing from the JKB version now in CIA files (DFS-2), as well as from the CIA cable translating it (DFS-3). It is however echoed in the Warren Commission version of her DFS statement (DFS-4), again

---

[23] 3 AH 83.

[24] The CIA also has some explaining to do. For example Headquarters cable DIR 84920 of 24 Nov 63 (241332Z), begins "After...reading the statement of Silvia Duran." Yet, according to the itemized file inventory and chronology supplied by the CIA, no full text of the Durán statement reached Headquarters until the JKB memo and attachment (DFS-2) were hand-carried to Langley on the night of November 26. A very terse account of her statement (DFS-1) had been forwarded in cable MEXI 7046 of 23 Nov 63 (240419Z). But the Headquarters cable does not refer to MEXI 7046, as would be the CIA practice when an earlier cable is being discussed.

[25] JKB memo, p. 5; CIA Cable 85758 of 29 November, 1963, p. 6; Warren Commission CE 2120, 24 WH 589. Cf. Lopez Report, 186-91.

[26] JKB memo, p. 6 ("jamas volvió a llamar"); CIA Cable 85758 of 29 November, 1963, p. 7; Newman, *Oswald and the CIA*, 407-09.

[27] 24 WH 590; cf. 688; Lopez Report, 190.

[28] MEXI 7046 of 24 November 1963, CIA Doc. #66-567. At the time both the leading Mexico City newspaper and the *New York Times* also reported that Oswald said he was a Communist. See *Excelsior*, November 25, 1963, in Mexico City Oswald FBI file at serial 105-3702-30; *New York Times*, December 3, 1963, reprinted at 24 WH 585.

[29] 3 AH 34; Warren Commission CE 2564, 25 WH 814-15.

robbed of its evidentiary significance: "she does not remember whether or not he said that he was a member of the Communist Party."[30]

It would appear from this history of alterations to the same statement that the fourth version (DFS-4), though still falsely dated November 23, 1963, has been revised to fit with the Warren Report version of Oswald as an isolated lone assassin. It is particularly unlikely that Durán on November 23 did not remember "whether or not [Oswald] said that he was a member of the Communist Party." Only a few hours before she had pulled the Oswald file, with the visa application on which she herself had typed, six weeks earlier, the following observations:

> The applicant [Oswald] states that he is a member of the American Communist Party and Secretary in New Orleans of the Fair Play for Cuba Committee....He displayed documents in proof of his membership in the two aforementioned organizations and a marriage certificate.[31]

The equivocations in the DFS-4 version are devious and dishonest. DFS-2 and DFS-3 transmit the significant fact that in November Durán had just checked Oswald's file (chequeo sus datos; checked his data).[32] DFS-4 replaces this statement, which would have made her alleged memory lapses even less credible, by the innocuous one that in September she "took all his data" (tomó todos sus datos) to fill out the application.[33] We can assume that Durán had not forgotten a few hours later Oswald's claim to be a Communist, which she had no trouble recalling in 1978. Thus the missing first version of the same statement ("said he Communist") is probably the most credible one. The Review Board should try to obtain it.

I conclude that these successive alterations to the "November 23" DFS text were deliberate, and designed to suppress the following facts:

1) Durán's original description of him (as a short, poorly dressed blond) did not resemble that of the Dallas Lee Harvey Oswald.

2) Oswald's visa business in the Cuban Consulate began and ended on September 27, 1963, meaning that an alleged third visit the next day did not actually occur.

3) Either from this visit or some earlier event, the visitor to the Embassy was known to authorities as "Harvey Lee Oswald."

4) The visitor said he was a Communist.

The corroboration of the suppressed testimony by the original visa application suggests that a fifth fact was also being suppressed:

5) The visitor supported his visa application with an American Communist Party card.

Other Sources for the Suppressed Testimony of Silvia Tirado de Durán.

Much of this suppressed material was recovered (and augmented) by Silvia Tirado de Durán (by now remarried as Silvia Tirado de Bazan) in her 1978 interview with three members of the HSCA Staff. In this interview she again said that the visitor's hair had been blond (*rubio*).[34] She now

---

[30] 24 WH 589; cf. 688.

[31] WR 303; 25 WH 814-15. Durán later confirmed writing the words: 3 AH 29, 38, 40; cf. 3 AH 137, 142.

[32] She unambiguously confirmed this in 1978: "I went to the Consulate and I look in the Archivos and I saw the application, I saw that it was the man and I went to the Embassy and I talked to the Ambassador.." (3 AH 79).

[33] 24 WH 671, 688.

[34] 3 AH 69-70.

said that Oswald had visited the Embassy three times (rather than twice, as in all the DFS versions). She was emphatic, however, that all of Oswald's visits were on the same day, September 27, that he did not return the next day (when the Consulate was closed), and that she did not phone the Soviet Embassy on the next day, Saturday September 28, as one of the supposed Oswald telephone transcripts alleged.[35]

Silvia Tirado further testified that Oswald said he was a member of the Communist Party ("He said he was a member of the Party, of the Communist Party, the American").[36] According to the Lopez Report, Silvia testified further that Oswald showed her the following supporting documents: his Russian labor card, his marriage certificate, "his American Communist Party membership card, and his 'Fair Play for Cuba' membership card."[37] When however we turn to the same testimony as published by the HSCA, the reference to the Communist Party card is missing from the list.[38]

Having reflected much about this, I have concluded that Silvia did mention the Communist Party card in 1978, just as she had on the application in 1963. If so, the HSCA must have responded to Silvia's testimony about Oswald's professed Communism in the same way as the DFS, by altering, and in effect suppressing, this detail.

Testifying later in Cuba, two other witnesses, Consul Eusebio Azcue and his successor Alfredo Mirabal Diaz, both had no trouble recalling the Communist Party card.[39] Mirabal's testimony was particularly vivid, reinforced as it was by a very sensible skepticism which Silvia shared:

> I noticed that he presented a card or credentials as belonging to the Communist Party of the United States....I was surprised by the fact that the card seemed to be a new card. I must say that I also have been a Communist for a number of years and that generally we do not use credentials or a card to identify ourselves as members of the party.[40]

Silvia Durán also communicated very similar suspicions:

> When he said he was a member of the Party, of the Communist Party, the American, I said why don't they arrange, the Party, your Party with the Cuban Party, and he said that he didn't have the time to do it....It was strange. I mean because if you are a Communist and you're coming from a country where the Communist Party is not very well seen, and in Mexico City that the Communist Party was not legal at that moment -- crossing the border with all of his paper, it was not logical. I mean, if you're really Communist, you go with *anything*, I mean just nothing, just your passport, that's all.... it was strange, travelling with all of his documents just to prove one thing....He said that he was a Communist. That was strange. Because it would be really easy for him to get the visa through the Communist Party.[41]

If the visitor did present a card, and if Edwin Lopez (who was present) is correct in saying that Tirado testified to this in 1978, then we have a parallel cover-up in successive alterations of Tirado's statements outside the DFS, analogous to the successive alterations of the "November 23" DFS statement.

It would seem appropriate therefore for the Review Board to seek and review all the successive reports of Tirado's statements and testimony. Some of these documents are currently in Cuba and have never been published in the United States. Known documents include:

---

[35] 3 AH 25, 31, 49-51; cf. 3 AH 114. In all of these details Tirado, interviewed in Mexico City, was corroborated by former Consul Eusebio Azcue, testifying in Washington, except that Azcue speculated that Oswald's third visit could have occurred on September 28 (3 AH 130-33, 136, 151).

[36] 3 AH 34; cf. 33.

[37] Lopez Report, 192, citing Duran testimony, p. 28.

[38] 3 AH 33 (Duran testimony, p. 28): "He show me letters to the Communist Party, the American Communist Party, his labor card... his uh, marriage pact...and a card saying he was a member of the Fair Play for Cuba."

[39] 3 AH 130-31, 142 (Azcue); 3 AH 176 (Mirabal).

[40] 3 AH 176.

[41] 3 AH 34, 35, 57, 58.

ST-1. Cuban Embassy Confidential Report 125. Sent from Cuban Ambassador Hernández Armas to Havana after interviewing Durán on November 25, after her first DFS arrest and interrogation [Not seen].[42]

ST-2. Telephone conversation of 26 November between Ambassador Hernández Armas and Cuban President Dorticos. Having spoken to Durán, Hernández told Dorticos that the DFS asked her concretely "if she had personal relations and even if she had intimate [i.e. sexual] relations with him. She denied all that." He also spoke of the bruises inflicted on her by the DFS.[43] This aggressive line of DFS questioning was later confirmed by Silvia to the HSCA.[44]

ST-3. Statement prepared by Durán in response to request from Ambassador on November 26 [Not seen].[45]

ST-4. Durán's interview with a CIA Mexico City station asset, LIRING-3, on May 26, 1967. She told LIRING-3 that in her DFS interrogation she had been "interviewed thoroughly and beaten until she admitted that she had an affair with Oswald".[46]

ST-5. Tirado's first American press interview, with Ron Kessler of the *Washington Post*. In this interview she said that Oswald "claimed to be a member of the American Communist Party."[47]

ST-6. Tirado's HSCA interview, as summarized by Edward Lopez in the Lopez Report (according to which Silvia testified that Oswald showed her "his American Communist Party membership card").[48]

ST-7. Tirado's HSCA interview, as published by the HSCA, in which the reference to the Communist Party card is missing.[49]

ST-8. Tirado's interviews with Anthony Summers, 1978, May 13, 1979, and January 31, 1995. In 1995 she was adamant that Oswald did not return to the Consulate on September 28, when it was closed.[50]

This fragmentary review of what we have of these non-DFS Tirado records is enough to cast further doubt on the version of her "November 23" statement (DFS-4) published by the Warren Commission. It also strengthens the impression that the subject of the Communist Party card was an extremely sensitive matter, possibly an intelligence matter, being protected by government censorship as late as 1978.[51]

The two series of records taken together (the DFS series and the ST series) suggest that some members and/or employees of the CIA Mexico City station, acting in concert with some members of the Mexican DFS, were guilty of falsifying the facts concerning Oswald's visit, and above all that

---

[42] Mentioned in MEXI 7068 of 26 November 1963, p. 2. It is probable that the Ambassador had sent an earlier report after Durán went to him with information about Oswald on November 23.

[43] English translation of intercept transmitted in MEXI 7068 of 26 November 1963.

[44] 3 AH 86; cf. Lopez Report, 254.

[45] CIA Document #133-594, translation of part of Dorticos-Hernández Armas phone conversation of November 26, 1963.

[46] Memo of 26 May 1967, "Meeting with LIRING-3," forwarded under HMMA-32243 of 13 June 1967; CIA Document #1225-1129, cf. #1084-965.

[47] *Washington Post*, November 26, 1976, A7; 3 AH 34 (1978).

[48] Lopez Report, 192, citing Duran testimony, p. 28.

[49] 3 AH 33 (Duran testimony, p. 28).

[50] Newman, *Oswald and the CIA*, 368; cf. Summers, *Conspiracy*, 582.

[51] The HSCA may possibly have been motivated (in this and other details of decorum) out of desire to protect Tirado, who unlike the other witnesses still lived in Mexico and indeed worked for the Mexican Government. To say this is not to explain away the initial sensitivity of the CP card issue.

this falsification antedated the assassination.

Conflicts between Durán's Statements and the Alleged CIA Intercepts

In particular these documents raise questions about the CIA's intercepted telephone conversations concerning Oswald from September 27 to October 1, 1963. The authenticity of the alleged September 28 conversation has already been challenged on these and other grounds by John Newman. A transcript prepared at the time by the CIA claims that Durán and someone, whom CIA Station employees later "determined" to be Oswald, phoned from the Cuban consulate to the Russian consulate on Saturday, September 28 (when both consulates were closed).[52] But according to the consensus of documents in both sets of the Durán records (DFS-2, DFS-3, ST-6, ST-7), Durán's position is that Oswald did not return after September 27, and specifically not on September 28. DFS-4, the Warren Commission version, is not credible in its revised language, that "she could not remember."

Newman's plausible hypothesis is that two of the speakers in the September 28 conversation, "Durán" and "Oswald," are impostors.[53] But CIA station employees, listening to the tapes, decided that the man who telephoned the Soviet Embassy on October 1, and identified himself as "Lee Oswald," was the same as the man who phoned on Saturday.[54] In other words, if the September 28 intercept is a fabrication involving a false "Oswald," so are the intercepts from October 1. This is an important finding, inasmuch as the only pre-assassination information about Oswald to go outside the CIA Station, all of it provocative, was based on these intercepts alone. The other family of intercepts, referring to Oswald's visa application on September 27, were for some unexplained reason not shared with CIA Headquarters or the FBI until late November 23.[55]

The two apparently fabricated intercepts between them suggested that a Soviet KGB member, Valeriy Kostikov, had sent a cable to Washington at Oswald's request. The September 28 transcript was so mysterious as virtually to defy summary: it had Oswald saying, "I went to the Cuban Embassy to ask them for my address, because they have it."[56] Transmitting this information to the FBI, CIA Headquarters commented, "From the gist of this conversation, it appears that the 'North American' expected to be at some location fixed by the Cuban Embassy and wanted the Russians to be able to reach him there."[57] By the time the FBI had this information, a Headquarters CIA Counterintelligence Officer, Tennant H. Bagley, had already identified Kostikov to the FBI as a KGB officer linked to "the KGB's 13th Department (responsible for sabotage and assassination)."[58]

For six weeks the CIA Station in Mexico had known from the September 27 family of transcripts (the "visa" family, as opposed to the apparently fabricated "non-visa" family) that Oswald's business was the relatively innocuous matter of a visa application. This clarifying information was conspicuously withheld, indeed denied, in a memo which the CIA Station passed in mid-October to the FBI in Mexico City:

---

[52] Newman, *Oswald and the CIA*, 364-68.

[53] Newman, *Oswald and the CIA*, 365-66. Newman considers it "improbable" (p. 368) that the third voice speaking from the Soviet Consulate "was also an impostor." However in the preceding sentence he invokes the claim of former Soviet Consul (and KGB member) Oleg Nechiporenko, that "the call could not have gone through because [on Saturday] the switchboard was closed." Quite clearly, if we accept Nechiporenko's statement, the whole of the alleged Saturday transcript has to be an artefact (fabrication).

[54] Lopez Report, 78, 171.

[55] MEXI 7033 of 23 November 1963, 232246Z, CIA Document # 55-546.

[56] MEXI 7023 of 23 November 1963, 231659Z, CIA Document # 49-545. Transcript reprinted in Newman, *Oswald and the CIA*, 364.

[57] DIR 84915 of 23 November 1963, 232200Z, CIA Document # 45-17.

[58] SX-25550, Memo from Tennant H. Bagley, Chief, SR/CI, 23 November 1963. The Review Board should ascertain when the CIA and FBI first linked Kostikov to Department 13 and assassinations. One reason may be the very circumstantial argument presented in DIR 82312 of 17 November 1963, that an individual who had met Kostikov in February 1963 had met three months later in New York with Oleg D. Brykin "of Thirteenth Department of First Chief Directorate of KGB."

This officer determined that Oswald had been at the Soviet Embassy on 28 September 1963 and had talked with Valeriy Vladimirovoch [sic] Kostikov, a member of the Consular Section, in order to learn if the Soviet Embassy had received a reply from Washington concerning his request. We have no clarifying information with regard to this request.[59]

Asked by the House Committee to explain "why the 10/16 memo said that there was no clarifying information on Oswald's 'request' when it was known by this time that he was seeking a visa," the memo's author (wife of the Station's expert on Soviet affairs) "said that 'They had no need to know all those other details.'"[60]

One concludes from all this that employees of the Mexico City Station were manipulating information about Oswald even before the assassination, and advancing data from the false (non-visa) intercepts in place of the more accurate data from the visa intercepts of September 27. Even the September 27 intercepts, however, appear questionable when we focus on the various versions of Durán's DFS statement.

Was the Durán Statement Based on the Oswald Visa Application?

DFS-3, the CIA cable translating the Spanish of DFS-2, contains one sentence that is a translation of something else:

Oswald was told that the aid which could be given to him was to advise him to go [to] the Russian Consulate. *The Consul then* spoke by telephone to the person in charge of that office, and was informed that the case would have to be referred to Moscow and that there would be a four month delay.[61]

There is no textual support for this reference to the Consul speaking by telephone in the Spanish original, which should perhaps be translated:

Oswald was told that the aid which she could give him was to advise him to go to the Russian Consulate, *for which reason* (para lo qual) she spoke by telephone to the person in charge of that office, and was informed that the case would have to be referred to Moscow and that there would be a four month delay.[62]

Silvia Durán objected to the DFS-4 version of this statement: "the declarant [i.e. Durán], *admitting that she exceeded her duties*, unofficially called the Russian Consulate."[63] In denying that she had either exceeded her duties or admitted this, Durán confirmed that she had telephoned the Consulate.[64]

Why then should we waste time on the unsupported statement in DFS-3 that "the Consul [not Silvia] then spoke by telephone?" The first reason is that, for some unexplained reason, the language of DFS-3, although not supported by the language of the DFS-2 version it purports to translate, almost exactly tracks the language typed on to Oswald's visa application, and signed by Consul Alfredo Mirabal:

---

[59] Memo of 16 October 1963 for the Ambassador from [redacted], Subject: Lee Oswald/Contact with the Soviet Embassy, CIA Document #9-5; filed in the Mexico City FBI Oswald file as 105-3702-1.

[60] Lopez Report, 171; quoted in Newman, *Oswald and the CIA*, 367. "They" here clearly refers to the Mexico City Ambassador and FBI, the recipients of the memo. Newman for some unexplained reason equates "They" with "the HSCA investigators" some fifteen years later.

[61] DIR 85758 of 29 November 1963, p. 6.

[62] Attachment to JKB memo of 26 November 1963, p. 5.

[63] 24 WH 688.

[64] 3 AH 99. Durán also objected to the sentence in DFS-4 that Azcue said to Oswald, "'people like you, instead of helping the Cuban Revolution, only do it harm,' it being understood that in their argument, they were referring to the Russian Socialist Revolution and not the Cuban Revolution" (24 WH 688, cf. 590, WR 302). Her response to this sentence was that the Azcue-Oswald conversation "was exclusively with the Cuban Revolution" (3 AH 100-01).

We [*Nosotros*] spoke to the Consulate of the USSR and satisfied ourselves that they had to wait for authority from Moscow to grant the visa and that there would be an approximately four month delay.[65]

The similarity is striking, and one is moved to ask if the CIA Station had not already acquired a copy of this visa application. Such a possibility reinforces another one, reported by John Newman from an FBI source, that "Silvia Duran was possibly a source of information for Agency or the Bureau."[66] An alternative possibility, no less suggestive, is that the CIA had obtained it from Oswald himself.

There is a second reason to believe the DFS-3 version is correct in alleging that the Consul had spoken to the USSR Consulate by telephone. This is that Consul Mirabal testified under oath that he had indeed talked with the Soviet Consul, and learned "it would take about 4 months to obtain a response."[67] One should not make too much of this corroboration. Testifying fifteen years later in 1978, Mirabal may have been influenced by the visa application in his hands.

The same might be said of Consul Azcue, who testified that it was he who received the call:

I received a telephone call from the consulate of the Soviet Union.... And the consul tells me that apparently the documents... attesting to his residence in the Soviet Union and his marriage certificate...are correct.... But without a doubt he cannot issue the visa without consulting Moscow.[68]

But Azcue's testimony is more credible for supplying details not summarized in the visa application observations: that he "received" rather than made the call, that the Soviet documentation was considered valid, and finally that Silvia "might have transferred the call to me."[69]

In the light of the contemporary evidence from the visa application, it is easy to imagine that Silvia did, in fact, transfer the call she received on September 27 to one or both of the consuls. The problem is that there is no trace of this transfer in the CIA transcript of the call, which shows Silvia alone talking, and closing off the conversation in a routine way ("No bother, thank you very much.")[70]

The CIA transcript is at odds with the visa application data in another respect: according to it the Soviet consul said (twice) that authorization had to come from Washington. Against this version of what was said we have the united testimony of the visa application, of Silvia Durán (in DFS-2 and DFS-3, but not in DFS-4), and of Consul Azcue in 1978, that the Soviet Consul said (what one might normally expect) that the authorization had to come from Moscow.

I cannot determine from the available evidence whether or not the transcript can be believed in its divergent reference to "Washington." It is likely however that the disappearance of the word "Moscow" from the DFS-4 version of Durán's testimony, like the insertion of her alleged memory lapse about whether Oswald called back, was a conscious editing to efface the conflicts between her original statement and the CIA transcripts.

---

[65] Oswald visa application, 3 AH 129; cf. 137, 25 WH 814: "*Nosotros llamanos al Consulado de la URSS y nos contestaron que ellos tenían esperar la autorización de Moscú para dar la visa y que tardería alrededor de 4 meses.*"

[66] Newman, *Oswald and the CIA*, 388, reporting what FBI SA Larry Keenan heard from the Mexico City Legal Attaché, Clark Anderson. A newly released note from David Phillips to Win Scott might seem to imply that Durán was provisionally considered for recruitment, but not after the assassination made her notorious ("She doesn't seem to me to have any target potential now, if she ever did, with all the confusion surrounding her;" hand-written note, date-stamped November 24, 1963, appended to MEXI copy of DIR 84921 of 24 November 1963; duplicate of CIA #68-554). But, given Phillips' record of phase-two prevarication, one could just as easily argue the opposite: that this note is yet another Phillips cover-up, intended to deceive.

[67] 3 AH 176.

[68] 3 AH 132; cf. 142.

[69] 3 AH 132, 142.

[70] CIA transcript from Soviet Embassy, September 27, 1963, 4:26 P.M., Oswald Box 15b, folder 56, CIA 1/94 release. Cf. MEXI 7033 of 23 November 1963.

What Were the CIA Station and DFS Up To?

It is clear, furthermore, that one of the editing changes to DFS-4 had the effect of effacing a nasty DFS secret, one which also may have concerned both agencies. This had to do with Silvia's alleged characterization of her own political position. In DFS-2 and DFS-3, she allegedly said of herself that "She has a leftist ideology, by conviction, and is in accord with Communism, but does not belong to any political group."[71] Just as Oswald's alleged self-profession of Communism vanished by revisions (in Mexico and also in Dallas), so also, in DFS-4, did Silvia's. Like Oswald's her "Communism" was converted on paper to "Socialism:" "That, as she had already stated, the declarant had been a follower of Socialism and the Marxist doctrine for several years."[72]

To understand what is at stake here, we must go back to the statement in ST-2 (the telephone conversation of 26 November between Ambassador Hernández Armas and Cuban President Dorticos) that the DFS asked concretely "if she had personal relations and even if she had intimate [i.e. sexual] relations with him. She denied all that."[73] In confirming this aggressive line of questioning to the HSCA, Silvia also supplied the context of a Communist conspiracy that the DFS were also hoping to establish:

> Cornwell: Did the officers from the Seguridad Department ever suggest to you during the questioning that they had information that you and Oswald had been lovers?
>
> Tirado: Yes, and also that we were Communists and that we were planning the Revolution and uh, a lot of false things.... Because all the time they tell me that I was a Communist and I said I'm not a Communist... I believe in Socialism but I'm not a Communist; and they insisted that I was a very important people for the government, the Cuban Government, and that I was the link for the International Communists---the Cuban Communists, the Mexican Communists, and the American Communists, and that we were going to kill Kennedy, and I was the link. For them I was very important. Of course, it was not true.[74]

At the time the Mexican CIA Station transmitted the misleading DFS-2 statement about Durán's alleged "accord with Communism," not only the Station Chief (Win Scott), but also the Ambassador (Thomas Mann) were pushing hard to obtain corroboration for what they called the Durán family's "apparent conspiracy with Oswald."[75] As I have noted earlier, they recommended not only that the DFS rearrest Durán, but that they "break" her under interrogation -- i.e. use torture.[76]

It is possible that Mann, Scott, and the Mexicans hoped by their talk of international conspiracy to provoke war against Cuba. But Mann and the Mexican Secretary of Gobernación Gustavo Díaz Ordáz were both good friends of the new American President Lyndon Johnson, and in fact the three men had met together repeatedly on Johnson's ranch.[77] It is also possible that their promotion of international conspiracy had a lesser goal in view: not war, but the apparent phase-one risk of war which Johnson was already exploiting as his case for establishing a Warren Commission.[78] (To say

---

[71] DIR 85758 of 29 November 1963, p. 5.

[72] 24 WH 687. For the extensive revision of testimony from many witnesses about Oswald's self-professed Communism," see Chapter VII, "Oswald, Harvey Lee Oswald, and Oswald's Communist Party Card."

[73] MEXI 7068 of 26 November 1963.

[74] 3 AH 86, 91; cf. Lopez Report, 254. In other words, this particular revision in DFS-4, unlike the others, was closer to what in all probability Durán actually said. At the same time, it significantly altered what the DFS November 23 statement originally reported.

[75] MEXI 7104 of 27 November 1963, CIA Document #174-616, p. 5.

[76] MEXI 7072 of 26 November 1963, CIA Document #128-590; see Chapter IV. Cuban Ambassador Hernández Armas had already described, in the conversation overheard and transmitted by the CIA, the bruises which the DFS had inflicted on Durán in her first interrogation (MEXI 7068 of 26 November 1963, p. 4).

[77] Dick Russell, *The Man Who Knew Too Much*, 454.

[78] See discussion above in Chapter VII, "Oswald...and Oswald's Party Card," 71-72.

this is not to accuse these three men of involvement in the assassination itself. The false "phase one" story, and its goal of inducing a Warren Commission, may conceivably have been designed as a *triage* operation: to restore faith in a badly shaken U.S. body politic, rather than for the conspiratorial goal of protecting guilty individuals.)

Along with other strange activities conducted by Ambassador Mann and the Mexico City Station, the DFS-2 allusion to Durán's "Communism" made phase-one speculation possible; the later DFS-4 effacement of this allusion brought her statement into line with the phase-two sentiments that were by now the U.S. government line. While Win Scott and station sources continued to promote the false story of Durán's affair with Oswald, as late as 1967, there was no longer any desire to promote such stories in Washington.[79]

To sum up: it would appear that the post-assassination hype about conspiracies was piggy-backed upon a pre-assassination operation, and that the successive alterations to Durán's statement were made by the CIA and the DFS to protect this operation.

What was this operation, and was it the CIA's? With good supporting evidence, John Newman has asked: "Could Oswald's trip have been part of a CIA effort at countering the FPCC in foreign countries and 'planting deceptive information which might embarrass' the FPCC?"[80] He has also argued that the phone calls of September 28 and October 1 (the non-visa family of phone intercepts) may represent a second operation (involving an Oswald impostor), piggy-backing, from outside and with limited information, upon the CIA's Oswald operation.[81] He does not speculate who may have been behind this second, unauthorized operation. I shall argue shortly that the Chicago mob may have had inside access, through the DFS, making it possible to plant false intercepts, creating the false impression of an Oswald-Kostikov contact. For the DFS had both CIA and mob links dating back virtually to its formation after World War II.[82]

Is there corroboration elsewhere for the suppressed intelligence operation (involving Oswald's visa application) which I have deduced from the rewriting of Durán's November 23 statement? There is perhaps some. If in fact a "Harvey Lee Oswald" did present a Communist Party card in support of his visa application, this operation, as I argued a year ago, would provide a source for the otherwise anomalous information in a November 22 Army cable from Texas (from Army Intelligence sources) that "Oswald, Harvey Lee... is card carrying member of Communist Party."[83]

It seems likely that the FBI in Mexico City knew about Harvey Lee Oswald's "Communist" activity in the Cuban Consulate, and knew to keep quiet about this otherwise explosive allegation. One suppressed document in the Mexico City FBI file on Lee Harvey Oswald (File 105-3702) was originally assigned to another file on "Harvey Lee Oswald" (File 105-2137).[84] To judge from this lower number, the file on Harvey Lee Oswald was older than the file on Lee Harvey Oswald, and would thus also date from before the assassination.

---

[79] See Chapter IV; Newman, *Oswald and the CIA*, 377-91. Newman writes (p. 391) of the "unsavory possibility" that "the story may have been invented after the Warren Commission investigation to falsely implicate the Cuban government in the Kennedy assassination." The record unambiguously shows that Durán was interrogated about this story by the DFS on November 23, 1963 (3 AH 86), and that this interrogation and accompanying abuse were discussed by Cuban Ambassador Hernández Armas three days later (MEXI 7068 of 26 November 1963). In 1967 she told a CIA station asset, LIRING-3, that in her DFS interview she had been "interviewed thoroughly and beaten until she admitted that she had an affair with Oswald" (Memo of 26 May 1967, "Meeting with LIRING-3," forwarded under HMMA-32243 of 13 June 1967; CIA Document #1225-1129, cf. #1084-965).

[80] Newman, *Oswald and the CIA*, 394; quoting from FBI memo in Schweiker-Hart Report, 65.

[81] Newman, *Oswald and the CIA*, 364-68.

[82] Scott, *Deep Politics*, 104-05, 142.

[83] U.S. Army Cable 480587 from Fort Sam Houston, Texas, to U.S. Strike Command, McDill AFB, Florida, 230405Z (Nov. 22, 10:05 CST): "Following is additional information on Oswald, Harvey Lee.... Don Stringfellow, Intelligence Section, Dallas Police Dept., notified 112th Intc Gp, this HQ, that information obtained from Oswald revealed he had defected to Cuba in 1959 and is card carrying member of Communist Party."

[84] Mexico City FBI file 105-3702 on Lee Harvey Oswald (opened 10/18/63): Serial -254, information from "Wesley." At bottom: "File 105-2137 (Harvey Lee Oswald)" [file # crossed out and changed to 3702].

One year ago I petitioned the Assassination Records Review Board for the review and release of this file, and all other files and records pertaining to Harvey Lee Oswald. I would now appeal to the Cuban Government for all pertinent documentation which it holds on this matter, specifically the records which they have of what Silvia Durán and other Embassy officials told them about Durán's DFS arrest and interview.

To learn where the original records of Durán's interview now can be located, the Review Board should also identify and interview those, like "JKB," who were responsible for them and for the altered and presumably falsified later versions. This list of witnesses would include the Mexican DFS officials involved, including Deputy Director Fernando Gutiérrez Barrios, who signed and attested to the falsely dated Warren Commission version.[85]

It should be easy to locate Gutiérrez as a witness: from 1989 until 1994 he served as Mexico's Secretary of Gobernación (Minister of Interior).[86] To persuade him to testify now on such a delicate matter will no doubt prove more difficult, for what is at stake is no less than the good faith between his government and that of the U.S. The Mexican officials must somehow be made to understand that the only hope for a healthy future, for both governments, lies in a full and frank disclosure of facts which have been poisonously falsified for far too long.

Gutiérrez' private secretary in 1963 was a young protege, José Antonio Zorrilla Pérez, who (as we shall see) was revealed in the 1980s to have been deeply implicated with Mexico's leading drug traffickers. It is at least possible that international drug traffickers exerted their influence on the DFS in 1963 as well, through the intervention of personnel recruited and trained by Chicago mobster Richard Cain.

The DFS, the Intercepts, Richard Cain, and the Chicago Mob

I have suggested that the progressive alterations of Silvia Durán's DFS statement of November 23 indicate two distinct levels of falsification. That is, one or more of the changes made to the DFS-4 or Gutiérrez Barrios version of her statement were apparently designed to preserve the credibility of a previously falsified pre-assassination telephone intercept transcript, that made on September 28. In making these changes, the DFS was in effect performing a service for the CIA; and it may well have have received guidance in this matter from the CIA (as it did in the original interrogation of Silvia).[87]

But the new CIA releases confirm earlier published reports that the DFS itself was involved in the pre-assassination LIENVOY telephone intercepts; and thus, if so, the DFS was protecting itself as well. In a book dealing with the DFS involvement with drug traffickers, Elaine Shannon alleged that the CIA entrusted the DFS with the task of collecting and transmitting these transcripts.[88] Philip Agee's book corroborated this allegation of DFS involvement. He described the wire-tap operation, LIENVOY, as a "joint telephone-tapping operation between Mexico City station and Mexican

---

[85] Gutiérrez's signed statement begins, "At 6 p.m. on November 23, 1963...I, the undersigned, Captain Fernando Gutiérrez Barrios...certify that Mrs. Silvia Tirado de Durán...drew up this instrument" (24 WH 686, cf. 669). Ms. Tirado testified in 1978 that she was arrested at lunch time on November 23 (3 AH 80-81), that she was interviewed until past midnight (3 AH 85-86, 101-02), that the DFS made a stenographic machine record (3 AH 83). Above all she took strong issue with the Warren Commission version of her statement, and denied making some of the statements in it attributed to her (8 AH 99-102). Specifically, she denied that she had admitted exceeding her duties in phoning the Soviet Consulate (3 AH 99; WR 302, 24 WH 589, 688) and that Azcue had reproached Oswald in the name of the Russian (as opposed to the Cuban) revolution (3 AH 101; 24 WH 589, 688).

[86] *Wall Street Journal,* March 16, 1989, A1.

[87] Among the CIA documents are lists of questions which the CIA Station prepared for Silvia's interrogation. See Mexico Station Dispatch of 13 November 1963 and attachments, CIA Document #404-750; also CIA Document #103(?)-42.

[88] Elaine Shannon, *Desperados* (New York: Viking, 1988), 180: "The DFS passed along photographs and wire-tapped conversations of suspected intelligence officers and provocateurs stationed in the large Soviet and Cuban missions in Mexico City."

security service:" "The station provides the equipment, the technical assistance, couriers and transcribers, while the Mexicans make the connections in the exchanges *and maintain the listening posts.*"[89]

Several CIA Documents released in September 1995 make it clear that in 1963 the Mexican Gobernación (Interior Ministry, in which the DFS was housed) also had access to the information product from the LIENVOY phone tap operation.[90] On the night of November 23-24 the Station notified Headquarters they had canceled their surveillance of Kostikov, having noticed that the Mexicans also had him under physical surveillance. They speculated that the Mexicans were "reading same [redacted] take as Station."[91]

Critics like myself, who have treated the LIENVOY intercept program as a CIA operation, have missed the important point that in fact it was staffed and monitored in part by the DFS.[92] This is important, because the DFS was already deeply involved in corruption and organized crime. Thus the LIENVOY operation, so often described as "the CIA's," was not only technically insecure, it was potentially open to manipulation by criminal elements. Those manning the listening posts in particular were apparently Mexican and not under CIA control.[93]

One can see how, under such conditions of divided responsibility, opportunities for mischief could proliferate. The CIA Station itself seems to have treated LIENVOY as insecure. On November 23 (?), in a memo listing Support Activities Assignments regarding the assassination, electronic surveillance of the Soviets was tasked to an older phone intercept program, LIFEAT.[94]

The Review Board should review and release CIA documents with respect to the LIENVOY operation, which may have been used to document a false Oswald-Kostikov link, and thus pressure the U.S. government into covering up the crime of its President's murder. It is particularly important to learn by whom, and under whose higher authority, the personnel were recruited who may have supplied falsified intercepts.

One man who may have been involved is Richard S. Cain (alias Scalzetti), the notorious Chicago mob figure and right-hand man to Sam Giancana who was also an FBI informant, and at the very least, a CIA contact. The CIA's own files show that Cain visited the CIA's Mexico City Station in April 1962, at which time "he stated that he had an investigative agency in Mexico...for the

---

[89] Philip Agee, *Inside the Company: CIA Diary*, 613, 532. Agee further claims that Mexican President Adolfo Lopez Mateos, a "close collaborator of the Mexico City station," received the cryptonym LIENVOY-2 (p. 614). Although Lopez Mateos was witting of the LIENVOY operation, recent CIA releases suggest that his cryptonym may have been different (Dir 85245 of 27 Nov 63, CIA Document #176-619).

[90] Dir 85245 of 27 Nov 63, CIA Document #176-619, NARA #104-10015-10188, PDS 62-116. Cf. XAAZ-35907, "Summary of Relevant Information on Lee Harvey Oswald at 0700 24 November 1963:" "Mexican authorities, [redaction dealing with sensitive sources and methods] and who had noticed the name of Lee OSWALD in it, arrested Silvia Duran" (CIA Document # 130-592, NARA #104-10015-10359, PDS 62-137). It was of course the DFS who arrested and interrogated Silvia Durán. Cf. also NARA #104-10004-10199, PDS 62-13,22; NARA #104-10018-10040, pp. 3, 10, PDS 62-144,151. Redacted references in these two documents to "the 1 October intercept on Lee Oswald" raise the possibility that although the station copy of this tape was indeed destroyed (as reported in MEXI 7054 of 11/24/63), the LIENVOY center manned by the Mexicans then supplied a duplicate copy (the one which was subsequently listened to by Warren Commission counsels Coleman and Slawson).

[91] MEXI 7041, 24 Nov 63, CIA Document # 74-555, NARA Record # 104-10015-10070. Earlier, in MEXI 7029 of 23 Nov 63, the Station reported to Headquarters that they had suggested to a Mexican official (Echeverria?) that Durán be arrested immediately and held incommunicado. The cable noted that the official "can say D.F.S. coverage revealed call to him if he needs to explain."

[92] Cf. *Deep Politics*, 41, where I write of "a CIA recording of the alleged Lee Oswald's voice." See also Newman, *Oswald and the CIA*, 355: "This call was recorded by the CIA's Mexico City station." The CIA itself is the source of this false impression: e.g. "On 1 October 1963, our Mexico City Station intercepted a telephone call Lee OSWALD made" (Headquarters CIA Report of about 13 Dec 1963, NARA # 104-10004-10199, p. 1).

[93] See e.g. handwritten appendix to NARA # 104-10095-10001, PDS 62-197: "The Mexican monitors (according to [redaction], outside Staff Agent) said caller (who called himself Oswald) had difficulty making himself understood both (as I recall) in English and in Russian."

[94] Memo of 23 (?) November 1963, TX-1939, NARA # 104-10015-10061, PDS 62-69. Of course the CIA may have had some other reason for not using LIENVOY that day. It is striking that the same memo says nothing about surveillance of the Cubans.

purpose of training Mexican government agents in police methods, in investigative techniques, and in the use of the lie detector."[95]

Cain's expertise was in electronic surveillance, most notoriously the tapping of telephones. In the period 1950-52 he had tapped the telephones of Cuban revolutionary leaders in Miami on behalf of Batista; in 1960 he was approached by his former employer to install phone taps on behalf of former Cuban President Prío.[96] According to an obituary notice in the *Chicago Tribune*, the CIA had engaged Cain in 1960 because of his Havana mob contacts, and also to wiretap the Czech embassy in Havana.[97] Thus Cain would appear to be a likely candidate to supply the "technical assistance" which Agee says the Mexico City CIA station provided the DFS on the LIENVOY operation.

We do not learn as much from the released CIA documents on Cain, but its clear that these have been bowdlerized. According to one document,

> The [CIA] Office of Security has a file on Subject CAIN which in summary reflects that...in 1963, while with the Cook County Sheriff's Office [and also working for Gian-cana], he became deeply involved in the President Kennedy assassination case.[98]

Yet the only example I have seen of this deep involvement is Cain's report to the Chicago CIA office that at a secret meeting in February 1963 of the Fair Play for Cuba Committee in Chicago, "the assassination of the President of the U.S. was discussed."[99] It is indeed interesting that Cain supplied this information (or disinformation). There are further hints in the same memo that Cain's "contact clearance" in September 1963 (which "furnished eight reports concerning exile Cuban activities in the Chicago area") may have produced additional information (or disinformation) which was later interwoven into the complex assassination stories involving Abraham Bolden and Dr. Paulino Sierra.[100] But there is nothing in these records to justify the claim that Cain was "deeply involved."

We see the same bowdlerization with respect to Mexico. Cain himself claimed "he had done some work for CIA in Mexico."[101] According to Agency documents, Cain's contact with CIA there was an unprovoked walk-in to the CIA Station, shortly before "he was deported from Mexico for carrying a loaded revolver and brass knuckles, for impersonating a Mexican government official, and for violating his tourist permit."[102] In a *Chicago Tribune* obituary notice that we read that Cain was ousted from Mexico for having trained anti-Castro Cuban exiles there, for a future invasion.[103] According to a follow-up article, Cain "did have repeated traffic with the CIA in Chicago and Mexico City," reporting on Castro spies in anti-Castro exile groups.[104]

The CIA was clearly evasive, even in its own internal documents, about its true relationship with Richard Cain. (One memo-writer observed, "I see no need or obligation on the part of the Agency to acknowledge [to an outsider] our past 'contact' relationship" with Cain; his superior,

---

[95] CIA memo to Chief, SRS, from M.D. Stevens, 9 October 1967, Subject: CAIN, Richard S., p. 2. Cf. Memo for Chief, LEOB/SRS, 11 December 1967, Subject: New York Times article of 6 December 1967 (on Abraham Bolden), p. 3.

[96] 10 AH 172. The HSCA listed Cain's employer's name in 1950 as William "Buenz." It is more likely that this was the William J. Burns Detective Agency, the firm for whom he worked at this time in Dallas and Chicago (*Chicago Tribune*, December 21, 1973).

[97] *Chicago Tribune*, December 28, 1973, p. 16.

[98] Memo for Director of Security, 19 December 1969, Subject: CAIN, Richard Scully...#272 141, pp. 1-2.

[99] Memo for Chief, LEOB/SRS, 11 December 1967, Subject: New York Times article of 6 December 1967 (on Abraham Bolden), p. 3.

[100] Ibid. Cf. Dick Russell, *The Man Who Knew Too Much*, 635 (Bolden); Peter Dale Scott, *Deep Politics*, 89-91, 329-30, 371; 3 AH 371-89 (Sierra). At least one of these eight reports produced a CIA name search for Arturo Olivera, one of the DRE's Chicago members (cf. CD 1085D3.2).

[101] Memo for Director of Security, 19 December 1969, Subject: CAIN, Richard Scully...#272 141, p. 1.

[102] Ibid.

[103] *Chicago Tribune*, December 28, 1973, p. 16.

[104] *Chicago Tribune*, December 31, 1973, p. 10.

Steven Kuhn of the Security Research Staff, concurred.)[105] The documents show nothing pertinent to
Time's allegation that in 1960-62 Cain was recruiting for anti-Castro operations:

> With the consent of the CIA, intelligence sources say, Detective Cain began recruiting
> Spanish-speaking toughs on the Windy City's West Side. Some of the hoodlums were
> sent to Miami and Central America for training in commando tactics....U.S. sources say
> that the CIA spent more than $100,000 on the operation, while Giancana laid out $90,000
> of the Mob's own funds for Cain's expenses.[106]

However, *Time*, as much as the CIA, may have had a motive to cover up the past relationship
between Richard Cain and its parent, Time-Life. The FBI heard in 1960 from Cain and another
source that he was planning to parachute into Cuba to take photos of anti-Castro guerrilla operations
on behalf of *Life*.[107] Such "covert operations journalism" was regularly conducted for Time-Life by
journalists and organized crime figures, such as John Martino; and regularly there was CIA support
for these operations as well.[108]

From all this we see, even from CIA files, indications of Cain's involvement with the Mexico
City CIA station and its operations. Let us for the time being hypothesize that Cain's firm, Accurate
Detective Laboratories, had a contract with the DFS to train (and possibly recruit) personnel to man
the electronic listening posts at the Soviet and Cuban consulates. This could mean that the operation
which produced falsified transcripts from Mexico City with respect to Oswald had been set up by a
man, Richard Cain, with links to the Chicago milieu of Jack Ruby. For Cain's firm, Accurate
Defense Laboratories (described in a CIA memo as "an investigative agency in Mexico with branches
in Chicago and Los Angeles") had its Chicago office in the back of a mob juice operation, Frontier
Finance Corp. And the owner of Frontier Finance, Fiore Buccieri, was later indicted with Ruby's old
friend and 1963 contact, Lenny Patrick.[109] The President of Frontier Finance, former Chicago Police
Captain John Scherping, also ran the Chicago office of Accurate Laboratories, which hired Cain as its
general manager.[110]

The Richard Cain-Lennie Patrick-Dave Yaras segment of the Chicago mob had connections in
1963 not only to Ruby but to Sam Giancana, and above all to mob activities in Cuba.[111] It is of
course unlikely that they could by themselves have originated a sophisticated message linking
Oswald to Kostikov, whose potential for blackmail depended on knowledge of what was contained
about Kostikov in government files. But if Cain recruited and/or trained those who were in the DFS
intercept program, then we may have isolated the matrix for a sophisticated CIA-Mafia assassination
plot in 1963, one whose target was ultimately deflected from Castro to Kennedy. Such a matrix could
have connected activities that on the surface would seem wholly unrelated, from sophisticated intelligence manipulations in Mexico City to the crimes in Dallas of Jack Ruby and his associates.

For Cain, unlike Buccieri and Patrick, appears to have been close to, if not inside, the highly
sensitive CIA-Mafia connection that in 1960-61 recruited Cain's boss Giancana and Santos
Trafficante for the assassination of Fidel Castro. An HSCA staff report presents credible arguments
that Cain's own mission in 1960 may have been part of the CIA-Mafia plots against Castro, and that
Cain himself may have been the "assassin-to-be" mentioned by his boss Giancana on October 18,
1960.[112]

[105] Memo for Director of Security, 19 December 1969, Subject: CAIN, Richard Scully...#272 141, p. 3.

[106] *Time*, June 16, 1975; quoted in Hinckle and Turner, *The Fish Is Red*, 78.

[107] 10 AH 173; FBI files HQ 105-93264 and Chicago 139-1403; cf 92-12846, all on subject: Cain. The Review
Board should obtain these files. Cain told the FBI he was in touch with Manuel Antonio de Varona, who was (as
ZR/RIFLE-2) involved in the 1960-61 CIA-Mafia assassination plots.

[108] See Scott, *Deep Politics*, 113-20.

[109] CIA memo to Chief, SRS, from M.D. Stevens, 9 October 1967, Subject: CAIN, Richard S., p. 2 ("agency");
Chicago Tribune, December 31, 1973, p. 10 ("Buccieri"); Chicago Crime Commission, Annual Report, 1966, p. 104
("Patrick"); Scott, *Deep Politics* 152, AR 151 ("1963 contact").

[110] Ovid Demaris, *Captive City*, 292.

[111] 4 AH 567, 9 AH 948; Scheim, *Contract on America*, 132-37; Scott, *Deep Politics*, 158-63, 172, 192, and
passim.

[112] 10 AH 172-73. The same memo argues that Cain may have been the "J.W. Harrison" whose bugging es-

At least in 1961-62, this highly restricted operation was run out of the CIA's Staff D (FI/D), headed by William Harvey.[113] Ostensibly Staff D "was a small Agency component responsible for communications intercepts."[114] However the restrictions on clearances for COMINT (communications intelligence) made FI/D an ideal hiding place for sensitive operations that CIA officials wished to hide from the rest of the Agency. One of these was ZR/RIFLE, Harvey's project for an "Executive Action Capability," i.e. assassinations. Thus it was an FI/D workshop that, for example, provided AM/LASH with a poison pen device in November 1963.[115]

FI/D was definitely responsible for the LIENVOY intercept program in Mexico City. LIEN-VOY reports were filed regularly to FI/D (and thus at one time to Harvey) at Headquarters. More significantly, Ann Goodpasture, the Station employee who brought the DFS intercept product into the CIA station, was an FI/D employee.[116]

In other words it is entirely plausible that FI/D would turn to Cain, when developing the LIEN-VOY program in the early 1960's. A CIA component willing to collaborate with Giancana's men in assassination would certainly have no problem in recruiting Giancana's electronic expert for a wire-tap operation.

But this collaboration looks more sinister in 1963, when LIENVOY produced false intercepts concerning Oswald and Kostikov. Ann Goodpasture played a role in the falsification of the record; it was she, for example, who supplied the mistaken identification in the station's original Oswald cable, making Oswald appear to be "age 35" and balding.[117] The introduction of the impostor intercepts into the CIA's files must have involved, similarly, people inside the Station as well as the outside. If Richard Cain helped recruit the latter, then we may be looking at an FI/D disinformation operation at both the DFS end and also inside the Station.

To sum up, in the the LIENVOY Project we may have isolated a key pressure point in the manipulation of an authorized intelligence operation into an illegal assassination plot. The false October 1 CIA-DFS intercept contributed to the false Oswald-Kostikov link that was eventually used to provoke an official cover-up of the assassination.

The Review Board should regard this CIA-DFS connection as relevant, perhaps central, to the Kennedy assassination plot. It should pursue the relevant documents with those elements in the Mexican Government now seeking to purge the tradition of criminal influence and corruption from their country's politics. Personnel of the DFS have played, and apparently continue to play, a crucial role in that tradition.[118]

capade in Las Vegas, on behalf of Maheu and Giancana, led to an effective CIA immunity for Giancana (10 AH 173-74). General Fabián Escalante Font of the Cuban Interior Ministry charged in a 1993 Cuban television documentary that Richard Cain was one of the marksmen, along with Leonard Patrick, who shot President Kennedy in Dallas (Reuters, 11/27/93; cf. Claudia Furiati, *ZR Rifle: The Plot to Kill Kennedy and Castro*, 140, 165). For reasons too lengthy to explore here, I doubt that Cain and Patrick were shooters on November 22.

[113] I.G. Report, 37.

[114] David Martin, *Wilderness of Mirrors*, 121; quoted in Newman, *Oswald and the CIA*, 374.

[115] I.G. Report, 92-93; Martin, *Wilderness of Mirrors*, 121; Newman, *Oswald and the CIA*, 375.

[116] Newman, *Oswald and the CIA*, 374. Newman falls into a common mistake in calling the Oswald transcripts "Cuban Consulate transcripts." In fact the CIA has supplied us with transcripts from the Soviet Embassy alone; intercepts of Oswald from the Cuban Embassy phones have for some unexplained reason never been released. Cf. Lopez Report, 81 (almost entirely deleted). In 1976 all but ones of the CIA officers queried by CIA Legal Counsel Scott Breckinridge apparently told him that "the Cuban tap" was not active "at the time Oswald visited Mexico" (Memo for the Record of 3 Dec 1976 from Scott D. Breckinridge, OLC; NARA # 104-10095-10001). We know however that on September 27 (at the time of Oswald's visit) there was an active tap on at least one Cuban Embassy telephone, 25-09-14. (The transcripts are in the National Archive, JFK Collection, Box 7, Folder 30). The intercepts include a call from Silvia Durán at 10:54 am, asking another officer, Guillermo Ruiz, for the Consulate number. The number supplied by Ruiz (11-28-47) is that given by Silvia to Oswald (presumably in her office at that time), and that afternoon, in connection with Oswald, to the Soviet Consulate. Cf. 16 WH 54 ("11-28-47" in Oswald's notebook); MEXI 7033 of 23 Nov 1963 (phone call to Soviet Embassy); Lopez Report, fn. 319 (transcript). This phone call is hard to reconcile with Durán's testimony to the HSCA that she gave out the telephone number "so many times" (3 AH 21) "to all the people" (3 AH 51).

[117] Lopez Report, 136-39.

[118] Regrettably the Board has already acceded to CIA withholding with respect to "the 1 October intercept on

The DFS and Crime, 1947-94

In Mexico, to be sure, a DFS scandal involving forged and altered documents will seem almost trivial in the light of later DFS scandals. The DFS was already linked to drug-traffickers by the late 1940s, when the DFS founder retired to work with Mexico's leading international drug kingpin.[119] The Chicago mob had been supplied with drugs from Durango, Mexico, from as far back as 1947, in a major Mexican government-protected connection that appears to have involved Jack Ruby.[120] By the 1960s Durango and Chicago were joined in a heroin connection, dominated at both ends by the family of Jaime Herrera Novales. Herrera Novales, a Mexican, was protected by his badges as a member of the State Police and also the DFS.[121] Chicago mobsters were simultaneously involved in smuggling stolen cars to Mexico, in an international ring which appeared to overlap with narcotics operations.[122]

Mexico's culture of political corruption attracted Sam Giancana when he fled from U.S. Justice in 1966. Protected by a lawyer close to President Echeverría, it was easy for him to continue to run his world-wide gambling operations from Mexico City and then Cuernavaca. Cain introduced Giancana to this lawyer, Jorge Castillo; and eventually, after Cain was released from jail in 1971, Cain became Giancana's courier.[123] It is possible that Giancana's activities in Mexico also involved narcotics. Drug trafficker Alberto Sicilia Falcón, a Bay of Pigs veteran, is said to have been in regular contact with Giancana in Cuernavaca, in the same period that he had Echeverría's Secretary of Gobernación, Mario Moya Palencia, as a passenger on his private plane.[124]

In the 1970s an offshoot of the DFS, the Brigada Blanca, formed death squads to eliminate the violent left.[125] In the early 1980s no less than thirteen DFS officials were indicted in California for their active involvement in a major international stolen car ring; Miguel Nazar (or Nassar) Haro, by then the DFS Director (and in 1978 the man who helped frustrate the visit of HSCA investigators to Mexico) was initially protected from indictment by the CIA, because of his alleged "indispensability as a source of intelligence in Mexico and in Central America."[126] Nazar Haro "was also linked in U.S. court testimony to selling protection to cocaine smugglers."[127]

The scandal of the DFS' long-time involvement with international drug trafficking came to a head under Nazar Haro's successor, José Antonio Zorrilla Pérez. Zorrilla in 1963 had been private secretary to his political mentor, Fernando Gutiérrez Barrios.[128] By the 1980s the DFS zone

---

Lee Oswald," the next review being projected in the year 2017. See NARA #104-10004-10199, PDS 62-13,22; NARA #104-10018-10040, pp. 3, 10, PDS 62-144,151.

[119] Scott, *Deep Politics*, 142.

[120] Scott, *Deep Politics*, 131, 138-41. In 1947 Ruby was involved, probably as an FBN informant, in a major Mexican opium-smuggling case. A man whom Ruby met in Chicago, Taylor Crossland, was subsequently arrested by the FBN (on a tip from "underworld sources") after arriving in the U.S. from Durango, Mexico (*Chicago Tribune*, August 30, 1947). Paul Roland Jones, the key figure arrested in this case, contacted Ruby, for the first time in ten years, shortly before the Kennedy assassination (Scott, *Deep Politics*, 143).

[121] Elaine Shannon, *Desperados*, 58-59, 180.

[122] Demaris, *Captive City*, 337; cf. Chicago Crime Commission, Annual Report, 1966, 53-54. Gerald Covelli, arrested in 1963 for his role in the stolen car ring, was a former business associate of Paul Labriola and James Weinberg, who had come down from Chicago to Dallas along with Paul Roland Jones and Jack Ruby (Demaris, *Captive City*, 336; Scheim, *Contract on America*, 110, 9 AH 155). Covelli's ring exported stolen cars to Guatemala and to Mexico, where top police officials were later indicted for receiving stolen U.S. cars (see below). A continent-wide stolen car ring had functioned in Chicago since the 1940s; see *Chicago Tribune*, August 30, 1947.

[123] Brashler, *The Don*, 290-93; *Chicago Tribune*, December 21, 1973, p. 8.

[124] James Mills, *The Underground Empire*, 548-51, 839-40; Henrik Krueger, *The Great Heroin Coup*, 178.

[125] Elaine Shannon, *Desperados*, 180; Rogelio Hernández, *Zorrilla: el Imperio del Crimen*, 24-25.

[126] When Associate Attorney General Lowell Jensen, alerted to the CIA interest in Nazar Haro, refused to permit Nazar's indictment, the U.S. Attorney in San Diego, William Kennedy, publicly exposed the CIA's role in obstructing justice. For this Kennedy was fired. See Elaine Shannon, *Desperados*, 181-83; Peter Dale Scott and Jonathan Marshall, *Cocaine Politics*, 36.

[127] Philip L. Russell, *Mexico Under Salinas*, 6.

[128] Rogelio Hernández, *Zorrilla: el Imperio del Crimen*, 13.

commanders along the U.S. border were all suspected by DEA officials of complicity in the growing drug traffic; and Zorrilla himself was reportedly receiving payoffs from the Guadalajara drug kingpin Rafael Caro Quintero.[129] When a former friend of Zorrilla's, the journalist Manuel Buendía, began to explore the relationships between Mexican police, CIA, and drug traffickers, he was shot down in the streets of Mexico City. Zorrilla and other DFS agents were the first to arrive on the scene, and also to ransack his office.[130] Zorrilla, who was soon a suspect, retired abruptly as DFS Director in February 1985; and the DFS was dissolved. Four years later he was arrested with at least four other DFS officers for involvement in Buendía's murder.[131] Opposition legislators demanded that Zorrilla's superior in 1984, Fernando Gutiérrez Barrios, be forced to testify as to his "possible knowledge" about the case.[132]

The U.S. press hailed Zorrilla's arrest as a sign that the new Mexican government of President Carlos Salinas de Gortari might crack down on organized corruption. However Zorrilla's arrest closed, rather than opened, the doors on a larger investigation of all those involved, including his superiors. And Salinas' first choice for head of the Intelligence Directorate, successor organization to the DFS, was Miguel Nazar Haro. (Nazar Haro soon retired again, when old charges were revived in the press about his use of torture as DFS director.)[133]

Since then it has become clear that the dark shadow of the longtime DFS-drug connection continues to haunt Mexican politics. In August of this year the *New York Times* revealed that a former DFS agent, Fernando de la Sota, who was later also a CIA agent, had been arrested and convicted for lying about his presence at the assassination in 1994 of Mexican presidential candidate Luís Donaldo Colosio.[134] According to the Mexican weekly *Proceso*, the briefly arrested "second gunman" in the case, Jorge Antonio Sánchez, turned out to be an agent of the Center of Investigations and National Security (CISEN), the current successor organization to the DFS. Reporting this in the *Nation*, Andrew Reding further referred to the "trails of evidence" leading to top officials of the Salinas administration, like José Cordoba Montoya, Salinas' coordinator of the intelligence agencies, including CISEN.[135] The mystery of the Colosio assassination is still further heightened by the interest in it of Miguel Nazar Haro, privately investigating the murder as he did earlier that of Manuel Buendía.[136]

It is perhaps hopeful that the new Mexican President, Ernesto Zedillo, has distanced himself from this DFS tradition, by appointing an opposition party member as his new Attorney General. A better understanding of DFS irregularities in 1963 should be welcomed in 1995 by those forces in Mexican politics who are seeking to limit the influence of corruption and assassinations.

But what should most concern us in this deep political interaction between the CIA and a criminal DFS is the CIA's protection of at least one guilty DFS leader (Miguel Nazar Haro) from deserved prosecution in U.S. courts. This protection should be evaluated in the light of the CIA immunity granted to Sam Giancana in 1961 (in which Cain may have played a role) and the FBI and Warren Commission's false isolation of Ruby from the Giancana-Yaras-Patrick Chicago mob in 1964.[137]

---

[129] Elaine Shannon, *Desperados*, 184-86, 263-64.

[130] Elaine Shannon, *Desperados*, 202; Rogelio Hernández, *Zorrilla: el Imperio del Crimen*, 37-39.

[131] Elaine Shannon, *Desperados*, 263; *New York Times*, June 15, 1989; *San Francisco Chronicle*, June 30, 1989. Two of the arrested officers, Juventino Prado and Raul Pérez Carmona, had earlier been indicted in the stolen car ring case (*Washington Post*, June 26, 1989, A15).

[132] *Christian Science Monitor*, July 10, 1989.

[133] *Washington Post*, June 26, 1989, A15.

[134] *New York Times*, August 3, 1995, A5. De la Soto was dropped from both the Mexican and the CIA payroll in 1992, after he was suspected of being paid off by the leading drug trafficker in Ciudad Juárez (Rafael Aguilar Guajardo, the former DFS commander in Durango). Cf. Elaine Shannon, *Desperados*, 185, 263.

[135] Andrew Reding, "Narco-Politics in Mexico," *Nation*, July 10, 1995, 53-54.

[136] *New York Times Magazine*, August 21, 1994, 38; Rogelio Hernández, *Zorrilla: el Imperio del Crimen*, 52.

[137] In 1963-64, and again in 1993, a key figure in presenting Ruby as a loner appears to have been former Chicago FBI Agent William Roemer. In 1963 Roemer was the FBI expert on Sam Giancana, in part because Roemer's chief mob informant (and close friend) was Richard Cain (cf. Roemer, *War of the Godfathers*, 141, 220). Soon after Ruby killed Oswald, Roemer's young partner John Bassett helped elicit from Giancana-Patrick associates like Dave

Yaras the assurances that Ruby "was not outfit connected" (22 WH 372, cf. 317, 357) that later found their way into the Warren Report (R 790). After this false picture was demolished by the HSCA, Roemer himself revived it for Posner in 1993. Roemer told Posner that Ruby's Junk Handlers Union local "was a legitimate union when Jack was involved" (Posner, p. 352). This demonstrable falsehood (cf. 22 WH 438) was based on earlier FBI misinformation (22 WH 320) from a witness, Ted Shulman, who had once been closely interrogated by McClellan Committee Counsel Robert Kennedy about his "collusive deals" with mob figure Paul Dorfman (Scott, *Crime and Cover-Up*, 39; McClellan Committee, 16084-16103). Roemer also told Posner that "Ruby was absolutely nothing in terms of the Chicago mob....We talked to every hoodlum in Chicago after the assassination, and some of the top guys in the mob, my informants, I had close relationships with them -- they didn't even know who Ruby was" (Posner, p. 354). This evasion was clearly deceptive: some of the "top guys" talked to, and specifically Yaras (22 WH 372) and Patrick (22 WH 318, cf. 9 AH 948-52), freely admitted knowing Ruby for years.

APPENDIX I: REVISING THE OSWALD LEGEND: A "MARXIST," NOT A COMMUNIST

A: WITNESSES CLOSE TO OSWALD

WITNESS NO. 1: Ruth Paine:

Phase One: Ruth Paine to James Hosty, 11/5/63: "Mrs. PAINE then expressed the opinion that she considered LEE OSWALD to be an illogical person and recalled that he admitted to her being a 'Trotskyite Communist'." (23 WH 508, 17 WH 777, 23 WH 459, etc.)

Ruth Paine's brother to FBI, 12/2/63: "He could not recall his sister mentioning the name Oswald at that time, but said that the woman's [Marina's] husband was a Communist" (SAC Cincinnati to DIR, 12/3/63, FBI HQ 105-82555-146)

Phase Two: Ruth Paine to Warren Commission, 3/19/64: "Representative Boggs. Did he ever express any political opinions to you? Mrs. Paine. Yes, he called himself a Marxist." Cf. 3/20/64: "I thought he considered himself a Communist by ideology, certainly a Marxist. He always corrected anyone who called him a Communist and said he was a Marxist" (3 WH 108).

WITNESS NO. 2: Michael Paine:

The revision of her husband's views reportedly underwent a similarly striking metamorphosis in just four days:

Phase One: Michael Paine to FBI (Harrison), 11/22/63: "Oswald has indicated to him to have read extensively of Communism and appeared to him to have Communistic ideas" (WCD 5.201)

Deputy Sheriff Walthers: "I said, 'How does the guy [Oswald] think, what is he, what does he do?' He [Michael Paine] said, 'He's a Communist. He is very communistic minded. He believes in it'" (7 WH 549; describing meeting on November 22).

Phase Two: Michael Paine to FBI (Odum and Hosty), 11/26/63: "Oswald stated that he became a Marxist in this country and that he learned Marxism from reading books" (WCD 5.207)

Michael Paine to Warren Commission, 3/18/64: "I thought to myself if that is the way he has to meet his Communists, he has not yet found the Communist group in Dallas (2 WH 408).

Warren Report, citing Michael Paine and his friend Frank Krystinik: Oswald "expressed Marxist views and declared he was a Marxist, although denying that he was a Communist" (WR 739).

WITNESS NO. 3: Frank Krystinik:

Phase One: Krystinik to FBI, 11/25/63: "Krystinik asked Oswald about his political belief and Oswald stated that he was a 'Marxist.' Krystinik then asked 'Does that mean you are a Communist?' Oswald then said 'All right, if you want to call me that, that is what I am, I'm a Communist" (SAC Dallas to DIR, 12/3/63, FBI HQ 105-82555-158). Cf. WCD 6.188.

Phase Two: Krystinik to Warren Commission, 3/17/64: "Mr. Liebeler: In the course of the conversation with Oswald at the ACLU meeting, did he tell you he was a Marxist? Mr. Krystinik: Yes. It seems to me that I commented to him that, 'You are a Communist and I am a Capitalist,' and I can't remember exactly what it was, but he corrected me and he said, 'I am a Marxist.' When I addressed him as a Communist, he said, 'I am a Marxist.' Mr. Liebeler: He corrected you then when you said he was a Communist and indicated he was not a Communist? Mr. Krystinik: Yes." (9 WH 466)

Warren Report: "Oswald expressed Marxist views and declared that he was a Marxist, although denying that he was a Communist" (WR 739)

WITNESS NO. 4: John A. McVickar:

A key witness to Oswald's 1959 defection in the U.S. Moscow Embassy, John A. McVickar, underwent the same phase-one/phase-two Communist/Marxist conversion over in the State Department:

Phase One: McVickar to FBI, 11/23/63: "Oswald was arrogant, 'mad' and threw his passport on the desk....McVickar said Oswald spoke as a trained communist as he repeated 'the party line.' He said he felt Oswald and Webster were both used by Soviet intelligence for interrogation only" (FBI WFO Airtel to DIR, 11/23/63; FBI HQ 105-82555- 9th no. 49)

Phase Two: McVickar to State Dept., official memo of 11/27/63: "Oswald was extremely arrogant, truculent [sic] and unfriendly to America....He gave the impression of being very angry about something or things which had happened to him during his childhood or during his duty in the Marine Corps. He said however that he was a 'Marxist'....He gave evidence of some education in the rudiments of Communist dogma....It seemed to me that he could have acquired all these ideas himself....On the other hand, there also seemed to me to be the possibility that he was following a pattern of behaviour in which he had been tutored by person or persons unknown. For example, in discussing Marxism and the legalities of renunciation he seemed to be using words which he had learned but did not fully understand" (Memo of 11/27/63, 18 WH 154-55)

McVickar to State Dept., Confidential memo of 4/7/64: "I am afraid that I remember only very little of the actual statements in Communist terms which Oswald made to justify his desire to renounce his citizenship. I recall he said that he wanted to renounce 'because he was a Marxist'....It seemed to me then that he was using words that he did not fully understand, but this does not necessarily mean that he was taught to say them...he might have read some books himself" (Memo of 4/7/64, 18 WH 334)

McVickar to Warren Commission, 6/9/64: Does not mention either "communist" or "Marxist;" "It occurred to some of us that it may be that he had some coaching from somebody; but also, I must say, he was an unusual person and apparently sort of an ingrown person, and so it may be that he had conceived and carried out all these things by himself" (5 WH 302-03)

WITNESS NO. 5: Kerry Thornley:

Phase One: Kerry Thornley to Secret Service, 11/25/63: Thornley "had made this comment to Oswald, that he [Oswald] was a Communist" (11 WH 95)

Phase Two: Kerry Thornley to Warren Commission: "I certainly didn't think he was a Communist and I certainly didn't tell him so.... At the time I just thought -- well, the man is a nut" (11 WH 95-96)

CASE NO. 6: The Glover Party, 2/22/63:

Phase One: "Florence McDonald" to FBI, 11/29/63: "Oswald informed all in attendance that he was a Communist and had attempted to join the Communist Party while he was in Russia" (WCD 5.192)

Richard Pierce to FBI, 11/29/63: "recalled that Oswald did not hesitate in stating he was a Communist and sympathetic to the views of Communism" (WCD 5.194)

Phase Two: Alexandra Taylor to FBI, 12/1/63: Oswald "considered himself a socialist" (FBI HQ 105-82555-140)

Elke and Norman Fredricksen to FBI, 12/4/63: "Fredricksens did not recall that he said he was a Communist or member of.... [second page of teletype missing] (FBI HQ 105-82555-160)

Neither McDonald nor Pierce testified to the Warren Commission. McDonald was called "Betty McDonald" by Glover (10 WH 25) and "Elizabeth McDonald" by Michael Paine (9 WH 452). The Warren Report Index to Volumes 1-15 fails to distinguish her from the Betty Mooney MacDonald who hanged herself in a cell after serving as alibi for the accused shooter of a witness in the Tippit killing (WR 663; Meagher, 293-97).

Phase Two: Everett Glover to Warren Commission, 3/24/64: "This may be partly as a result of questioning some of the people present, but among the things that came out was that...he was apparently a Marxist....I do remember that he [Volkmar Schmidt or Richard Pierce] said he was a Marxist. Mr. Jenner. What impression did you have of the distinction, if any, between Marxism and Communism? Mr. Glover. Well, with reference specifically to the so-called Communist regime, the impression I got was that he was a Marxist theoretically, but he did not like what he saw in Russia" (9 WH 25-26)

Ruth Paine was interviewed at length about this party, where she first met the Oswalds, and which lasted five hours (2 WH 435-43). Her closest testimony on Oswald's politics at the party was to Mr. McCloy, as follows: "Mr. McCloy. [He] had an affinity for what might be called the Marxist system, is that right? Mrs. Paine. Right. Mr. McCloy. That is all the questions that I have" (2 WH 441)

George and Jeanne de Mohrenschildt were interviewed about this party (9 WH 256-59, 318-19), but not about Oswald's politics. Their daughter Alex (Taylor) Gibson was not asked about the party at all (11 WH 123-53).

B. WITNESSES AND SOURCES HOSTILE TO OSWALD

Two examples only will be cited here, because their sources, military intelligence and the Cuban anti-Castro Revolutionary Student Directorate (DRE), were perhaps the most prolific source of pernicious phase-one stories hostile to Oswald in the first days after the assassination.

Original Source: Air Force Intelligence (OSI): Major Crawford Hicks, Sixth District OSI, Robbins AFB, Macon Ga.

Witness: Palmer McBride, Patrick Air Force Base, Florida.

Phase One Story: Oswald "according to McBride, was preaching the Communist doctrine and stated he would like to kill President Eisenhower" (FBI airtel November 22, FBI HQ 105-82555-6th no. 50)

FBI Intervention: interview by Tampa FBI Agent John Palmer, November 23.

Phase Two Story: "I, Palmer E. McBride hereby furnish the following free and voluntary statement to John R. Palmer....Oswald was very serious about the virtues of Communism....In another conversation Oswald stated to me he was not a member of the Communist Party but he suggested both of us should join to take advantage of their social functions. I did not join the Communist Party, but I do not know whether he did or not" (WCE 1386 of 11/26/63, WCD 75.251-53, 22 WH 710-11).

Warren Report: "Oswald praised Khrushchev and suggested that he and McBride join the Communist Party 'to take advantage of their social functions'" (WR 384).

Original Source: DRE, CIA-backed anti-Castro group

Phase One Story: "Oswald acted as Chairman of the Fair Play for Cuba Committee, a well-known communist organization, in New Orleans....In the debate [with Carlos Bringuier of DRE, Oswald] proclaimed himself as a marxist-leninist and profound follower of Fidel Castro" (DRE Publication *La Trinchera*, 11/22/63)

Jose Antonio Lanusa, Intelligence Officer for DRE, reportedly told Daniel James, Executive Secretary of Citizens Committee for a Free Cuba "Oswald definitely a Communist and supporter of Castro" 9SAC WFO Airtel to Dir FBI, 11/23/63, 8:59 PM; FBI HQ 105-82555-8th no. 50)

FBI Intervention: Lanusa interviewed by Miami FBI Nov. 23; report is silent about Oswald's politics (SAC Miami to DIR FBI, 11/24/63; Miami FBI 105-8342-1). Evelio Ley interviewed by Miami FBI Nov. 23, describes Oswald as "a pro Fidel Castro" (SAC Miami to DIR FBI, 11/23/63; FBI HQ 105-82555-10th nr 50; 62-109060-820).

Phase Two Story: "In the debate...Oswald denied his membership in [*su filiacion al*] the Communist Party but affirmed himself to be a Marxist (DRE Newsletter of 11/26/63, obtained from Lanusa by Miami FBI Agent James J. O'Connor; Miami FBI 105-8342-53).

APPENDIX II: THE DOCUMENTARY LIFE OF HARVEY LEE OSWALD

A. In Mexico

Mexico City FBI file 105-3702 on Lee Harvey Oswald (opened 10/18/63): Serial -254, information from "Wesley." At bottom: "File 105-2137 (Harvey Lee Oswald)" [file # corrected to 3702]. Bill Turner (ex-FBI) is sure that these files would be numbered in consecutive order, so that 2137 would be earlier than 3702.

CIA Doc. #131-593; JKB memo of 11/26/63 and 10-page attachment: Summary of first Mexican interview of Silvia Duran et al, pp. 7 (twice), 8, 9, 10: "Aseveró no conocer a Harvey Lee Oswald." Versions of this sentence are used five times in all in this document, in statements of Ruben Duran, Betsy Serratos, Agata Roseno, Barbara Ann Bliss, and Charles Bentley.

B. In the Oswald Family

26 WH 765; CE 3119; Secret Service Report of 11/30/63: Mrs. Hazel Oswald (aunt) "told Harvey that she had a large, framed picture of his father.... William Stout Oswald...stated that although Harvey Lee Oswald is said to be his second cousin, he had never met him nor had he known Harvey was also employed by the William B. Reily Coffee Company....As Henry Davis had accompanied William to the office, he was interviewed on 11-23-63. He said that he did not know Harvey Lee Oswald."

21 WH 127; Pic Exh. No. 60 (Pic address book): (Mostly in LHO handwriting): "P.O. Box 2915 Dallas, Texas   O - Harvey." (11 WH 60-61 explains that Secret Service in San Antonio introduced marks "to identify the handwritings in the book... with the circle being the handwriting of Lee Harvey Oswald" 11 WH 60). Re last page ("O - Harvey"), Pic testifies: "This is the identifying mark in the hand of Secret Service Ben A. Vidles, in San Antonio, Tex." (11 WH 61). *** What this all means is that Oswald on Thanksgiving Day 1962 entered his name in his half-brother's address book as "Harvey."

Secret Service Interview of Marina Oswald, 11/25/63, WCD 344.9: "After you married Harvey, where did you and Harvey maintain your address or residence?"

C. In the Marines

8 WH 319 (affidavit of Paul Edward Murphy): "Oswald was nicknamed 'Harvey' after 'Harvey the Rabbit,' a movie which was then circulating. So far as I know, Oswald acquired this nickname for no reason other than that it was his middle name."

8 WH 317 (affidavit of Peter Francis Connor): "Oswald was nicknamed 'Harv.' This was a shortened version of his middle name; for some reason it upset him to be called by it."

FBI HQ 105-82555-204 (Memphis newspaper interview of Memphis patrolman J.E. Pitts, 11/24/63): "Oswald...had an intense hate for anyone that called him by the nickname of 'Harve' or by his middle name of 'Harvey' and he wanted to fight anyone that did it."

Pitts in Epstein, *Legend*, 282: "the guys found out he didn't like being called Harvey or Harve, so that's what a lot of guys called him."

Cf. 8 WH 270 (Daniel Patrick Powers): "He had the name of Ozzie Rabbit, as I recall."

Epstein, *Legend*, 68: "He [LHO] would mimic Bugs Bunny...earning him the nickname Bugs."

D. In the Soviet Union

18 WH 450; CE 985: State Dept. translation of 3/61 LHO medical records from Minsk: "Name: Oswald, Harvey Alik" (also "A. Oswald). Cf. 18 WH 454: "Name: Oswald, Harvey A....Oswald, H.A." (The Russian originals were not supplied to the Warren Commission, and hence not published.) Medical records of 10/28/59 from Botkin Hospital, Moscow (18 WH 461, 466) have "Name: Oswald, Lee Harvey." A medical card of Feb. 3?, 1962, has "Lee Hardy Oswald" (18 WH 474-75).

State Department Security Office Memo from Emery J. Adams, SY/E, to Passport PPT, 3/2/61 (covering FBI memo from WFO 2/27/61): "It is requested that the recipients advise if the FBI is receiving info about Harvey on a continuing basis."

16 WH 234; CE 72: Letter of 5/3/61 to LHO from P. Chikarev (but signed Voloshin): "Esteemed citizen Harvey Oswald" Cf. Epstein, *Legend,* 111; CD 206.360; WCD 1084 (e), 122-23 (as indexed to Mary L. Petterson, before being dropped and replaced by old pp. 124-25 (24 WH 631; CE 2121)

Cf. 18 WH 433; CE 985: Document # NO/4522 12/11/61 as translated by State Dept, Doc. 8A: "Citizen Harvey Lee Oswald." BUT original at at 18 WH 434 has (in Russian) "Citizen Lee Harvey Oswald."

4 AH 210 (=3 AH 572): CIA Doc. #435-173A, covering memo of 25 November 1963: "It was partly out of curiosity to learn if Oswald's wife would actually accompany him to our country, partly out of interest in Oswald's own experences in the USSR, that we showed intelligence interest in the Harvey story."

E. On Return to the United States - Pre-Assassination

4 WH 432; Testimony of FBI Agent John Lester Quigley, who interviewed Oswald 8/10/63: "[T]he jailer brought in an individual who was then introduced to me by Lieutenant Martello as Harvey Lee Oswald. I then identified myself by credentials to Lee Harvey Oswald. Mr. STERN. You said Harvey Lee Oswald. Mr. QUIGLEY. I beg your pardon. Mr. STERN. You meant Lee Harvey Oswald? Mr. QUIGLEY. Yes; Lee Harvey Oswald." (If Quigley could be believed on this point, Martello's would be the earliest reported use by law enforcement of the the name "Harvey Lee Oswald.")

3 WH 8; Testimony of Ruth Paine, 3/19/64: "He [LHO in New Orleans, August 1963] went out to buy groceries, came in with a cheery call to his two girls, saying 'Yabutchski,' which means girls, the Russian word for girls, as he came in the door. It was more like Harvey than I had seen him before." Cf. 17 WH 185.

24 WH 732; 24 WH 745: CEs 2137, 2138; FBI interviews 12/20/63 and 2/6/64 of Mrs. Lee Dannelly of Austin re "the person who contacted her giving his name as HARVEY OSWALD on or about September 25, 1963."

26 WH 178; CE 2789; CD 205-629-32: Leonard Hutchinson story to FBI about LHO's attempt to cash check for $189 payable to "Harvey Oswald." Cf. WR 331-32.

F. Post-Assassination: CIA

CIA Doc. #1277-1025; Memo of 25 Mar 1964 from A.E. Shrout to Chief/Employee Activity Branch. Subj: Bielefeldt, Talbot, who reported contact with Mrs. Carol Hyde, "mother of Ruth Payne.... Mrs. Payne is the former landlady to the Harvey Lee Oswald family." ["Payne," like "Harvey Lee Oswald," is a recurring anomaly.]

"CIA #180" (in CIA 1975 release): CIA memo of 30 Dec 1963 in LHO 201 file: "Reference is made to [redacted] an incoming [redacted] telegram dated 19 December 1963, in connection with the Harvey Lee OSWALD Case [redacted] This telegram concerns a Mr. and Mrs. DEMOHRENSCHILDT who appear to have lived in Dallas, Texas, but on 2 June 1963 went to Haiti."

CIA Doc. #435-173A; Memo of 12 Dec 1963 from [redacted]; covering memo of 25 November 1963: "Subject: Mr. Lee Harvey Oswald.... It was partly out of curiosity to learn if Oswald's wife would actually accompany him to our country, partly out of interest in Oswald's own experiences in the USSR, that we showed intelligence interest in the Harvey story." 3 AH 572; = 4 AH 210.

G. Post-Assassination: Military Intelligence

U.S. Army Cable 480587 from Fort Sam Houston, Texas, to U.S. Strike Command, McDill AFB, Florida, 230405Z (Nov. 22, 10:05 CST): "Following is additional information on Oswald, Harvey Lee.... Don Stringfellow, Intelligence Section, Dallas Police Dept., notified 112th Intc Gp, this HQ, that information obtained from Oswald revealed he had defected to Cuba in 1959 and is card carrying member of Communist Party."

ONI Teletype of 11/27/63 (272130Z) from NAVCINTSUPPCEN.3 to DIO 8ND: "Subject: OSWALD, HARVEY LEE." (ONI-229)

ONI Teletype of 11/27/63 (272210Z) from DIO 8ND to NAVCINTSUPPCEN.3: "Subject: OSWALD, HARVEY LEE." (ONI-230)

H. Post-Assassination: FBI

First question of FBI to Robert Oswald 11/22/63 in Dallas Police Station: "'Is your brother's name Lee Harvey Oswald or Harvey Lee Oswald?... We have it here as Harvey Lee.' 'No,' I said, 'it's Lee Harvey Oswald.'" (Robert Oswald, *Lee: A Portrait of Lee Harvey Oswald* [New York: Coward-McCann, 1967], 18). (This agent may have been SA Charles T. Brown: cf. 15 WH 619, testimony of Detective Roy Standifer.)

FBI HQ File 105-82555-88, Cable # 241 from Legat Bern to DIR: [Title] "Changed. Lee Harvey Oswald, aka Harvey Lee Oswald, Internal Security - R and Cuba. Title changed to show correct sequence of first and middle names"

FBI HQ File 105-82555-1st no. 96, Urgent 5-11 PM 11-24-63 from SAC New York to HQ, HQ file 100-3-7717: "Allegations that Lee Oswald is a Communist have created panic among members of National Board of CP, USA." Unrecorded copy to HQ Oswald file on 12/11/63 with handwritten notation, "Harvey Lee Oswald."

Paul Scranton Memo to SAC Miami 11/27/63 (FBI Miami 105-8342-29): "Informant advised that SALVAT told him the DRE has a tape recording of HARVEY LEE OSWALD's trial at New Orleans [i.e. the radio debate] in which OSWALD states he is not a Communist but a Marxist. This tape is in the possession of LUIS FERNANDEZ ROCHA."

SAC New Orleans to DIR 11/27/63, FBI HQ 105-82555-166 (response to Alvarado story): "HARVEY LEE OSWALD"

23 WH 207; CE 1711; CD 84.177-79: LA FBI interview in Sherman Oaks, CA, 11/29/63 of Herbert Eden: Ruby's "action in shooting HARVEY LEE OSWALD is the result of a 'brooding sick man.'"

23 WH 373; CE 1763; CD 223.65-67: (informed) FBI interview in Mobile 12/26/63 with Jack Hardee; says "the police officer whom HARVEY LEE OSWALD allegedly killed...was a frequent visitor to Ruby's night club."

FBI Report of Frederick Slight, Tampa, 1/30/64 on Fair Play for Cuba Committee, Tampa Division (10/17/63-1/14/64), p. 12: "A DON SIDER, who claimed to be a representative for 'Time' magazine contacted MANUEL AMOR at which time he told AMOR that it was his understanding that HARVEY LEE OSWALD had been connected with the FPCC at Tampa and wanted to know if this was true."

FBI #836: Enrique Lorenzo-Luaces y Vilaseca saw Robert Taber of FPCC with Harvey Oswald.

I. Post-Assassination: Dallas Police

19 WH 438; Dean Exhibit No. 5009; CD 85.325: FBI copy of DPD Sergeant P.T. Dean memo of 11/26/63 (see below, 24 WH 87): re "the transfer of Harvey Lee Oswald, W/M/24."

24 WH 87; CE 2002, p. 27; Patrick Dean memo of Nov. 26, 1963, about his assignment re "the transfer of Harvey Lee Oswald, W/M/24, to the County Jail."

24 WH 142; CE 2002, p. 76; memo from Detective Louis D. Miller re "Shooting of Harvey Oswald;" mentions "prisoner Harvey Oswald."

24 WH 259; CE 2003, p. 125; Westphal/Parks memo of Nov.22 thru Lt. Jack Revill to Captain W.P. Gannaway of SSB, re TSBD: first name is "HARVEY LEE OSWALD 605 ELSBETH" (*Deep Politics*, 277).

24 WH 329; CE 2003, p. 252; F.M. Turner report of his duties: "On November 25, 1963, we took a picture of Harvey Lee Oswald, DPD #54018 and showed it to witness Ronald Fischer."

J. Post-Assassination: Secret Service

16 WH 721; CE 270: Transcript of Secret Service Agent J.M. Howard interview 11/25/63 with "Mrs. Marguerite Oswald, mother of Harvey Lee (replaced by "Lee Harvey") Oswald:" "This is an interview with Mrs. Marguerite Oswald, mother of Harvey Lee Oswald."

16 WH 749; CE 270: Transcript of Secret Service Agent J.M. Howard interview 11/25/63 with "Robert Lee Oswald, brother of Harvey Lee (replaced by "Lee Harvey") Oswald:" "This is an interview with Robert Lee Oswald, brother of Lee Harvey Oswald." (Both interviews refer to LHO as "Lee" [Marguerite] or "Lee Harvey" [Robert]).

26 WH 30-31; CE 2675 "Title or Caption Harvey Lee Oswald." Interview 2/28/64 by Secret Service Austin TX of Billy Joe Lord "regarding his and Harvey Lee Oswald's trip to France aboard the SS Marion Lykes" in 1959. "Harvey Lee Oswald" used a total of nine times.

K. Post-Assassination: Warren Commission Testimony

4 WH 32; Testimony of Sebastian Latona, FBI HQ fingerprint expert, 4/2/64: "Mr. EISENBERG. And whose prints were they? Mr. LATONA. The fingerprint was identified as Harvey Lee Oswald. Mr. EISENBERG. That is Lee Harvey Oswald? Mr. LATONA. That is right. Mr. EISENBERG. And the palm? Mr. LATONA. The palmprint was identified also as Harvey Lee Oswald. Mr. EISENBERG. Again Lee Harvey Oswald? Mr. LATONA. That is right.

4 WH 38: Mr. LATONA. Exhibit 649...has been identified as a palmprint of Harvey Lee Oswald, the right palmprint. Mr. EISENBERG. That is Lee Harvey Oswald, Mr. Latona? Mr. LATONA. That is right, Lee Harvey Oswald." (Compare J.C.Day at 4 WH 261.)

4 WH 261; Testimony of J.C. Day, DPD fingerprint expert, 4/22/64: "Mr BELIN: What was your opinion so far as it went as to whose [fingerprints] they were? Mr. DAY. They appeared to be the right middle and right ring finger of Harvey Lee Oswald, Lee Harvey Oswald." (Compare Latona on fingerprints above.)

6 WH 438; Testimony of Mrs. Earlene Roberts, 4/8/64: "Mr. BALL. And the police officers came out there? Mrs. ROBERTS. Yes, sir. Mr. BALL. Do you remember what they said? Mrs. ROBERTS. Well, it was Will Fritz' men [DPD Plainclothesmen Senkel, Potts, and Cunningham, joined later by F.M. Turner]....They asked him [Mr. Johnson] if there was a Harvey Lee Oswald there....Mr. BALL. And you didn't have that name.... Mrs. ROBERTS. No -- he registered as O.H. Lee and they were asking for Harvey Lee Oswald." N.B. Senkel is the partner of F.M. Turner (above at 24 WH 329).

12 WH 51: "Mr. HUBERT. Let me mark this document, then -- I am marking it...as Exhibit 5323, Deposition of Sheriff J.E. Decker....It is called Acco Press on the inside and bears the label on the outside, "Harvey Lee Oswald, WM 24, Murder--11-22-63 of John Fitzgerald Kennedy...." Deposition as reproduced bears title "Lee Harvey Oswald" (19 WH 54).

L. Since the Warren Commission

Robert Kennedy to Jeff Greenfield, 1968 (after the assassination of Martin Luther King): "'You know that fellow Harvey Lee Oswald, whatever his name is, set something loose in this country.' The first stories after Dallas, Greenfield remembered, had so miscalled Oswald. 'That's the way he remembered [the name] because obviously he never took another look at it again." Arthur M. Schlesinger, Jr., *Robert F. Kennedy* (New York: Ballantine Books, 1978), 941-42; citing Jeff Greenfield recorded interview of 1969, RFK Oral History Program.

William George Gaudet to Fensterwald, 1975: speaks of "Harvey Oswald"

Ray Zauber to Peter Dale Scott, 1977: speaks of those who knew "Harvey Oswald"

APPENDIX III: "HARVEY" AND "HARVEY ALIK OSWALD" IN THE SOVIET UNION

References to Oswald as Harvey antedate his Fall 1963 visit to Mexico City. The earliest documentary references to Oswald as "Harvey" are from 1961, when there are at least four from a ten-month period. In the State Department's Security file on Oswald, there is a March 1961 internal memo from Emery J. Adams of the Security Staff, asking the Passport Bureau to advise "if the FBI is receiving info about Harvey on a continuing basis."[1] There is no known bureaucratic precedent for calling Oswald "Harvey," although two years later a CIA officer would write that his division had "showed intelligence interest in the Harvey [i.e. Oswald] story.[2]

But Mr Emery Adams may have had better intelligence of Oswald than we know of today. (The State Security Staff had close liaison with the CIA's Office of Security, and indeed a number of CIA officers went overseas under State Department Security Staff cover.) Less than one month after Mr. Adams wrote his memo, Oswald checked into a Minsk hospital, not as "Lee Harvey Oswald" (the name he had used in a Moscow hospital in 1959), but as "Oswald, Harvey Alik" ("Alik" being the name he had come to substitute in Russia for the Chinese-sounding "Lee").[3] Oswald must have used the name "Harvey" to other Soviet officials at this time as well. In May he received a letter, addressed to "Esteemed citizen Harvey Oswald," in which an administrator called Voloshin told him officially that he was not eligible to study at Patrice Lumumba University in Moscow.[4] This letter is ignored in the Warren Report's biography of Oswald, but we hear from Edward Jay Epstein that it was taken much more seriously by at least one of the Oswald-watchers in CIA counterintelligence (who claimed to have thought that Voloshin could have been Oswald's Soviet recruiter).[5]

We have to place in context these Soviet references in March, April and May 1961 to a "Harvey Oswald," or "Harvey Alik Oswald," which can be seen as anomalous. Most of Oswald's Soviet documentation is in the name of "Lee Harvey Oswald," including his work papers and most significantly his marriage certificate of April 30, 1961.[6]

At the same time, if we consider Oswald stay in Minsk, the "Lee Harvey Oswald" documentation can also be seen as anomalous. He was not called "Lee" by his friends in Minsk, he was called "Alek;" "Alek" was indeed the name by which he was introduced to Marina in March 1961.[7] All of the published letters and notes written to or from Oswald by friends in Minsk (some fifteen in all) use the name "Alek" (except for one addressed to "Marina" and "Olegushka").[8] When Marina visited her aunt in Kharkov in October 1961, Oswald's letters to her bore the return address "A. Oswald"

[1] State Department Security Office Memo from Emery J. Adams, SY/E, to Passport PPT, 3/2/61 (covering FBI memo from WFO 2/27/61).
[2] 4 AH 210 (=3 AH 572): CIA Doc. #435-173A, covering memo of 25 November 1963: "It was partly out of curiosity to learn if Oswald's wife would actually accompany him to our country, partly out of interest in Oswald's own experences in the USSR, that we showed intelligence interest in the Harvey story."
[3] 18 WH 450; CE 985: State Dept. translation of 3/61 LHO medical records from Minsk: "Name: Oswald, Harvey Alik" (also "A. Oswald"). Cf. 18 WH 454: "Name: Oswald, Harvey A....Oswald, H.A." (The Russian originals were not supplied to the Warren Commission, and hence not published.) Medical records of 10/28/59 from Botkin Hospital, Moscow (18 WH 461, 466) have "Name: Oswald, Lee Harvey." A medical card of Feb. 3?, 1962, has "Lee Hardy Oswald" (18 WH 474-75).
[4] 16 WH 234; CE 72: Letter of 5/3/61 to LHO from P. Chikarev (but signed Voloshin): "Esteemed citizen Harvey Oswald;" WCD 206.360.
[5] Cf. Epstein, Legend, 111: "Oswald's attempt to enroll himself... in Patrice Lumumba University, where reportedly he was friendly with several foreign students, including Mary Louise Patterson, the daughter of William L. Patterson, who was then serving on the executive committee of the Communist Party in the United States." Epstein wrote in New York magazine that "I got a CIA 'trace' on Voloshin, and he turned out to be a KGB officer who had been in the Far East at the same time Oswald was there....One former CIA counterintelligence official suggested to me that Voloshin might have been the person who recruited Oswald or arranged for his defection" (New York, February 27, 1978, p. 37. Cf. WCD 1084 (e), 122-23 (as indexed to Mary L. Patterson, before being dropped and replaced by old pp. 124-25 (24 WH 631; CE 2121).
[6] 22 WH 72; cf. 18 WH 531-33.
[7] 1 WH 91 (Marina Oswald's testimony); 18 WH 552, 600 (narrative written by Marina Oswald).
[8] 16 WH 162-226, passim; 16 WH 232.

(16 WH 197), or "A.H. Oswald" (16 WH 219).

It would appear that Oswald named himself in two different ways for two different audiences. Officially, whether addressing the Soviet or the American authorities, he was "Lee Harvey Oswald," or "L.H. Oswald."[9] Unofficially, to his friends, he was "Alek," or "A.H. Oswald."

But this distinction does not begin to explain his hospital registration as "Harvey Alik Oswald," and "H.A. Oswald," or the letter from Patrice Lumumba University to "Esteemed citizen Harvey Oswald." We have as it were a second family of Oswald records from Minsk, in which the order of the forenames is mysteriously reversed.

I will now mention a tiny clue which makes the "Harvey Alik Oswald" records more credible, at least for me. I have already mentioned that Oswald's Minsk hospital records carry the name variants "Harvey Alik Oswald," "Harvey A. Oswald," and "H.A. Oswald."[10] There is one added note and name variant: "Money, documents and other valuable were left with the patient. A. Oswald."[11] In other words, Oswald was registered with the name "Harvey" first, but those working with him, including the nurse who took his valuables, knew that he was addressed familiarly as "Alik."

This is a common enough American phenomenon, even among government personnel and covert operatives (the names of E. Howard Hunt and G. Gordon Liddy come to mind.) Oswald would be completely familiar with this habit from the case of his own father. Officially, beyond question, his father was "Robert Edward Lee Oswald."[12] Familiarly, however, Robert E. L. Oswald was known to his wife, close family and friends, as "Lee," or "Lee Sr."[13]

The available evidence further suggests that in the Marines Oswald himself, enrolled as "Lee Harvey Oswald," was more commonly known as "Harvey," or as "Harv," than as "Lee." Nelson Delgado, perhaps Oswald's closest friend at Santa Ana (and certainly the Marine who testified at greatest length about him to the Warren Commission) lived in the same Quonset hut, yet "didn't even know his name was Lee."[14] Like most Marines, Delgado called him "Oswald," "Os," or "Ozzie."[15] As for the name "Lee," there was just one fellow-Marine, Peter Connor, who told *Life* magazine that Oswald "used to bring up this stuff about his name, Lee...because he said he was named after Robert E. Lee."[16] The same Peter Connor told the Warren Commission, however, that "Oswald was nicknamed 'Harv.' This was a shortened version of his middle name."[17] The nickname "Harvey" or "Harv" was corroborated by two other Marines.[18] For whatever reason, it seems to have been the custom to call Oswald, like his father, by his middle name.

---

[9] CE 1314, a paper retrieved from the Paine home, is apparently a rough draft of his resignation letter in May 1962 from the Minsk Radio Factory. He uses the names "Lee H. Oswald" and "L.H. Oswald" (22 WH 486).

[10] 18 WH 450, 454.

[11] 18 WH 450.

[12] For "Robert Edward Lee Oswald," see e.g. 25 WH 88 (FBI transcript of his marriage record in the Trinity Evangelical Church book of Baptisms, Marriages, and Deaths); 1 WH 225, 268 (testimony of Marguerite and Robert Edward Lee Oswald, Jr.) (In saying this we can ignore the false variant of his name, in the files of the FBI, CIA, and IRS, as "Edward Lee Oswald". This variant originated in the 1960 interview of Marguerite Oswald by FBI agent John W. Fain: see Fain FBI Report of 5/12/60, "Funds Transmitted to Residents of Russia," pp. 1, 6 (17 WH 700, 705); INS information request on Oswald of 12/17/61; both contained in CIA's Oswald 201 file, Warren Commission CD 692.

[13] "Lee:" 1 WH 253 (Marguerite), 8 WH 104 (Lillian Murret, Marguerite's sister), 26 WH 764 (Mrs. Hazel Oswald, sister-in-law, to Secret Service); "Lee Sr." 23 WH 717 (Mrs. Hazel Oswald, sister-in-law, to FBI).

[14] 8 WH 264.

[15] 8 WH 264; cf. 8 WH 270 (Daniel Powers); 8 WH 317 (Donald Peter Camarata); Epstein, *Legend*, 74 (Zack Stout).

[16] *Life*, February 21, 1964, 74A; reprinted at 16 WH 807. Cf. Connor's affidavit to the Warren Commission: "He claimed to be named after Robert E. Lee" (8 WH 317).

[17] 8 WH 317.

[18] Paul Edward Murphy (8 WH 319), J.E. Pitts (Epstein, *Legend*, 282; FBI HQ 105-82555-204). Both Connor and Pitts related that Oswald disliked being called "Harvey," perhaps because (according to Murphy) he was nicknamed "'Harvey' after 'Harvey the Rabbit,' a movie which was then circulating" (8 WH 319). Powers recalled that "He had the name of Ozzie Rabbit" (8 WH 280, cf. 287). Owen Dejanovich remembered him as "Bugs," after Bugs Bunny (Epstein, *Legend*, 82; cf. 68).

In other words, there was family and personal precedent for the privileging of Oswald's middle name in the Minsk hospital record, listing Oswald as both "Harvey Alik" and also as "A." (Alik). This follows the same general pattern as the application form filled out by Marguerite in 1942 to admit Oswald's brother, Robert E. Lee Oswald, Jr., to a Lutheran Orphan Asylum. Marguerite entered the father's name (in inadequate space) as "Robert Ed. Oswald;" her own, as "Mrs. Lee Oswald."[19]

The hospital document, in other words, familiarizes and privileges the middle name in a way that is entirely credible within the traditions of the Oswald family. What makes the hospital document so very credible is that this same habit is also completely un-Russian, because the Russian middle name is always a patronymic. To conform to Russian conventions, Oswald's middle name would have had to be "Robertovich," or possibly "Leeovich," or (at a stretch) "Aleksandrovich;" but two of these names are grotesque inventions, and the third inappropriate. To call himself "Harvey Lee," or eventually "Harvey Alik," seems a more reasonable compromise -- especially when you consider that this gave to the patronymic place in his own name the familiar name of his father or its Russian equivalent. (Writing as "Lee Harvey Oswald," Oswald had been forced on official forms to write "Harvey" in the space for "patronym" ("Otchestvo"), an absurdity alleviated by the name "Harvey Alik.")[20]

Those close to him would understand and accept his American-only habit of calling himself by his middle name "Alik." Those far off, whether Emery Adams in the State Department or the unknown "Voloshin" at Patrice Lumumba University, would assume from the name "Harvey Alik Oswald," naturally but perhaps wrongly, that the person's preferred given name was "Harvey."

I would now like to propose a solution, simple but potentially far-reaching, for the paradox that we are faced with two conflicting families of Oswald documents for the Minsk period: an almost excessive trove of "Lee Harvey Oswald" documents, and a much smaller family of "Harvey Alik Oswald" documents. The key is that the second family comes primarily from U.S.S.R. government sources, specifically under cover of a diplomatic note of May 5, 1964 from the Soviet Ambassador to the U.S. Secretary of State.[21] It seems clear from this Soviet note alone that Oswald in Minsk used both variants of his name, and I have no reason to assert that in the Minsk period there is any covert significance to the two variants.

It is what happened later, I suspect, that made the difference significant. And these subsequent events appear to have resulted in the suppression of the source documents which resulted in the widespread use of the name variant, "Harvey Lee Oswald." I suspect, however, that there must have been at least one such archetypal source in the State Department. Why else would the State Department translator, faced with a 1961 routine report about Lee Harvey Oswald at the Minsk radio plant, have mistranslated "Lee Harvey Oswald" as "Harvey Lee Oswald"?[22]

[19] Pic Exh. No. 3; 21 WH 57.

[20] See for example 18 WH 408, 412, 415, 419, 421.

[21] Warren CE 985, 18 WH 403. The U.S.S.R. note seems to be aware of the paradox, but minimizes it. The appended "Lee Harvey Oswald" documents are listed in the note under the name "Lee H. Oswald." The "Harvey Alik Oswald" documents are listed as "Oswald." One cannot accuse the Soviet Union of making propaganda out of the difference (18 WH 404-07).

[22] 18 WH 433; CE 985: Document # NO/4522 of 12/11/61 as translated by State Dept, Doc. 8A: "Citizen Harvey Lee Oswald." Original at 18 WH 434 has (in Russian) "Citizen Lee Harvey Oswald."

APPENDIX IV. CASE CLOSED? OR OSWALD FRAMED?

A review of Gerald Posner, *Case Closed: Lee Harvey Oswald and the Assassination of JFK* (New York: Random House, 1993).

Posner's *Case Closed* is a special book about a special case: the two, indeed, are part of a single phenomenon. From the outset, the Kennedy assassination has attracted -- along with cranks, ideologues, paranoid obsessives, charlatans, and a clairvoyant -- two special kinds of student: the lawyers and the scholars. From the outset there have been reasons (persuasive reasons) of state to close the case; and from the outset there have been glaring problems with the evidence which have kept it open. Over the years there has been no shortage of people (not just lawyers) meeting the persuasive needs of state, nor of people (including some lawyers) following the lure of truth.

If anything has become more clear about the case since the Warren Report, it is that officials of many government agencies have lied, sometimes repeatedly, to maintain the Warren Commission's conclusions. Congressional Committees have established that FBI agents lied about Oswald's visit to the Dallas FBI office before the assassination, and that CIA officials gave false statements (even within the Agency) about CIA surveillance of Oswald at the Cuban and Soviet Embassies in Mexico City.[1] These official lies have created a touchstone against which new books about the assassination can be tested. Are lies transmitted uncritically, in lawyerly fashion, as evidence? Or are they exposed by scholarly investigation? As we shall see, Posner's performance is a mixed one (he deals with the FBI falsehoods, but not the CIA ones). On balance, unfortunately, it is a lawyerly performance.

Case Closed may seem to uninformed readers to be the most persuasive of the succession of books that have urged readers to accept the lone-assassin finding of the Warren Report. But to those who know the case it is also evidence of on-going cover-up. For Posner often transmits without evaluation official statements that are now known to be false, or chooses discredited but compliant witnesses who have already disowned earlier helpful stories that have been disproven. He even revives a wild allegation which the Warren Commission rejected, and reverses testimony to suggest its opposite.

These are serious charges. There are in fact books on both sides of the Kennedy assassination controversy about which similar accusations could be made, and normally one might conclude that such books did not merit a serious rebuttal. But *Case Closed* is a special book, in which Posner more than once acknowledges help from "confidential intelligence sources."[2] It has since been granted major publicity in the media, from *U.S. News and World Report* to the *Today* show and *20/20*.

There are many places where one can agree with Posner's rebuttal of particular critics on particular points (such as the Garrison investigation, and its as-yet unproven allegation that Oswald knew another alleged suspect, David Ferrie). Concerning the physical and medical evidence, he promotes new arguments by others which appear to be worthy of serious consideration. One must grant also that on a topic of this range and complexity no one's book will be flawless.

But in *Case Closed* some of the weakest sections of the Warren Commission argument have been strengthened by suspect methodologies and even falsehoods, so systematic they call into question the good faith of his entire project.

On the now-hoary question of whether Oswald's protector in Dallas, George de Mohrenschildt, had a CIA relationship, Posner reverts to the Warren Commission method of letting the CIA answer the question: "CIA officials have provided sworn testimony that there was no de Mohrenschildt-U.S. intelligence relationship."[3] That will not work in 1993. In 1978 the House Select Committee on

---

[1] U.S. Cong., Senate, Intelligence Committee, *Performance of Intelligence Agencies*, Appendix B; House, Judiciary Committee, *FBI Oversight Hearings*, October 21 and December 11, 1975; Posner, 215-17 (Oswald and FBI in Dallas); House, Select Committee on Assassinations, "Lee Harvey Oswald, the CIA and Mexico City," Classified Staff Study (cited henceforth as Lopez Report, declassified 1993), 123, 164, 183-84, etc. (Oswald in Mexico City).

[2] Posner, pp. 511, 514, etc.

[3] Posner, 86.

Assassinations revealed that, when leaving Dallas in May 1963 for Haiti, de Mohrenschildt traveled to Washington and took part in a Pentagon-CIA meeting with de Mohrenschildt's business ally, a Haitian banker named Clemard Joseph Charles. A former CIA contract agent has since suggested that one of de Mohrenschildt's purposes in moving to Haiti was to oversee a CIA-approved plot to overthrow Haitian dictator Francois "Papa Doc" Duvalier.[4]

There is no excuse for Posner's repeating, uncritically and without footnotes, another old CIA claim, that at the time of the assassination, "Oswald's CIA file did not contain *any* photos" of Oswald.[5] This false claim is an important one, since the CIA has used it to justify the false description of Oswald which it sent to other agencies on October 10, 1963, six weeks before the assassination. But as Anthony Summers pointed out thirteen years ago, the CIA pre-assassination file on Oswald contained four newspaper clippings of his defection to the Soviet Union in 1959, and two of these contained photographs of him.[6] One could argue that the original error arose from an innocent oversight; although this is unlikely, since it is part of a larger pattern of CIA misrepresentations concerning the photos.[7] One cannot offer such an innocent defense for Posner's repetition of the falsehood. His discussion of the photo issue is a running argument with Summers'; and indeed in this section he repeatedly disputes Summers' allegations.[8]

In short, this book is not "a model of historical research," as the historian Stephen Ambrose has claimed. It is a lawyer's brief.

Reversing the Verdict on Jack Ruby and Organized Crime

One would have thought that one issue now resolved beyond question is that Jack Ruby indeed had, as the House Select Committee on Assassinations concluded, a "significant number of associations" with organized crime leaders both nationally and in Dallas (AR 149). Eight pages on this topic in the House Committee Report were supplemented by a staff volume of over a thousand pages. Once this important point is conceded, it is hard not to agree that the Warren Commission's portrait of Ruby as a loner, based on misleading reports and suppression of evidence by the FBI, was a false one.

To avoid this problem, Posner has produced a witness who revives the Warren Report's portrait of Ruby as "a real low-level loser," -- adding that only "conspiracy theorists" would "believe that Ruby was part of the mob." The witness is Tony Zoppi, whom Posner describes as a former

---

[4] 12 AH 55-57; Summers, 248; Dick Russell, *The Man Who Knew Too Much* (New York: Carroll and Graf, 1992), 318-19; Warren Hinckle and William Turner, *The Fish Is Red* (New York: Harper and Row, 1981), 210 (contract agent); Peter Dale Scott, *Deep Politics and the Death of JFK* (Berkeley and Los Angeles: University of California Press, 1993), 78. There is also the problem of the alleged KGB defector, Yuri Nosenko, who came to America in 1964 with the claim that the KGB had had nothing to do with Oswald. There are issues here that will probably never be resolved, but Posner, in order to close the case, makes light of them. He spends most of his time confirming what he calls "Nosenko's bona fides" (p. 41), and his arguments are quite persuasive. But even if Nosenko were a bona fide defector, it does not follow that all that he says about Oswald is true. On the contrary, the House Committee reported "significant inconsistencies" in statements Nosenko had given the FBI, the CIA, and the Committee (AR 102). Posner makes the valid rebuttal point (p. 45) that a 1967 CIA review found "massive errors in the translations of the interviews conducted before and during Nosenko's imprisonment." But he does not reveal to his readers that this finding related to CIA interviews only, leaving unexplained the reported major discrepancies between Nosenko's statements to the Committee and to the FBI. Thus there is still little justification for Posner's having relied so heavily on Nosenko as a principal source.

[5] Posner, 186n; emphasis in original. This false claim was originally made within the Agency by an anonymous official to CIA General Counsel Lawrence Houston. See Anthony Summers, *Conspiracy*, (New York: McGraw-Hill, 1980), 381.

[6] Summers, 381; Warren Commission Document 692; CIA Document 590-252.

[7] Lopez Report, 137-41. The Lopez Report called explanations offered by CIA employees on the matter of the false Oswald description "hard to accept" (139) and "implausible" (140).

[8] Posner, 191 (footnotes 99 and 100), 193 (footnote 105). These cite pages in Summers immediately before and after the account of the photos in Oswald's file.

"prominent entertainment reporter for the Dallas Morning News."[9] He does not mention that Zoppi had been the source of an innocent explanation for Jack Ruby's 1959 visits to the Havana casinos, an explanation so swiftly demolished by the Committee that Zoppi himself retracted it. Thanks to this episode we now know that Zoppi, as well as Ruby, was close to a casino employee of Meyer Lansky's called Lewis McWillie, and was himself working for a mob casino in Las Vegas, the Riviera, by the time the Committee interviewed him in 1978.[10]

Why would Posner choose a discredited casino employee to claim that Ruby was not connected to the mob? The answer, surely, that he is a lawyer out, like the Warren Commission, to "close" a case. Posner opposes the thousand pages of House Committee documentation, not with new rebuttal documentation, but by extended oral interviews with just four witnesses, each of them dubious. One is Jack Ruby's brother Earl, investigated by the House Committee because of allegations that his business and personal incomes increased after Oswald's murder (AR 159). Another is former FBI Agent William Roemer, from the Chicago FBI Office that covered up Ruby's organized crime links in the first place. (The House Committee concluded that the FBI "was seriously delinquent in investigating the Ruby-underworld connections;" AR 243.)[11]

The fourth is Dallas Deputy District Attorney Bill Alexander, who on November 22, 1963 "decided to 'shake things up a bit,'" and told his friend Joe Goulden at the *Philadelphia Inquirer* "that he intended to indict Oswald for killing the President 'in furtherance of a Communist conspiracy.'"[12] Posner transmits Alexander's admission to him (in the second of four interviews) that he has been an important liar about the case.[13] And yet Posner interviewed Alexander over "several days" (503), and cites him, as a "significant source," on at least sixteen different occasions.

Crucial to closing the case is rebuttal of the House Committee's finding that Ruby may have had "assistance" from Dallas policemen in entering the Dallas Police Basement (AR 157). It learned that doors to another stairway had apparently been left unlocked, and the men guarding these doors reassigned elsewhere shortly before the murder. It learned also that "the Dallas Police Department withheld relevant information from the Warren Commission," particularly that at the time the sergeant responsible for the reassignments, Patrick Dean (an acquaintance of Dallas mob boss Joe

---

[9] Posner, 355, 361.

[10] Scott, 198-99; 5 AH 170ss; 9 AH 164-69. The stake of Meyer Lansky, Moe Dalitz, and the Chicago mob in the Riviera is confirmed by one of Posner's other Ruby witnesses, William Roemer, *War of the Godfathers* (New York: Donald I. Fine, 1990), 82, 167.

[11] In 1963 Roemer was the FBI expert on Sam Giancana, in part because Roemer's chief mob informant (and close friend) was Giancana's close associate Richard Cain (cf. Roemer, *War of the Godfathers*, 141, 220). Soon after Ruby killed Oswald, Roemer's young partner John Bassett helped elicit from Giancana-Patrick associates like Dave Yaras the assurances that Ruby "was not outfit connected" (22 WH 372, cf. 317, 357) that later found their way into the Warren Report (R 790). Roemer told Posner that Ruby's Junk Handlers Union local "was a legitimate union when Jack was involved" (Posner, p. 352). This demonstrable falsehood (the mobster Paul Dorfman had already moved in; cf. 22 WH 438) was based on earlier FBI misinformation (22 WH 320) from a witness, Ted Shulman, who had once been closely interrogated by McClellan Committee Counsel Robert Kennedy about his "collusive deals" with Paul Dorfman (Scott, *Crime and Cover-Up*, 39; McClellan Committee, 16084-16103). Roemer also told Posner that "Ruby was absolutely nothing in terms of the Chicago mob....We talked to every hoodlum in Chicago after the assassination, and some of the top guys in the mob, my informants, I had close relationships with them -- they didn't even know who Ruby was" (Posner, p. 354). This evasion was clearly deceptive: some of the "top guys" talked to, and specifically Dave Yaras (22 WH 372) and Lennie Patrick (22 WH 318, cf. 9 AH 948-52), freely admitted knowing Ruby for years.

[12] Posner, 348n. Alexander actually said that he would "charge Oswald with murdering the President 'as part of an *international* Communist conspiracy'" (William Manchester, *The Death of a President* [New York: Harper and Row, 1967], 326; Scott, *Deep Politics*, 270). Alexander's recollection of the reaction from his superiors ("What the hell are you trying to do, start World War III?") is accurate, and hardly trivial: the risk that local officials would provoke a war was Johnson's excuse for federalizing the murder case and giving it to the Warren Commission.

[13] "Shortly after the *Inquirer* incident, Alexander and two local reporters concocted a story that Oswald had been FBI informer S-179 and had been paid $200 a month. Lonnie Hudkins, one of the reporters, printed the story, attributing it to an unidentified source. The fallout was so great that the Warren Commission held a January 22, 1964, executive session to discuss the issue. 'I never much liked the federals,' Alexander says. 'I figured it was as good a way as any to keep them out of my way by having to run down that phony story'" (Posner, 348n). One of those who printed the "phony story" was Joe Goulden (*Philadephia Inquirer*, December 8, 1963).

Civello) had been given, and failed, a polygraph test (AR 158).

Posner ignores these disturbing indications of conspiracy. He writes (p. 393) that "it was never clear whether the door near the public elevators was properly locked," but offers no reason to counter the admission by Sergeant Dean, the officer in charge, that the door was not locked. Like the Warren Commission, he concludes that Ruby entered by a different route, a vehicle ramp, even though no witnesses saw Ruby enter that way and eight witnesses (Posner mentions only two) said that he did not.[14] His only evidence for the ramp route is the Warren Commission's: Ruby's own say-so, as testified to later (but not at the time) by four Dallas policemen, one of them Dean.[15]

Here again Posner downplays an important Committee finding, by turning again to questionable witnesses, and totally ignoring the evidence of official cover-up, in this case by the Dallas Police.

Repeating Stories Which Even the Warren Commission Rejected

This lawyerly habit of preferring convenient but discredited witnesses is widespread throughout the book. With respect to Oswald's prior use of weapons (another highly disputable area) he accepts, as did the Warren Commission, the testimony of Marina Oswald. In so doing he does nothing to rebut the finding of Warren Commission Counsel Norman Redlich in February 1964, that Marina "has repeatedly lied to the Secret Service, the FBI, and this Commission on matters which are of vital concern."

Given this unrebutted memo, it is hard to excuse the Warren Commission for relying on Marina's testimony that the Mannlicher-Carcano "was the 'fateful rifle of Lee Oswald.'"[16] But Posner resuscitates a story from Marina which even the Warren Commission, knowing the story's history, discounted as having "no probative value."[17]

> Marina said, "Then he got dressed and put on a good suit. I saw that he took a pistol. I asked him where he was going, and why he was getting dressed. He answered, 'Nixon is coming...'" She did not know who Nixon was, but was determined that Lee should not leave the house with the pistol. She asked him to join her in the bathroom, and when he entered she jumped out and slammed the door shut. Bracing her feet against the nearby wall, she struggled as hard as she could to keep the door closed against his efforts to push out. "I remember that I held him," she said. "We actually struggled for several minutes and then he quieted down....At first he was furious, but as he calmed, Oswald agreed to strip to his underwear, and stayed home reading the remainder of the day.[18]

We can only repeat here a few of the problems with this story, which at the time engendered a number of supporting statements to the FBI that were later hastily recanted:

> According to one version of this latest story from Marina, Oswald had "intended to shoot Nixon" in Dallas; and she "had locked Lee Harvey Oswald in the bathroom the entire day...to prevent him from doing so"....Faced with the fact that the Oswald bathroom, like all others, locked from the inside, Marina then told the FBI...that in April 1963 "she forcibly held the bathroom door shut by holding on to the knob and bracing her feet against

---

14 Posner, 395; G. Robert Blakey and Richard N. Billings, *The Plot to Kill the President* (New York: Times Books, 321-22.

15 Posner, 395-96. Posner says "three" Dallas policemen, instead of four. Is he mindful of the problem with Dean's testimony which he does not share with his readers? Accepting Jack Ruby's version as if it were authoritative, Posner also claims (396n) that the House Committee "ignored the fact that Secret Service agent Forrest Sorrels also said he heard Ruby tell [the Dallas police]... that he had come down the ramp (*Dallas Morning News*, March 25, 1979)." He thus rebukes the Committee for ignoring a "fact" that emerged after their report was published. In 1964 Sorrels testified under oath that he did not recall hearing Ruby comment on how he got into the basement area (13 WH 68).

16 WR 128, citing 1 WH 119, 14.

17 Warren Report, p. 189.

18 Posner, *Case Closed*, 120.

the wall".... Finally she would tell the Warren Commission... that she and her much stronger husband "struggled for several minutes" *inside* the bathroom....Faced with other, irreducible difficulties in this Nixon story, the Warren Commission discreetly concluded it was of "no probative value."[19]

Note here that Posner has glossed over the inconsistencies in two incompatible stories by attempting to present them as one. In fact if Marina was outside holding on to the knob, she could not have simultaneously been inside struggling with her husband.

Twisting Testimony to Imply (or Even State) Its Opposite

But Posner's worst abuse of testimony occurs with respect to Oswald's location before the fatal shots. Posner inherits the Warren Commission's problem that a number of credible witnesses placed Oswald on the first or second floor of the School Book Depository, both shortly before and shortly after the fatal shots were fired from the sixth floor at 12:30 pm. The FBI Summary Report of December 1963 suggested that Oswald had been observed on the fifth floor between 11:30 and 12:00; but the Warren Commission added that he had been seen (by Charles Givens, of whom more below) on the sixth floor. Posner, like earlier advocates of the lone assassin theory, reports another such alleged sighting as fact: "At 11:40 one of the workers, Bonnie Ray Williams, spotted Oswald on the east side of that floor, near the windows overlooking Dealey Plaza."[20]

The problem with this convenient story is that Williams, as if to satisfy his exigent examiners, had apparently changed his story not once but twice. An earlier FBI interview on November 23 had reported Williams as saying that he had seen Oswald on the fifth floor about 11:30 am; and that Williams had returned to the sixth floor about noon *and seen no one*.[21] One day earlier, only a few hours after the assassination, Williams had signed and sworn to a Dallas Police affidavit, stating categorically that "I didn't see Oswald any more, that I remember, after I saw him at 8 am."[22]

The Warren Commission was quite aware of this problem. It quizzed Williams about his conflicting earlier statements to the FBI (though not to the Dallas police); and then discreetly declined to use his belated story about the sixth floor. And yet relied heavily on Williams' account (in another story he had failed to report earlier) of *hearing* the shots fired from one floor above him while watching the motorcade with two co-workers on the fifth floor. Commission Counsel Belin elicited vivid testimony from Williams on this point: "It sounded like it was right in the building....it even shook the building, the side we were on. Cement fell on my head."[23]

Williams's earlier amnesia about what he heard is compensated for by elaborate corroboration from his two alleged companions, "Junior" Jarman and Harold Norman. Indeed the corroboration is so precise that one's suspicions are raised, especially since none of the three had reported their important earwitness accounts to the Dallas police.[24] We even find these suspicions voiced by Stephen White, in one of the many earlier books which, like Posner's, has tried to persuade the American public that the Warren Commission was right:

Any student of the Report...must become uneasy at the testimony of the three men who stationed themselves at a fifth floor window in the Depository to watch the motorcade go by. Their stories dovetail admirably: The each heard three shots; they believed they were

[19] Scott, *Deep Politics*, 271, 289; cf. discussion at 289-91; 22 WH 596, 786; 5 WH 389-90.

[20] Posner, 225; cf. 22 WH 681 (FBI interview of March 19, 1964); 3 WH 165.

[21] WCD 5.330, emphasis added; cf. 3 WH 169.

[22] 24 WH 229.

[23] 3 WH 175; quoted in Posner, 242. Cf. 3 WH 179: "I heard three shots. But at first I told the FBI I only heard two -- they took me down -- because I was so excited, and I couldn't remember too well. But later on, as everything began to die down, I got my memory even a little better than on the 22d, I remembered three shots."

[24] Like Williams, Norman, when testifying to the Warren Commission, recanted details of an earlier statement he had made under oath (3 WH 194; cf. 17 WH 208).

fired above them; one of them heard three shells hit the floor above them. It may well be so, but uneasiness is engendered when one learns that the Warren Commission stimulated their memories by a reenactment that duplicated in detail the account to which the investigators themselves were by then committed, and in so doing may have made concrete a recollection that had earlier been vague and indistinct.[25]

The Warren Commission needed an eyewitness to Oswald on the sixth floor, in order to rebut three eyewitness stories that Oswald had spent this period on the first or second floor of the building. Posner has no better rebuttal for one of these three downstairs witnesses (Eddie Piper) than to say that "Piper... is clearly mistaken as five witnesses had placed Oswald on an upper floor, left behind by the elevators by that time."[26] The big problem here is that the witness score of five (for upstairs) versus three (for downstairs) had originally been one, or later two (for upstairs) versus four (for downstairs). The problematic nature of this evidence had been noted in an early Warren Commission internal memo of February 25, 1964.[27] All five who had declared for upstairs by March had changed their stories to do so. None had done so more suspiciously than the one witness, Charles Givens, whom Posner chooses (without any hint of this problem) as his main source.

There are three possible responses to the confusion and conflict in witness testimony about Oswald's location. There is the judicious or common sense response (which was that of the House Committee): to conclude that the "inconsistencies in the statements...created problems that defied resolution 15 [now 30] years after the events in Dallas."[28]

There is the scholarly response: to gather more evidence, whether as to what happened inside the Depository, or about the alterations in the witnesses' stories, or about the forces which led to these alterations. Sylvia Meagher in 1971 looked more closely at "The Curious Testimony of Mr. Givens," which changed at least four times in five months, and ended up with his switch from being a downstairs to an upstairs witness. According to an FBI memo of November 22, Givens had told the FBI that at 11:50 am he had seen Oswald reading a paper in the "domino room" on the first floor. In his Warren Commission testimony of April 8, 1964, Givens told counsel Belin that he had never made the earlier statement, and claimed (for the first time in the official record) that he had seen Oswald on the sixth floor just before noon.[29]

Meagher also reprinted an intervening statement on February 13, 1964 to the FBI by Dallas Police Lt. Jack Revill (a narcotics detective), "that Givens had previously been handled by the Special Services Bureau on a marijuana charge and he believes that Givens would change his story for money." And she denounced as "patently false" Revill's testimony to the Warren Commission (on May 13, 1964), that Givens had told him on November 22 he had seen Oswald on the sixth floor, on the grounds that Givens had never said this until April 1964.[30]

---

[25] Stephen White, *Should We Now Believe the Warren Report?* (New York: Macmillan, 1968), 57-58.

[26] Posner, 227. For just some of the many problems of the alleged Oswald-by-the-elevator encounter (later doubled to become two Oswald-by-the-elevator encounters), see Gordon Miller, *The Third Decade* (September 1993), 33-35. Miller does not mention that Bonnie Ray Williams (3 AH 168) attributed to the first encounter an exchange of words between Givens and Oswald which Givens (6 AH 351) attributed to the second encounter (when Williams was not present). Posner, undaunted, reports both elevator-encounter stories, along with the Givens version of the exchange of words, as if they were incontestable facts. Posner also names Jack Dougherty as a witness to an 11:45 am elevator-encounter, citing (without page reference) an "affidavit of Jack E. Dougherty, November 22, 1963" (Posner, 540, footnote 12). When Posner omits page references, one's suspicions are rightly aroused. The affidavit (24 WH 206) says nothing about an elevator encounter at all. There is also no elevator in the testimony (6 WH 377-78), where Dougherty stated, "It was about 11 o'clock -- that was the last time I saw him."

[27] Summarized in Sylvia Meagher, "The Curious Testimony of Mr. Givens," *Texas Observer*, August 13, 1971; reprinted in Peter Dale Scott, Paul L. Hoch, and Russell Stetler, *The Assassinations: Dallas and Beyond* (New York: Vintage, 1976), 246-47.

[28] AR 50.

[29] 6 WH 345-56; WR 143; cf. WCD 5.329 (FBI interview of 11/22/63); all summarized in Meagher, 245-47.

[30] WCD 5.330 (FBI memo of 11/22/63); 6 WH 345-56, WR 143 (Givens testimony); WCD 735.296-97 (Revill to FBI), 5 WH 35-36 (Revill to Commission); Meagher, in Scott, Hoch, and Stetler, 245-48.

Finally there is the lawyerly approach: to tell less, not more, to suppress the difficulties with the testimony that is preferred, and to invent non-existent problems with the testimony of witnesses one wishes to discredit. This is the approach of Posner in *Case Closed*. Instead of admitting, and discussing, the problems with the sixth floor witnesses who recanted their own testimony, Posner completely ignores these problems, and creates the false impression that it is a key first floor witness who has contradicted herself.

Posner is especially concerned to impeach the testimony of Carolyn Arnold, which corroborated Oswald's own account of having lunch on the first floor, in opposition to the Warren Commission account of Oswald waiting on the sixth floor. In Posner's words:

> Carolyn Arnold, a secretary to the Depository's vice-president, told Anthony Summers in 1978 that at 12:15 she entered the second-floor lunch room and saw Oswald sitting in one of the booths. "He was alone as usual and appeared to be having lunch," Arnold said. Her interview with Summers was the first time she ever publicly told the story about seeing Oswald in the lunch room. But Arnold had given two different FBI statements shortly after the assassination. In one, she said she "could not be sure" but might have caught a fleeting glimpse of Oswald in the first-floor hallway, and in the second statement said she did not see him at all. Arnold told Summers the FBI misquoted her, though she had signed her statement as correct. Four other women worked with Arnold and watched the motorcade with her that day. They support her original statements and not the story she told fifteen years later. Virgie Rachley and Betty Dragoo accompanied her when she left the second floor at 12:15. They did not see Oswald in the lunch room.

After this apparent demolition of Arnold, Posner dismisses the other two witnesses in a footnote:

> William Shelley and Eddie Piper also thought they saw Oswald on the first floor shortly before noon. But Shelley later admitted he saw him at 11:45 A.M., *before* others noticed him on the sixth floor. Piper thought he saw Oswald at noon filling orders on the first floor, but he is clearly mistaken as five witnesses had placed Oswald on an upper floor, left behind by the elevators at that time.[31]

(These five witnesses had come up with the elevator story long after the assassination; and one of them, Charles Givens, had originally placed Oswald on the first floor).[32]

But the apparent problem with Arnold's testimony is an artefact of Posner's own lawyerly imagination:

1) Arnold never told the FBI "she did not see [Oswald] at all." She said that she "did not see Lee Harvey Oswald *at the time President Kennedy was shot*."[33] This was in response to a narrow question asked of all Book Depository witnesses by the FBI, in accordance with a request from the Warren Commission. Similar if not identical answers were given by Roy Truly, who according to Posner saw Oswald two minutes (some say 90 seconds) after the assassination, and by five of Posner's alleged upper floor witnesses.[34]

2) It is highly misleading to say that "Arnold told Summers the FBI misquoted her, though she had signed her statement as correct." Here Posner conflates two different FBI statements, one of November 26 about seeing Oswald on the first floor (where she later claimed to have been

---

[31] Posner, 227; emphasis added.

[32] Posner does not supply a footnote for his statement that Shelley saw Oswald "at 11:45 A.M." What Shelley told the Commission, unambiguously, is that he saw Oswald on the first floor at "about ten to twelve."(6 WH 328). The difference of five minutes, trivial in practice, is devastating to Posner's logic; for 11:50 is the Commission's time for the first encounter at the elevator on the fifth floor. In other words, Shelley's testimony cannot be written off as compatible with the highly dubious elevator story.

[33] 22 WH 635; FBI interview of March 18, 1964, emphasis added.

[34] 22 WH 634 (Arce), 22 WH 645 (Dougherty), 22 WH 649 (Givens), 22 WH 655 (Jarman), 22 WH 666 (Norman); cf. Howard Roffman, *Presumed Guilty* (Rutherford, NJ: Fairleigh Dickinson University Press, 1975), 185.

misquoted), and one of March 28 about not seeing Oswald at the time of the assassination (which she had signed as correct).

3) Thus there is no evidence that Arnold ever contradicted herself. One might normally suspect witnesses who denied making statements attributed to them by the FBI. But Posner has no grounds for doing so in this case. As he is quite aware, three of his upper floor witnesses (Givens, Williams, and Norman, whose final stories he reports as gospel) had denied under oath making earlier statements attributed to them by the FBI and/or Secret Service.[35] Arnold's different memory after fourteen years is hardly comparable to the the dramatic differences in reported stories from Givens after a few weeks, or even hours.

I call Posner's treatment lawyerly, because he is trying both to make some very problematic sixth floor witnesses seem clearer than they were, and to make a first floor witness seem more problematic than she really was. But at times his abuse of evidence goes beyond legal propriety. On the same page, for example, he tries to rebut Oswald's own statement that he took his lunch in the first-floor domino room by a seemingly persuasive barrage of conflicting testimony: "Danny Arce, Jack Dougherty, and Charles Givens [all three of them upper floor witnesses who had changed their stories] also ate in the first-floor room up to 12:15 and said there was no sign of him."[36] The footnoted citation for this statement from Givens is to the Warren Commission Hearings, Volume Six, p. 352. But on that page we find the exact opposite testimony: "Mr. BELIN: On November 22 did you eat inside the building? Mr. GIVENS: No Sir." After this discovery, one can raise questions about the other alleged witnesses as well.[37]

Not every page of Posner's book is as full of distortions as this one. Even here I have focused on the worst handling of evidence; there are indeed other credible witnesses who create problems for those who believe that Oswald in fact spent this time on the first floor.

But I have no trouble admitting that the evidence is confused, and the Depository witness testimony problematic. It is Posner, in his desire to find the case closed, who must introduce a false simplicity that in fact is not to be found. There will be those who argue that Mr. Posner is after all a lawyer, and we should expect no better of him.

But my complaint is about the national media pundits who (like Tom Wicker) have hailed this book as "thoroughly documented" and "always conclusive." My complaint even more is with the prominent academics who (like Professor Stephen Ambrose) have hailed it as "a model of historical research." The case will certainly never be closed as long as the media tout such misrepresentations as the proper answer to the critics.[38]

Postscript

A review in an academic journal by the historian Thomas C. Reeves, published after the above had appeared, praised *Case Closed* as "a masterpiece of solid research, objectivity, and careful reasoning." The same review faulted Sylvia Meagher as an example of the "conspiratorial theorists

---

[35] 6 WH 354 (Givens); 3 WH 168, 171-72, 173, 180 (Williams); 3 WH 194 (Norman).

[36] Posner, 227.

[37] Givens' testimony is consistent with his original affidavit to the Dallas Police on November 22 that at twelve noon he took his lunch break and left the building. A very similar statement ("At lunch time at 12:00 noon I went down on the street") had been signed and sworn to by Danny Arce (24 WH 199). Arce's different statement to the Warren Commission, that he ate lunch in the "domino room" (6 WH 365), is thus open to question. This leaves only Jack Dougherty, a witness the Warren Report very understandably calls "confused" (WR 153) and who testified twice to Warren Commission Counsel Ball that the shots were fired "before I ate my lunch" (6 WH 379).

[38] Since this review was first published, Prof. David Wrone has noted yet another instance of Posner's misrepresentations (*Journal of Southern History*, February 1995, 186). Posner cites an FBI report for the claim that Oswald ordered the printing of Fair Play for Cuba Committee handbills at the Jones Printing Company in New Orleans (Posner, p. 127). In fact the cited witness told the FBI, when shown a photo of Oswald, that "she could not recognize the person represented in the picture as the person who placed the order for the handbills" (22 WH 797).

whose reputations have been demolished by Posner."[39] I enquired of Prof. Reeves his reasons for preferring Posner to Meagher, and invited him to look more closely at his treatment of her, as follows.

Here is the first of Posner's alleged demolitions: "Sylvia Meagher... writes, 'There is, then, no basis in any of the available medical or psychiatric histories for allegations that Oswald was psychotic, aberrant, or mentally unsound in any degree.' Meagher's conclusion is contradicted not only by [Dr. Renatus] Hartogs but also by two Soviet psychiatrists who evaluated Oswald...in Moscow" (Posner, 13n).

Dr. Renatus Hartogs had diagnosed the 13-year-old Oswald in April 1953, after his truancy from school. He found Oswald to be "functioning presently on the bright normal range of mental efficiency." He added that "no finding of neurological impairment or psychotic changes could be made," but diagnosed Oswald as "personality pattern disturbance with schizoid features and passive-aggressive tendencies" (20 WH 89-90). Posner quotes chiefly from Hartogs' much more dramatic testimony to the Warren Commission eleven years later, about "definite traits of dangerousness" and "potential for... assaultive acting out" (Posner, 12; 8 WH 217, cf. 219). The later testimony is of course at odds with Meagher.

However, when confronted with his own original report, Hartogs conceded that it "contradicts" his later recollection: "I didn't mention it [the potential for violence] in the report, and I wouldn't recall it now" (8 WH 221). The Warren Report itself (a model of judiciousness, when compared to Posner) noted that "Contrary to reports that appeared after the assassination, the psychiatric examination [by Hartogs in 1953] did not indicate that Lee Oswald was a potential assassin, potentially dangerous" (WR 379). Meagher recorded Hartogs' retraction and cited the Report; Posner suppresses all reference to both. It would appear that Meagher's summary language was closer to the truth than Posner's expanded report of a charge which (as he typically fails to tell us) was almost immediately retracted.

We find a similar perversity in Posner's allusion to the Soviet psychiatrists. As a lawyer, he prefers to quote a hearsay account of two reports filed by psychiatrists from Moscow's Botkin Hospital ("Both concluded he was 'mentally unstable'" [Posner, 51]). This hearsay is from a witness, Yuriy Nosenko, whose credibility was impeached by both the FBI and the CIA, and in whose diverse statements to various agencies the House Committee found "significant inconsistencies" (AR 102). Why does Posner rely on hearsay, when (as he knows, p. 514) we have the actual reports from Botkin Hospital?

Meagher quotes from these reports (p. 244), Posner does not. The reports found Oswald "not dangerous to other people...of clear mind, no sign of pyschotic phenomena...no psychotic symptoms," and his attitude "completely normal" (18 WH 464, 468, 473). Once again, Posner's "demolition" is achieved by substituting erroneous recollections for the known truth.

Posner is not always so dishonest, and Meagher is not always faultless. Posner does quote one sentence from Meagher which is technically inaccurate, in connection with the Tippit killing. Here it is: "Benavides, the man who had the closest view of the murder, did not identify Oswald at that time or even when he was shown a photograph of Oswald months later during his testimony for the Commission" (Meagher, 256; Posner, 276n). But Meagher's only error here is to speak of a photograph of Oswald, instead of photos of the clothing he was wearing that afternoon (to which Benavides responded, "I think the shirt looked darker than that," 6 WH 453). The big point, which still stands, is that neither the Dallas Police nor the Warren Commission ever asked the only true eyewitness to the shooting to identify Oswald or his photograph.

Prof. Reeves has declined to respond to the above comparative evaluation of Posner and Meagher.

---

[39] *Journal of American History*, December 1994, 1379-80.